Modern Myths, Locked Minds

Modern Myths, Locked Minds

Secularism and Fundamentalism in India

T. N. MADAN

ಐಲಿ

DELHI
OXFORD UNIVERSITY PRESS
CALCUTTA CHENNAI MUMBAI
1998

Oxford University Press, Great Clarendon Street, Oxford OX2 6DP

Oxford New York
Athens Auckland Bangkok Calcutta
Cape Town Chennai Dar es Salaam Delhi
Florence Hong Kong Istanbul Karachi
Kuala Lumpur Madrid Melbourne Mexico City
Mumbai Nairobi Paris Singapore
Taipei Tokyo Toronto

and associates in
Berlin Ibadan

ISBN 0 19 564707 6

Typeset by S.J.I. Services, B-17, Lajpat Nagar Part 2, New Delhi 110024
Printed at Pauls Press, New Delhi 110015
and published by Manzar Khan, Oxford University Press
YMCA Library Building, Jai Singh Road, New Delhi 110001

*To the memory of Tathya
and for Vibhas*

Their own mode of representing things is the more deeply imprinted
on every nation, because it is adapted to themselves, is suitable to their
own earth and sky, springs from their mode of living, and has been
handed down to them from father to son.
JOHANN GOTTFRIED HERDER, *Ideas for a Philosophy of the
History of Mankind*

Preface

Reflection on secularism, and more recently on religious pluralism and fundamentalism, has been one of the abiding concerns of Indian intellectuals through the years since independence nearly half a century ago. Personally, I became interested in the nature and significance of secularization in the course of my work on modern occupations and the professions in the late 1960s and 70s. It was then that I realized that the processes of secularization do not necessarily generate world images or worldviews that may be called secular in the nineteenth-century Western sense of the term, conveying a turning away from religion at the levels of meaning, purpose and practice. I wrote a short paper for a seminar in 1978 arguing for the importance of historical specification in the study of secularization in India.

It was only in 1984, however, after the traumatic events that summer in Amritsar, that I came to appreciate the close if not causal relationship between secularism and fundamentalism. It was then that I decided to undertake a study of these ideologies. My immediate focus was on the Sikh predicament, but it was clear to me from the very beginning of my studies that Hinduism and Islam also would have to be considered.

I have worked on this book at a deliberately leisurely pace, combining it with other academic pursuits, administrative responsibilities, and travel. The work involved more than a considerable amount of reading and reflection. The writing of the various drafts of the chapters, some of which were published in books and journals, and are included here in revised form, took a long time, in fact ten years. This is nearly the same length of time as one takes to complete school education in India. For me the writing of this book has been in a sense like going to school, to begin with the rudiments and then move on to what I trust are deeper understandings. I am aware that mistakes of fact and interpretation are not wholly avoidable in a book of broad scope such as this. I look forward to their identification.

I would like to emphasize that the descriptive or evaluative statements in this book do not at all reflect my own personal religious beliefs, or lack of them. If I find the ideologies of secularism and pluralism flawed, as indeed I do, this does not imply the merit of any particular religious point of view. My characterization of them as 'modern myths' and 'locked minds' underscores both their importance in the contemporary world and their limitations or, in the case of fundamentalism menacing character, as worldviews.

Finally, I should point out that words from languages classical are italicized in the text, but they have not been provided with diacritical marks. All important words have been, however, collected in the glossary, and transcribed in a standard manner. Quotations have been reproduced without any alteration.

T.N. Madan

Delhi—Shimla—Austin
1986–1995

Acknowledgements

In the preface I compared the writing of this book to going to school. My teachers have been the many authors on whose work I have depended for information and illumination. They are too many to be thanked individually: my indebtedness to them marks every page of this book. I would like to warmly thank by name all those generous colleagues and friends who read parts of this book while it was in preparation, or my published work related to its themes, and favoured me with their advice and criticisms through personal communications or published comment. They are: Seema Alavi, Scott Appleby, Alan Babb, Fred Bailey, Jerry Barrier, Upendra Baxi, André Béteille, Jan Bjorkman, Daya Krishna, M.S. Dhami, Louis Dumont, V.N. Dutta, Gopal Krishna, Stephen Graubard, Robert Hardgrave Jr., M.S. Jain, Raymond Jamous, Mark Juergensmeyer, Sudipta Kaviraj, Frédérique Marglin, Barbara Metcalf, Gail Minault, Harbans Mukhia, Ashis Nandy, Philip Oldenberg, Neil O'Sullivan, Bhikhu Parekh, Joyce Pettigrew, R. Sundara Rajan, Francis Robinson, Bill Roff, Ramashray Roy, Lloyd and Susanne Rudolph, Satish Saberwal, Sudhir Chandra, Tejeshwar Singh, Stanley Tambiah, Jit Singh Uberoi, Ashutosh Varshney, and Nur Yalman. I am particularly indebted to Satish Saberwal for reading the whole work and offering incisive criticism and helpful advice.

I had already been working on this book when I was invited in 1988 to contribute a paper to the first volume of an encyclopaedic survey of fundamentalisms sponsored by the American Academy of Arts and Sciences under the directorship of Professors Martin Marty and Scott Appleby. Soon afterwards I was asked to become a member of the project's steering committee. I benefited enormously from this four-year long association with a large number of distinguished scholars from various parts of the world.

Some of the chapters of this book appeared in earlier versions in various books and journals. The consent of the editors and publishers concerned for the inclusion here of these materials is gratefully acknowledged. The details are as follows.

Chapter Two was published in *Social Compass: International Review of Sociology of Religion* (Louvain, Belgium), vol.33, no.2–3, 1986, pp.257–73, under the title of 'Secularization and the Sikh Religious Tradition'.

Chapter Three appeared in *Fundamentalisms Observed* and Chapter Four in *Fundamentalisms Comprehended*, both edited by Martin E. Marty and R. Scott Appleby, and published by the University of Chicago Press in 1991 and 1995 respectively. The original titles were, 'The Double-edged Sword: Fundamentalism and the Sikh Religious Tradition', and 'From Orthodoxy to Fundamentalism: A Thousand Years of Islam in South Asia'. © 1991, 1995 by the University of Chicago. All rights reserved.

Chapter Eight is based on 'Whither Secularism in India?' in *Modern Asian Studies* (Cambridge, England), Vol.27, no.3, 1993, pp.667–97.

Some of the materials used in this book were presented as lectures at four institutions. I would like to place on record my gratitude to the following colleagues for their invitations and hospitality: Professors Elizabeth Hopkins and Frédérique Marglin of Smith College, Northampton, USA, where I was the Neilson Professor in Fall 1990; Professor Ratna Naidu at the University of Hyderabad, India, where I occupied the Radhakrishnan Centenary Chair in Winter 1995; Professor Mrinal Miri, Director of the Indian Institute of Advanced Study, Shimla, where I was Visiting Professor in Summer 1995; and Professors Richard Lariviere and Patrick Olivelle of the Asian Studies Department of the University of Texas at Austin, where I was Visiting Professor during Fall 1995.

Among institutions, it is the Institute of Economic Growth, Delhi, to which I am most heavily and happily indebted. For close to three decades the Institute has provided me freedom and support to pursue my research insterests. I am particularly grateful to the late Professor V.K.R.V. Rao and Professor P.N. Dhar for their encouragement and many kindnesses. Among my colleagues at the Institute, the economists have been indulgent and the sociologists supportive. I thank them all.

For nearly twenty years now Aradhya Bhardwaj has rendered me valuable research assistance, finding books, checking references, correcting proofs, and preparing indexes. Her skills have gone into the making of this book also. I have found in Satya Narain the perfect amanuensis: he reads my handwritten manuscripts with remarkable ease and fidelity and transforms them into error-free print on the wordprocessor. I am grateful to both of them.

Finally, a word of thanks to Uma, as usual, for her advice and patience and much more.

Contents

Chapter One

Introduction
Scope, Concepts, Method

A very popular error: Having the courage of one's convictions; rather, it is a matter of having the courage of an "attack" on one's convictions!
FRIEDRICH NIETZSCHE, *Notebooks*

Interests, material as well as ideal, not ideas directly control action. But world images, which are the production of ideas, have often served as the channels along which action is moved by the dynamics of interests.
MAX WEBER, 'The Social Psychology of World Religions'

Thus I saw the moving drama of the Indian people in the present, and could often trace the threads which bound their lives to the past, even while their eyes were turned to the future. Everywhere I found a cultural background which had exerted a powerful influence on their lives.
JAWAHARLAL NEHRU, *The Discovery of India*

This is a book about the 'ideologies' of 'secularism', and 'fundamentalism', discussed in the setting of 'the religious traditions' of India. The setting is not extraneous: the specific meanings of secularism and fundamentalism that seem most appropriate derive their appositeness from these very traditions or, more precisely, from the dialectic of the cumulative traditions and a particular historical situation. This is not less true of secularism—the antinomy of the sacred and the secular notwithstanding—than it is of fundamentalism. In other words, the mode of inquiry is concrete or context-sensitive rather than abstract or theoretical. Cultural specificities remain opaque, however, unless we employ general concepts to interpret them. The procedure implies some measure of controlled comparison and generalization. This is a book of cultural sociology rather than social theory or the history of particular religious traditions.

I would like to begin the discussion by clarifying briefly (in the following section) my use of the terms 'ideology' and 'religious tradition'. Later (in the next three sections), I will introduce the terms 'secularism', 'fundamentalism', and 'pluralism' in that order, considered as ideologies, indicating the departures that I have made from the generally prevalent usages. Finally (in the last section), an outline of the structure of the book and of the method of interpretation will be presented.

Ideology: Religious Tradition

The word ideology, as is well known, has many connotations in social science literature; it is not my intention to survey or evaluate them here. I would like to stress, however, that in my use of it, the critical attitude that has for long characterized use of the term (and not in Marxist sociology alone in which it is the *camera obscura*) is retained here (see Thompson 1990). My primary aim, however, is to understand and interpret, rather than to praise or denounce, the ideologies or social phenomena generally designated as secularism and fundamentalism. A sceptical stance will be maintained, questionable assumptions highlighted, and hidden agendas exposed. I will also query some of the current usages of these terms because they seem unclear or incoherent to me, and not merely because they are ideological. Ideologies are not, of course, neutral: they convey value judgements of various kinds. Bringing out these evaluations or ideological implications of particular conceptions of secularization, secularism, and fundamentalism is part of the task of interpretation being undertaken here.

In my use of the term, an ideology has, first of all, a substantive content of ideas, world images, and value judgements (affirmations or rejections). It is not simply descriptive of the' contemporary situation, but its justification or critique. Every ideology is rooted in historical experience, but it is futuristic even when it calls for a return to fundamentals of one kind or another. It is a link between identity and aspiration. Secondly, and following from the foregoing, an ideology is a comprehensive, even totalizing, blueprint for living and for action, whether to preserve elements of the status quo, or to revive elements of a past that are considered weakened or lost, or to proceed towards a newly visualized future. Not all of an ideology's objectives are, however, explicit.

Thirdly, ideology is rhetorical in form: it seeks to convince and persuade people about the desirability of a particular world image, and mobilize them for action to achieve the stated objective. Communication is used in a rational manner to appropriate existing symbols, signs, idioms, expressions, and meanings, or to invent them. It follows that a concern with the social distribution and purposive use of power—not naked power but power legitimized by religious or secular criteria such as divine dispensation or popular will— is central to the notion of ideology adopted here. One set of people seeks to exercise power over others, and make them believe and do various things through rhetoric or discursive action. It is not the other's mind or body—their thought or behaviour—alone that is sought to be controlled, but both.

It may be added that I do not look upon ideology as 'superstructure' in the sense of an epiphenomenon or, worse, as a distorted or misrecognized image of the social reality. I rather consider it one of the many significant social forces that are operative at the global or intraglobal level in society, and which contribute to its constitution. In doing so I acknowledge the influence of Louis Dumont's seminal comparative studies of ideology or social thought. Further, I follow Max Weber in affirming the relevance of both the materialist and idealist interpretations of social reality in both its structural and processual aspects, and repudiate the methodological reductionism that derives the allegedly 'real' meaning of ideologies from economic and/or political structures.

It is well known that both religion and science have been presented as ideologies in particular historical settings by interested groups, such as political parties, or by charismatic individuals. I am not concerned with the ideological uses of science in this book except very indirectly insofar as I am interested in secularism. The focus on religion is sharper, and this brings me to the notion of religious tradition.

The preference for the idea of religious tradition over religion derives from the nature of my concern, which is not with the substantive content (cosmological, theological, and metaphysical) of any religion (Hinduism, Islam, or Sikhism), or with its ritual aspect, but with the relationship of the sacred and the secular according to it. More specifically, the concern is with spiritual authority, exercized by religious functionaries of one kind or another (prophets, priests, scriptural specialists, etc.), in relation to temporal power, vested in traditional kings or the modern state.

In this context, it is the dynamic aspect of the relationship between the sacred and the secular (understood as practical modes of being rather than as abstract realms of value) that is most significant. Dynamism means openness, or the scope for revision and restatement: what one may do tomorrow cannot be foretold today in its entirety. It also means accumulation or tradition. In the words of Wilfred Cantwell Smith, who breaks up the omnibus category of religion into 'faith' and 'tradition'—that is matters 'internal' and 'external'—a religious tradition 'is a part of this world, it is a product of human activity; it is diverse, it is fluid, it grows, it changes, it accumulates' (1978: 159). When this dynamism is frozen, we arrive at one kind of fundamentalism. At the same time, it should be recognized that a runaway or radical dynamism would mean the absence of continuity or tradition. In all three major religious traditions of India under study, there is a discernible coherence and continuity of ideas regarding the relationship of the sacred and the secular. This encourages me to undertake the inquiry that constitutes the scope of this book.

I would like to point out here that it is misleading and meaningless, if not virtually impossible, to impose upon the religious traditions under consideration a radical dichotomization of the religious and non-religious aspects of culture. As I have written elsewhere, to speak about religion in India, without querying the notion of religion as a discrete element of everyday life is to yield to the temptation of words (see Madan 1989: 115). My use of the term religious tradition here should be read, therefore, as a condensed expression for social-cultural-religious tradition. Thus, when one discusses organizational pluralism characteristic of Hindu society, one hardly begins to understand it without prior knowledge and understanding of certain critical notions that are considered religious, such as the notions of retribution or purity and pollution. On this point I follow the path laid out by Max Weber (1958), M.N. Srinivas (1952), and Louis Dumont (1970b).

Secularization, Secularism, the Christian Tradition and the Enlightenment

Secularization, secularity, and secularism are multivocal words. While some scholars consider this a limitation on their usefulness as naming words or, more so, as analytical categories, others have argued that their strength lies in this very flexibility or ambiguity of connotation.[1] I recognize the danger of premature fixation of meanings that goes with an uncritical essentialism, but I also believe that it is important that when we use words referentially, or more significantly as concepts, we should know what we are talking about. I will, therefore, try to clarify briefly the use of the above set of terms in the context of, first, the Judeo-Christian tradition and the Enlightenment and, then, sociological and political thought. The involvement of sociological and cultural anthropological theories of religion with Christianity—not only in the nineteenth century but also in our own times—is sufficiently well-known (see e.g. Evans-Pritchard 1965; Asad 1993) for me to dwell on it here.

To begin, let me say, that (1) secularization ordinarily refers to socio-cultural processes that enlarge the areas of life—material, institutional and intellectual—in which the role of the sacred is progressively limited; (2) secularity is the resultant state of social

---

1. In 1965, David Martin, a sociologist, noting the lack of fit between empirical data and the counter-religious notion of secularization, proposed erasure of the word from the sociological vocabulary (see Martin 1965). About the same time, Larry Shiner, a professor of religion in the USA, suggested that 'we drop the word entirely and employ instead terms such as "transposition" or "differentiation", which are both more descriptive and neutral' (1967: 219). The word secularization is, of course, still in use. Martin has even given us a book, outlining 'a general theory of secularization', and presenting a wide range of empirical possibilities within the West (see Martin 1978). More recently, André Béteille (1994), has argued forcefully that words as concepts often derive their usefulness from their ambiguity, and holds this to be true of secularism.

In our own time, secularization has acquired the status of a 'social myth' that contains elements of truth, namely the empirical processes that constitute it, as well as distortions of that truth, all in the service of diverse, even mutually opposed, ideological positions. While the so-called conservatives see secularization as a threat to their conceptions of the good, moral life, robbing it of its ideas of sacredness and value, the secularists look upon it as an anti-religious, emancipatory, historical process. The latter consider urbanization, industrialization and modernization as the causes and symptoms of the 'secularizing fever' that grips our societies today (see Glasner 1977).

being; and (3) secularism is the ideology that argues the historical inevitability and progressive nature of secularization everywhere. While modern secularists generally see the three concepts as mutually entailed or harmoniously integrated elements of a preferred world image, some contemporary scholars of Christianity have written about secularization as the will of God, but denounced secularism as ungodly.

The English word 'secular' is derived from the Latin *saeculum*, which means 'an age' (for example, *in saecula saeculorum*, for ever and ever, Timothy I, 1: 17), or 'the spirit of an age'. It has the same meaning as the Greek 'aeon' (*aion*), which is used in the New Testament for an 'age' or 'era': more precisely, 'the present time between the times when men are pilgrims and sojourners in the terrestrial city' (Shiner 1965: 280). By extension the word also denotes 'the world', located not only spatially as the Greek cosmos, but also temporally. Throughout the Bible, the notions of time and history, contrasted with timeless myth, are pervasive. The Lord's act of creation takes six days to complete; the departure of Abraham from Mesopotamia and of Moses from Egypt, both are events in space and time; Jesus moves in time with his people towards his Kingdom.

Besides the notions of time and history, the Bible also introduces in the very first verse of the Book of Genesis, the idea of the world as divine creation. Being created, the earth and all that is on it are separated from divinity and made available for human mastery (Genesis 1: 28). In other words, they are secularized. As Peter Berger, a social theorist, puts it, the seeds of secularization were sown in the Old Testament in the form of 'a God who stands *outside* of the cosmos, which is his creation, but which he confronts and does not permeate' (1973: 121). This opens the way for what he calls 'historization', that is man's self-making activity. 'It may be said that the transcendentalization of God and the concomitant "disenchantment of the world" opened up a "space" for history as the arena of both divine and human action' (ibid.: 124). Berger concludes by saying that, closely related to the foregoing two ideas is the motif of 'ethical rationalization in the old Testament (in the sense of imposing rationality on life)' (ibid.: 125).

Friedrich Gogarten, a Christian theologian, elaborates the significance of human action. He draws attention to verses 1–5 in Chapter 4 of the Galatians (in the New Testament) to point out the significance of God sending forth his son, born of a woman and under the Jewish law; namely that those subject to the law may be redeemed, and guided to graduate from being minors, who are no different from slaves, to the status of sons. To attain such status is to assume responsibility, about the scope of which St Paul said, 'all is permitted'. According to Gogarten, 'this statement opens up a fully new religion of man in the world, the face of the world has been completely changed', and 'the basis is laid for the lordship over the world and its powers that the human spirit is later to achieve' (see Shiner 1964: 33–4). Gogarten locates the Christian roots of secularization in his notion of human nature as the unity of receptivity and creativity: man is defined not only by 'his openness to other than men and to the mystery of his being in the world', but equally by his ability 'to respond as one who can give or withhold himself' (ibid.: 28). The scope for the exercise of human responsibility is indeed immense.

The underlying idea of two domains of action is repeatedly stated in the New Testament. Thus, we read about the things that are God's and those that are Caeser's (Luke 20: 25), and about the two swords (Luke 22: 38). Jesus is said to have acknowledged to Pilate that he was the King and clarified that his Kingdom was not of this world (John 18: 36). In course of time, the two worlds were sought to be brought together, first of all by Constantine I, who became a Christian early in the fourth century, and attempted to make Christianity the official religion of Rome. Until Constantine's conversion there was a tension in the dualism of God and Caesar, for Jesus Christ as 'King of kings' was superior to any earthly king, who would be 'served' but surely not 'worshipped': whatever was due to Caesar was first due to God. This conflict was resolved when Constantine declared his own allegiance to Jesus Christ (see Pelikan 1987: 48–50).

A powerful champion can be a master too. It was now the turn of popes, claiming their mandate from Peter, to characterize earthly government as a mere instrument subordinate to the city of God. A celebrated formulation of this dichotomy is by St Augustine at the beginning of the fifth century: 'two cities have been formed by two loves: the earthly by the love of self, even to the contempt of God; the heavenly by the love of God, even to the contempt of the self' (1948, xiv, 29: 47). The stark opposition conveyed in this declaration reflects the negative, early Christian judgement of the secular world brought under the power of Satan. Augustine did not condemn civil authority, but saw in the need for it a departure from the ideal order of human affairs. Later, at the end of the fifth century, Pope Gelasius gave an explicit definition of the relationship under discussion, clarifying that 'the priestly power is much more important [than the royal power] because it has to render account for the kings of men themselves at the divine tribunal' (see Tierney 1980: 13).[2]

In the centuries after Gelasius, that is through the Middle Ages (*ca.* 700–*ca.* 1550), the character of the papacy was profoundly transformed by the decline of the Roman empire and resultant developments. The popes assumed the role of temporal governors of Rome and the surrounding areas, and continued to enlarge their influence. In course of time, they turned their back on the Byzantine emperors in the East, and the Roman Church emerged, if not as the only true state in the West, certainly as the most dominant institution. Indeed, the Church created a successor empire in alliance with the Frankish kings, and became identified with the whole of organized society. The kings sought and received sanctification—sacred relics, ecclesiastical vestments, holy anointment oils, etc. were employed for the purpose—at the hands of bishops, and government came to depend heavily upon the supernatural for legitimation even as the Church became deeply involved in secular matters. The sacred kings, however, turned out to be quite 'fragile'. As R.W. Southern (1970: 36–7) points out

[T]he growing complexity of society... called for organized government rather than ritual for the solution of its problems.... In the long run this discovery helped to enlarge the area of secular action and pointed forward to a purely secular state.... Moreover, with the secularization of the lay ruler, that whole broad stratum of society which he particularly represented—the laity—suffered a corresponding demotion.

The Church strengthened its hold over government through the late eleventh and early twelfth centuries by providing specialized knowledge through secular clergy—so-called and distinguished from monastic monks. It acquired 'the most formidable array of teeth', *but* 'they could seldom be used effectively against the current

2. According to Louis Dumont, the Gelasian formulation is of cross-cultural application: 'It is not unreasonable for us to suppose that the original sacred sovereignty (for example, that of ancient Egypt or of China), has in some cultures differentiated into two functions, as it did in India' (1986: 47). My own studies of the religious traditions of India in this book support this view.

of any widespread secular interest' (ibid.: 41). Among the religious forces of the times, the ecclesiastical hierarchy has been described as 'the greatest and the most fundamental' (Tillich 1968: 145). Inevitably, it came into conflict with civil hierarchies, as national governments were cropping up all over the place from the early twelfth century onward. Each hierarchy sought to establish an ordered Christian society, but from its own perspective, in which the religious and the secular could be combined. Over a period of nearly a thousand years, the sacred-secular relationship oscillated between a sharply defined dichotomy of roles and a mixture of functions. The bishop and the king each were conceived of as a *persona mixta*. Around 1100, 'the concept of the king as a person endowed with spiritual qualities was still in bloom', but 'the papal doctrine finally denied to the king a clerical character' (Kantorwicz 1981: 44–5). Gradually, by the early fourteenth century, towns and secular governments, which had meanwhile grown in size and scope, 'first found their voice' (Southern 1970: 45). They questioned 'sacerdotal supremacy' as well as 'papal secular pretensions'. 'Individual experience', 'the role of the community as the source of political and spiritual authority', and 'the values of secular life' generally became salient (ibid.: 48–9). Eventually, the collapse of the uneasy relationship of the ecclesiastical and secular hierarchies signalled the end of the Middle Ages.

Unlike the oscillations of the Latin West, a unity of domains throughout characterized the Orthodox East. This schism emerged early—for example, Peter's intermediary role was never recognized in the East—and crystallized by the end of the eighth century (see Herrin 1987: 443ff.). The two Christendoms were divided by theological, cultural and political factors. As Timothy Ware writes: 'The life of the Byzantium formed a unified whole, and there was no rigid line of separation between the religious and the secular, between Church and State; the two were seen as parts of a single organism' (1973: 49). The implication of this split is that our discussion of the relationship of Christianity and secularization holds good only with reference to the Latin Church. But, then, secularization made deeper inroads into the social and intellectual life of Western Europe than into the East, at least until the Leninist revolution.

In the dynamics of the relationship of the religious and the secular through the Middle Ages, it should be stressed that ideas alone were not the moving force. The evolution of institutions, enlargement of populations, the rise of urban settlements, general economic growth, and so on, also were significant elements of the situation. After the collapse of the Roman imperial authority, the Church played no mean role in fostering not only kingships but also the universities (see Saberwal 1995). Each institution—Church, state, university, etc.—nurtured its own autonomy.

The conflict between religious faith and human reason, which forms part of the background to the emergence of the modern ideology of secularism, surfaced in the late Middle Ages. It is an important chapter in the history of the relationship of Christianity and Greek philosophy. The ripening of this conflict, and the efforts of Thomas Aquinas and others to compose it, eventually led in the seventeenth century to the flowering of what is called 'modern' philosophy in the West (see Russell 1946 and Tillich 1968). This consisted of a serious attempt to construct a rational explanation of the universe on the basis of scientific or experimental knowledge, and to control it through technology. As Arnold Toynbee (1979: 168–9) puts it:

> [T]he traditional Christian panorama of the Universe, which had been built out of an amalgam of Christian myth, Jewish scripture, and Greek philosophy and science... ceased to command unquestioning assent in Western minds.... One practical expression of the moral revolt was a deliberate transference of seventeenth century Western Man's spiritual treasure from an incurably polemical Theology to an apparently non-controversial science.

The seventeenth century also saw the emergence of the notion of the perfectibility of man, not by scientific progress alone but also by social action. The Augustinian notions of human worthlessness and human impotence generated a reaction that drew upon Renaissance humanism, the spirit of which can be found in the New Testament epistles too. Jean Calvin was a major contributor to this reaction. 'God', he wrote, 'abolishes the corruptions of the flesh in his elect in a continuous succession of time, and indeed little by little' (see Passmore 1970: 157). The dependence of this gradualist perfectibilism upon divine grace was rejected by other thinkers, such as the Cambridge Platonists, who argued that, as rational beings endowed with free will, men have the option if not also the responsibility to take charge of their lives. The Graeco-Christian ideal of absolute perfection was replaced by an incremental, indeed endless, notion of multidimensional (physical, intellectual and moral) perfectibility, achieved in the course of self-directed everyday life (see ibid.: 149–70).

The foregoing and, doubtless, other developments strengthened incipient, post-Renaissance, secularist tendencies in western Europe and Britain. The Enlightenment, or the Age of Reason, inaugurated in the second half of the eighteenth century, created the intellectual ambience for the eventual formulation of a general ideology of secularism. No serious scholar anywhere believes any longer that Enlightenment philosophers—particularly the English and the Germans—rejected religion completely: they rather sought to bind it within 'the limits of reason alone' (Kant), as natural religion (Hume, Locke, et al.), rejecting 'revealed' religion and a transcendental justification for religion. Voltaire's dying declaration was of faith in God and detestation of superstition (see Ayer 1986). Kant repudiated all but the most abstract religion, but acknowledged the validity of religion as 'experience' (see Gay 1966). It has been said that the philosophers of the Enlightenment 'demolished the Heavenly City of St Augustine only to rebuild it with more up-to-date materials' (Becker 1932: 31).

Peter Gay has pointed out in his wide-ranging and authoritative account of the Age of Reason that, although it was still a religious age, secularization involved 'a subtle shift of attention: religious institutions and religious explanations of events were slowly displaced from the centre of life to its periphery' (1966: 338). To quote Kant *'Enlightenment is man's emergence from his self-incurred immaturity. Immaturity* is the inability to use one's own understanding without the guidance of another.... The motto of the Enlightenment is therefore: *Sapere aude*! Have the courage to use your *own* understanding'! (1991: 54, emphasis original).

This shift was, in Ernst Cassirer's (1968: 163) words, a change in 'the intellectual centre of gravity', bringing about an epochal break in the Western conceptions of ontology and epistemology. It was a call for human self-emancipation. Nature had been shorn of its mysteries—in Friedrich Schiller's phrase, it had been 'disenchanted'—and reconceptualized as 'self-supporting and self-explanatory'. The question of transcendence had been—or so the philosophers thought—set aside. The emphasis no longer was on the sacred things beyond, but on *saecularis*, or lasting worldly things judged as value, and on *saeculum*, or our age, here and now. Secularization encompassed everything including art, history, morals, politics, and of course science.

If secularism as an ideology is placed within the setting of the Enlightenment, as I think it should be, it is obvious that its roots are better defined positively as a reasonable theory about human agency, rather than negatively as merely an anti-religious ideology. Indeed, scholars from Max Weber and Ernst Troeltsch to Louis Dumont and Peter Berger have in their different ways pointed to the essential linkages among Protestantism, individualism, and secularization. In Berger's succinct summing up, 'Protestantism cut the umbilical cord between heaven and earth', and presented secularization as a gift to humankind (1973: 118). David Martin too proclaims that 'secularization initially occurs within the ambit of Christian societies' (1978: 2).

Earlier in this chapter, I briefly presented Peter Berger's argument about the secularizing influence of some Old Testament ideas, namely a strict monotheism, 'disenchantment' of the world, and 'historization'. He further maintains that early Christianity did not allow the blossoming of these key ideas. He adds: 'The Protestant Reformation, however, may...be understood as a powerful re-emergence of precisely those secularizing forces that had been "contained" by Catholicism, not only by replicating the Old Testament in this, but going directly beyond it' (1973: 123).

Thus, the idea of the privatization of religion, which is the minimal recommendation of secularists everywhere, owes its birth as much to the Protestant notion of the individual's assumption of responsibility for his or her own salvation without the aid of the Church, as to the secular notion of the perfectibility of humankind by social action mentioned above. The general secularization of life in the West after the Reformation is thus significantly, though only partly, an unintended consequence of a religious idea. More directly, Martin Luther strengthened the forces of secularization by maintaining that the Christian community exists solely by faith, trusting in God's saving grace, and that the Church possesses no jurisdictional powers. He maintained that it was the duty laid upon all true Christians in the New Testament that they submit to secular authorities, the range of whose powers he actually extended in ways that ruled out resistance. Similarly, Calvin recommended political dutifulness to the faithful without regard for the character, conduct, or religion of the ruler (see Hopfl 1991). The manner in which the Lutheran-Calvinist ideas of 'predestination' and 'calling' promoted the spirit of world mastery among the Puritans is the subject of Max Weber's famous thesis on the subject (see Weber 1930).

To conclude the present argument, I suggest that Luther and Calvin helped to usher in a modern, secularized age that they themselves would hardly approve of. Although religious ideas contributed to the strengthening of the processes of secularization in the West, the latter in turn, ironically, contributed to the erosion of religious beliefs, practices, and authority. In the words of the theologian Paul Tillich, Protestantism created a 'sacred void' in Western society, for it 'demands a secular reality', although within the 'Gestalt of grace' (1957: 213–14).

The word 'secularization' has been already used in this discussion. I should now point out that it seems to have been first employed in the course of the negotiations for the Peace of Westphalia (1648) at the end of the Thirty Years' War. Secularization referred to the transfer of lands and other church properties to the exclusive control of the princes.[3] Not all such transfers were opposed in the seventeenth century, but subsequently, Roman Catholic accounts of secularization, deemed them 'an unmitigated evil' (Shiner 1967: 208). It may also be noted here that, in the middle of the seventeenth century, secularization had not yet come to denote religious tolerance or indifference to religion. The conclusion of the Thirty Years' War, which was a war of religions, coincided with the reign of Louis XIV in France: a more cruel persecutor of religious minorities would be hard to find in the annals of Europe.

What was at first largely a matter-of-fact statement about certain events, later became, after the French Revolution, a value statement as well. In 1789, Talleyrand announced to the National Assembly that all ecclesiastical goods were at the disposal of the nation, as indeed they already should have been as a matter of principle.[4] Secularity now came to be considered as the rational basis of social life and therefore an imperative. Once such an idea is accepted, and secularization as a historical process brought under its control—that

---

3. It may be added here that such take-overs were not without precedent. In England, Henry VIII broke off from Rome, seized power over the Church, and secularized its wealth and personnel in a few swift moves (1532–36). He secularized the state also (see Somerville 1992: 11ff.). The most celebrated example from the twentieth century is Lenin's decree of 1918 declaring all Church properties to be publicly owned.

4. While a matter of principle was thus being emphasized, a practical purpose too was being served, for the extravagant Louis XVI had left the state coffers empty.

is, transformed into an ideology—there can be no looking back for the converted.[5] When George Jacob Holyoake coined the term 'secularism' in 1851, and led a rationalist movement of protest in England, secularization was built into the encompassing ideology of progress.[6]

Holyoake inherited from the Owenite and Utilitarian movements of England a naturalistic, ethical and social utopian rationalism. From the French Revolution he derived republicanism, anticlericalism, and an aversion to theology. His endeavour was 'to encourage men to trust Reason throughout and to trust nothing that Reason does not establish'. Besides, he advocated 'the fullest liberty of thought' and discouraged 'worship of supposed superior things' (see Campbell 1971: 46–57). More affirmatively, the 'essential principle' of secularism was 'to seek for human improvement by material means alone', which are adequate to secure 'the desired end' (Waterhouse 1921: 348). Holyoake's followers, never many in number, came from the working and lower middle classes. Not being an effective organizer, he was virtually displaced in the late 1850s by Charles Bradlaugh, who was prominent in the formation of the National Secular Society in 1866. The Secularists (so-called) have been described as 'republicans' in a devotedly monarchical country and 'atheists in a society which, outwardly at least, was profoundly religious' (Royle 1980: x). These developments in Britain and abroad were a spent force in half a century (see Royle 1974 and 1980), and are not relevant to the present discussion except very broadly.

The negative assessment of secularization as a general process among Christian theologians and lay scholars, referred to earlier, lasted more than two centuries. It was in the 1950s that some radical thinkers, including Friedrich Gogarten and Dietrich Bonhoeffer, offered a new perspective, asserting that secularization, but not

---

5. It would seem that the word secularization has been also used to describe the involvement of the Church with Greek thought (see Shiner 1965: 280).

6. The *Oxford English Dictionary* gives the following definition of secularism, which it dates from 1851: 'The doctrine that morality should be determined solely with regard to the well-being of humankind in the present life, to the exclusion of all considerations drawn from belief in God or a future state'. Needless to add, this is Holyoake's definition of the term. Holyoake had spent six months in prison in 1841, having been the last person to be thus sentenced in England for public blasphemy. It has been suggested that he may have been led to coin the neutral term secularism, as a substitute for atheism, to avoid further complications (see Saran 1982: 2).

secularism, should be accommodated within the Christian faith. To quote Gogarten (see Smith 1968: 41–2).

So long as faith and secularization remain what they are according to their nature, the relation between them cannot be one of contending with each other for the sphere belonging to them. If faith means keeping from secularization what is seized by it, faith ceases to be faith. If secularization begins to claim for itself that which belongs to faith, secularization does not remain within secularity, but becomes secularism.

For Gogarten secularism is 'erroneous secularization'. Other scholars make similar distinctions. Martin Marty, a historian of religion in America, does not consider secularization 'closed to faith', but criticizes secularism as 'self-contained, self-explanatory, self-enclosed', permitting 'no witness to the activity of God in history' (1965: 145). Harvey Cox, a Harvard theologian, maintains that, while secularization is 'an irreversible historical process' that has 'its roots in the biblical faith itself', secularism is an 'ism' and a 'closed world-view', which 'menaces the openness and freedom secularization has produced' (1965: 18–21).

The implication of the foregoing views obviously is that the basic flaw of the ideology of secularism is its holistic, non-dualistic character, and that the separation of the domains of the sacred and the secular must be acknowledged everywhere and in the same manner.[7] The problem with the acceptance of this position is that non-Christian religious traditions either do not make this distinction (e.g. Islam), or do it hierarchically (e.g. Hinduism), subsuming the secular under the sacred. If this dichotomy is employed by contemporary Christian theologians to protect Christianity against secularism—in fact from the erosive effects of secularization itself—it occurs in sociological literature in the opposite sense, that is, in the sense of putting the sacred in its place, which is the privacy of personal faith, or no place at all. Either ideological endeavour—privatization or abolition of religion—is characterized by doubt, I think, rather than confidence, although this is rarely acknowledged.

7. Not everybody finds the arguments about the compatibility of Christianity and secularization acceptable. Leszek Kolakowski puts it quite bluntly: 'In the hope of saving itself, [Christianity] seems to be assuming the colours of its environment, but the result is that it loses its identity, which depends on ...[the] distinction between the sacred and the profane, and on the conflict that can and must exist between them' (1990: 69).

Secularization and Secularism: Social Science Perspectives

As stated above, secularization, once it was transformed into a thesis or ideology, became an emotive word with many connotations, ranging from anti-clericalism to the liberation of knowledge from the false premises of religious dogma. From the latter arose the sociological concept of secularization which has been defined by Peter Berger as 'the process by which sectors of society and culture are removed from the domination of religious institutions and symbols' (1973: 113).[8] While the inner logic of the economic sector seems to make it the most convenient arena for secularization, other sectors—notably the political and the cultural—have been found to be less amenable to it. It is in relation to the latter that the ideology of secularism acquires the most significance.

The foundations of the sociological thesis of secularization were laid by Auguste Comte in a massive body of work from which I will mention just two points here. (1) His evolutionary paradigm of intelligence, or knowledge, progressing from the 'Theological, or fictitious' to the Metaphysical, or abstract', and finally to the 'Positive, or scientific' stage is well known. He located and named a new science 'sociology' in the domain of positive knowledge and committed it to a secularist rather than any available religious view of social reality. (2) All historical religions were, in Comte's judgement, theological, but religion was in principle associated with feeling or sentiment and was therefore potentially useful. He stressed that human reason was not boundless and society was possible only through emotional stimuli and by virtue of a moral consensus, which Comte considered inconceivable without 'the spiritual reorganization of the West' in the first place. This process was to embrace ideas, morals and ultimately social institutions. Hence Comte's fantastic project of founding a new religion of humanity on the basis of positive knowledge, with himself as its high priest. Comte's fantasies have a point, though. In the words of Bernard Reardon, 'His belief that the only real knowledge is that provided by science has been widely accepted', but it is equally important to note that 'he had sense enough to realize that of itself science is unable to answer all the

8. Cp. the definition given by Larry Shiner: 'secularization means the decline of conventional religiosity and the loss of respect for the higher powers of tribe and tradition' (1965: 280).

problems of human existence and that man cannot dispense with ideological goals' (1985: 236). Put simply, Comte was insightful enough to realize that 'religion was both intellectually obsolete and socially necessary' (Preus 1987: 109).

Comte's specific proposals for the future were of course fanciful, but many of his basic assumptions and assertions were endorsed by more disciplined thinkers, most notable among them all being Emile Durkheim (1881–1918). He maintained that, although the inroads of science into human affairs (that is, secularization) had proceeded far and deep by the end of the early twentieth century, yet it was forbidden entry into 'the world of religious and moral life'. Durkheim thought, however, that even this 'final barrier' would be overcome, and science would 'establish herself as mistress in this reserved region' also. Was it then all over for religion? Not quite. The uncertainty and ambiguity of the following declaration, from the same classic text from which I have just quoted, namely *The Elementary Forms of the Religious Life* (1915), is remarkable. Durkheim wrote: 'there is something eternal in religion which is destined to survive all the particular symbols in which religious thought has successively enveloped itself'. And so 'religion seems destined to transform itself rather than to disappear' (1965: 462–96). Building upon a tradition that was about three centuries old in the West, Durkheim looked forward to a purely secular but moral education to take on some of the social functions or responsibilities that religions—none of them false, in his judgement, all true in terms of their social function (see ibid.: 3)—had been performing for so long.

In one of his last statements on the subject, Durkheim warned against a complacent view of the secularization of morality. To guard against a secularized but 'impoverished and colourless morality', he said, 'We must seek, in the very heart of religious conceptions, those moral realities that are, as it were, lost and dissimulated in it.... In a word, we must discover the rational substitutes for those religious notions that for a long time have served as the vehicle for the most essential moral ideas' (see Pickering 1975: 196).

Durkheim's fairly accurate prognosis errs on the side of caution, I think, in relation to the survival of religion in human society. The point is perhaps best illustrated by what has been happening in North America in the years since World War Two. Robert Bellah's exposition of 'civil religion' (see Bellah 1967 and 1964) had already provided an insightful illustration of the transformation of religion within an evolutionary framework; but now we have Robert Wuthnow's (1989) richly documented work which underscores that a simple-minded, linear notion of secularization is wholly inadequate to capture the restructuring of American religion in our time in all its complexity and vibrancy (see also Demerath and Rhys 1992).

Max Weber (1864–1920) was less confident about the future of a secularized world than Durkheim. The key motifs of the process of rationalization in Weber's judgement were, first, a valorization of the means-end relationship (instrumental rationality) and, second, the exercise of reason as such on 'the image of the world', resulting in the replacement of religious primacy in society by economic primacy. The latter is qualified by the ways in which politics operates in modern society. Rationalization is a broader notion than secularization since it includes the systematization of religious ideas and the emergence of ethical rationalism. Secularization (in the sense used above in our discussion of Comte and Durkheim), however, lies at its core.

Once initiated, rationalization proceeds relentlessly: it eliminates magic and mystery from the world, but it also abolishes ultimate values, because the only values it knows are instrumental. A consequence of the decline of religion, according to Weber (1948: 155), is that:

The fate of our times is characterized by rationalization and intellectualization and, above all, the 'disenchantment of the world'. Precisely the ultimate and most sublime values have retreated from public life either into the transcendental realm of mystic life or into the brotherliness of direct and personal human relations.

'Science is meaningless', Weber approvingly quoted Tolstoy saying, 'because it gives no answer to our question, the only question important for us: "What shall we do and how shall we live?" ' (ibid.: 143). Needless to emphasize, this is a moral question—a question of values. In dismay, he warned that the 'almost superstitions venera- tion of science as the possible creator or at least prophet of social revolution, violent or peaceful' can only end in disappointment (1978, 1: 515).

As for power, which Weber placed at the very centre of a secularized world, he saw no evidence anywhere of its exercise totally divorced from religion. As he put it, 'the complete subordina- tion of priestly to secular power... can nowhere be found in its pure type' (1978, 2: 1158–60). Nevertheless, Weber's sociology fills the void caused by the retreat of religion in our time, through the increasing importance of politics, law, and bureaucracy. There is no turning back: and where the West leads, he believed, the rest of the world will follow, not under external impact alone, but also because 'disenchantment' ultimately overtakes all prophetic religions. But Weber's study of world religions persuaded him that rationalization as a historical process is context specific: despite formal similarities, it will not have the same content and significance everywhere.[9]

For a truly universal sociological theory of secularization we have to turn to Karl Marx (1818–1883). As Owen Chadwick puts it: 'Marxism was the most powerful philosophy of secularization in the nineteenth century.... Its power was intrinsic: the systematic and original exposition of a theory of secular society, based partly upon philosophical axioms and partly upon theories of contemporary economics' (1975: 66).

In Marx's perception, the phenomenon of secularization (or decline of religion) was not particularly complex. He did not write much on the subject, but he did indeed consider 'the criticism of religion' as 'the premise of all criticism'.[10] According to him the radical or correct understanding of religion consisted in demystifying it by locating the insights provided by Bruno Bauer and Ludwig Feuerbach regarding the illusory character of divinity, and therefore of religion, within a framework of class antagonism. Feuerbach had argued that the idea of an all-knowing and all-powerful divinity enables human beings to overcome, through projection, their own sense of inadequacy. The function of religion is not anthropological, Marx argued, but sociological. He wrote: 'Feuerbach resolves the religious essence into the human essence.... [He], consequently, does not see that the "religious sentiment" is itself a social product' (see Elster 1986: 22). More specifically, Marx writes (ibid.: 301):

Man makes religion, religion does not make man.... But man is no abstract being encamped outside the world. Man is *the world of man*, the state, society. This state, this society, produce religion, an *inverted* world-consciousness, because they are an

---

9. For a discussion of Weber's notion of rationalization see Schluchter (1984) and Mommsen (1989). The latter's disagreement with the former on certain points is of great interest.

10. It may be noted that, although Marx himself presented this formulation as relevant to Germany, its general applicability cannot have been absent from his mind. Indeed, it has been widely treated as such.

inverted world.... The struggle against religion is therefore a fight against the world
of which religion is the spiritual aroma (emphasis original).

Then follow the famous lines about religion as 'the sigh of the
oppressed creature', indeed 'the opium of the people', and the
recommendation for corrective action: 'To abolish religion as the
illusory happiness of people is to demand their real happiness. The
demand to give up illusions about the existing state of affairs is the
demand to give up a state of affairs which needs illusions'
(ibid.:301).

Marx's vision of the future is of a secularized world, pushed
forward through economic and social development towards a class-
less and unalienated society. But the irony of it all is that, in Owen
Chadwick's words, the idea of an 'awry world' that should be
'redeemed' is 'no irreligious idea. The whole idea of alienation is
unthinkable without Christian and Jewish axioms, and the coming of
its cure is sometimes expressed [by Marx] in terms which bear the
scent of older language of redemption' (1975: 68). What is more,
Marx himself had doubts about the future course of secularization.
He wrote: 'the fact that the secular foundation [of life] lifts itself
above itself, and establishes itself in the clouds as an independent
realm, is only to be explained by the self-cleavage and self-contradictoriness of the secular basis' (see Lowith 1949: 49).[11]

It should be clear from the above necessarily very brief exposition
of the sociological conception of secularization, as formulated by

---

11. Marx's views on religion were reinforced and restated by Friedrich Engels. He
wrote: 'When... man no longer merely proposes but also disposes—only then will the
last alien force which is still reflected in religion vanish; and with it will vanish the
religious reflection itself, for the simple reason that there will be nothing to reflect'
(1954: 440). He stressed the importance of the scientific education of the masses for
the ending of the mysteries and illusions which give rise to religious beliefs.
   The Marxist critique of religion found its most vehement statement in the views of
Lenin. For example:
   Those who toil and live in want all their lives are taught by religion to be submissive
   and patient while here on earth, and to take comfort in the hope of a heavenly award.
   But those who live by the labour of others are taught by religion to practice charity
   whilst on earth, thus offering them a very cheap way of justifying their existence
   as exploiters and selling them at a very modest price tickets to well-being in Heaven.
   Religion is opium for the people. [The altering of Marx's phraseology may be
   noted]. Religion is a sort of spiritual booze, in which the slaves of capital drown
   their human image, their demand for a life more or less worthy of man (Lenin 1962:
   2).

four major figures in the sociological tradition, that the endeavour to free society from its religious moorings—that is, to secularize it—is fraught with difficulties. The sociological perspective too suffers from (in Marx's phrase) self-contradictoriness. If seen as a secularized issuance of Christianity, and also influenced by Judaism, it retains a commitment to the religious foundations of society. If treated as a product of the Enlightenment, sociology appears before us as a commentary on secularization. In either idiom it remains partial in both senses of this word—incomplete and biased.

*   *   *

A final comment on secularization, considered in its institutional rather than the ideological aspect. Where do we locate 'the secular state'? This is not the place to go again into the more than a thousand years of struggle between the authority of the priest and the power of the king in the Christian West. Nor indeed may we undertake an excursus into liberal political philosophy. Suffice it to briefly note here a few parallel strands in the political thought of Thomas Hobbes and John Locke, two outstanding ideologues of the modern state in the second half of the seventeenth century.

Hobbes did not regard Christian doctrine as politically destabilizing, but considered the church a vested interest that had to be kept under the sovereign's control. To allow the church to be its own head would amount to creating an enemy of the sovereign, for sovereignty is indivisible. Indeed, he defined the church in *Leviathan* (1651) as a community of Christians, 'united in the person of one Sovereign; at whose command they ought to assemble, and without whose authority they ought not to assemble' (1991: 321). According to Hobbes, a divinely instituted spiritual authority independent of civil control had never existed in the Judeo-Christian tradition. Moses, Aaron, and the succeeding high priests had combined civil and ecclesiastical powers in their persons (ibid.: 357). As for the Kingdom of Christ, since it was not of this world, it could not serve as a model for it before the general resurrection (ibid.: 334–5.). Meanwhile, the sovereign would rule equally over secular as well as religious matters, and the role of the church would be that of a moral counsellor. Only the sovereign's command can make religious doctrines binding. 'Temporal and *Spiritual* government are but two words,' wrote Hobbes, 'brought into the world, to make men see double, and mistake their lawful sovereign' (ibid.: 322). The medieval distinction between the church and the state—*sacerdotium* and *regnum*—is here abandoned. The Hobbesian state is not, quite clearly, secular as we understand the term today: particularly if it is argued (as indeed has been done by some scholars) that self-interest alone did not constitute for Hobbes the notion of political obedience; divine command was an essential element in it (see Martinich 1992: chaps 3 and 10).

A problem with Hobbes' formulation is that it does not deal with the problem of religious difference: the church and the sovereign both are assumed to be Christian. Locke, in his *Letter Concerning Toleration* (1689) takes a broader view: 'I esteem ... toleration to be the chief characteristical mark of the true church' (1991: 14). He looked upon a church as any voluntary association of believers practising a religion, who are self-governing within the framework of civil society. The liberty of conscience, of which he was a great supporter, was to be accommodated within the necessary authority of the state, not outside it. He wrote: 'Things that are prejudicial to the commonweal of a people in their ordinary use, and are therefore forbidden by laws, those things ought not to be permitted to churches in their sacred rites' (ibid.: 37). Locke recognized, particularly in his later writings, the functional difference between the church and the state (see Mabbott 1973: 173–4), but insisted that human beings are not governed by the positive laws of civil society alone. Above such and other laws (namely 'fraternal' and 'private' laws), stands divine law, revealed to humankind but also discoverable through reason. Laws other than divine law were considered obligatory by Locke only derivatively: 'they do not bind men by virtue of their own innate force but by virtue of some divine precept on which they are grounded; nor are we bound to obey magistrates for any other reason than that the Lord has commanded it' (Locke 1967: 226). Although this position seems the opposite of Hobbes', it is not wholly so, for both recognize the priority of divine command in human affairs. We encounter in Hobbes as well as in Locke the notion of the functional preeminence of secular power, but not its autonomy.

It is only in the eighteenth century that a more consistent secularization of social and political thought begins to take shape (see Gay 1966, vol. 2, chap. 3), which in turn leads to widespread secularization of the European mind in the nineteenth century (see

Chadwick 1975). I have already discussed above the significance of the emergence of the sociology of religion in the work of Comte and his successors. As for the specific notion of the secular state, it would seem that, while the princes of Europe were deemed secular at various times, though not for the same reasons, it was the American and French Revolutions that eventually bestowed concreteness and precision on the idea. Both revolutions were based on, among other key concepts, the notions of the secular natural order and the political rights of the individual. Reliance upon Christian theology (such as had, for instance, helped shape revolutionary thinking in England in the civil war and in the revolution of 1688) was abandoned. In France, the constitution of 1791 secularized the state, the Concordat was signed in 1801, the Civil Code came in 1804, and eventually the separation of the church and the state became law in 1905 (see Bauberot, forthcoming).

The conception of the secular state that seems most relevant for characterizing the Indian polity is that of the First Amendment to the American Constitution enacted in 1791. What it implies is not of course unproblematic (see Swomley 1987), but two ideas stand out: 'non-interference' (the state, or more precisely the government, shall not establish a church) and 'entitlement' (the citizen has the in-alienable right to follow a religion of his or her choice, or none at all). This same right was also affirmed in the French Charter of the Rights of Man, though more in the name of individual freedom than that of religious tolerance.

It would seem that, at the very beginning the settlers in North America, the so-called Pilgrims, with a history of religious persecu-tion behind them—they would not accept the authority of the Church of England—were most concerned about religious freedom. The legislative background to the First Amendment was complex (the state too had to be protected), but the crucial thing was the first law passed by the General Assembly of the Commonwealth of Pennsyl-vania, at the behest of its founder, William Penn, guaranteeing the religious freedom of the individual (so long as he or she remained a monotheist!). Subsequently, Thomas Jefferson provided distin-guished leadership for bringing about the separation of the church and the state. He deeply cherished the ideals of the Enlightenment, and put his trust in human reason, which he did not consider opposed to natural (as against revealed) religion. Jefferson denied the state any right to have an opinion in matters of religion. 'It is error alone which needs the support of government,' he wrote, 'Truth can stand by itself'. He was therefore opposed to the continuance of the Anglican Church, which had been established early in the colony of Virginia and elsewhere. In 1777, he drafted a Bill for Establishing Religious Freedom that became law nine years later. This outcome owed much to the efforts of Jefferson's young friend James Madison. The Virginian statute became the model for similar enactments by other American states, and ultimately found its place in the United States Constitution through the First Amendment to the Bill of Rights, which stipulated that, 'Congress shall make no law respecting an establishment of religion, or prohibiting exercise thereof' (ibid.: 48). A decade later, in 1802, Jefferson, by then the President, summed it all up in the by now famous declaration that he contemplated 'with sovereign reverence that act of the whole American people' which amounted to 'building a wall of separation between the Church and the State' (see Greene 1941 and Cunningham Jr. 1991).

What the First Amendment allows or disallows continues to be debated to this day. Thus, is free exercise of religion an 'equality right' that 'protects both individuals and religious organizations from some of the regulation that is now imposed by the secular state... subject to the compelling government interest test... [which is intended] principally to prevent tangible harm to third persons who have not joined the faith' (Laycock 1994 : 886)? A Supreme Court ruling of 1990, which upheld the Oregon state ban on the use of the drug peyote in certain American Indian rituals, affirmed the 'equality right' interpretation. Following public protests, the Congress passed the Religious Freedom Restoration Act three years later, upholding the 'liberty right' view as correct.

The 'liberty right' view, it seems to me, is what the Indian Constitution envisages, embodying a vision of the combined principles of religious freedom and the secular state. The circumstances in which the task of constitution-making was undertaken, soon after the partition of the subcontinent on the basis of religious or civilizational difference, made the separation of religion and the state imperative. But the pervasive character of religion in the country—and indeed in all countries of South Asia—made the privatization of religion problematic and its abolition unrealizable. Moreover, the presence of a considerable number of minority religions, together accounting for 20 to 40 per cent of the total population (depending

upon whether the Scheduled Castes and Tribes are included with the
Hindus or not), made imperative the accommodation of specificities
of religious belief and practice. Thus was born the notion of the
secular state as one that is based on respect for all religions or
non-discrimination on the ground of religion (see Luthera 1964,
Smith 1963, and Chapter Eight).

Fundamentalism and Pluralism

Compared to secularization and secularism, revitalization and
religious fundamentalism are not only relatively more recent concepts, their connotations too are less clearly established. I will not
use the word revitalization in this book. In what follows I will try to
introduce the notion of fundamentalism and clarify my intended use
of it.

Fundamentalism is often employed in contemporary journalistic
as well as scholarly writings as a trendy substitute for communalism,
or simply as a term of abuse. This is regrettable because there is a
fair degree of consensus on the meaning of communalism in Indian
studies, though not on the best way of combating it (see, e.g., Bipan
Chandra 1984 and Pandey 1990). Insightful attempts to clearly
distinguish between communalism and nationalism are available
(see, e.g., Dumont 1964). Fundamentalism, however, remains a
rather vaguely defined omnibus word. A simple way to eliminate the
resultant confusion would be to avoid using the term, but this is no
more likely to succeed than earlier authoritative admonitions to
abandon keywords such as 'ideology', 'secularization', or 'religion'
(see Williams 1977: 55–71, Martin 1965, and Smith 1978).
Moreover, its ambiguity notwithstanding, or perhaps because of that,
fundamentalism points to a worldwide concern of our times. Recent
efforts to introduce some precision of usage are therefore welcome
(see, e.g., the essays dealing with India in Martin and Appleby 1991,
1992, 1993, 1994, 1995).

In trying hopefully to provide a clearer definition of fundamentalism in this book, I will select from two fundamentalist movements,
widely so called, certain key features that make a meaningful whole
when put together. In fact, the first of these movements, associated
with certain Protestant groups in North America, was fundamentalist
by self-ascription as well as other-ascription. The second case is the

Iranian Revolution of 1978–9, which has attained paradigmatic status as being fundamentalist in contemporary discussions of it and other similar movements. The term Islamic fundamentalism, however, is older, having been applied, for instance, to the teachings of Sayyid Abul ala Maududi in India (see Ahmad 1964).

In the late nineteenth and early twentieth centuries, a certain distrust of Romanism, ritualism and rationalism was voiced in certain quarters in England and the USA. The focus was on the implications of, first, certain trends in Biblical criticism and, second, materialist philosophies and the social sciences. At the centre of the argument was the status of the Bible as scripture and the admissibility or otherwise of modernist textual interpretations with the objective of overcoming the apparent conflict between Biblical teaching and scientific knowledge, represented most challengingly by the Darwinian theory of evolution. As scripture, the Bible had to be accepted by orthodox Christians as infallible or inerrant and as transparent, that is not in need of interpretation. In other words, the authority, inerrancy and transparency of the Bible were unquestionable. The hope of the people who declared their loyalty to the scripture was millenarian, and they gathered a large following among conservative Presbyterians and Baptists in North America.

A series of twelve pamphlets, entitled *The Fundamentals*, published between 1910 and 1915, gave expression to the above-mentioned concerns. What was under attack in these tracts was modernism rather than science, but the conception of science that the pamphleteers entertained was that of Baconian inductivism. Their principal concern was to oppose modernist criticism of the Bible. In their nine-point statement of faith, they stressed above all else the notion of the inerrancy of scripture. A World Christian Fundamentals Association was formed and, by the mid-1920s, the term 'fundamentalist' was in use. Fundamentalists were now being asked to do 'battle royal for the Fundamentals', which were chiefly doctrinal and intended to ward off 'the havoc' that 'rationalism' had unleashed (see Marty 1986: 237).

A climactic event in the midst of these developments was the so-called Scopes trial of 1925, which concerned the right of public school teachers to teach the theory of evolution in the classroom, if they felt so inclined. John Scopes was one such teacher in Tennessee, and he was convicted by a court of law for having violated a state law forbidding the teaching of evolution. Fundamentalists won a victory, even though a limited one, over modern science, but they were also exposed in public as ignorant bigots. Subsequently, the votaries of fundamentalism opted for a low profile, and liberals assumed charge of most large denominations. Fundamentalists re-emerged on the public scene in the 1960s and 70s, when the U.S. Supreme Court decisions banning prayer in public schools (1963), and permitting abortion on demand (1973), rekindled the clash of religious and secular values. Since then new varieties of Christian fundamentalism (associated with the names of Randall Terry, Jerry Falwell, and Bob Jones) have made their appearance in North America and elsewhere (see the essays dealing with Christian fundamentalisms in Marty and Appleby 1991, 1992, 1993, 1994 and 1995). Moreover, following the second Vatican Council's efforts (1962–5) at ecumenical reconciliation, and the compromise of the Church with modernity, conservative Catholics also began to voice their concern about the fundamentals of the faith.

The concept of fundamentalism, like that of secularism, had its birth in the ambit of Protestantism in the West. What began as a laudatory term in the 1920s was pronounced a bad word by James Barr, a Biblical scholar, half a century later, suggestive of 'narrowness, bigotry, obscurantism, and sectarianism' (1978: 2). Ten years later, Martin Marty, historian of religion in North America, called the original use of the term fundamentalism 'obsolete' (1988: 15). He recommended a comparative study of fundamentalist, or fundamentalist-like, movements that may be said to share a 'family resemblance' in the sense that they do not have a key feature, or all of a set of features, in common, but exhibit one or more characteristics that define the family. This approach has helped to spread the net wide, and the Fundamentalism Project of the American Academy of Arts and Sciences has yielded an encyclopedic survey of fundamentalisms around the globe (see Marty and Appleby 1991, 1992, 1993, 1994, 1995).

In this book, I would prefer to adopt a less open definition of fundamentalism, using some key features of Protestant fundamentalism described above, and supplementing the same by another set of features derived from the Iranian revolution of 1979. Following Barr (1978: 1 et passim), but not too closely, the key ideas that I have borrowed from the early American fundamentalists are: (1) Affirmation of the inspiration, final authority, inerrancy, and transparency of scripture as the source of belief, knowledge, morals, and manners;

(2) recognition of the reactive character of fundamentalism: it is not an original impulse as, for example, orthodoxy is, but a reaction to a perceived threat or crisis; and (3) intolerance of dissent, implying monopoly over truth.

To the above three defining ideas, I have added four more from the Iranian Revolution (which I discuss below). These are: (1) Cultural critique, that is the idea that all is not well with social or community life as lived at a particular time; (2) appeal to tradition, but in a selective manner that establishes a meaningful relationship between the past and the present, redefining or even inventing tradition in the process; (3) capture of political power and remodelling of the state for the achievement of the stated objectives; and (4) charismatic leadership.

All seven features are present in the Iranian Revolution. The modernization (or secularization) process in Iran under Reza Shah Muhammad Pahlavi's reign after World War Two carried forward the beginnings made in the revolutionary changes that occured in 1905–11. At that time, a socially and educationally backward society had opted for a Western form of government, glossing over the inherent conflict of principles between Islam and Western political systems (see Arjomand 1988). By the early 1960s Iran, alongside Egypt and Turkey, seemed set on the path of modernization conceived in terms of nationalism, urbanization, Westernization, etc. The happenings were analysed and celebrated in, among other books, Daniel Lerner's modern sociological classic, *The Passing of Traditional Society* (1958). We now know that he was celebrating too soon like the others who held the same or similar views. Secularization in Iran had been rapid and fairly wide-ranging, and yet it was partial. Most importantly, the civil code continued to be based on Islamic holy law (*sharia*), and Shia *ulama*, whose importance in Iranian public life dates back to the beginning of the sixteenth century, remained powerful. A reversal of modernization, and a going forward by another route, was already in the making.

An Iranian author, Jalal-e-Ahmad, published a book (in Persian) in 1961 entitled *Gharbzadegi*, that is 'stricken by the West'. The theme, comprising cultural critique as well as political revolt—in short, a repudiation of Western hegemony—received more scholarly treatment in the work of Ali Shariati, a sociologist of leftist leanings who was also a social reformer and religious revivalist (see Shariati 1979; Cragg 1985). Such reactions have, in turn, led to fundamentalism being described as a modern (i.e. contemporary) phenomenon that is antimodern (i.e. reactionary or regressive), 'inseparable from the spectre of its dreaded enemy: the Enlightenment', which is at once its 'precursor' and 'foil' (Lawrence 1989: 8). This characterization seems applicable to the Iranian case, but not necessarily to all situations that one might call fundamentalist.

The revolution symbolized and ultimately led by Ayatollah Ruhollah Khomeini sought to destroy the 'modern' Iran that the Shah and the urban, propertied, ruling class had tried to build. It was, first, a bloody reaction to the present and, only then, a return to the past or the fundamentals of Islam. Economic and political discontent contributed significantly to bring together landlords, the petty bourgeoisie, and the clergy, all of whom felt marginalized by the so-called 'white revolution' from the top (see Arjomand 1988: 99). Ideological support to the gathering storm was provided not only by fundamentalist clerics, but also by liberal Muslims and secular Marxists. The latter appreciated the importance of Khomeini's support—the clergy had deeper ties with the masses than the modern intellectuals—but they hoped eventually to be rid of him. As for the Ayatollah, he proclaimed in 1979 itself that Iran's 'sacred movement' was 'one hundred percent Islamic' (see Amuzegar 1991: 23). The constitutional system he established was, he said, inspired by the example of the Prophet and early Islamic governance. The idea of an autonomous secular state was rejected.

The book *Fundamentals of Islamic Thought* (1985), authored by Khomeini's protégé, Ayatollah Mutahhari, which served as a manifesto of the revolution, was indeed a 'challenge to modern, secular, scientific discourse'. The revolution also rejected the notion of Iranian secular nationalism that had been used by the Shah to build a modern nation-state. In other words, an *eidos*, or worldview, based on both Western science and Western political philosophy, was rejected. Also rejected was the Western *ethos*, or lifestyle, in its cultural, social and ethical aspects. It had been visibly though not most significantly symbolized by sartorial styles, particularly those of women, and these were sternly rejected. Khomeini's call was for adoption of 'the culture of the Quran'. Abandonment of Western-style neckwear by men and donning of the veil (*chadar*) by women became key symbols of cultural recovery.

The ideological foundation of the Islamic Republic of Iran is, of course, Islam. A formal return to religion—to its legitimizing role

rather than to any certainties that it might offer to the believer—that
lies at the core of the fundamentalist quest, alongside of other
concerns, makes no sense unless there is first a departure from it.
Such departures were precisely what Khomeini considered to be the
guilt of the secularized and secularizing Iranian ruling class. The
Islam to which the Ayatollah ordered the Iranians to return was Islam
as interpreted by him and his followers among the clerics in the city
of Quom. Khomeini was less of a scriptural literalist than, say,
Sayyid Abul ala Maududi of India (see Chapter Four), but he too
emphasized as a matter of principle that the teachings of the Quran
were self-evident. In his interpretations he rejected earlier liberal
exegeses by traditional Iranian scholars within the framework of the
relatively open Shia tradition. Khomeini's insistence that the final
source of the true Islamic life is the Quran and the exemplary actions
(*sunna*) and sayings (*hadis*) of Prophet Muhammad was in effect a
sunnification of Iranian Islam. For the Shia, the Quran is not a closed
book. Its acknowledged interpreter is the twelfth Imam (successor to
the Prophet), who, it is believed, has remained hidden since the
eighth century, and has ever since secretly guided a succession of
living interpreters, such as Khomeini.

Drawing presumably on the thirteenth-century Iranian theologian
Nasiruddin Tousi's neo-Platonic concept of the perfect man as the
perfect teacher, Khomeini put forward the doctrine of the guardianship of the jurist (*vilayet-i faqih*). According to it, legitimate governance on behalf of the Hidden Imam is best vested in the most
qualified jurist. In effect, this meant a clerical state of the kind that
Islam had never known before in all thirteen hundred years of its
history. It certainly was a radical departure from the Shia conception
of divinely inspired leadership, that is the Imamate. The Ayatollah
also gave his approval to a republican constitution that is in many
formal and substantive respects modern, and is indeed modelled on
Western democracies. To give but one example, the idea of a parliament elected by the citizenry can hardly be said to embody the
Islamic notion of *ijma* (consensus) among qualified people, whether
the *ulama*, that is the learned doctors of Islamic law, or the *fuqaha*,
or jurists. While the institution of monarchy was consistently attacked by Khomeini as un-Islamic, republicanism too found no place in
his most important work on the subject, namely *Hukumat-i-Islami*
(1971; see Khomeini 1979). There the emphasis is on the successors
of the Prophet being 'just jurisprudents' who are 'the ruler and the

successor in all affairs' (ibid.: 47). Indeed, it seems that Khomeini was criticized by some Islamic clerics for violating Islamic law (see Amuzegar 1991: 27).

In the employment of the notion of the guardianship of the jurist, we see selective retrieval of tradition and overwhelming emphasis on the importance of power. Indeed, it is the capture of power by the clergy in Iran that has been described as 'the most important inspiration' that the Iranian revolution has given to Muslims everywhere (see Keddie 1995: 124). The reactive character of the revolution and its concern with cultural critique—with arresting cultural decline and corruption of lifestyles—and with asserting the sanctity and ultimate authority of Islamic scripture (the Quran) has already been noted above. By acclaiming the perfection of Islam as religion (*din*)—this is certified in the Quran itself (5.3)— Khomeini implicitly ruled out the perfection of other religions. The believer in Islam, who is devout in belief and firm in practice, is thus assured that he or she, being properly guided, is in possession of the truth and therefore worthy of receiving God's benevolence (*barakat*).

To sum up: A brief examination of the beginnings of Protestant fundamentalism in the USA, and of the ideological underpinnings of the Iranian Revolution, has been attempted here to give content and meaning to the term fundamentalism. The intention is not, however, to impose a foreign set of ideas on developments within India's religious traditions, but to facilitate an understanding of the latter through controlled comparison. The encounter with the Indian reality should also help us to refine our use of the key terms 'secularism' and 'fundamentalism' as tools of descriptive analysis.

*   *   *

A final terminological clarification. One of the key concepts that is used in this book is religious pluralism, which stands in direct opposition to fundamentalism by denying that any one religion is in sole possession of the whole truth. In India, secularism has been defined by a wide range of scholars and politicians as equal respect for all religions—*sarva dharma samabhava*—on behalf of both the state and the citizenry. In the Preamble to the Constitution, secularism is rendered in Hindi as the neutrality of the state in relation to different religious communities (*pantha nirpekshta*), which is somewhat more precise than the notion of equal respect for all religions, but not clear enough (see Chapter Eight).

The notion of pluralism is not very much more precise than fundamentalism or secularism. Thus, it could stand for anyone of the following three positions. First, it may connote mutual exclusiveness or absolute difference, conveyed for instance in the Quranic declaration, 'To you your religion, to me mine' (109.3). To subscribe to it would amount to live in a state of mutual exclusion but not conflict.

Secondly, pluralism can stand for a convergence of the fundamentals of different faiths, although variously defined. Thus, there is the Rigvedic aphorism, 'The Absolute is but one, but the learned describe it diversely' (I.164.46). This is the position embraced by the exponents of neo-Hinduism, from Swami Vivekananda to Mahatma Gandhi (see Chapters Six and Seven). Maulana Abul Kalam Azad also subscribed to this view of religious pluralism, stressing the mutual compatibility of such key motifs as the unity of God (*tauhid*) in Islam and monism (*advaita*, non-dualism) in Upanishadic Hinduism (see Chapter Five). Although somewhat more outward-looking and therefore positive, this version of pluralism too remains trapped in exclusivism. Gandhi's distrust of voluntary religious conversion on the ground that one who is a sincere seeker will find the Truth in his own religion, for all religions are equally true, is the best possible expression of this second meaning of pluralism.

Thirdly, pluralism might mean that every religion requires the others, for no religion has a monopoly over the whole truth. The issue is not of tolerance or respect, but of understanding. The critical assumption is that acknowledgement of difference between two points of view, rather than their similarity alone, could be the basis of understanding. By this definition, a religious person will not merely respect religions other than his or her own, but actually seek to understand and experience them or, at least, learn from them. Gandhi at times came close to adopting this radical position, as when he maintained that the religion he lived by transcended Hinduism. More explicitly, he wrote : 'if only we could all of us read scriptures of different faiths, we should find that they were at bottom all one and *were all helpful to one another*' (Kher 1962: 26, emphasis added). Sri Ramakrishna, the mystic from Bengal, also had embraced this concept of pluralism when he chose to live for a while as a practising Muslim. More generally, he had a deep interest in both the so-called high (Vedantic) and low (puranic, folk) forms of Hinduism.

His personal vision was not translatable into a social creed, however; such mystical experiences rarely are. The inspiration behind Vivekananda's mission lay elsewhere, not in his master's personal experience or success (*siddhi*) (see Chapter Six).

The above discussion of pluralism does not address the question whether all religions may be *a priori* deemed to be equally true, metaphysically sound and morally valid. Such an undertaking is outside the scope of this book and also beyond my competence. Even a limited empirical investigation of the cognitive assumptions and moral precepts of India's major religions is not an objective of the present exercise. Its importance however, may not be denied. In the absence of an answer to the above question, the notion of religious pluralism remains ambiguous. It is obvious that an uncritical affirmation of pluralism may easily slip into a philosophically naive relativism, or sophistry, which acknowledges no values except relativism itself.

The current use of pluralism in India as one of the two elements of secularism—the other being a non-discriminatory state, misleadingly described as equal respect for all religions on everybody's part—does not inspire confidence that the implications of pluralism have been given the careful consideration that they surely deserve. The importance of such an exercise is underscored by the fact that, while the availability of ideas that could be called secular (in the Enlightenment sense of the term) in the Hindu and Islamic religious traditions of India is doubtful—the Sikh religious tradition presents other problems—the possibility of pluralism in Hinduism and perhaps Islam seems more promising.

Structure and Method

The scope of this book was described above as an inquiry into the ideologies of secularism and fundamentalism in the context of the religious traditions of India. Also, an attempt was made to provide working definitions of the main concepts or key words, namely ideology, religious tradition, secularization, secularism, fundamentalism, and pluralism. I would now like to outline the structure of the book and briefly describe its methodological orientation.

I begin with the Sikh religious tradition, which is in fact the tradition whose study helped me first to formulate my definitions of secularism and fundamentalism. As I have stated in the Preface, it was the developments in Punjab between 1978 and 1984 that persuaded me to undertake the present study, although my interest in the thesis of secularization had been aroused earlier. The fact that Sikhism is only about five hundred years old apparently made its study more manageable, but I was to discover soon that the Sikh oral tradition is no less complex and multivocal than the older Indian traditions of Hinduism and Islam. A point of entry was provided by the fact that many Sikh intellectuals consider their religion secular and describe it as such. I explore the meanings of secularism within the Sikh tradition in Chapter Two, beginning with Guru Nanak. Next, I discuss what seem to me significant restatements of the original teaching, but which are not considered so by Sikh intellectuals generally. The chapter concludes with a short account of Maharaja Ranjit Singh's multi-religious polity.

While discussing developments within the Sikh religious tradition, I emphasize sacralization of power at the hands of Guru Hargobind, which can also be viewed as the secularization of the sacred. This momentous development quite inevitably led to Guru Gobind's highly significant linking of identity and aspiration. I suggest in Chapter Three that Sikh fundamentalism had its birth then itself, but underwent further development in the hundred years from the 1880s onward. During the recent past, it reached its peak through an alliance with secessionist politics and generalized violence, and then suffered a decline. Currently, Sikh fundamentalism seems to have become inward looking, targeting deviations from orthodoxy, which is under continuous redefinition.

I would like to make a methodological clarification at this point. In the presentation of what seem to me significant developments in India's major religious traditions, attention has been focused here on certain critical events and on the contributions of particular individuals. I do not claim representativeness for any one of the latter, however, not even for the founding guru of Sikhism. Having adopted the notion of tradition as one of the key ideas for this study, I can hardly claim freedom from temporal situatedness for any historical figure, no matter how great, for tradition implies collectivity and diachrony. Some individuals, however, may well be judged as significant contributors to the development of a religious tradition in ways that appear not only historic in retrospect but also meaningful today. I should add that I have not attempted to construct anything like a roll of honour, for I am not writing history in the biographical mode, but only searching for answers to certain questions.

Turning to Islam in South Asia, in Chapter Four, I make a distinction between orthodoxy and orthopraxis, on the one hand, and fundamentalism, on the other. While the state was regarded as inimical to the purity of Islam by the guardians of the religious tradition, fundamentalism established a partnership between religion and power. It is the story of a thousand years, and has had to be told in terms of significant contributions of selected ideologues, including religious scholars, kings and emperors, and modern intellectuals. Condensation became inescapable, but I have tried to avoid abridgement such as would ignore any major developments recognized as such by the historians. Needless to add, I consider Islam as one of India's major religious traditions, for that is what it is sociologically and indeed historically.

From the Sikh case I had learnt the significance of looking for ideas and world images that might be seen as secular or secularizing in one sense or another. Such an investigation in respect of Islam was possible only in terms of the quest for relative autonomy from the control of religious specialists sought by the wielders of royal power. This search reached its limits in the person of Akbar: his confrontation with the doctors of religious doctrine was, I try to show, the crucial turning-point from orthodoxy to the beginnings of fundamentalism in Indian Islam. The most articulate spokesman for a full-blown Sunni fundamentalism, however, was Sayyid Abul ala Maududi, a journalist, in the middle of the twentieth century. Indeed, the impact of his pleading was felt even in the heartland of Islam, the Arab countries.

It is an irony of the times that one of the scholars who is said to have had an influence on Maududi was Abul Kalam Azad. Azad's own quest as an Indian Muslim, after a precocious start as a pan-Islamist, turned out to be for religious pluralism. I discuss in Chapter Five his efforts to find a religious as well as historical, but not a secular, basis for this position. It is the authenticity and sincerity of Azad's endeavour that matters rather than his failure to convince his co-religionists, whether the elites or the masses, about the importance of his exegesis. He was great enough to acknowledge the failure himself.

Pluralism is of course widely claimed to be inbuilt into the Hindu religious tradition. Similar claims about Hinduism—more precisely the Brahmanical notion of *dharma*, as this-worldly or secular, rather than other-worldly and theocentric—are also made. I pose two questions in Chapter Six: First, does the classical textual tradition contain the notion of autonomous secular power, independent of spiritual authority? Second, how tenable is the claim on behalf of modern Hinduism that it is pluralist in orientation and essentially tolerant of other religious traditions. The conclusions I arrive at are the following. First, classical Brahmanical thought was holistic and hierarchical; it recognized relations rather than essences and, therefore, did not grant absolute autonomy to secular power. Indeed, and contrary to what is often asserted, even the classical work *Arthashastra* does not warrant a view to the contrary. Second, while the principle of hierarchy, in thought as well as social action, does seemingly permit a pluralist orientation and generate intergroup interdependence, it does so in an inegalitarian manner. In the context of religious difference, the best we may expect within a Hindu framework is non-violent exclusivism or peaceful coexistence.

In Chapter Seven, I discuss Hindu revivalism in the nineteenth century, first in Bengal and then in Punjab. A striking feature of these revivalist movements was their concern with the identification of true scripture and with scriptural authority. This search reached its climax in the later writings of Dayanand Sarasvati. Besides, there was the concern with social reform. I take the position that the Arya Samaj movement did indeed have the markings of nascent fundamentalism, but the concern with political power remained somewhat mute. From muteness we move on to the concealment of political goals with the rise of the ideology of Hindutva, and the establishment of the Rashtriya Swayam Sevak Sangh in 1925. These developments signal the arrival of Hindu fundamentalism. I conclude with a discussion of Mahatma Gandhi's views of Hinduism and of transcendental religion; all historical religions were considered by him flawed expressions of the latter. As stated above, of all pluralists discussed in this book, it is he who comes closest to being a radical pluralist. Gandhi's assassination at the hands of a Hindu was more than a criminal or political act: it was an expression of the mutual exclusiveness of pluralism and fundamentalism.

Chapter Eight, which is devoted to an examination of the contemporary crisis of Indian secularism, defined as inter-religious tolerance, also opens with Gandhi's views, this time on secularism in the original, Western, sense of the term. I point out that he rejected the ideology of secularism—the secularization thesis—without any qualifications, but interestingly, and consistently, advocated a secular state completely detached from the religious concerns of the people. The major part of this chapter is devoted to a discussion of Jawaharlal Nehru's views on religion and his paradoxical endorsement of *Indian* secularism—inter-religious tolerance—after a life-long commitment to the ideals of the Enlightenment. He represents better than anybody else in India—and perhaps anywhere in the modern world—the predicament of modernity.

The Epilogue draws attention to some aspects of the ongoing debate on Indian secularism.

Before I close, a few observations about the kind of data that have gone into the writing of this book and on the manner of their use. Let me stress, first of all, that this is not a book on comparative religion. I am not concerned with an examination of India's major religions as reservoirs of theology, cosmology, mythology, and metaphysics, or as guides to the performance of ritual or the expression of religious devotion. I am rather interested in the evolution of religious traditions with particular reference to the emergence or absence of the ideologies of secularism, fundamentalism, and pluralism. To the extent to which this has required reference to certain theological or metaphysical ideas, these have been briefly considered.

Secondly, this is not a historical work in intention, scope or method. I am no more a historian than I am a student of comparative religion. Religious traditions are indeed considered here as historical constructions, but the intention is not to make a contribution to the history of Hinduism, Indian Islam, or Sikhism. Nor is the writing of regional history, say of Bengal or Punjab, the objective. I have not undertaken any archival research or discovered any unknown documents, but I have studied both original sources (in English, Hindi, and Urdu and, with the help of translations, also in Sanskrit) and secondary texts. The present work is interpretative in character and does not aim at narrative completeness. It bases the interpretations on carefully selected events and ideas in each case, taking care that the manner of selection is governed by the questions posed and is not capricious. It bears witness to how the past contributes to the making of the present, and conversely, how the past is continuously redefined in the light of the present. Although the various traditions are examined serially, the process of understanding through comparison, anticipated in this introductory chapter is sustained throughout the book.

From a specifically sociological point of view, the book is concerned with an examination of the thesis that secularization is a universal and cross-cultural process that generates in course of time its own universally applicable ideology. My conclusion is that the ideology of secularism, which the ruling classes have promoted in India in the half-century since independence in 1947, is ambiguous, being at times similar to, and at other times different from, the Western notion of secularism rooted in the Enlightenment. Moreover, it has become intertwined with religious fundamentalisms which are partly in the nature of a backlash. Those sections of intellectual opinion that embrace a Western conception of secularism, stressing the redemptive role of rationality and scientific temper—the desirability of cultivating the latter has been built into the Constitution—tend to concentrate on 'the sunny side' of the empire of reason and ignore what Stephen Toulmin (1990) has called its 'hidden agenda'.

I have gone into the question of the social organization of the religious traditions under study only in a limited way, indicating, for instance, the social bases of support of the various fundamentalist movements discussed. The analysis is not, however, quantitative in character.

I believe it would not be misleading to describe my method as interdisciplinary, but in a modest rather than an ambitious vein. To repeat, I seek to describe, analyze, compare, and interpret, rather than to prescribe. The quest is for understanding rather than a plan of action. Certain implications for action, however, are implicit in the analysis itself. I believe that if a question is posed clearly, it carries the possibilities of answering it in itself. Beyond that I hesitate to be specific. But I do think that whatever exists empirically, and not also culturally—because it is not rooted in social thought—exists but weakly. This is the critical weakness of secularism in India, howsoever defined. It would be a complete misreading of my intentions if the book is read as a celebration of the weakness of secularisms and the apparent strength of fundamentalisms. I present the situation as it is now: there is no such thing as the final interpretation. The world we live in is always on the move, and reinterpretation is an unending endeavour.

Chapter Two

The Sikh Religious Tradition
Meanings of Secularism

To conquer the mind is to win the world.
GURU NANAK DEV, *Japji* 28

One is religious to the extent of one's power.
SUKHA SINGH, *Gurbilas Dasvin Padshahi*

God wanted me to look upon all religions with one eye;
that is why he took away the light from the other.
MAHARAJA RANJIT SINGH *in conversation with a Muslim fakir*

It was pointed out in Chapter One that the notion of secularization as a self-consciously articulated theory of social change is relatively recent and of Western origin. The processes of secularization, however, are, if not exactly as old as human history, coeval with the rise of modern science and technology. As a modern theory, the thesis of secularization bears the imprint of the dialectic of religion and reason or, more precisely, Protestantism and the Enlightenment. In its utopian form it was put forward as the ideology of secularism, denying any legitimacy to religion in society. Our discussion underscored the importance of examining the on-going processes of secularization everywhere contextually, that is in relation to the 'local' religious tradition or traditions. In this chapter, I attempt an examination of the significance of the fact that, in the Sikh religious tradition, an original attitude of qualified world affirmation was, in the course of time, redefined to emphasize the unity of the spiritual and political functions in society, so that what might seem distinct and even contradictory in terms of the Western civilization is here sought to be reconciled. This development within the Sikh religio-political tradition cannot but be of deep interest to students of comparative religion and to theorists of secularization.

Sikhism as This-Worldly Ethic

Of the great religious traditions of humanity, Sikhism is one of the youngest, being barely five hundred years old. Its beginnings and development have been recorded in both oral narratives and literary texts, but these do not always speak with one voice. The fact that the founder of this religion, Nanak Dev, was literate, as were his nine successors, does not really prove helpful in this regard. Not only are non-Sikh scholars in disagreement over many issues, the Sikhs themselves also have found agreement hard to arrive at.[1] A major difficulty is that while the historian is sceptical about many details that comprise the tradition, because of lack of reliable evidence, the believer considers it self-validated. For the sociologist, while the qualms of the historian seem legitimate, it is tradition that matters, for it moves people and guides their actions. The most crucial illustration of this problem is the status of the biographical narratives called *janam sakhi*, which are anecdotal in character and combine the historian's hard facts with the people's sacred myths (see Mc-Leod 1976: 20–36). For the Sikh, it is not easily questionable that Nanak was a recipient of divine guidance; and, according to the *Miharban Janamsakhi*, God gave Nanak a cup of nectar (*amrit*) and ordained that his followers would be redeemed. There is also the question of the authorship of *Bachitar Natak* and *Dasam Granth*: tradition attributes these works to the last personal Guru, Gobind Singh, but modern scholarship is sceptical. The mysteries associated

---

1. Among knowledgeable 'outsiders' we find such sharp disagreements as are illustrated by, for instance, the assertion that the Sikh religious tradition evolved in the direction of creating 'almost a nation' (Eliot 1954: 272) contrasted with the judgement that the Sikhs 'are virtually a caste of the Hindus' (Toynbee 1954: 415). The disagreements among the insiders are equally acute and often on basic issues, such as the meaning of the word 'Sikh' itself. According to Khushwant Singh, the word is 'presumably derived ultimately from the Sanskrit *shishya*, disciple, or *shiksha*, instruction—Pali, *sikkha*' (1963: 36). While this is the generally accepted view, dissenting views include the following: 'The word "Sikh" ... derives its origin from Pali and means the same as in the great Buddha's Dhammpad—the elect, or in the Sikh parlance, chosen (by God), God's own' (Gopal Singh 1978: xxxv; see also Kapur Singh 1959: 276).

with the origin and development of a religious tradition should cause no surprise, for it is mystery that entails faith.

Given the ambiguities, the sociologist must self-consciously opt for versions of critical events that command general acceptance, and construct a coherent interpretation of the tradition. What follows is such an interpretative effort to examine the place of the sociological notions of secularization and secularism in the Sikh religious tradition.

While for the Sikh believer, this 'new' religious tradition begins with divine revelation, the sociologist must (following Max Weber) seek to supplement 'subjective understanding' (*verstehen*) with 'causal adequacy' as manifest in the relations between relevant historical events. In other words, one must define, if possible, the context for the revelation. Fortunately, it is possible to do so in the case of the Sikh religious tradition: the context for its emergence is provided by the interplay of the political, economic, social and cultural situations in Punjab in the late fifteenth century.

Ever since the first intrusions of invading Muslim armies in the eleventh century, Punjab had been subjected to much political turmoil and violence. The image of the king had come to be that of a 'butcher'[2], rather than that of the 'protector'. Nanak Dev (1469–1539), a pious, god-loving person of gentle disposition, had felt impelled, after witnessing the brutality of Babar's invasions of north India (in 1524–5), to cry in anguish: 'It was Death, disguised as the Mughal that made war on us./When there was such slaughter, such groaning,/Didst Thou not feel the pain, O Lord?' (Harbans Singh 1966: 5). Nanak's grievance was not only against the invader but also against native Hindu kings who had abandoned their moral duty of protecting their subjects (who in Hindu political thought are the king's 'children' rather than 'subjects'). While his wail is also a prayer to God to redeem his creatures, implicit in it is a call to man to assume the duty of self-protection—an idea which is in harmony with Nanak's concept of human dignity.

The people among whom Nanak sought to arouse this sense of responsibility were largely the agricultural, artisan, and merchant castes of Punjab; Nanak himself belonged to the Hindu trading caste of Khatris.[3] The former were the economically exploited class. It

---

2. Guru Nanak Dev, the founder of Sikhism, is said to have lamented: 'This age is a knife, kings are butchers; justice hath taken wings and fled' (Macauliffe 1909: I, xliv).

3. See footnote 10.

would be misleading, however, to attribute to him class consciousness in the sociological sense of the term; his references to God
as 'magnate' are significant (see Hans 1985: 213). Besides, the
people he addressed were enmeshed in religious observances and in
the grip of degenerate Brahman priests, who themselves were
patronized by Hindu kings—such as those who survived in the hills
in the east—and Hindu landlords. Fortunately, the caste system in
Punjab had already been weakened by the spread of the anti-caste
Buddhist religious tradition in north India in the pre-Muslim period.
Subsequently, the socio-cultural life of the people had, during the
medieval period, come under the influence of both the Hindu
egalitarian socio-religious movement of *bhakti* ('devotionalism',
according to which all are made equal in their love of god) and the
pan-theistic movement of the Muslim Sufi orders. The Brahmanical
tradition and the social organization associated with it were also
under pressure from within as a result of the growth (during the
fourteenth and fifteenth centuries) of sectarian cults of renouncers
(*sannyasis*) and occultists (*yogis*). These three streams of religious
thought and practice, *bhakti*, Sufism, and *hatha-yoga*, in synthesis
gave rise to the 'Sant' tradition that provided Nanak the materials
out of which he produced a reinterpretation for those who chose to
become his followers. One may say that Punjab was waiting for
Nanak (see Ray 1970: 7–45).

It was in 1499 that Nanak is believed to have given his first
message after, he said, God the supreme preceptor (guru), had passed
on the holy word (*shabad*) to him. The message was: '*na koi hindu
na musalman*': there is no Hindu and no Muslim.[4] That is, no true
followers of the Hindu and Islamic faiths are to be found any more.
Or, alternatively, being a Hindu, or a Muslim, is meaningless: what
matters is that one must be a true devotee of God and realise that the
practice of truth is the highest morality: 'Truth above all,/above truth,
truthful conduct (*sachon ore sabh ko/ upar sach achar*)' (see Khushwant Singh 1963: 43). Though the former interpretation has been
generally favoured in the Sikh tradition (see Macauliffe 1909: I, 37),
the latter seems equally plausible when read alongside other related

---

4. We are on slippery ground here. Authoritative opinion is certain that these are
not Nanak's own words: they are attributed to him in the *Puratan Janamsakhi*.
Identical words are traditionally believed to have been an utterance of Kabir (early
fifteenth century).

pronouncements, such as the following: 'Neither the *veda* nor the *kateb* know the mystery'. While the *veda* comprise the oldest sacred texts of the Hindu religious tradition, the word *kateb* is used by Sikh theologians to refer to the Torah, the Psalms, the Gospel, and the Quran (see McLeod 1968:161). This is not the place, however, to go into the controversial issue of how new this religious perspective (it was not yet a tradition) was, and whether it was more Hindu or Muslim or Buddhist, or an attempted synthesis of Hinduism and Islam.[5] I will rather concentrate on the essentials of the teachings of Nanak Dev,[6] who, in his own lifetime, it seems, was known as Baba rather than Guru. The latter appellation came to be applied to him retrospectively after his death, when the chain of gurus came to be established. Babas were wandering holy men. The most significant period of his life, 'in terms of his posthumous influence' (ibid: 230), however, was the twenty years of settled domestic and community life at the village of Kartarpur on the river Ravi. Nanak's thought, like traditional thought generally, was marked by comprehensiveness and consistency: its theology entailed its sociology, or, to put it the other way round, its sociology is incomprehensible without reference to its theology.

To begin with Guru Nanak's concept of God, it is clear that his view of the world was theocentric. God is the creator (*kartar*) of everything that exists. It follows that everything is sacred or holy, and the dualistic notion of the religious *versus* the secular is inadmissible. Man is, however, an easy prey to temptations and readily lapses into immorality.[7] His worst error is egoism or hubris (*haumai*): 'Devoted to pride, I weep in sorrow, saith Nanak. How shall deliverance be obtained?' (see Macauliffe 1909: I, 170). It is thus

5. For the argument in favour of a strong Muslim influence, see, e.g., Khan 1967. McLeod (1968) has, however, argued against it and contended that a third way, based on the rejection of both Hinduism and Islam, rather than a synthesis of the two, was intended by Nanak. This is also the conclusion at which J.S. Grewal (1979) arrives in his study of Nanak. Kapur Singh (1959) has put forward an interesting argument in favour of Buddhist influences.

6. For accounts of Nanak's teachings I have depended upon his own Japji and other sayings (in various English translations): see Khushwant Singh (1963), McLeod (1968), and Ray (1970). Also, I have drawn upon notes of interviews I conducted with a dozen educated Sikh gentlemen in Delhi in the summer of 1985.

7. Nanak warned: 'This God-built house of the body,/ of which the soul is a tenant, has many doors./ The five temptations that the flesh is heir to/ Make daily raids upon it' (Trilochan Singh et al. 1960: 84).

that man becomes separated from his Maker: 'O my Lord, who can comprehend Thy excellences! None can recount my sinfulness'(see McLeod 1968:177).

Man is, however, born to be saved. Nanak taught the notion of 'divine commandment' (*hukam*), which entails the idea of divine initiative for the salvation of man: 'Nanak, the True King Himself unites (the believer) with Himself' (ibid.: 175). Although divine initiative comes first, man too must strive for his own salvation: 'The sweat of labour is as beads/Falling by the ploughman as seeds sown./We reap according to our measure/Some for ourselves to keep, some to others give' (see Khushwant Singh 1963: 47, n.41). What God intends for man is his *hukam*: this is revealed to man through *shabad* (the holy word) with the guidance of the preceptor (guru) and by meditation on God's name (*nam*): 'For a diseased world the remedy is the Name' (see McLeod 1968:195).

The primacy of Nanak's concern with individual salvation need hardly be emphasized (see Ray 1970: 61); what must not be overlooked, however, is the fact that he did not teach a selfish concern for one's own salvation alone, but rather the moral responsibility of the true believer for the salvation of fellow human beings as well. According to tradition, Nanak summed up his teaching very simply: *kirt karo, nam japo, vand chakho:* work for your living; abide in meditative recitation of God's name; share what you have with others (see Khushwant Singh 1963: 47). The *self* is thus seen in relation to the *divine* and the *social*, so that a withdrawal from either of these relationships must spell one's extinction. It is this combination of piety and practical activity (in the form of worldly labour) which is the essence of Nanak's this-worldliness.

Some Sikh intellectuals find the seeds of secularism in such an ethic of world-affirmation. We must be wary, however, about jumping to conclusions. The guru's world-affirmation was not absolute but explicitly qualified. As divine creation, the universe is real, he taught: 'Whatever is done by Thee is real: all Thy reflections too are real'. At the same time, he insisted that God alone is 'eternal' and, as such, He is distinct from the universe. What is impermanent is also in a sense false, and dangerous, since it may turn out to be a snare. Nanak acknowledged the traditional Brahmanical notion of five obstacles to the path of virtue, namely lust (*kama*), anger (*krodha*), covetousness (*lobha*), attachment to worldly things (*moha*), and egotism (*ahankara*). Detachment is, therefore, the supreme value (see Grewal 1979: 267): this-worldliness encompassed by detachment. Borrowing a famous formulation of Max Weber (1930) about Christian asceticism, we may say that Nanak sought to fashion 'a life in the world, but neither of nor for this world'.

Like the devotees of the Sant tradition, Nanak emphasized that man's ultimate goal should be to merge with God, but unlike some of them he affirmed the worth of man's worldly existence while it lasts, and repudiated the Brahmanical ideal of renunciation as long as it remains confined to external behaviour, like leaving one's home. 'Having renounced the life of the householder (*grihastha*) why go begging at the householder's door?' he asked. 'Of all renunciations, the best is to give up lust, anger and greed' (see Jodh Singh 1967: 41). He 'rejected altogether the practice of celibacy and asceticism, of penances and austerities, of pilgrimages and formal religious exercises, worship of images, and the authority of the so-called sacred texts' (Ray 1970: 57). By abandoning both ritualism and occultism, Nanak turned his back on magic and miracles and on the social universe of castes and sects. Instead he extolled the virtues of the company of godly people (*sadh sangat*) which, alongside the repetition of God's name, absolute truthfulness, contentment, and restraint of the senses, he regarded as the five pathways to union with the divine (see Khushwant Singh 1963: 42–3). A concomitant of the holy assembly or congregation (*sangat*) was the institution of the community kitchen (*guru ka langar,* the guru's kitchen) which dealt a severe blow to Brahmanical notions of purity and pollution and commensal exclusivism. Sitting down to eat together in a single row (*pangat*) was the secular aspect of *sangat*—the material representation of the moral or spiritual idea of equality, and became a powerful cementing force among Nanak's followers. In short, Nanak held up the ideal of *raj mein jog* (detachment in the midst of worldly involvements) for his followers to pursue. The way to truth lay for him through the life of a virtuous householder.[8]

---

8. Cf. Talib 1969: 95 'Over the life of the recluse the Guru has exalted the station of the *Grihasti* [householder].... The *Grihasti* is the person fixed amidst moral duty, which he must face and assume even at the cost of suffering. The Guru's meaning is unmistakably clear: our life is circumscribed by material surroundings, yet man must transcend these to affirm spiritual and moral fulfilment'.

It is debatable if Nanak thought of himself as the founder of a new religion[9]; he surely would not have wanted to form a new sect. He did, however, want the disciples who had gathered around him to continue to live differently from the others (Hindus, Muslims), and in a state of social and spiritual communion (*ap japo aura nam japao*: remember God and make the others too remember Him). He also named a successor, Lehna (1504–52), whom he renamed Angad (literally, 'part of my body') (see Khushwant Singh 1963: 49). By this single but momentous act, he planted the seeds for the growth of a new religious community, a corporate body such that the distinction between one and the many—whether the gurus over time or the Sikhs at a particular time—was abolished. According to the Sikh religious tradition, Angad and the subsequent eight gurus, though nine different human beings, were but one person and that person was Nanak, who was guided by God, the supreme Guru. Therefore, whatever their teachings and actions, these have to be acknowledged to be in essence and indeed in truth Nanak's. The Sikhs have tried thus to overcome the problem of reconciling the teachings and actions of the different gurus. It seems to me, however, that, in the context of the problem set for the present discussion (namely secularism and secularization), these differences are of critical importance. In fact, they could not but be so, given the changes that took place in the internal composition of the Sikh community and in its socio-political environment over the 150 years or so following Nanak's death.

As stated above, Nanak belonged to a Khatri caste: he was a Bedi. The Khatris were a congeries of castes (*jatis*, to be precise) comprising the traditional Vaniya (or Baniya) trading and commercial castes, agriculturists and artisans. All these communities, unlike the Brahmans and the Kshatriyas (the two highest ranked castes of priests and warriors respectively), had well-developed ethics of work and a

---

9. To call 'the gentle and intense Indian mystic', Nanak, 'the "founder of Sikhism", as is often done, is surely to misconstrue both him and history. He was a devotee (*bhakta*) who... attacked religious formalism of all kinds. Several generations later his followers were religiously formalised, systematised.... Out of this was born what we call "followerism"' (Smith 1963: 66f). Toynbee (1960: 9) refers to Nanak as the 'founder' of Sikhism but adds that Nanak himself would perhaps not have agreed. Most Sikh intellectuals disagree, and reject the notion of the emergence of a 'new religion' as a gradual process that is still in progress.

market orientation.[10] Expectedly, they often did well by themselves in economic terms (judging by the standards of the medieval period), but they lacked the status of high castes; in fact many of the craftsmen were considered unclean by the two top castes (see Ray 1970: 14). It is they who became the first disciples of Nanak and in large numbers. There was no love lost between him and the Brahmans and the Kshatriyas.

The relationship between Guru Nanak and his followers was of mutual advantage. His egalitarian social outlook and ritual-free religious faith offered them release from their relatively low status and the control of the Brahmans. His message made their work respectable as well as profitable. On their part, they not only provided a following for the new guru, but also the material means to operate the quite revolutionary institution of the community kitchen, which provided free food to those followers who needed or wanted to take advantage of the facility. According to a Sikh historian, the Khatri traders found in the teachings of the early gurus 'exactly what they sought and consequently lent their powerful support to the Sikh movement imparting to it the character of an urban or town-based movement'. Subsequently the agricultural classes also came in. 'Their joining the movement was facilitated partly by the hold the commercial classes had on the cultivating classes' (Fauja Singh 1969: 3). It was thus that the Sikh innovation became a broad-based social movement of immense potential. Reversing the well-known Weberian argument about the relationship between the Puritan ethic and the spirit of capitalism (see Weber 1930), I would suggest that, in Punjab, the market-cum-profit oriented Khatris ensured the success of the religious faith pronounced by Nanak. Their secular outlook converged with Nanak's.

Nanak's choice of Angad as the second guru, instead of one of his sons, in his own life time, is attributed by historians to the former's high spiritual qualities, but some of them also mention that Lehna had a sizable personal following and this may have weighed with the

10. All ten of the Sikh gurus were Khatris. The tenth and last, Gobind, was of the Sodhi subcaste. He maintained, however, that both the Bedis and the Sodhis were Kshatriyas and indeed descended from the lineage of the divine avatar Rama of the Hindu religious tradition (see Grewal and Bal 1987: 109). It may be noted here that, notwithstanding the image of Khatris as traders, some of them were originally Kshatriyas (see Puri 1988), a category which has long been open to a variety of groups.

Guru (see Khushwant Singh 1963: 49). The Sikh community did, in fact, prosper in both numbers and resources under Angad. As a result the institution of the community kitchen (*langar*) became stabilized. He also established the practice of collecting the offerings made by the Sikhs, and there is reason to believe that he may have encouraged the keeping of accounts in the manner of Khatri accountants.[11] He also placed a great emphasis upon physical fitness among his followers who were encouraged to engage in drill, wrestling, and competitive games. He thus planted the seeds of what was to flower into one of the most deeply ingrained self and other ascribed images of the Sikhs as a people of exceptional valour, or, as the British liked to call them, a 'martial race'. By all accounts, Angad was not only a worthy spiritual guru but also a worldly man and an able organizer of men and institutions. Under his guidance the secular component of Nanak's teaching does indeed seem to have been strengthened.

The size of the following and the resources they commanded had grown so large by the time of Amar Das (1479–1574), the third guru, that special measures for their organization and use had to be taken, and he proved equal to the task. He divided his wide-spread followers into twenty-two parish-like groups called *manji*, and placed each *manji* under an agent, called *masand*, who collected the offerings from the followers and also provided them spiritual guidance. An equal emphasis upon the secular and religious functions of these agents is noteworthy. If a tilting of the balance did occur, it would seem to have been in favour of the secular function.

In this connection, a most noteworthy incident has been preserved in the Sikh tradition. Pointing out that Amar Das 'emphasized the need and sanctity of secular activity among the Sikhs', Gopal Singh writes: 'When Gango, a Khatri, came to see him and asked, "What shall I do to save myself?", the guru replied, "Go and open a bank at Delhi and dwell upon the name of God"' (1978: I, xii). The story may well be apocryphal, but its currency itself is significant. It reminds one of the kind of advice which Puritan pioneers such as Benjamin Franklin gave to the newly settled 'pilgrims' in North America (see Weber 1930: 50ff.). It has also been recorded that Amar Das stressed

---

11. Guru Angad evolved the Gurmukhi script using for this purpose basically the script employed by Khatri traders to maintain accounts (see Gopal Singh 1978:1 xl). It is obvious that he must have been familiar with account-keeping.

social egalitarianism by insisting that his visitors first eat in the community kitchen before meeting with him,[12] and this rule is believed to have been applied even to the Mughal emperor Akbar when he visited the Guru. Moreover, though the fare served in his kitchen was rich, Amar Das himself ate frugally and only what he himself earned by his own labour (Harbans Singh 1964:24).

Although asceticism was rejected, austerity was acknowledged as a personal virtue in the lives of these early gurus. At the same time the exhortation to their followers was to strive for worldly fortunes. The fourth guru, Ram Das (1534–81), a builder of cities and towns, including Amritsar, which is the holy city most revered by the Sikhs, invited traders from wherever his message could reach to settle down there.

The Guru asked his Sikhs to help each other in founding business houses and pray for their success. The Sikhs from now on remained no longer small farmers or petty shopkeepers, but went as far as Kabul to buy and sell horses, and become jewellers, embroidery workers, carpenters and masons, bankers and wholesalers (Gopal Singh 1978: I, xli).

With the passing away of Ram Das the first phase of the evolution of the Sikh community came to an end. During this phase the two most significant factors in the evolutionary process were, first, the unusual personal qualities of the gurus, who combined their spiritual quest with an affirmation of the worth of mundanity in a seamless worldview, and second, the social composition of the early followers. These factors were able to operate in unison in relatively well-settled political conditions, particularly during the long and highly tolerant reign of the great Mughal king, Akbar.

Ram Das broke with tradition when he chose his son-in-law as the next guru; the succession thereafter went from father to son while the first three gurus had strictly avoided this choice. Moreover, after Akbar's death the political environment within which the Sikhs had to operate became increasingly hostile, compelling them to abandon their early pacifist ways. Finally, the social composition of the community underwent a radical transformation with the massive infusion of the Jats. In choosing to cope with adverse circumstances from a position of strength and engaging in politics, the Sikh gurus,

---

12. *Pehle pangat piche sangat:* first sit down in a row [to eat with others]; only then may you sit [with the Guru].

from now on, contributed to the making of what, borrowing once again the phraseology of Max Weber (1930: 181), one may call the Sikh 'iron cage'. The Sikhs themselves generally conceive of it as their call to destiny. Increasingly, they became involved with secular power and ultimately sacralized it. More about this below.

Arjan Mal (1563–1606), fifth in succession, was a great consolidator. Nanak had given the new message for whosoever would listen and bound them in the act and symbolism of the common meal. Angad gave the Sikhs a distinctive script. Amar Das gave them a place of pilgrimage at Goindwal, where he constructed a sacred well (*baoli*). Although this was against the letter and the spirit of the teachings of Nanak, it fulfilled the traditional aspirations of the people. Ram Das became the instrument of a miracle, for the tank which he dug out at his new city of Chak Ram Das is believed by pious Sikhs to have been filled miraculously by the will of God. Its waters are thus no less than *amrit*, the holy water that bestows immortality: hence the renaming of the city as Amritsar, the pool of ambrosia.

Guru Arjan's contributions were a fitting capstone on this edifice. He constructed a temple in the holy tank known as Harmandar Sahib, 'the honoured temple of God', and he gave the Sikhs their Holy Book the *Adi Granth* ('the original book') by committing to writing the prayers, hymns and sayings of the first four gurus, his own, and those of many Hindu saints and Muslim sufis of the Sant tradition from various parts of the country. This eclecticism has been described as 'an effort to extend the Sikh constituency' (Hans 1985: 215). It may be added here that it was Nanak himself who started the practice of using his own compositions in prayers or worship (see Grewal 1979: 284).

Arjan converted the traditional voluntary offering to the guru into an obligatory tithe (*dasvandh*), showing a concern for money obtained by open but somewhat coercive means. This gave a new definition to the relationship of the Sikh guru and his followers. Needless to emphasize, money is a key symbol of a secularized world (see Weber 1930: 174). An indefatigable traveller, Arjan won for the Sikh faith the following of thousands of Jats. By now Sikhs were to be found in many north Indian cities, often as traders. His achievements were recognized widely and he accepted the honoured sobriquet of *Sacha Padshah*, 'the true emperor', for himself, signifying the unity of the sacred and the secular functions. He also got involved in contemporary politics, and took the side of the rebel prince Khusrau against his father, the emperor Jahangir. This cost Arjan his life, but in the process he gave the Sikhs their first martyr, establishing yet another significant element of the Sikh tradition, namely the call to martyrdom, which continues to be a powerful motive force in the lives of many Sikhs until today. In fact, the symbolism of martyrdom, which became highly valorized as a result of the killing of the ninth and tenth gurus as also the latter's sons, has been invoked by Sikh fundamentalists in recent years (see Chapter Three).

I must pause here to explain the significance of the infusion of the Jats into the Sikh fold which was mentioned above. Although originally pastoralists in Rajasthan, the Jats had moved into Punjab from the ninth century onward, and established themselves as very hard-working and successful peasant cultivators. Although they had prospered economically, they suffered from a stigmatized identity in relation to caste Hindus.

With their strong rural base, their martial traditions, their normally impressive physique, and their considerable energy the Jats have for many centuries constituted the elite of the Punjab villages. They are also noted for their straightforward manner, for a tremendous generosity, for an insistence upon their right to take revenge, and for their sturdy attachment to the land (McLeod 1976: 11).

The Khatris were the money-lenders and mentors of the Jats and the first three Sikh Gurus, themselves Khatris, hailed from the Jat country in central Punjab. It was this human component (66 per cent of all Sikhs at the 1881 census) of the burgeoning Sikh heritage which Guru Arjan, who attained martyrdom in 1606, bequeathed to his son with the message 'to sit fully armed on his throne and to maintain an army to the best of his ability' (Field 1914: 19). And Hargobind did exactly as he was told, signifying a major turning point in the continuing redefinition of secularism in the Sikh religious tradition.

The Doctrine of Two Swords

Hargobind (1595–1644), though only eleven years old when he became the sixth guru of the Sikhs, spoke in the accents of a mature man, according to Sikh oral tradition: 'My *seli* [rosary worn as a necklace by the previous gurus symbolizing their spiritual pursuits] shall be a sword-belt, and my turban shall be adorned with a royal aigrette' (Macauliffe 1909: IV, 2). At his investiture he carried two swords in his swordbelt and explained the significance of his action: 'one to avenge my father, the other to destroy the miracles of Muhammad' (Narang 1960: 60). In other words, while the one symbolized his temporal power (*miri*),the other stood for his spiritual authority (*piri*).[13]

Even more portentous was Hargobind's decision to have a new temple erected facing the Harmandar Sahib (but outside the holy tank of Amritsar), which he called the Akal Takht, 'the Throne of the Immortal God'. Therein he had his own throne built higher than the throne of the Mughal emperor in Delhi. '[I]nstead of chanting hymns of peace, the congregation heard ballads extolling feats of heroism, and, instead of listening to religious discourses, discussed plans of military conquests' (Khushwant Singh 1963: 63). He asked his agents (the *masand*) to fetch him tribute in men, horses and arms. He raised an army and built a small fortress, Lohgarh (the steel castle), in Amritsar. Hargobind had an ambivalent relationship with the emperor Jahangir (who had had Hargobind's father tortured to death), suffered imprisonment, and finally during the time of the next emperor, Shahjahan, came into open conflict with the imperial troops on three occasions. The Sikhs acquitted themselves well in these clashes, though they also suffered heavy losses (see Harbans Singh 1964: 33). By 1634, Hargobind obviously had second thoughts about continued conflict with the imperial power, and withdrew into a quieter way of life in the Himalayan foothills in east Punjab. He stayed there until his death ten years later. Apart from the conflict with the Mughal emperors, he also had to grapple with the organizational problems generated by an expanding and an increasingly heterogeneous following including the Jats and 'superstition-ridden Hindus' (Khushwant Singh 1963: 66), and even 'criminals and fugitives' (Cunningham 1955: 50).

What is the significance of 'the call to arms' given by Guru Hargobind in the general context of the evolution of the Sikh community, and in terms of the processes of secularization? The estab-

---

13. It is not clear how exactly Hargobind defined the relationship between spiritual authority and temporal power. His religious tradition had paid little attention to the latter; in fact, Nanak had ridiculed and reviled kings, saying even worms were better, for kings forget God. In this connection the significance of building the Akal Takht separately, outside the holy tank, may not be minimized. In the comparative context Dumont (1983: 15) has observed that the 'logical' relation between the two functions is one of 'hierarchical complementarity with *auctoritas* encompassing *potestas*'.

lished opinion of Sikh scholars themselves flows from their the-oak-tree-in-the-acorn position: 'We do not see any essential difference in the outlook of Guru Hargobind from his predecessors' except perhaps in emphasis which was of course the need of the time' (Gopal Singh 1978:1, xlii). Some non-Sikh historians echo this judgement when they maintain that Hargobind, and later Gobind Singh (the tenth Guru), did not deviate 'from the great ideal of Guru Nanak' by transforming 'a purely pietistic faith and society to a militant and crusading one directed towards temporal ends': they are said to have only elaborated 'in the context of a somewhat different socio-political situation, what Guru Nanak stood for in his own time and space' (Ray 1970: 86). Two interrelated issues of interpretation are involved here: one theological and the other sociological. Sikh hermeneutics has had to reckon with Nanak's admonition, 'fight with no weapons except *shabad* [the holy word]' (Cunningham 1955: 40), and an explicit formulation on this issue had to await Gobind Singh.

From the sociological point of view the apparently contextualist approach of scholars such as Gopal Singh and Niharranjan Ray seriously minimizes the significance of both the changing composition of the Sikh community (its internal order) and its relations with the Mughal empire (its external order) and, therefore, provides us with emasculated history. They uncritically echo the traditional Sikh point of view, which discerns even a political dimension to Guru Nanak's concerns, by recalling that he made certain statements about the state and that he too has long been referred to as 'the True King' (*Sacha Padshah*). The most authoritative scholarly opinion is best stated by J.S. Grewal, who maintains that 'man's moral commitment is given a clear primacy over his political obligations' in Nanak's teaching (see Grewal 1979: 165)—that 'true sovereignty' according to the Guru was not all political (ibid.: 166). In other words, society was to be saved by virtuous people and, above all, God, and not by secular power such as that of kings.

From the specific point of view of the present discussion, therefore, a critical change in the character of secular outlook, and in the process of secularization, must be acknowledged. Nanak's moral this-worldliness, summed up as 'work, worship, and sharing', and faith in divine grace, are from Hargobind's time redefined in terms of temporal power, honour and revenge. To use a sociologist's phrase, hope has become political (see Martin 1978: 63), and when this happens, the encompassing character of spiritual authority as opposed to temporal power, even if acknowledged, is, in fact, undermined. Writing from the perspective of the historian of religions, Toynbee has observed: 'While it is manifest in the case of Judaism, Christianity and the Mahayana that a higher religion was being diverted from its mission by being exploited politically, this is not less true, though it may be less obvious, in the case of Islam and Sikhism' (1979: 110).

The transformation brought about by Hargobind was radical: its most important characteristic was an emphasis upon the unity of religion and politics, but in a manner that the primacy of the former was weakened. It could also be construed as a process of sacralization, indicative of the elevation of the secular world to a position it had not occupied before: pursuit of power (in the sociological sense of the word) could now pretend to be on par with the religious quest—a thing of value—and even overshadow it. This new worldview found its full expression in the words and actions of the tenth and last Guru, Gobind Singh, but not before another and a truly glorious martyrdom had taken place.

Hargobind's three immediate successors (his grandson, greatgrandson, and son, in that order) are of no particular interest for this discussion, beyond the fact that, though they could not completely withdraw from political involvements, they stressed the pietist-pacifist element of the Sikh religious tradition more than its martial fervour. In 1675, Tegh Bahadur, the ninth guru, suffered martyrdom defending the sanctity of a people's religious faith. The efforts of the fundamentalist Muslim emperor Aurangzeb to bring Tegh Bahadur, who was widely respected not only by Sikhs but also by Hindus generally, under the heel were successfully resisted by the saintly guru until he was executed in Delhi.[14]

Govind Rai (1666–1708) was only nine years old when he was called upon to cremate his father Teg Bahadur's severed head, which had been carried in secrecy to Anandpur (east Punjab). Ever since the retreat of Hargobind into the Shivalik Hills, the Sikh gurus had imbibed the local Hindu cultural and religious ethos. Significant elements of this ethos were the Puranic story of Krishna as a divine

---

14. The importance of the evolving significance of the notion of martyrdom in the Sikh politico-religious tradition is illustrated by Khushwant Singh's translation of a verse attributed to Guru Gobind on the ninth Guru's execution: 'He suffered martyrdom for the sake of his faith' (1963: 74–5). This is not a literal translation.

incarnation and the cult of Shakti, that is the divinity conceived of as 'power' and represented as the goddess. The Hindu concept of power is, of course, total and not to be equated with the notion of political power in the Western civilization. 'The Shakti blended easily with the Jat cultural patterns which had been brought from the plains. The result was a new and powerful synthesis which prepared the Panth [the Sikh community] for a determinative role in the chaotic circumstances of the eighteenth century' (McLeod 1976: 14).

Gobind's upbringing in Patna (in eastern India) and Anandpur took place in a Hindu environment, and he attained a considerable knowledge of the Hindu as well as the Sikh religious traditions. He defined his own role almost literally in terms of Hindu scripture. Echoing the *Bhagavad Gita*, he wrote: 'For this purpose was I born: To uphold righteousness, to protect those worthy and virtuous. To overcome and destroy the evil doers'(Harbans Singh 1966: 176).[15] He, however, repudiated the Hindu idea of avatar: 'Whoever calls me the supreme Being shall suffer in hell. Recognise me as God's servant only' (ibid.: 13).

Gobind was obviously deeply impressed by the Hindu cult of the goddess of destruction, and is believed to have written long poems in praise of her: his first composition and only major Punjabi work, 'Var Sri Bhagautiji ki', is based on the *Markandya Purana*, a Brahmanical text. Subsequently, he wrote a poem in Hindi also, 'Chandi Charitar', honouring the goddess. His designation of the sword as 'Bhagauti', the goddess, recalls the fact that the sword is her symbol in Hindu mythology. He also called god *sarbloh*, 'all steel' (pure steel). The supplicatory prayer, *ardas*, which he composed, begins thus: 'Having first remembered the Sword, meditate on Guru Nanak'. Another well-known prayer composed by him concludes with these words: 'Hail! hail to the creator of the World,/ The Saviour of Creation, my Cherisher,/ Hail to thee, O Sword' (see Harbans Singh 1966: 47). In an earlier composition, 'Shastar Nam Mala', containing the names of various weapons, Gobind had identified these with divinities and even personified them.

Guru Gobind's inspiration was taken more from his grandfather, Hargobind, than his father, and he waged war against the Mughals.

---

15. Cf. the *Bhagavad Gita* (IV.7–8): Whenever righteousness wanes and evil prevails, I go forth from age to age to protect the good, punish the wicked, and re-establish the sovereignty of good.

He introduced the notion of *dharmayudda*, 'holy war' or 'war to uphold righteousness', into the Sikh religious tradition, drawing upon, once again, Hindu sources. At the end of his rendering of the story of the avatar Krishna, he is believed to have written: 'I have cast into the popular tongue the story of Bhagvata./ This I have done with no other purpose, Lord, except to glorify the 'holy war'' (see Harbans Singh 1966: 48). His justification of the theology of the sword (obviously mindful of Nanak's exhortation to his followers to wield no weapon and rely solely on the recitation of God's name) was also conveyed, so it is said, in a message called the 'epistle of victory' (*zafarnama*), which, tradition has it, he sent to Aurangzeb: 'when all avenues have been explored, all means tried, it is rightful to draw the sword out of the scabbard and wield it with your hand' (see Khushwant Singh 1963: 78, n. 5). As Khushwant Singh notes, 'It would be idle to pretend that this change of emphasis was purely theological' (1963: 89).

Ultimately, in 1699, Gobind instituted baptism for the Sikhs to constitute a community of the 'pure' (*khalsa*), in deference to God's command, he said. He employed a double-edged sword (*khanda*) to prepare the baptismal water. The baptized Sikh was to call himself Singh (literally, 'lion') in the manner of the Hindu Rajputs (warrior caste) of north India. One of the symbols of an initiated man, he prescribed, should be the sword (*kirpan*), or an emblem of it, which a Sikh was exhorted to always carry on his person.[16] The emphasis on the sword symbolized the value of valour, and also pointed to a political goal as a part of the religious quest. J.S. Grewal observes: 'More than ever before the activities of Guru Gobind Singh's Sikhs now appeared fraught with political implications, and the stage was set for a deeper conflict with contemporary powers' (1987: 126). But conflict is never a goal in itself; this could now only be the acquisition of political power—the establishment of a Sikh state. Not long afterwards, the words *raj karega Khalsa*, 'the pure (baptised) Sikhs

16. The emphasis originally was on the symbolic rather than a real sword; Guru Gobind himself used to wear a miniature sword in his hair. The other related symbols are, as is well-known, *unshorn hair* tied into a knot with *a comb* placed in it, a *steel bracelet* worn on the right forearm, and *knee-length trousers*. Gobind laid down the wearing of unshorn hair as an obligation; the other items are not mentioned in the code of conduct (*rahitnama*) he had drawn up for the Sikhs (see Khushwant Singh 1953, 1963). For two different and unusual interpretations of the five symbols see Kapur Singh (1959: 137–54) and Uberoi (1991: 320–32).

will rule' were added to the daily prayer (*ardas*) by one of his followers. A most significant instrument of the quest for power was to be the band of warriors (*jatha*), modelled on the congregation (*sangat*), bound by codes of conduct (*rahitnama*). Together these concepts emphasized collective identity and common purpose rather than individual leadership or following. Guru Gobind Singh announced closure of the canon (*gurbani*) and declared that, after his death, spiritual authority would vest in the Holy Book (*Guru Granth*). Temporal power for the furtherance of Sikh secular interests, he declared, would be exercised by the Khalsa (*Guru Panth*), represented at any place and time by five baptized Sikhs.

To say that the significance of Gobind Singh's achievements for the evolution of the Sikh religious tradition and the Sikh community was enormous would be an understatement. The passage from Guru Nanak's pietist and pacifist message of salvation and qualified world affirmation to Guru Gobind's call to his followers to take charge of their destiny as a self-ascribed community, and to take up arms if necessary to achieve their objectives, was *the passage from sacralized secularity to secularized religion*. Using the criteria developed in the Introduction (Chapter One), the revolutionary steps taken by the tenth guru could be said to be fundamentalist in orientation. Scripture was concretized (through the closure of the *gurbani*) and elevated to the status of the spiritual guru. The sense of community bonding was greatly strengthened through a variety of measures including personal and collective names (Singh, Kaur, Khalsa), a ritual of baptism replete with rich symbolism, and a code of conduct. These key elements helped define an exclusive way of life and also provided the basis for cultural critique. Guru Gobind did not hesitate to place power in the centre of the scheme of things. In doing this he was reacting to the situation in which he found himself as the guru of a demoralized following. To the extent to which the situation demanded in his judgement a reshaping of the religious tradition, he responded with vision and vigour. He emerged as a role model for succeeding leaders, but none of them has ever come anywhere near him in achievements (see Chapter Three).

The Secular State of Ranjit Singh

The effort to establish a Sikh state succeeded almost immediately after the death (by murder) of Guru Gobind Singh in 1708. His chosen successor to carry on the 'holy war'—ironically a Hindu renouncer—felt free to define his own identity. He cast himself in the kingly role, although he said that he was no more than a slave (*banda*) of Gobind Singh. Banda Bahadur, 'brave slave' (that was the name he chose for himself), moved swiftly, incited an agrarian uprising, fought Muslim armies, and captured the province of Sirhind from the Mughal governor in 1710, less than two years after Gobind Singh's death. Banda now assumed the title of *padshah*, the emperor, and even issued coins to mark the inauguration of his rule. All this was very short-lived, however, and Banda was executed in 1716. But the consciousness generated by Guru Gobind Singh survived—consciousness of the Khalsa not only as a repository of spiritual knowledge, but also of political will.

Eighty years and more had to pass before a genuine state was established by a Sikh in 1799, when the eighteen year-old Ranjit Singh (incidentally a Jat) captured the city of Lahore from three squabbling Sikh sardars who were in control of it (see Khushwant Singh 1963: 196ff.). A valiant soldier, a shrewd administrator, and a sagacious ruler, Ranjit Singh unified Punjab and the adjoining areas under his direct rule, or under other rulers who acknowledged his over-all sovereignty and paid tribute to him. Ironically, Ranjit Singh's state was not a Sikh state, but a monarchy, and the prophecy that the Khalsa would rule had not been fulfilled. In fact, it has been asserted that the 'republicanism' of Gobind Singh was 'compromised', 'gradually, progressively and purposely' (Kapur Singh 1959: 352), by Ranjit Singh, who assumed the title of Maharaja at a Brahmanical coronation ceremony in 1801. 'Within a few years after his coronation, he reduced into desuetude the supreme authority of the Sikh polity, the *Gurumata* [the collective will of the community treated as the opinion of the guru], and entrusted the control of the government of his expanding territories to a cabinet of his own choice, in accordance with the ancient Hindu monarchical tradition', though personally 'he never claimed independence from the *Gurumata*' (ibid.: 360).

We have here an important concept, namely the secular state, which was new in the evolution of the Sikh religious tradition: a gulf was created—a wall erected—between the polity and the personal religious faith of the ruler. Ranjit Singh's first act on entering Lahore had been to 'pay homage' at two of the city's mosques associated with its Muslim rulers (see Khushwant Singh 1963: 197). He persevered in a broadly defined policy of non-discrimination towards all communities by personally celebrating their religious festivals, and by proclaiming the equality of all citizens before the law (ibid.: 203). Although such pluralism could not be said to be alien to the Sikh religious tradition,[17] it did entail serious compromises: the notion of the Khalsa as the repository of political power (*Guru Panth*) was one of the casualties.

'The factor which contributed most to Ranjit Singh's success', writes Khushwant Singh, 'was his respect for all faiths.' He further points out that 'Ranjit Singh's court reflected the secular pattern of his state', and that 'there were no forced conversions' in his time. 'This attitude won the loyalty of all his subjects' (1963: 294–5). But, and as already pointed out above, other Sikh historians contest this judgement on one crucial point: according to them Ranjit Singh's secularism was against the Sikh religious tradition (see Kapur Singh 1959: 284–387), for it destroyed the hierarchical unity of spiritual authority and temporal power. Contemporary historians also have been somewhat sceptical about his fair treatment of Muslims. Nevertheless, Ranjit Singh may well be considered a precursor of the secularism of Jawahrlal Nehru and the Constitution of the Republic of India (see Chapter Eight). Nehruvian secularism, however, is anathema to those who claim to speak in the name of the Sikh religious tradition (see Chapter Three).

Ranjit Singh died in 1839 and the kingdom he had built collapsed in 1846, creating a situation in which the Sikhs, shorn of political power, sought refuge in their religious faith, but found it much diluted. The 'iron cage' of worldly involvements had gradually confined the faith too narrowly. Like the Muslims who, in a similar situation of loss of political power, had earlier turned to the

17. Gobind wrote in his 'Akal Utsat': 'Recognise all mankind, whether Hindus or Muslims, as one./ The same Lord is the Creator and Nourisher of all,/ Recognise no distinctions among them./ The monastery and the mosque are the same,/ So are the Hindu worship and the Muslim prayer./ Men are all one' (Harbans Singh 1966: 3). He is said to have echoed the Quran (109: 3) and said to a Muslim *qazi* (judge): 'Your religion is good for you and our religion for us'. A modern Sikh commentator calls this a 'strange twist' to Guru Nanak's mission (Hans 1985: 218).

'purification' of their religious life (see Chapter Four), the Sikhs too sought solace in reviving the orthopraxis entailed by their orthodoxy. This involved, among other things, reassertion of the supreme position of the guru, elimination of those elements of Hindu ritualism which had reasserted their sway in the everyday life of the Sikhs and, freeing of the Sikh temples from the control of priests who were not baptised Sikhs. The socio-political concomitant of these moves was the redefinition of Sikh identity in the negative slogan 'We are not Hindus', necessitated not only by the inner urge for reform but also the external pressure exercised by the revivalist Hindu Arya Samaj (see Chapter Seven). Religion thus became a 'sign' of distinction between Sikhs and Hindus, and was reduced to being its own 'shadow' (to borrow a formulation from Dumont 1970a: 91).[18]

Through the Gurdwara Act of 1925, the control of the temples passed into the hands of a democratically elected body, namely the Shiromani Gurdwara Prabandhak Committee (SGPC), and the political movement against British imperialism and Hindu cultural hegemony was taken charge of by the exclusively Sikh political party, Akali Dal (see Khushwant Singh 1966: 193–216). Although the Sikhs were nearly unanimous in relation to their religious goals, they found themselves divided politically. Events that could be seen as a reassertion of Sikh republicanism also carried in them the seeds of disruptive politics. The partition of the subcontinent in 1947 was a deadly blow to the Sikh community, which found itself driven out of areas that had been its home since the very beginning. The sense of political grievance deepened with the passage of time, and the Akalis repudiated any notion of the separation of religion and politics and the state that political analysts derived from the Constitution of

---

18. For a different interpretation of the events of the second half of the nineteenth century, see Oberoi 1994. He questions the thesis of the cultural decline of Sikhs, and regards the same as a construction of the British and the new elites who spearheaded the Singh Sabhas (see Chapter Three). While Oberoi pays due attention to the opportunities that the British rulers generated (and not in the armed services alone), I think he plays down the impact of the collapse of the kingdom bequeathed to the Sikhs (indeed all Punjabis) by Ranjit Singh. There is a strong similarity between this situation and the downfall of the Mughal empire in the early eighteenth century. In both cases many community leaders linked loss of power to a decline in the quality of the religious life, and initiated corrective steps along both the cultural and political routes (see Chapter Four).

India. This repudiation became the basis for the demand for a Sikh homeland (see Nayar 1966 and Harbans Singh 1983: 343ff.).

Simultaneously with these political developments, large land-owners, mainly Hindus but also Sikhs, became the principal beneficiaries of the successful Green Revolution in Punjab, and expanding opportunities in industrial enterprise and the urban professions. As world-wide opportunities for secular success beckoned, the Sikhs responded enthusiastically, but at a price, namely the increasing 'incidence of apostasy': 'the sense of belonging to the Sikh community requires both the belief in the teachings of the *Adi Granth* and the observance of the Khalsa tradition initiated by Guru Gobind Singh' (Khushwant Singh 1966: 303). In the circumstances it seems that the Sikh faith will survive only if it is enforced by the state, and this could only be done by a Sikh state (see ibid.: 305).

The most serious threat to religious faith is modernization, which includes secularization in the sense of a restricted role for religion in the life of the individual, but the Sikhs, with their this-worldly tradition are unlikely to turn their back on the modern world. If this indeed be so, then it is only to be expected that 'fundamentalism', which often is an expression of a guilty conscience, will characterize Sikh public life for quite some time to come. In the eyes of the orthodox, the three values of 'work, worship, and sharing' have been displaced by 'parasitism, godlessness, and selfishness' in the lives of many apparently successful and modernized Sikhs. Hence the call, 'Be good Sikhs', given by the fundamentalists.

*　　*　　*

To conclude: In this chapter I have been concerned with an examination of the Sikh religious tradition with a view to finding out what it teaches us about the patterns and processes of secularization. This is a particularly worthwhile exercise in view of the assertion of many Sikh scholars that, while their religious faith postulates the unity of religion and politics, it is at the same time a 'secular religion'. In fact it has been argued that 'this comingling of motifs [spiritual authority and royal power] makes for a certain secularization of faith in Sikhism' (Attar Singh 1973: 22), so that confidence is expressed that 'the Sikh faith has an in-built mechanism that can absorb successfully the essential spirit of secularism' (Samundari 1973: 6).

The foregoing discussion suggests that there are three possible meanings of secularism within the Sikh religious tradition, and a fourth one outside it but affecting Sikh life today. Each connotation derives from a particular pattern of secularization, which in turn is causally linked to certain, antecedent critical events in a manner observed elsewhere (see Martin 1978). These are: (1) world-affirmation or 'mundanity'; (2) the unity of religion and politics and therefore of the *gurdwara* and the state; (3) religious pluralism and the separation of religion and politics; and (4) a narrowing of the role of religion in society. Of these, the first meaning does not by itself entail the second: in fact, and as noted by a number of Sikh scholars, the merger of functions 'ultimately weakened the original religious impulse' (see Attar Singh 1973: 22). As for the third and the fourth patterns of secularization, it is obvious that they are at variance and even in conflict with the first and the second, and have been, therefore, rejected by orthodox Sikhs.

In the context of interreligious comparison, it is obvious that, confident theories of modernization notwithstanding, a hiatus exists. The 'translation' of ideas from one civilizational setting to another, even after the 'transfer' of related institutions (most notably the 'modern' state) has formally been achieved, is not easy. India's major religious traditions—Hinduism, Islam, and Sikhism—do not provide the kind of idiom which the Christian tradition, before and after Luther, did for secularization in its European manifestations. And yet it is these that are recommended as universally valid by modernization theorists. Needless to add, idioms are only part of the story, the part on which the foregoing discussion has focused. Idioms go with institutions, and may even evolve from the latter. The sociological perspective is committed to the importance of institutions, and this has been explored often, most recently and ably by Satish Saberwal (1995) in his comparison of India and Europe.

Chapter
Three

The Sikh Religious Tradition
Fundamentalisms, Old and New

Learn the religion of the age, brothers, from the perfect guru.
ADI GRANTH, M3, Gauri 3

There is no such thing as a clean-shaven Sikh.
KHUSHWANT SINGH, *A History of the Sikhs*

We are always affected, in hope and fear, by what is nearest to us, and hence
approach, under its influence, the testimony of the past. Hence it is constantly
necessary to inhibit the overhasty assimilation of the past to our own expecta-
tions of meaning. Only then will we be able to listen to the past in a way that
enables it to make its own meaning heard.
HANS-GEORG GADAMER, *Truth and Method*

Fundamentalists or Defenders of Faith?

Alone among the countries of South Asia, India is a secular state by
constitutional proclamation. The Preamble to the Constitution refers
to India as 'a sovereign secular socialist democratic republic'. As
pointed out in Chapter One, the secular state in the context of India's
major indigenous religious traditions—namely Hinduism and Sikhism—does not mean that a constitutional wall separates the state
from the church here as it does, for instance, in the United States, for
none of these religions is associated with an institutional structure
comparable to the Christian Church. The Sikh *gurdwara* (temple) is
sometimes loosely called a church, but such a comparison is misleading, for the *gurdwara* is a place of worship rather than an organ of
institutional control. Also, secularism does not mean in India that
religion is privatized: the idea is alien to the indigenous religious
traditions, which are holistic in character and do not recognize

dualistic categories such as sacred versus profane, religious versus secular, or public versus private.

The freedom to hold any religious beliefs and engage in related religious practices has, however, given rise to one of the most agonizing dilemmas of the Indian polity: how to cope with the demand of some religious communities, notably the Sikhs, for the recognition of their 'right' to repudiate the separation of religion and politics in the conduct of their own community life.[1] There is an apparent contradiction here: while religious identities are sought to be neutralized at the national level, it is demanded that such an identity should be allowed to become the basis of the political structure at the regional or state level because politics should not be separated from religion. If a religion does not allow autonomy to politics, can the state forge an identity as powerful as the one offered to a people via their religious community? The assumption has been that it can and it should do so. The main means to this end have been identified as the promotion of civic ties and class interests to take the place of the primordial bonds of race, language, and religion. Judging by what we know, the effort has not been a total success anywhere in the Western world; when it has been pursued relentlessly, the consequences, whether under fascism or communism, have been horrendous. It is, morever, by now widely recognized that 'political modernization' and 'economic development' are Western notions and do not have easy passage in non-Western settings. This conflict of worldviews and desired futures provides the setting for one of the most tragic events in the nearly half-century old history of independent India.

Given the self-proclaimed secular character of the Indian state, it might well appear both puzzling and shocking that in June 1984 the government of India should have ordered units of its regular army (including Hindu, Sikh, and Muslim servicemen), under a chain of command consisting at the top of three generals (two Sikhs and a Hindu),[2] to storm the precincts of the holiest of Sikh shrines, the

---

1. Tradition-oriented or orthodox Muslims also adhere to the same position, though with one qualification. While they reject the separation of religion and the state in principle, they accept it as an arrangement for Muslims living in a non-Islamic state (see Chapter Five).

2. It should be stressed that the composition of these units and of the chain of command *happened* to be as described here: no special efforts were made for them to be so composed.

Golden Temple at Amritsar, to clear it of elements which the government considered to be in unlawful possession of it. The military action, code-named Operation Blue Star, resulted in extensive damage to the buildings in the complex and the killing of over a thousand people, including pilgrims. It shocked Sikhs everywhere and saddened millions of Indians.[3]

A few words about the character and historical importance of the Golden Temple (so called because of the gold plate cover of its dome) will be apposite at this point. Since the Sikh religion is, unlike Hinduism, against anthropomorphic representation of divinity, and therefore also idolatry in principle, a Sikh place of worship, the *gurdwara* (gateway to the guru or preceptor), is a place for congregational listening to readings from the Sikh Holy Book (the *Adi Granth* or the *Granth Sahib*), and for saying prayers. The only true object of

---

3. Among India's religious minorities, Muslims and Sikhs have been politically the most active. Muslim separatism developed in less than a hundred years into a very powerful force in the Indian subcontinent and was mainly responsible for the partition in 1947 and the creation of Pakistan. However, there are today more Muslims in India (102 million or 12 per cent of the total population of India, according to the 1991 official census) than in any other country except Indonesia and perhaps Bangladesh.

By comparison, there are not many Sikhs—only 16 million or 2 per cent—but they have much greater social visibility and political weight than numbers alone would lead one to expect. Actually there are more Christians in India (20 million) than Sikhs, but neither they nor the smaller religious minorities—Buddhists, Jains, Zoroastrians, etc. (about 2 per cent)—stand out as prominently as the Sikhs. The latter with their characteristic unshaven beards, unshorn hair, and carefully tied turbans, are readily distinguishable from other Indians. Besides, the Sikhs are a geographically mobile people: although concentrated in Punjab (about 80 per cent), they are found all over the country, mostly in urban areas. Many Sikhs have travelled abroad in search of job opportunities: their numbers are estimated to be well over a million.

A few words about the social composition of the Sikh community. One of the first principles on which the Sikh community was founded was the rejection of caste, but they retain a memory of caste origins, and their daily social conduct is influenced in significant ways by caste traditions and stereotypes. Thus, Sikhs of the Jat caste, who account for 50 to 60 per cent of all Sikhs, do not look kindly upon menial work and favour agriculture, their traditional occupation. The first Sikhs came from the upper castes, as indeed did the ten gurus. Conversions from among Hindu 'scheduled' (low) castes occurred around the beginning of the twentieth century in large numbers. Today these converts are estimated to account for 12 per cent of the Sikh population. The intermediate artisan castes also are present. Intercaste marriage is still uncommon, but hereditary occupational specialization is on the decline. Politically Sikhs are a divided people and have supported not only the Akali (exclusively Sikh) parties but also the Congress and the Communist parties.

veneration is the *Granth Sahib* itself as the embodiment of divinely revealed knowledge, or the holy word (*shabad*). The temple was built with the help of common people by Guru Arjan (1563–1606), the fifth of the ten Sikh gurus (see Chapter Two). Located in the middle of the sacred tank (*sarovar*) of Amritsar, constructed earlier, it was named Harmandar, the temple of god. Its construction was begun in 1588 and the unusual architectural style, marked by a doorway on each of the four sides, stressed that the new faith was open to everybody. According to tradition, the Guru said: 'My faith is for the people of all castes and creeds from which ever direction they come and to which ever direction they bow' (see Gopal Singh 1988: 177).[4]

Arjan's son, Guru Hargobind (1595–1644), built a second temple (*ca.* 1606) facing the original shrine and outside the sacred tank; it was called Akal Takht, 'the throne of the immortal god'. Here, as stated earlier (Chapter Two), 'instead of chanting hymns of peace, the congregation heard ballads extolling feats of heroism, and instead of listening to religious discourses, discussed plans of military conquests' (Khushwant Singh 1963: 63). Besides the tank and the two temples, the sacred complex includes the walkway (*parikrama*) to enable pilgrims to circumambulate Harmandar Sahib as an act of piety.

In its present form, the Golden Temple dates back to the early nineteenth century, having been rebuilt by Maharaja Ranjit Singh after suffering damage at the hands of Muslim invaders. Today, while Harmandar houses the Granth Sahib by day, Akal Takht is the home of traditional weapons associated with the sixth and tenth gurus, and it is here that the *Granth Sahib* is kept at night. The rituals, called *maryada* (tradition), consist mainly of daily veneration of the holy book, including readings from it. Apart from daily worshippers and occasional pilgrims who visit the Golden Temple for religious devotions, many Sikh functionaries concerned with its maintenance and other laymen are allowed by a legally constituted managerial body, called the Shiromani Gurdwara Prabandhak Committee (SGPC), to stay in the buildings that constitute the outer quadrangle of the sacred complex. In June 1984 such residents included armed

---

4. According to Sikh tradition, unsupported by historical evidence, the foundation stone of the Golden Temple was laid by a Muslim Sufi, Mian Mir. It bears testimony to the traditional Sikh approach to religious differences that such a story should be believed.

Sikhs who formed part of a statewide militant movement for the assertion of the political and economic rights and religious prerogatives of the Sikhs, which, they maintained, were in danger.

Their leader was a charismatic Sikh preacher, Jarnail Singh Bhindranwale (b. 1947), who, fearing arrest by the government had actually taken sanctuary in the Akal Takht late in 1983 and had had it fortified. Both the occupation of the temple and its fortification were unprecedented. Bhindranwale and his associates carried on their persons not only the traditional Sikh sword as a part of their religious obligation, but also modern firearms. They were trained in the use of the latter by a former Sikh general of the Indian army, who had been dismissed from service by the government on charges of corruption.

In the judgement of the government, largely shared by the public (including many Sikhs), Bhindranwale was a fundamentalist. In India, a fundamentalist is a person who employs religious appeal to mobilize his co-religionists for·political action. The goals of such action are usually a mixture of religious objectives (pursuit and propagation of the traditional way of life and of the Truth as stated by the proponents) and the furtherance of politico-economic interests of one's own community as against those of similarly defined other communities. The government, too, is opposed if it comes in the way. Fundamentalists are seen by their critics as closely associated with, or as being themselves, political extremists (those who press communal or regional demands against the state so hard as to constitute a threat to political stability) and, in certain situations, terrorists (who use different forms of terror, including murder, to further political ends). In Punjab, Bhindranwale had himself been charged twice with complicity in political murders, but had not been prosecuted for reasons of expediency. The fundamentalist is very much a creature of his situation rather than a pure traditionalist, and fundamentalism is not pristine orthodoxy. Sikh orthodoxy would in fact discourage fundamentalism if the teachings of the gurus are our guide, for they advocate catholicity and not narrowness of the mind.

The situation in Punjab just before Operation Blue Star is summed up thus by Murray Leaf, an American anthropologist (1985: 494):

There does not seem to be any doubt that Bhindranwale was the main organizer of a terrorist campaign that was responsible for the murder of several hundred innocent Hindus and that in publicly wearing arms and defiantly proclaiming his willingness to use them he was making himself a target for retribution. Moreover, by setting up his headquarters in the Golden Temple he was in effect daring the authorities to violate the temple in order to capture him. Neither the people of Punjab nor the precepts of the Sikh religion condone murder.

Patwant Singh, a Sikh author, concurs: 'Jarnail Singh Bhindranwale did what no Sikh had done in the past: he placed the supreme emblem of Sikhism in the direct line of fire' (1988: 415). When the Indian army finally mounted an assault on the temple complex on 5 June 1984—a siege had begun two days earlier—Bhindranwale was killed, along with many associates and pilgrims, who had come there to commemorate the fifth guru's day of martyrdom.

Bhindranwale and his associates were fundamentalists and terrorists in the judgement of the government and of their critics. There is no doubt, however, that they considered themselves true Sikhs (*gursikh*), defenders of the basic teachings of the Sikh gurus (*gurbani*) and promoters of the economic interests of the Sikh community (*qaum*). It is noteworthy that Bhindranwale was referred to and addressed as 'Sant' by his followers. This usage is of considerable significance in Sikh cultural and political history.

Traditionally, *sant* means a seeker of truth and salvation, who devotes himself individually as well as in the company of fellow seekers to acts of piety, notably the remembrance of god through the repetition of his name (*namsimran*) and the singing of hymns (*kirtan*). The hymns are usually from the *Granth Sahib*. The original usage of around the fifteenth century was gradually transformed so that by the nineteenth century *sant* became the designation of religious teachers who gave spiritual discourses and provided scriptural commentary and exegesis. This is the current usage too, though it must be added that since India's independence, some *sants* (notably Sant Fateh Singh and Sant Harchand Singh Longowal) have become actively involved in politics (see McLeod 1987: 256–61 and Kapur 1986: passim). The preachers in some cases have been associated with a seminary-like institution, significantly known as the *taksal* (mint), where pupils receive rigorous religious instruction in the traditional style. Bhindranwale was a product and since 1977 head of the Bhindranwale or Damdama *taksal*, but had no more than about five years of modern primary-school education. He gained considerable prominence in 1978 and the following years as a result of his involvement in Punjab politics. It is ironical that Bhindranwale's prominence in the politics of the state should have owed a great deal to early support by the Congress Party, which was interested in playing the communal card to erode the support base of the Akalis (see Kapur 1986).

What happened in Punjab in 1978 is important to our attempt to understand the character of contemporary Sikh fundamentalism. At that time the state was governed by a coalition government formed by two religion-based political parties, the Sikh Akali Dal and the Hindu Jana Sangh (the latter had merged into the larger, professedly secular Janata Party before withdrawing into what is today called the Bharatiya Janata Party). This was a curiously opportunistic alliance between political rivals with the sole aim of holding power. Allegedly under the pressure of its Jana Sangh members, the coalition government gave permission to the Nirankari sect to hold their annual convention in the city of Amritsar, the home of the Golden Temple. The Nirankaris believe in a living guru, so repudiating the ruling of Gobind, the tenth Sikh preceptor, that after his death the *Granth Sahib* would be the spiritual guru, and temporal authority would vest in the community. The Nirankaris have also made additions to the Sikh holy book. This is, from the orthodox point of view, apostasy, for the tenth guru had also announced the closure of the canon (*gurbani*, or the spoken word of the guru) and had refrained from including any of his own numerous compositions in it. Besides these two very serious lapses, not all Nirankaris strictly follow currently prevalent Sikh injunctions about personal appearance. In the eyes of the orthodox and orthoprax Sikhs, these unforgivable sins of commission and omission make Nirankaris obnoxious foes of the true faith.

To prevent the annual convention, which attracts thousands of people from far and wide, Bhindranwale marched from the Golden Temple to the site of the meeting at the head of a procession, shouting anti-Nirankari slogans, and vowed not to allow the convention to take place. The processionists mutilated a shopkeeper on the way and finally made an unsuccessful attempt on the life of the head of the Nirankari sect. In the violence that ensued, swords and firearms were used freely by both sides: three Nirankaris and a dozen Sikhs lost their lives. Both sides complained of lack of protection by the police. Bhindranwale, who was a relatively unknown preacher until then, became suddenly famous as a religious leader with political ambitions. Soon afterwards he became embroiled in party politics (see Tully and Jacob 1985).

Bhindranwale's close association with Amrik Singh, son of the previous head of the Damdama seminary, whom he considered his ritual brother, turned out to be immensely useful. In 1978 Amrik Singh became President of the All-India Sikh Students Federation (founded in 1943 by the Akali Dal). In that capacity he had mounted an offensive against the influence of the communist parties among Sikh students and achieved considerable success. Membership of the Federation rose from 10,000 to 100,000 in a couple of years (see Sharma 1981: 121). Although Amrik Singh's father had nominated Bhindranwale rather than him as his successor, the former remained close to Bhindranwale, placing the institutional resources and networks of the Federation at the latter's disposal. Amrik Singh was an educated youth and his followers included diverse elements, ranging from idealists to extremists. They were drawn from Punjab's middle and lower-level peasantry and from among agricultural workers. Between 1980 and 1984, the Federation was the backbone of Bhindranwale's movement. Amrik Singh died with him in Operation Blue Star.

Bhindranwale's call to the faithful was to return to the fundamentals or true teachings of Sikhism, adhere to the codes of conduct, and find through them the good, moral life. In his speeches Bhindranwale laid more stress on conduct than belief, talking little of theological or cosmological ideas as such, and more about behavioural matters and politico-economic issues. Commentary on such ideas, it may be noted, would have been a major concern in his earlier role as a *sant*, i.e. Sikh preacher, speaking to largely rural audiences. The change of substance did not, however, alter the style. There was a rustic simplicity about his utterances which gave them immense appeal. 'You cannot have courage without reading *gurbani* [the sayings of the gurus, i.e, the scripture]. Only the bani-reader can suffer torture and be capable of feats of strength' (see Pettigrew 1987: 5). The derivation of behaviour (feats of strength) from the reading of scripture comes close to reducing scripture to behaviour. I have been told by many educated Sikhs that the refrain of Bhindranwale's speeches was *tusi change sikh bano* (you should become good Sikhs): 'Who would object to that?', ask my informants. The proof of one's religiousness is thus seen to lie in correct practice. The priority of the canon is, however, unquestionable in principle, for without orthodoxy there can be no orthopraxis. Let me elaborate.

To take the scripture first. As was noted earlier (Chapter Two), Guru Nanak, the first Sikh preceptor, repudiated the authority of the written word, whether that of the Brahman's Veda or the Muslim's Quran. The emphasis was on interiority, on listening to the holy word (*shabad*) with the inner ear, rather than reading it or listening to it with the external ear. The idea of a holy book came later: it was the third guru, Amar Das, who had a two-volume hymnal compiled consisting of the devotional poems of the first two gurus, earlier medieval religious poets, and himself. According to Sikh tradition, an enlarged edition was prepared by the fifth guru, Arjan. It would seem that his 'enemies...were circulating spurious works bearing the name of Nanak in order to seduce Sikhs from their loyalty to the legitimate succession. In order to combat this threat to his authority Guru Arjan decided to prepare an authorized text bearing his own imprimatur' (McLeod 1976: 60). This was done in 1603–4, and the holy book was placed in the Golden Temple.

In the next hundred years, the main interest seemed to lie in who had possession of the *Granth Sahib*. Thus, the sixth guru, Hargobind, removed it from the Golden Temple and kept it in his own home. The tenth guru, Gobind, had new copies made, according to tradition, relying upon his memory. He did something more important: he announced the closure of the canon and invested the holy book with personhood, declaring it to be the guru after his death. It thus became Sri Guru Granth Sahib, the auspicious and revered guru: 'I abolish from now on the succession of persons through heredity or selection. The God's Word as enshrined in the Adi Granth (original book) will be the eternal and the spiritual Guru and the secular Guru will be the Panth, or the whole community of the Khalsa' (see Gopal Singh 1987: 27).

It was another 175 years or so before the scriptural guru acquired its present position of supreme authority. The context in which this happened was the emergence of Sikh fundamentalism in the late nineteenth century. A definitive text of the holy book, being the recension believed to have been prepared by the tenth guru and containing the compositions of the first five and ninth gurus, was finalized as recently as 1962. The uncertainty about its precise contents has not, however, stood in the way of the deepest reverence for the *Granth Sahib*. We have here a historic example of the supremacy of symbol over substance.

Turning to behavioural matters, on which Bhindranwale laid the greater stress, the beginnings of a code of conduct may be traced to the momentous happening of 13 April (some say it was on 30 March) 1699, when the tenth guru, Gobind, instituted the order of baptized Sikhs, namely, the Khalsa, and laid down directions for proper behaviour (see Chapter Two). The principal emphasis seems to have been on being unshorn. When asked by what marks his Sikhs were to be recognized, Guru Gobind is said to have replied: 'My Sikhs shall be in their natural form, that is, without the loss of their hair or foreskin, in opposition to the ordinances of the Hindus and the Muhammadans' (see Macauliffe 1909: vol.5, 99). The concern was with physical identity and to that extent it was political rather than spiritual. Khuswant Singh (1953) maintains that the guru wanted to raise a body of men who would not be able to deny their faith when questioned, but whose physical appearance would invite persecution and also breed courage to resist it.

Although the core of a code of conduct is fairly clear, the details are not so. As Gopal Singh (1987: 191) puts it:

The Rahitnamas (Sikh codes of conduct) were all written by the Sikhs after the demise of the last Guru and do not tally with one another, except in some basics. That is why the Gurdwara act of 1925 defined the Sikh as "one who believes in the Ten Sikh Gurus and the Guru Granth Sahib and has no other religion"... Up to now, in spite of several attempts by Sikh intellectuals, the SGPC has not been able to issue a certified code of Sikh conduct, as there was great difference of opinion among the participants themselves. When we talk, therefore, of Sikh fundamentalism, we do a great disservice to this great, catholic, all-inclusive faith.

And yet Bhindranwale did have a clear concept of who was a good Sikh and who his enemies were. In his numerous speeches between 1978 and 1984, he identified three principal foes of Sikhism. These were, first, the apostates (*patit*) or, in his own words, 'Those who profess Sikhism but do not behave as Sikhs' (see Pettigrew 1987: 15). The emphasis on behaviour, on orthopraxis rather than orthodoxy, is noteworthy. Not only are Nirankaris and other heretical sects the target of attack, but also those Sikhs who have modernized or secularized their lifestyle. Bhindranwale demanded strict adherence to the codes of conduct which had evolved during the eighteenth and nineteenth centuries. He promised political and economic rewards and not merely spiritual good in return for it. The emphasis on behaviour goes well with material gain.

Here is a typical exhortation (quoted by Pettigrew ibid.):

We shall only rule if we become Khalsa [pure or true Sikhs].... i.e. keep unshorn hair and take amrit ['nectar,' baptismal holy water]. Being the sons of Sikhs you are trimming your beards. We ourselves are ruining Sikhism.... The communists have started telling boys at school and students that they are not slaves and therefore they need not follow this [Bhindranwale's] movement.... I will tell you how we are slaves: We have a minority complex. But don't consider yourselves a minority. We are not losers. A loser is a man whose Father is weak... Our Father says, "When I make my single Sikh fight against 125,000 enemies only then do I deserve to be called Gobind [the reference is to the tenth guru]". What a great promise that was!

Similarly, he mocked his audiences: 'You people cut your beards, do you think you resemble the image of Guru Gobind Singh? And if you don't and He was your Father then what does that make you? I hesitate to say what you should be called' (ibid.). Here is a third example of Bhindranwale's rhetoric regarding the Sikh way of life: 'Young men: with folded hands, I beseech you.... Until we enter our home, until we have swords on us, shorts on our bodies, Guru's word on our tongues, and the double-edged sword in our hands, we shall get beatings. It is now up to you to decide... the decision is in your hands' (see Juergensmeyer 1988:70).

Bhindranwale repeatedly drew pointed attention to the traditional symbols of Sikh identity (notably the beard, the sword and the shorts—all three indicative of the fighting spirit) and added new ones of a similar kind, the motor-cycle and the revolver. Here is another typical harangue: 'for every village you should keep one motorcycle, three young baptized Sikhs and three revolvers. These are not meant for killing innocent people. For a Sikh to have arms and kill an innocent person is a serious sin. But Khalsaji [O, baptized Sikh], to have arms and not to get your legitimate rights is an even bigger sin' (see Tully and Jacob 1985: 114).[5]

Not only did the fallen Sikhs have to be brought back to the true path—by exhortation, persuasion, ridicule, and if necessary, the threat of violence—the enemies from without also had to be faced with full might. What his opponents saw as the practice of terrorism,

---

5. Cf. another version of the same quotation in Juergensmeyer (1988: 86). 'It is a sin for a Sikh to keep weapons, to hurt an innocent person, to rob anyone's home, to dishonor anyone or to oppress anyone. But there is no greater sin for a Sikh than keeping weapons and not using them to protect his faith'.

he himself considered the call to heroic action. Who were these external enemies?

First, those Hindus who denied Sikhs a separate socio-religious identity, and second, the central and state governments which gave protection to apostates and other 'enemies' of the Sikhs, and denied the latter the opportunity to put their religious beliefs into practice. The religious beliefs that were singled out by Bhindranwale above all others were, first, the inseparability of religion and the state or politics, tracing this teaching to the sixth guru, Hargobind, and second, the indivisible or corporate character of the Sikh community, deriving it from the praxis of the tenth guru, Gobind. More than any other gurus, including the first, it was these two and certain elements of their teachings which Bhindranwale recalled *selectively* to emphasize militancy as righteous action. The fundamentals or basic teachings of Sikhism were thus given an intentionally specific, if not narrow, definition.

Speaking of the external foes, Bhindrawale said: 'They are perpetrating atrocities on us, exterminating our youth, burning our Holy Book, and insulting our turbans. When this is so you don't need to file a writ or a suit. There is no need to get a licence for arms. Neither Guru Hargobind took a licence from Jehangir nor Guru Gobind sought one from Aurangzeb' (see Pettigrew 1984: 113).[6] Similarly, 'the Hindus are trying to enslave us, atrocities against the Sikhs are increasing day by day under the Hindu imperialist rulers of New Delhi: the Sikhs have never been so humiliated, not even during the reign of Mogul emperors and British colonialists. How can the Sikhs tolerate injustice?' And so 'it should be clear to all Sikhs... that we are slaves and want liberation at any cost. To achieve this end, arm yourself and prepare for a war' (see Kapur 1986: 227). In one of the last messages to his followers he said: 'Peaceful means—*shanti mai*—these words cannot be found together in any part of the Sikh scriptures in the history of the Gurus nor in the history of the Sikhs'(see Pettigrew 1987: 4). The words about peace as formulated by Bhindranwale may indeed be absent; but he surely went against the spirit of *gurbani*.

In interpreting the basic teachings of the Sikh religious tradition in such militant terms, Bhindranwale was making a careful and

---

6. Jahangir (ruled 1605–27) and his grandson Aurangzeb (r. 1658–1707) are counted among the great Mughal emperors of India. See Chapter Four.

calculated choice. Like any other tradition, the Sikh cultural tradition has its 'pasts', not a single past, and selective retrieval is possible: indeed this would seem to be essential to all fundamentalist movements. A careful student of the scriptures and religious history of the Sikhs, John Archer, has observed (1946: 170):

Although neither in Nanak's *Japji* (recited by all practising Sikhs as their morning prayer) nor in Arjan's *Sukhamani* (psalm of peace) is there a hint that war is a just expression of Sikh power and a righteous means of accomplishing Sikhism's mission, the martial mood was nevertheless in the making—to be seen as the guruship itself continued. Not one of the first five gurus ever handled arms—in general there was no occasion for it. Arjan himself had declared "the divine Guru is Peace". Guru Nanak had previously said, as the legend has it: "Take up arms that will harm no one; let your coat of mail be understanding; convert your enemies into friends; fight with valor, but with no weapon but the word of God".

When the occasion arose for it, the last guru, Gobind, is believed to have written to Aurangzeb that if all else fails, it is but righteous to lift the sword in one's hand and fight (see Chapter Two). Militancy is advocated but only as the last resort.

It is noteworthy that, while some Sikhs, who today take very seriously the task of religious revival, turn to the militant strand in their tradition, their critics, who accuse them of being fundamentalists, are at great pains to argue that there is an alternative tradition which is older and ethically superior. These critics, whether Hindus or Sikhs, would all go along with fundamentalism if it were to mean the pacifism, piety, and inter-religious understanding of the earlier gurus. While they agree that the struggle between good and evil is a recurrent phenomenon in human history, and has been recognized as such by all ten gurus, they deny that violent action is an essential element of the tradition. Bhindranwale too employed the rhetoric of good versus evil, but he interpreted it through the lens of militancy.

Exclusive Sikh Identity

The issue of a return to the fundamentals or true teachings acquired great salience for the Sikhs in the second half of the nineteenth century. The kingdom that Ranjit Singh (1780–1839) had established at the end of the eighteenth century, and in which Sikhs were prominent but not dominant, collapsed in 1846, within seven years of his death. Punjab then came under British rule. Large numbers of

Sikhs from among those who had taken to following the codes of conduct in the years of Ranjit Singh's rule reverted to their earlier easier ways. The process was apparently highly noticeable, for the British Governor-General, who visited Punjab in 1849, observed that the Sikhs were gradually relapsing into Hinduism. Four years later (in 1853) a secretary to the government, Richard Temple, wrote (see Kapur 1986: 8).

The Sikh faith and ecclesiastical polity are rapidly going where the Sikh political ascendancy has already gone.... The Sikhs of Nanak, a comparatively small body of peaceful habit and old family, will perhaps cling to the faith of [their] fathers, but the Sikhs of Gobind... who are more specially styled the Singhs or Lion, and who embraced the faith as being the religion of warfare and conquest, no longer regard the Khalsa now that the prestige has departed from it. These men joined in thousands, and they now depart in equal numbers. They rejoin the ranks of Hinduism.

Half a century later the situation seemed no better. Max Arthur Macauliffe, a British civil servant devoted to the cause of the Sikhs, who authored a monumental six-volume work on Sikh religion, wrote: 'Truly wonderful are the strength and vitality of Hinduism. It is like the boa constrictor of the Indian forest...Hinduism has embraced Sikhism in its folds; the still comparatively young religion is making a vigorous struggle for life, but its ultimate destruction is, it is apprehended, inevitable without State support' (1909: vol.1, vii). Macauliffe had first used this rather dramatic imagery to describe the Hindu-Sikh relationship about forty years earlier.[7] Obviously he chose to ignore two major developments of the previous fifty years when he repeated this judgement. He played down, first, the very support of the state (i.e., the British government of India) to the Sikhs, which he strongly advocated, and second, the emergence of sectarian and socio-religious reform movements among them, seeking a return to the basic teachings and a purification of Sikh prayer and practice. State patronage and the birth of fundamentalism reinforced the concern for an exclusive Sikh socio-religious identity.

The British were at first wary of recruiting Sikhs into the army and debarred veterans of the old Sikh army, but gradually they were allowed entry. This was done at least partly in recognition of the support the Sikhs had given to the British during the 1857 Mutiny, of which the symbolic figurehead was the Mughal 'emperor'.

---

7. Personal communication from N. Gerald Barrier, November 1988.

Mughals were the traditional foes of the Sikhs: the fifth guru had been tortured to death and the ninth beheaded on the orders of Jahangir and Aurangzeb respectively. The tenth guru had spent a good part of his life in militant defiance of the latter. What is more significant is that the British encouraged baptized Sikhs to adhere to their code of conduct and, once they were recruited, disallowed the abandonment of the conventional marks of Sikh identity (see Kapur 1986: 11, 24). Building upon the tradition emanating from the sixth and tenth gurus, the British helped in shaping the notion of the Sikhs as a martial race and indeed as a distinct and separate nation.[8] The Singh or 'Lion' identity of the baptized Sikhs thus gained ground.

Apart from recruitment to the army, collection of revenue and other civil matters brought the administration into daily contact with the Sikhs. The bureaucracy tended to be friendly toward the Jat Sikhs, the demographic core of the community, enabling them to maintain their prominent position in the countryside. Besides, many favours and honours, including land grants (*jagir*), were bestowed upon loyal Sikhs. The propagation of the Sikh religion received official support, and the government sponsored two English translations of the *Granth Sahib*. The first, by Ernest Trump (in the 1870s), turned out disastrously from the intended point of view: he maintained that the gurus had not intended to found a new religion and spoke disparagingly of the 'contents and style' of their hymns (see ibid.: 19). The second was by Macauliffe at the turn of the century (see Macauliffe 1909, 5 Vols; Barrier 1988a: 507–8). Macauliffe was untiring in his efforts in the cause of the religion of the Sikhs and in his patronage of them.

State support, however, is by itself never sufficient to galvanize people. Despondency over the reversal of worldly fortunes understandably leads to spiritual soul-searching. Two major sectarian movements emerged in Punjab in the 1850s and 60s with the avowed purpose of purifying the Sikh way of life and returning to the fundamentals. These were the Nirankari and Namdhari movements, but they had only limited influence among the masses. Moreover, and ironically, while they began as purificatory or fundamentalist

---

8. Wrote D. Petrie: 'Sikhs in the Indian army had been studiously nationalized or encouraged to regard themselves as a totally distinct and separate nation. Their national pride had been fostered by every available means' (see Wallace and Chopra 1988: 474).

movements, they ended up being heretical, the Nirankaris reinstating a living guru and the Namdharis predicting the rebirth of the tenth guru (see Khushwant Singh 1966: 123–35; Gopal Singh 1988: 602–25).

More significant than these sectarian movements was the emergence of, first, social reform organizations called Singh Sabhas in the 1870s and, second, Hindu-Sikh estrangement in the following decades. In addition to the crisis in the Sikh body politic, the activities of the Christian missions aided by the administration,[9] proselytization by a new Hindu organization known as the Arya Samaj, and the rationalism that came with the introduction of scientific ideas into everyday life through the English-medium schools and the press, also contributed to the weakening of the cultural values of the Sikh community (see Barrier 1995). Harjot Oberoi considers this sense of decline more an elitist perception than a general consensus: those responsible for articulating it were the leaders who formed the Singh Sabhas (see Oberoi 1994: 235 et passim).

In such a setting a combination of religious and secular concerns was a precondition for the success of any movement or organization. Thus the first Singh Sabha, founded at Amritsar in 1873, had as its main objective efforts 'to arouse the love of religion among the Sikhs,' followed by efforts 'to propagate the true Sikh religion everywhere' and to bring out 'the greatness and truth of the Sikh religion.' The distinctiveness of Sikhism from Hinduism was not, however, a major concern. In fact, some if not the majority of the leaders of this rather elitist Sabha were quite willing to see themselves and the Sikhs generally as reformists among Hindus. They came to be known as *sanatan*, or traditional Sikhs. As such they were pluralists, accepting the legitimacy of several traditions and multiple sources of authority within the Sikh community (*Panth*) (see ibid.: 254–5,396). They were also conservationists, believing themselves to be 'under seige as a result of British expansion in Punjab' (ibid.: 257). Friendly Hindus agreed, saying that the Sikhs were a Hindu sect. To achieve its goals, the Sabha envisaged educational, literary, journalistic, and social activities. It laid emphasis not only on the learning of Punjabi in Gurmukhi script, but also on inter-religious tolerance, and resolved not to come into conflict with the government

---

9. Oberoi (1994: 218) writes: 'In Punjab the Raj and Church advanced side by side.... The two fused together for the glory of God and the Queen'.

(see Barrier 1970: xxiv–v). Loyalty to the British rulers was maintained throughout the quarter century that the Sabhas were active. The British recognized this: in 1890 the viceroy Lord Lansdowne had declared that the government was sympathetic to the Singh Sabha movement (see Gopal Singh 1988: 625).

A second Singh Sabha came up in Lahore in 1879. Its lower-caste and middle-class leadership emphasized the need for reform, which included a call for simplification and purification of social customs and, as a prerequiste to these aims, 'an assertion of Sikh separateness' (Barrier 1988b: 171). Contrary to the eclecticism of the *sanatan* Sikhs, the new leaders emphasized the purity of doctrine and practice and presented the same as true Sikhism or 'Tat Khalsa' (see Oberoi 1994 and Barrier 1995). Expectedly, the two Sabhas were embroiled in conflict over issues of doctrine and authority, and made efforts to mobilize support for their respective positions among urban and, in the course of time, rural Sikhs. But this conflict was not wholly destructive. The Singh Sabhas established schools, a college, orphanages, archives and historical societies, and produced voluminous polemical and scholarly literature on the Sikh tradition. They also co-operated with each other in facing up to the upsurge of Hindu fundamentalism represented by the Arya Samaj. By the close of the century there were over a hundred Sabhas all over Punjab, together contributing to the tide of Sikh separatism (see Barrier 1988a, 1988b, 1995).

On a superficial view, the Singh Sabha movement could be said to have remained true to the orthodox tradition of 'no guru save the *granth*', and 'met the challenges of modern times with modern weapons' (Khushwant Singh 1966: 122), most notably modern education in combination with religious instruction. A more balanced judgement would be that the Sabhas played a 'complex role and, instead of a lost orthodoxy, put together elements from diverse and often conflicting traditions so as to enhance the distinct nature of the religion. This resulted in a new and different Sikh identity complete with ideology and practices commonly associated with Sikhism today' (Barrier 1995: 193).

As a result of the efforts of the Sabhas, the *Granth Sahib* began to be freely available in printed editions and acquired a new salience. *Granthis,* that is, specialists who could read the multilingual holy book, also gained in social visibility—a process of which we en-

counter certain unintended consequences today in the post-
Bhindranwale period.

When the first Singh Sabha opted for inter-religious tolerance, it
had not reckoned with the emergence of the revivalist Hindu Arya
Samaj, which was brought to Punjab in 1877 (see Jones 1976 and
Chapter Seven). Although many Sikhs reacted to it positively in the
beginning, welcoming its anti-ritualistic, anti-idolatrous, and social
egalitarian emphases, it soon became apparent that not only did the
Arya Samajists not hold the Sikh religion and its gurus in high
esteem, they also denied the autonomy of the Sikhs as a socio-cultural community. The crucial development in this context was the
purificatory (*shuddhi*) movement launched by the Arya Samaj. It was
at first aimed at preventing the conversion of Hindus to Islam and
Christianity. Later the objective became bolder and envisaged purification and reconversion. It was during this phase that Arya Samajist
Hindus, who split among themselves into militant and moderate
factions, came to be seen as enemies by the Sikhs. Samajist polemics
often became disrespectful of the gurus and insulting toward the
Sikhs, and the latter were dismissed as lacking true knowledge. In
1900 the Arya Samaj performed the purificatory ritual for a group of
outcaste Rahtia Sikhs: their heads and beards were shaved to transform them into pure caste Hindus (see Jones 1968: 50). The importance of unshorn hair for Khalsa Sikh identity has been mentioned
above. Inevitably, the Singh Sabhas retaliated and attempted to win
latitudinarian (*sahajdhari*) Sikhs and Hindu admirers of the faith into
the fold of the baptized (*amritdhari*) and the unshorn (*keshdhari*).

The breach between Hindus and Sikhs found manifold expression,
including pamphleteering and legal battles, and has never been
healed. Puzzlement and incomprehension of one another's intentions
and actions were the dominant emotions, but hostility and hatred
were not altogether absent. Each side resorted to the reconstruction
of history in a partisan spirit, presenting Sikhism as a new religion,
or as reformed or debased Hinduism. There were two fundamentalisms here, each seeking supremacy over the other. While Hindu
publicists wrote pamphlets under the title of *Sikh Hindu hain* (the
Sikhs are Hindus), a scholarly Sikh of high position, Kahan Singh,
published a pamphlet entitled *Ham Hindu nahin* (we are not Hindus),
which became very influential (see Khushwant Singh 1966: 147).

Harjot Oberoi has recently drawn attention to the radical character
of Kahan Singh's tract, which, he points out rightly, brought four

centuries of Sikh tradition to an end. Prior to the Singh Sabha movement, Sikhs and Hindus not only lived together in Punjab, but also shared a common cultural life, with common symbols and common cognitive and affective orientations. Moreover, most Sikhs identified themselves variously in terms of village, cult, lineage, or caste, depending upon the context, and did not project a single Sikh identity. No single source of authority within the Sikh tradition was recognized, and thus several competing definitions of who was a Sikh were possible. This was in conformity with the general social situation in India, where religious identities are usually defined regionally and even locally (see Oberoi 1988: 136–40; 1994).

The sociological approach helps us to appreciate better the role of the new social and cultural elites that constituted the leadership of the Singh Sabha movement. These elites cut across the primordial ties that had long provided the bases for identity definition. Perceptively, they focused on pluralism as the target of their attack. From then onward, Sikhs, in Oberoi's words, 'were required to speak and dream through one language', and this was the language of cultural elites. A Sikh Great Tradition was being invented, and those Sikhs who did not fall in line were sidelined and even excluded from the emergent mainstream. Oberoi (1988: 149) adds:

The older forms of Sikhism were displaced forever and replaced by a series of inventions: the demarcation of Sikh sacred space by clearing holy shrines of Hindu icons and idols, the cultivation of Punjabi as the sacred language of the Sikhs, the foundation of cultural bodies exclusively for Sikh youth, the insertion of the anniversaries of the Sikh Gurus into the ritual and sacred calender and, most important of all, the introduction of new life-cycle rituals.

To meet the challenges of the times (not merely the Hindu challenge but also that of new opportunities), the Singh Sabhas, which were brought together under the umbrella of a new body called the Chief Khalsa Diwan in 1902, opted for the Tat Khalsa sub-tradition as the genuine Sikh tradition. As noted earlier, the Khalsa, or the community of the pure, baptized Sikhs, was instituted by the tenth guru, Gobind. He had not, however, prescribed more than a minimal code of conduct, and had not excluded from the Sikh fold those who were reluctant or slow to conform. In other words, in the name of conforming to the Great Tradition, a tradition was now being slowly constructed from selected old elements and newly invented ones. Devotion to the three Gs—*Guru, Granth, Gurdwara*—became the core of the new emphasis in Tat Khalsa praxis (see Oberoi 1994: 316–7).

Other things were added. Thus it was the Chief Khalsa Diwan which, though accommodating in its overall approach, was instrumental in having Hindu idols removed from the Golden Temple in 1905, and a special marriage ritual enacted as law (the Anand Marriage Act) four years later (see Gopal Singh 1988: 603–4).[10] The five symbols of Sikhism (the so-called k's) were no longer deemed enough, and the body as such and the life-cycle associated with it acquired a new importance. Even more self-consciously, the Tat Khalsa encouraged the rewriting of history through narratives about martyrs and historical novels (see Oberoi 1994: 330). What began as the dream of a minority regarding Sikh identity became, by 1910, a general ideal among the Sikhs.

It is clear from the above that in the manner in which it came to be established in the late nineteenth and early twentieth centuries, Sikh fundamentalism had its character fixed not as a return to fundamentals—an original doctrine—but as a bending of traditional elements to contemporary uses. This is what is happening today. We have, however, some more ground to cover before we return to the present situation.

Gurdwara Agitation

In the drive to establish an exclusive Sikh identity and make some fundamentals of belief and behaviour its basis, the Singh Sabhas, and subsequently the Chief Khalsa Diwan had their eyes on the *gurdwaras*, particularly the Golden Temple, as very visible means of mobilizing the community. In utilizing this powerful symbol, they had to reckon with two impediments: the government, which was becoming increasingly suspicious, and the hereditary temple custodians *(mahant)* and priests *(pujari)*, who were openly hostile. The government had handled the Sikhs with caution, combining patronage with control. Pro-British groups and important individuals

10. The short and simple *anand* marriage ceremony, which may be performed in a *gurdwara* or at home and does not require any priests, was devised by a son of the founder of the Nirankari sect. The *sanatan* Sikhs ridiculed it as 'a bizarre innovation', lacking any 'intrinsic worth compared to the virtues of the customary rite' (Oberoi 1994: 386).

were the recipients of this patronage. In return they were expected to help in keeping volatile elements under control. This was perhaps best exemplified by the fact that the government never allowed the management of the Golden Temple to completely go out of its hands. It thus stood behind the *mahants*, who were almost invariably unbaptized Sikhs (though claiming affiliation with the Udasi sect founded by one of the sons of the first guru) or plain Hindus. They kept alive idolatry and a great deal of Brahmanical ritual in the temples, and were considered venal by the purists. The managers of the Golden Temple were particularly disliked, not only for their Hindu origin and ways, but also for their loyalty to the British.

The support of the temple custodians and priests was one of the many miscalculations of the British in Punjab. It led to what has been called the third Sikh war, but it was a war with a difference.[11] It is here necessary to cut one's way through a great deal of detail and focus on the issue of the promotion of the purity or fundamentals of faith within the community. The first critical event was very visible and dramatic. It happened in 1914. The construction of the new imperial capital had commenced in South Delhi, and in the clearing operations for the construction of the viceregal palace, the government demolished a boundary wall of the *gurdwara* at Rikabganj with the concurrence of the custodian. The opportunity to cry sacrilege and challenge both the guilty parties had been offered on a platter, as it were. The situation was prevented from escalating into open conflict by the outbreak of the war in Europe. The agitation was resumed in 1918, and the government yielded: the wall was rebuilt and the displacement of the custodian by a committee, which had meanwhile occurred, was recognized. Radical Sikhs felt emboldened to ask for community control of all their *gurdwaras*. This actually happened at a few places.

The situation took a decisive turn late in 1920. First, in October there was a congregation of Sikhs at Jallianwala Bagh, in Amritsar, where a very significant decision was taken, that is, to administer baptismal water to Sikh converts from among the so-called Hindu untouchable castes, and then lead them for prayers into the nearby Golden Temple. The custodian-priests resisted the proposed entry,

11. The expression 'the third Sikh war' was used by Sardul Singh Caveeshar, a participant. The two earlier wars, which were wars in the usual sense of the word, were fought by the Sikhs against the Muslims and then the British.

pronouncing it an act of desecration. The *Granth Sahib* was consulted, using the traditional method of interpreting the first verse on a particular page. The verdict went in favour of the congregation and against the priests. The choice of the venue of the gathering too had been significant. It was here that a British general had, the previous year, ordered the machine-gunning of a peaceful crowd, mostly Sikhs, on a festival day, killing 309 and injuring one thousand. He was later honoured by the custodian of the Golden Temple!

Then, in November, a proclamation from the Akal Takht, the seat of temporal authority, set up a committee for the community management of all Sikh shrines. It was called Shiromani Gurdwara Prabandhak Committee (SGPC). Almost simultaneously, in January 1921, the Akali Dal (band of immortals) was set up for the forcible eviction of the custodians wherever necessary. Both institutions were envisaged as instruments of the Sikh community for the furtherance of a purified way of religious and social life, without idolatrous priests and in repudiation of ritualism and caste distinctions. Such indeed had been the fundamental teachings of the gurus. Fundamentalism at this time was primarily religious, but it was soon to regain its political accent.

In the following year, the Akalis came into conflict with the custodians, first at Taran Taran and then at Nankana Sahib, the birthplace of the first guru. The custodian at the latter *gurdwara* and his mercenaries resisted with savage force a band of 150 Sikhs who sought entry into the temple, resulting in the death of over 130 of them. (According to some accounts there were no survivors.) Mahatma Gandhi commended the non-violent approach of these Sikhs and called their self-sacrifice exemplary. He also invited the Sikhs to see their struggle to cleanse the *gurdwaras* as inseparable from the cleansing of the 'bigger gurdwara', i.e., India. This was the typical Gandhian view of the inseparability of religion and politics (see Chapters Seven and Eight). The SGPC leadership accepted this advice and formally associated themselves with the national movement. Fundamentalism and nationalism thus became allies.

Alarmed by these developments, the government made one last bid to keep control of the Golden Temple by appointing a custodian, thus preventing its take-over by the SGPC. The keys of the treasury became the symbol of a new agitation which was completely peaceful: thousands of Akalis courted arrest and refused to co-operate with the government. Both weapons were taken from the Gandhian armory. The government had to yield once again, and the keys were handed over to the SGPC. Its president received a telegram from Gandhi: 'First battle for India's freedom won. Congratulations'!

More was to follow in 1922. Conflict between the Akalis and one more government-backed custodian, this time at Guru-ka-Bagh, resulted from the latter's refusal to allow Sikhs to use firewood cut from temple land. For several months unarmed protestors marched to the *gurdwara* only to be beaten there by government police or to be arrested and whipped in jails. They remained non-violent, however, and won countrywide admiration for their fortitude. Eventually, the government yielded once again. By the end of January 1923, about one hundred *gurdwaras* were under the control of SGPC. It is noteworthy that the backbone of these peaceful agitations, involving much hardship and suffering for the protestors, was the Sikh peasantry. It was not, however, a peasant movement.

By 1924, another Akali agitation against the British was mounted, this time for the restoration of the authority to the deposed Sikh ruler of the state of Nabha. The espousal of a purely political cause resulted in a split among the radicalized Sikhs and the domination of the SGPC by the Akali Dal. Already disturbed by the pressure tactics that had emerged as a characteristic feature of Akali movements, and concerned about the communalization of Punjab politics with Hindu or Sikh concerns overriding common or national interests, Gandhi called for the abandonment of the movement, saying it had nothing to do with religion, which was what the SGPC should be concerned with. This has been seen by many Sikhs as a volte-face by Gandhi. They ask, was it not Gandhi who first asked the Sikhs to link their *gurdwara* reform movement to larger political issues? One can argue both ways, but this is not the place for it (see Mukherji 1984: 58–77).

The *gurdwara* battle was finally waged on the floor of the Punjab Legislative Council with the support of non-Sikh (Hindu and Muslim) nationalist leaders and won. The Gurdwara Reform Act of 1925 placed the control of all Sikh shrines of Punjab in the hands of SGPC. Statutory restraints (see section 108[3] of the Act) were placed upon the participation of the SGPC in politics. These were to be, however, honoured more in the breach than in compliance. From then on, the Akali Dal (as a political party) and the SGPC (as custodian of the shrines), though by definition concerned with two different areas of activity, were in practice to work in tandem. In fact the political party established complete control over the religious body.

Sikh Separatism

Fundamentalism among the Sikhs came to serve two ends in the twenties: first, the establishment of the control of the community over the *gurdwaras*, and second, the maintenance of the boundary that distinguished Khalsa Sikhs from Hindus. The definition of the boundary became increasingly political, but politics itself did not emerge as an autonomous domain, the encompassing *ambiance* of the movement for independence notwithstanding. Instead of religion providing the value premises of politics, as Gandhi had envisaged and advocated, religion came to be used to further political ends. This happened at the national level no less than at the regional level. To use a perceptive observation of Louis Dumont (1970a: 91), made in another context (and cited earlier), religion was thus reduced from being 'the essence and guide of life in all spheres' to 'a sign of distinction' between politically organized communities. In this sense religious fundamentalism is really anti-religious. If this appears to be an overly reductionist view of the Akali position (and for that matter of the Arya Samaj position too), it should be made clear that we are not concerned here with ideology in the abstract but rather with how it is used in real-life situations.

During the two decades between the passing of the Gurdwara Reform Act in 1925 and the independence of the subcontinent in 1947, Sikh public life became polarized between the fundamentalists (Akali Dal), who retained control of the SGPC, and the secularists (the Congress and the Communist Party), who dominated politics. Each party sought legitimacy by invoking its own reconstruction of the Sikh religious tradition, its own strategy of remembering and forgetting. It is significant that each side emphasized the secular character of the tradition, but while this meant for the Akalis the religious legitimacy of worldly (political and economic) interests (see Chapter Two), and therefore the inseparability of religion and politics, for the Congress and the Communist Party it meant the separation of religion and politics. Reconstructions of tradition in such circumstances are naturally partial in both senses of the term: they are selective and they are partisan. This does not, however, mean that such reconstruction is illegitimate. The issue is not to press rhetorically for legitimacy, contrasting living movements with dead traditions: it is rather recognizing that the selection is presented as the Truth, single and whole.

The Akali Dal, with membership which is exclusively Sikh, has inevitably been led to political separatism which has depended upon fundamentalism for its hoped-for success. To hold one's religious beliefs and pursue religious practices without any hindrance, it is argued, one needs the protection of the state: the demand for a state where the Sikhs will rule is therefore considered a religious demand. In fact, as was noted earlier (in Chapter Two), those Sikhs who say their daily prayers include the words *raj karega khalsa* (the community of baptized Sikhs will rule) in the last prayer: they even seek to attribute this slogan without evidence to the tenth guru himself (see Khushwant Singh 1963: 90, n.29).

Although the Akali movement of the 1920s was directed against the government, and was brought close to the national movement by Gandhi, it nevertheless acted as a pressure group on behalf of the Sikhs. But gradually, as the Muslim demand for a separate state where Muslim cultural, religious, and economic interests could be safeguarded gathered momentum, the Akali Dal too began to stress increasingly the religious and political autonomy of the Sikhs. The case for political autonomy was more difficult to establish, since both the Muslims and the Hindus, each community by itself, outnumbered the Sikhs. The Akali Dal therefore put forward in 1943 the demand for an independent Punjab state so constituted that the Sikhs, comprising 20 per cent of the population, would hold the balance between the Hindus and the Muslims (40 per cent each). A year later (in 1944), the Akali Dal leader Tara Singh put forward the demand for a separate Sikh state.

This demand was given explicit formulation in a 1946 resolution of the Akali Dal (see Nayar 1966:89):

Whereas the Sikhs being attached to the Punjab by intimate bonds of holy shrines, property and language, traditions and history claim it as their homeland and holy land...and whereas the entity of the Sikhs is being threatened on account of the persistent demand of Pakistan by the Muslims on the one hand and of danger of absorption by the Hindus on the other...the Akali Dal demands for the preservation and protection of the religious, cultural, and economic and political rights of the Sikh nation, the creation of a Sikh state.

Although the demand was not conceded by the British, it has never really died down, notwithstanding a great many changes in its formulation. Incidentally, the notion of a homeland that is also a holy land was obviously borrowed from the right-wing Hindu Mahasabha (see Chapter Seven).

Loyalty to a common religion, namely Sikhism, has not generally been stressed explicitly as the sole or real basis for regional autonomy or for an independent Sikh state. Such political aspirations, whether limited or separatist, have usually been expressed through a rhetoric about the preservation of cultural identity based on the Punjabi language written in the Gurmukhi script. The insistence on Gurmukhi has been of crucial importance, because Punjabi is as much the language of the Hindus of Punjab (and of the Muslims across the international frontier in Pakistan's Punjab province) as it is of the Sikhs. But the argument has not been entirely convincing: although the Sikh holy book is written in Gurmukhi, there is no evidence of the use of the script among the Sikhs for secular purposes ever having been widespread or, until recently, of any general ability among them to read it. More to the point therefore has been the demand for the protection of the economic interests of the Sikhs against those of Hindu landowners and traders. Thus, religion, culture, or economic interests have in turn, or in various combinations, been emphasized as the key element in the demand for autonomy or independence.

The face is the same, but the masks worn over it have been various. Thus, the Akali Dal leader Tara Singh said in 1955: 'The cover of a Punjabi-speaking state slogan serves my purpose well since it does not offend against nationalism' (see ibid.: 37). The fear of loss of identity remains crucial. To quote Tara Singh again: 'the Sikhs are Hindus and I feel they are so. But I do not say so, as in that case the Hindus would absorb the Sikhs' (ibid.: 72). The language argument finally won and a Punjabi state was carved out of the Indian half of the original Punjab in 1966. This was the second partition of Punjab, the first having taken place in 1947 at the time of the creation of Pakistan. It is important to note that the shift in emphasis from religion to language coincided with the displacement of Tara Singh, a schoolteacher by profession, from a position of dominance in the Akali Dal by Fateh Singh, a *sant* (religious teacher). It would be fair, and not from a fundamentalist point of view alone, to regard the Sant's strategy of separating religion from language as chicanery. Punjabi, written in Gurmukhi script developed by the second guru is the sacred language of the Sikhs, being the mother tongue of the gurus and one of the vernaculars in the *Granth Sahib*. It symbolizes the availability of revelation (*shruti*) through the speech of ordinary people no less than it represents (using contemporary idiom) the right of nationalities to self-determination.[12]

The Punjabi state was of course not a Sikh state. It could not be, for despite the redrawing of boundaries, Sikhs in the new state could not account for more than 54 percent of the population as against the 44 percent share of the Hindus. In fact, when elections were held in the reorganized state, the avowedly secularist Congress succeeded in electing more Sikh legislators than the Akali Dal, and the latter had to seek the support of the right-wing Hindu party, Jana Sangh, and the Communists to form a coalition government. Such a coalition was bound to be short-lived.

The Akalis now turned to grievances on the economic front and launched a series of mass agitations against the central government during the 1970s and 1980s. The new manifesto was an Akali Dal resolution adopted in 1973 at Anandpur Sahib, a place associated closely in Sikh tradition with the last two gurus. It was here that the tenth guru proclaimed the formation of the Khalsa. The text of the resolution has been a matter of controversy. The central issues are, however, quite explicit: they include the assertion that Sikhs need 'a congenial environment and a political set-up for the preservation of their religion and culture and they need more resources and administrative freedom for their socio-economic development' (see Kapur 1986: 218ff.).

Based on the Anandpur Sahib resolution, several sets of demands were put forward after 1980, when the Congress returned to power in the state of Punjab and in New Delhi. The situation escalated into a confrontation with the state and central governments despite divisions among the Akalis. In 1981 the demand for an independent Sikh state, to be called Khalistan, was first voiced at an educational conference and then significantly on a festival day (Holi) at Anandpur Sahib by extremist (Dal Khalsa) and militant (Nihang) elements. Various Akali factions dissociated themselves from this demand, but as the pressures built, they came together and announced in 1982 the beginning of a righteous battle (*dharma yuddha*). Seeking to contain the movement, the Congress had earlier (1978–80) pushed Bhindranwale into politics, hoping that his religious influence among the Sikh masses would be greater than that of the Akalis. And so it was, but he turned against his promoters, that is, the Congress

12. I owe this formulation to J.P.S. Uberoi. It may be noted though that, as stated elsewhere in this chapter, today specialists are needed to read and interpret these centuries-old texts.

politicians, in 1980, and outdid the Akalis in the vehemence and violence of his own campaign for the acceptance of the demands, religious as well as economic. Early in 1984 Bhindranwale broke with the Akalis: he had by then entrenched himself inside the Akal Takht and become a phenomenon in his own right.

Several scholars have maintained that Bhindranwale used the language of religion to give utterance to genuine and widespread economic grievances of the Sikhs of both rural and urban areas. It is argued that had the central government been responsive and taken adequate steps to remove the causes of discontent, the secular bases of Sikh identity would have been strengthened. The government's indifference and ineptitude opened the way for Bhindranwale to present the issue of center-state relations in a religious framework—as discriminatory treatment of a religious minority by the government and as a threat to their cultural identity. It was therefore a matter of general concern to the entire Sikh community. Needless to say, the religious idiom proved to be most effective for general mobilization of support (see Pettigrew 1984: 113, 1987:20).

It is not our intention here to deny that the Punjab economy had run into a development crisis by the 1980s, arising from the tapering off of the gains of the Green Revolution and their unequal distribution, intersectoral imbalance, rising unemployment, etc. Applauded at home and abroad for its success in increasing agricultural productivity, and achieving a three-fold rise in production between 1966 and 1980 (with the use of high-yielding varieties of seeds and other inputs), Punjab ironically remained trapped in agriculture: half of its domestic product came from this source and supported almost 60 per cent of the labour force. The state lagged behind in industrial development, and this become a major grievance. People complained that the surplus generated by the Punjabi agriculturist was drained off and used as investment elsewhere in the country. Further, it was argued that the rich had become richer and the poor, poorer. Thus, while relatively larger farmers (with holdings of 20 acres and more) were making good profits, small farmers (with holdings of less than five acres) were actually net losers (see Gill 1988). Moreover, benefits were unevenly distributed between the districts. Gurdaspur and Amritsar performed poorly in terms of average farm income, ranking eighth and ninth among twelve districts. The majority of the militants at the height of the upsurge were Jat Sikh youths from the farming families of these very districts (see Grewal and Rangi 1983:64).

Yet another grievance of long standing pertains to alleged discrimination by the centre against Punjab in the allocation of irrigation and hydel power. This problem has its roots in the first and second partitions of the state. The overall picture then is that while, compared to many other states, Punjab is a success story in the field of economic growth, within the state itself there are complaints about inadequate and unbalanced development and inequitable distribution. The central government and a succession of state governments (formed by the Congress) are blamed for the state of affairs.

Some social scientists have rightly argued that one of the routes that leads to communalism or fundamentalism runs via economic discontent, which is of course a subjective feeling, although it may be based on objective facts.[13] But it is not our concern to apportion blame between the government and Sikh politicians. It is more important for the present discussion to emphasize that, contrary to what is sometimes suggested, Akali demands have at no stage been purely secular: they could not be, because Akalis of all shades of opinion consider the inseparability of religion and politics the first article of their faith. The economic situation therefore will not by itself help us to understand the character of the present expressions of Sikh fundamentalism.

After Operation Blue Star, 1984–94

The foregoing discussion brings us to Bhindranwale again, and he takes us back to the sixth and tenth gurus: to Guru Hargobind's

13. According to many observers, the emergence of fundamentalism and extremist politics as a result of economic hardship is particularly regrettable because it is alien to the Sikh way of thinking. Professor M.S. Dhami, political scientist (formerly of Guru Nanak Dev University, Amritsar) writes (in a personal communication of 11 September 1989):

Peasantry, especially small peasants, who comprise about 90 per cent of the Punjab peasantry, have been one of the pillars of secularist forces in Punjab. They were recruiting ground for diverse Marxist-Communist groups. It is true that when peasantry is under the pressure of adverse economic forces, they do produce in critical times 'bandits' about whom Hobsbawm has written. Their ideology may be coloured by their religious traditions, as in rural Punjab, under specific circumstances. Some of the terrorist groups are versions of the old bandit groups. But to resort to extremism and fundamentalism does not amount to ideological commitment. It is more a symptom of social and political decay.... Today an additional factor is state terrorism.

doctrine of the unity of temporal power and spiritual authority (*miri-piri*) and to Guru Gobind's practice of righteous war (*dharma yud-dha*), both discussed in the preceding chapter. The Sikhs will wage battle for their rights, Bhindranwale said, and they will do so from the Akal Takht, for the temple is also the fort. This is not politics, he maintained but religion, the true teaching. And in our words, this is fundamentalism. When the government and the so-called moderate Sikhs protested the fortification of the Akal Takht and its occupation by armed Sikhs, calling these actions desecration, Bhindranwale was supported by many Sikhs, who said that he was actually safeguarding the sanctity of the temple, which was likely to be violated by the government by sending the police or the army into the complex.

That is what ultimately happened during Operation Blue Star, in which Bhindranwale lost his life. The storming of the temple complex, and that too on Guru Arjan's martyrdom anniversary, turned out to be a severe blow to the Sikh psyche, a wound which has still not healed. It has given new and unprecedented power to the managers (*jathedar*) and scripture readers (*granthi*) of the *gurdwaras* in the political affairs of the Sikh community. It has led to the revival of several Sikh institutions of critical importance, notably the *sarbat khalsa*. The latter is a general gathering of Sikhs called by the *jathedar* of the Akal Takht for ascertaining the collective will of the community of believers, which would then be deemed to be the guru's decision (*gurmatta*), according to the teaching of the tenth guru, and would result in orders (*hukamnama*) to various individuals or groups. The manner in which these gatherings have been convened and their frequency have, however, violated the relevant conventions. Similarly, the declaration of particular Sikhs as *tankhahiya* (those who have sold their faith), and in some cases their subsequent rehabilitation, have been done in a far from prescribed or serious manner.

The Sikhs are a dynamic people and frozen states of inactivity are unheard of in Akali politics. A little over a year after Operation Blue Star, and the subsequent retaliatory assassination of Prime Minister Indira Gandhi (31 October 1984), Prime Minister Rajiv Gandhi signed an 'accord' with Sant Harchand Singh Longowal, a moderate Akali leader, in July 1985, for redressing Sikh grievances.[14] A few

14. The main sources for this account of the events from 1984 onward are the *The Times of India* and the newsmagazine *India Today*. These are not cited in the text to avoid unnecessary accumulation of references. Short accounts may be seen in Mohinder Singh (1988) and Patwant Singh (1988).

weeks later Longowal too was killed by Sikh militants. His supporters won the elections to the state legislative assembly, however, and his principal political associate Surjit Singh Barnala became the Chief Minister. The militants were not, however, a spent force.

On 26 January 1986, a *sarbat khalsa*, which had not been convened properly, was held within the precincts of the Golden Temple under the auspices of two organizations associated with Bhindranwale, namely, the Damdama *taksal* and the All-India Sikh Students Federation, to give the call for the resumption of the struggle for the leadership of the Sikh community. Besides, the intruders performed two symbolic acts of great visibility to give expression to their defiance of the state. First, they burnt the national flag from the balcony of the Akal Takht and hoisted a Khalistan flag atop the temple. Second, five Sikh priests, representing, according to tradition, the Sikh community inaugurated the demolition of the *Akal Takht*. This shrine had been extensively damaged during Operation Blue Star and subsequently repaired quickly at the initiative of the Government of India, but with much publicized public participation (*kar seva*), another Sikh tradition associated with the building of *gurdwaras*. This symbolic support had been made possible by the co-operation of a leader of the militant Nihang Sikhs who had stood aloof from Bhindranwale. Now, in 1986, it was the head of the Damdama *taksal* who led the demolition so that the temple could be reconstructed by true, and not *tankhahiya*, Sikhs, who invited the charge of being paid agents of the government.

A rapid flow of events during the following year included the proclamation of Khalistan, or the autonomous Sikh state, at the temple complex on 29 April, followed the next day by an unsuccessful attempt by the civil police to clear the area of intruders. Chief Minister Barnala's decision to send the police into the temple complex split the ruling Akali Dal. In February 1987, five so-called high priests, under the leadership of the custodian of Akal Takht, excommunicated Barnala, charging him with religious misconduct. They dissolved all competing Akali political parties (*dal*), replacing them by a unified Akali Dal, of which Bhindranwale's father was made the figurehead.

In a bizarre turn of events a few months later, the custodian of Akal Takht, finding himself unable to control the extremists, withdrew from the scene. This was an unprecedented act and highlighted the emergence of several centres of Sikh fundamentalism.

These were Akali politicians, 'high priests', and extremist-terrorist elements. As we have seen, the religious basis of Akali politics goes back to its beginnings in the early 1920s. Akali politicians are the original fundamentalists and have a large following, but they have been rendered ineffective by internecine factionalism, which continues unabated until today. Extremism rather than moderation seems to have emerged as the litmus test for identifying a true Akali. Sant Longowal paid with his life for his moderation, and Barnala's political career floundered. Meanwhile, terrorism has been brought under control by a determined central government, aided enormously by the disillusionment of the Sikh masses with militancy. Peace and the normal electoral process came back to Punjab in 1993, when elections at various levels (from the local to the state) brought the Congress back to power and Sardar Beant Singh became Chief Minister.

Sikh fundamentalism today survives around the custodians (*jathedars*) of the three major temples of Amritsar (Akal Takht), Anandpur (Sri Keshgarh Sahib), and Bhatinda (Damdama Sahib), and the *granthis* of Harmandar Sahib and Akal Takht. Sikh tradition recognizes five *takhts* (thrones), i.e., seats of temporal authority. These include, besides the first three temples just mentioned, the shrines at Patna (Bihar) and Nanded (Maharashtra). The *jathedars* of Patna and Nanded, being located outside Punjab, have been excluded from consultation by the other three custodians.[15] But since five Sikhs are needed to represent the will and authority of the community, the *granthis* of the two Amritsar shrines have been roped in. It is these five personages who are generally but quite erroneously

15. The history of the *gurdwaras* and the *takhts* and the manner in which they have been made a part of Sikh consciousness is an important subject. Of the five *takhts*, three, namely, those at Anandpur, Patna, and Nanded, are deeply interwoven with the biography of the tenth guru. Guru Gobind himself never visited the Akal Takht or Harmandar Sahib: in fact none of the last four gurus did so. The events of the last one hundred years have seen changes in the importance of the various temples. The process of redefinition of sacred places is not confined to the shrines but is comprehensive and includes the land of Punjab itself. Thus Oberoi perceptively observes (1987: 27–8):

> Surprisingly, despite [many] historical linkages with the Punjab, for most of the Sikhs' history, territory has not played a key role in their self-definition. It was only in the 1940s... when the cold truth dawned that the Punjab may after all be divided, that the Sikhs with a tragic desperation began to visualize the Punjab as their homeland.... It is the intersection of history and geography, discourse and space, territoriality and metacommentaries, that has transformed the Punjab into Khalistan.

referred to as the Sikh 'high priests'. Although Sikh temple rituals are a departure from the teachings of the early gurus, they are quite simple and not dependent upon ritual specialists. It is therefore a misnomer to refer to *gurdwara* custodians and scripture readers as 'high priests'. They have, nevertheless, acquired political clout and follow Bhindranwale's strategies of mobilization: they articulate the grievances of Sikhs against the government, caution the faithful about the poison of heresy and secularization, and warn them about the ever-present danger of absorption into Hindu society. The call to return to fundamentals arouses hope in some and guilt in others.

Such religious rhetoric is, however, explicitly interwoven with politics. Political parties, extremist groups, and others seek to gain control of the SGPC and have their own nominees appointed as *jathedars* and *granthis*. Alternatively, the SGPC is by-passed and efforts are made to have the positions filled through other means. The appointees are then expected to make political pronouncements and give directions to political parties or the general public along lines previously laid down. The terrorists and the government too have tried to make use of these so-called high priests, who have thus emerged as a crucial group of fundamentalists among the Sikhs today.

It would be a mistake, however, to consider the *jathedars* and *granthis* simply as usurpers. When the tenth guru declared closure of the lineage of personal gurus, his intention was to do away with intermediaries between the One True Guru (God) and the community of believers. As already stated, the *Granth Sahib* was proclaimed the spiritual guru and temporal authority was vested in the community. Given the length and linguistic diversity of the holy book it may be read and chanted properly (which it is meant to be) only by those who have been trained as *granthis* or *ragis* (singers of *raga* music). Ironically, the *granthis* have emerged as intermediaries through their special reading ability, and so have the *jathedars* through their responsibility for organizational matters connected with the *gurdwaras*, including the daily routine (*man-maryada*) connected with the veneration and reading of the *Granth Sahib*. Traditionally these functionaries have not been highly educated people or conversant with economic matters or political issues. Their roles and responsibilities, like those of the *sant* preachers, have been not only specific but also limited. In today's situation they are also called upon to pronounce on the very matters which lie beyond their ken. They thus become tools in the hands of others, who, needless to say, are far removed from the religious life as usually understood.

In the recent past (1993–94), two issues have attracted the attention (and even wrath) of the new guardians of the fundamentals of the Sikh faith. These are, first, the preservation of the supreme sanctity of the Sikh scripture and, second, adherence to the correct procedure in the ritual process (*maryada*) at Harmandar Sahib. The former is obviously the more general and therefore the more important issue.

Around the time Bhindranwale's career as a fundamentalist leader had reached its peak in early 1984, the editor of Punjab's oldest literary magazine, *Preet Larhi*, was shot dead near Amritsar, as his innovative interpretations of the Sikh religious tradition (including theology) were considered sacrilegious by the new guardians of the faith. Bhindranwale's directive in respect of such cases was clear: it was a moral obligation to kill them (see Oberoi 1993: 258). Many such killings occured in a summary fashion. Judging by recent events, to which I now turn, the fundamentalist conception of reverence for the scripture survives, although the tactics of enforcing it seem to be changing in the direction of non-violent but stern coercion.

In early 1993, Professor Manjit Singh, head priest of Takht Keshgarh Sahib was given by the Sri Gurdwara Prabandhak Committee (SGPC) additional responsibility as the *jathedar* of the Akal Takht. He marked his installation by issuing a warning to Sikh scholars not to treat the *Granth Sahib* as just a book that could be the subject of research in a routine manner. As divine revelation, the scripture could not be said to have a history, which is a secular concept. Textual studies that create uncertainty and anguish in the minds and hearts of the believers were sacrilegious and would not be allowed to proceed. The version of the *Granth Sahib*, based on the so-called Kartarpuri *beer* (manuscript), accepted as authentic was to be acknowledged as such by all Sikhs. The provocation for the warning was the impending publication of a history of the Sikh scripture, entitled *Gatha Shri Adi Granth*, by a senior Sikh scholar, Dr Piar Singh. It had also become known that a younger Sikh historian, Dr Pashaura Singh, had prepared a doctoral dissertation on the text and the meaning of the holy book at a Canadian university.

At the time the controversy became public (February 1993), about a hundred scholars, nearly all of them Sikhs, were reported to be working on different aspects of the Sikh religious tradition at the three universities in Amritsar, Chandigarh, and Patiala. Several senior scholars criticized the attitude of Manjit Singh who had, however, the backing of the SGPC. They pointed out that, while it was imperative that the text approved by the SGPC be acknowledged as the authentic one for ritual purposes, research such as Pashaura Singh's, also was desirable from the scholarly and historical perspectives. He had examined the text of the holy book to conclude that Guru Arjan, the original compiler, had altered and improved the language of certain passages and, perhaps, also amended the text of the foundational formula (*mul mantar*), believed by the Sikhs to have been received as divine revelation by Guru Nanak.

Protests by many university scholars notwithstanding, the committee of 'scholars' appointed by Manjit Singh found both Piar Singh and Pashaura Singh guilty of sacrilege against the scripture. Both were ordered to repent, which they did, or face excommunication. Thus, Pashaura Singh, a professor at the University of Michigan appeared before Manjit Singh at the Akal Takht on 27 June 1994, and admitted his 'mistakes', 'lapses', and 'wrong descriptions'. He was awarded purificatory punishment that was to last seven days, and included listening to holy hymns (*shabad kirtan*), reciting Guru Nanak's composition, *Japji*, dusting the shoes of visitors to the Harmandar Sahib, and washing the walkway (*parikrama*) at the temple. These incidents indicate a greater emphasis on the sanctity and finality of the scripture, as also its transparency, which renders all interpretations of surface meanings in order to arrive at latent meanings not only unnecessary but also illegitimate. Such an attitude to the reading of the canon is a critical feature of fundamentalism, for which the Sikhs have now adopted the Punjabi term *mulvad* as a literal equivalent. To emphasize its denotation, it is contrasted to *adharma*, or the absence of virtue, which is translated by them into English as 'secularism' (see Oberoi 1993: 257). In the words of Harjot Oberoi, 'fundamentalism has become an autonomous and authoritative discourse in the Punjab; it has subsumed other ideologies, particularly Sikh ethno-nationalism.... [It] is quickly maturing as an ideology and now offers seemingly attractive solutions for the everyday life of both the weak and the powerful' (ibid.: 279).

Characteristics of Sikh Fundamentalism

To conclude, I will try to highlight some of the major points that have emerged from the foregoing discussion.

Fundamentalism in the broad sense of insistence on certain basic beliefs and practices is perhaps an essential component of all religious traditions. What is specific to a particular fundamentalist movement is, I think, no less significant for understanding it than what it shares with others. Fundamentalism as a forceful affirmation of religious faith and cultural identity, combined with a militant pursuit of secular interests, is associated in the Sikh cultural tradition with the tenth guru. Let me hasten to recall that I am not using the word 'fundamentalism' as a condemnatory term. Sikh fundamentalism is not therefore a recent phenomenon. However, its expressions, shaped by changing historical circumstances, have been varied. The situation in the wake of the decline of Ranjit Singh's kingdom, including the threat of the Raj-Church nexus and the rise of Hindu fundamentalism in the late nineteenth century, was quite different from that faced by Guru Gobind Singh two hundred years earlier. The current manifestations of Sikh fundamentalism have several characteristics in common with the earlier ones, but they also have distinctive features. In what follows I concentrate on Sikh fundamentalism today.

Sikh fundamentalism is a reactive phenomenon, a defense mechanism. Its apparent confidence hides many doubts and its aggressiveness is a cover for fear and anxiety, fear of the threatening 'Other'—seen as people, namely nonconformist Sikhs, secularists of all communities, and communal Hindus, and as certain processes, notably heresy, modernization, cultural disintegration, and political domination. Of course, not all Sikhs experience these fears and anxieties about cultural identity, but the fundamentalists (in their own eyes, true Sikhs) would want everybody to do so. I would stress, however, that any attempt to explain religious fundamentalism in terms of states of mind alone amounts to reductionism and is therefore just as fallacious as economic determinism. Complex phenomena, needless to say, have multiple causes.

While mono-causal explanations of fundamentalism must be rejected, the claim of fundamentalists to be in sole possession of the Truth should be noted if we are to understand what motivates them and how they mobilize and hold their following. This does not mean that we recognize their claim as valid. In relation to their followers, fundamentalists do not allow the legitimacy of dissent and multiple opinions or individual judgements: a single judgement representing the collective will must prevail. This is considered axiomatic. It follows that Sikhs must have political power in order to enforce conformity. In the words of Khushwant Singh, 'in the Sikh state the Sikhs would not only be free of Hindus and Hindu influences, but the Sikh youth would also be persuaded (if necessary, compelled) to continue observing the forms and symbols of the faith' (1953: 84ff.). This implies that if Sikhs are not rulers, they must be rebels; but when they establish the 'just order' and become rulers, they cannot be rebels against themselves. In short, fundamentalism is totalitarian.

As a response to circumstances that are believed to be adverse, Sikh fundamentalism is marked not so much by deep theological concerns or intellectual vigour as by religious fervour and political passion. Sikh fundamentalists have not evolved a comprehensive worldview, but only an abridged ideology. Modern scholars generally serve it; they do not lead or guide it. Thus, scholastic efforts have been made to argue that although the Sikh scripture contains many words and phrases (such as *shabad, shunya, shiva, shakti*), which are also found in the Hindu and Buddhist religious traditions, they do not mean in Sikhism what they mean in the other religions (see Trilochan Singh 1969). Similarly, the roots of Sikhism in the *sant* tradition of socio-religious reform are played down, but this is not easy, for the *Granth Sahib* itself, which includes many compositions by devotees belonging to this tradition, bears witness to them. The first guru certainly made his choices regarding theological, cosmological, social, and other matters, but he made them out of the traditions with which he was most familiar, namely Hinduism and Islam, in that order. According to Grewal, 'it was a rich and lively religious atmosphere. And it was this atmosphere that Guru Nanak breathed' (1979: 140). But such scholarly disputations are of only limited interest to the fundamentalists or their lay followers, who think in stark black-or-white terms which alone, they seem to believe, facilitate action. It may be noted here that, with some exceptions, scriptural exegesis has not been a major concern of Sikh intellectuals. Inside the *gurdwaras* scripture is read, chanted, and venerated (very much as idols are in a Hindu temple); there are no discourses on it.

Understandably, therefore, it is not so much to the canon or scripture that Sikh fundamentalists turn for authority as to the tradition about what particular gurus or martyrs are believed to have said *and* done. Sikh fundamentalism is orthoprax rather than orthodox. The emphasis is upon action and the expected fruits of action, and these fruits are this-worldly—economic and political. Piety or conformity to codes of behaviour is seen as valuable in instrumental terms. For the orthodox, who do not think of belief and practice in dualistic terms, piety is its own reward. If action is motivated by the desired fruits, it is propelled by its situational logic. In the recent past, it is the tradition of violent action, characterized as righteousness and retribution for any attack on Sikh honour, that has been emphasized. Joyce Pettigrew (1975) has shown how deeply rooted these values are, though not in scripture but in the cultural tradition of the Jats, who account for the great majority of the Sikh community. The assassination of Indira Gandhi, prime minister at the time of Operation Blue Star, by her own Sikh bodyguards, and of General Vaidya, then the chief of the Indian army, are notable acts of revenge which the fundamentalists consider honourable, for they consider these two persons responsible for the attack on the Golden Temple complex. The same is true of the assassination of Sant Harchand Singh Longowal, within weeks of his having entered into an accord with Prime Minister Rajiv Gandhi in July 1985, which the pro-Bhindranwale Sikhs considered a betrayal of the cause of the community. Betrayal by anybody is bad, but by a leader it is particularly grievous.

Sikh fundamentalism depends upon charismatic leaders who are seen in the image of the sixth and tenth gurus as saint-soldiers (*sant-sipahi*). Such a leader must be willing not only to kill but also to die for the cause. Thus Bhindranwale said, using the words of Guru Gobind: 'when the struggle reaches the decisive phase may I die fighting in its midst' (see Juergensmeyer 1988: 65). And he did, achieving for himself the halo of a martyr among his followers. There has been official confirmation that Bhindranwale's men inside the Akal Takht, many of whom were hardly virtuous persons, fought with uncommon bravery to the last man. They also inflicted heavy casualties on the government troops. How important the role of a charismatic leader is, has been borne out by the relative ease with which the Punjab armed police were able to flush out in May 1988 (Operation Black Thunder) the terrorists who had reoccupied the Golden Temple complex in 1986.

But, as Bhindranwale's case so well illustrates, charisma needs material and institutional resources for its magic to work. He had the support of the institutional apparatus of the All-India Sikh Students Federation; besides, well-to-do Sikhs in India and abroad (UK, USA, Canada) provided him and his supporters with money to buy arms and for other activities. Since Bhindranwale's death in 1984, no comparable leader has appeared amongst the fundamentalists. It is not therefore surprising that the fundamentalist rhetoric has lost some of its force.

The strategy of the fundamentalist leader, as is well borne out by Bhindranwale's speeches and actions, is characterized by a selective appropriation of the tradition in a manner which is simultaneously revivalist and futurist. The notion of a Sikh state perhaps took shape in the tenth guru's time, or soon after, but the hope has not been realized. Guru Gobind's avenger, Banda Bahadur, conquered territory but hardly established a state (see Chapter Two and Khushwant Singh 1966: 107ff.). Maharaja Ranjit Singh's kingdom (1799–1839) was multi-religious. Fundamentalism today nourishes the hope of a Sikh state and points to destiny: the Khalsa will rule! Fundamentalism everywhere is explicitly soteriological.

The revivalist-futurist vision is not, however, unproblematic. On the one hand, the Sikh religious tradition is presented as a perennial philosophy; on the other, sensitivity to contextual variation is stressed. While the Sikh way of life is said to be unaffected by space-time (*desh-kal*) differences, Sikhs try to establish a territorial state of the true (baptized or Khalsa) Sikhs, namely, Khalistan. As Pettigrew has pointed out, 'Temporal power was vested in the Panth, but precisely what this meant was difficult to ascertain, since Panth was the religious community of all Sikhs and not the localized community' (1987: 6ff.). Similarly, Gopal Singh asks: 'if the Sikh must combine [religion and politics], what about others who must live in their realm' (1988: 833)? In other words, the fundamentalist strategy for political autonomy depends more upon emotive appeal than rational argument or—a much harder task—willingness and capacity to confront contradictions within the Sikh tradition.

Contradictions also mark the present expressions of Sikh fundamentalism. This is most obvious in the attitudes to science and technology. In principle, the modern secular and rational *weltanschauung* is opposed to any religious worldview, and since technology is the applied aspect of science, this too should be suspect. But the Sikh fundamentalists' interest in general issues—the principles of things—is overshadowed by their pragmatic concerns. The Sikh is a doer, typically a farmer, carpenter, or soldier—all three well-known and much admired images—or, nowadays, an entrepreneur. While voicing their concern about the erosion of traditional belief and practice in modern lifestyles, they have not hesitated to use science and technology in the specific contexts of their own needs. One of the demands written into the Anandpur Sahib resolution is for the installation of a radio transmitter at the Golden Temple for readings from the *Granth Sahib* and the singing of hymns to be broadcast. Bhindranwale allowed his speeches to be recorded and sold on cassette tapes. His exhortations to Sikh youth included appeals for motorcycles and firearms. During the worst days of terrorist violence, the most effective mode of killing used by militants was shooting by the pillion-rider on a motorbike. A highly respected retired police officer, K.F. Rustamji, a member of the minuscule Parsi community, observed (1988: 8): 'For a number of years, the dominant image in the minds of people of India will be that of a young Sikh spraying a group of people with an automatic, and killing women and children mercilessly. And along with it may appear the thought that few Sikhs condemn them'. The image of the non-violent Sikh protestor of the 1920s, who had won the admiration of Gandhi, was temporarily and aberrantly replaced by that of the killer. This goes hand-in-hand with the displacement of the brave Sikh (the Singh or 'Lion') by the Sikh as victim, which was a recurrent theme of Bhindranwale's speeches. It may be said, however, that he was perhaps only recalling the self-images that occur in the daily Sikh prayer (*ardas*)—in which the Sikh is 'powerless', 'dishonoured', 'without shelter', and a supplicant for divine grace—but doing so with a purpose.

The valorization of violence as righteous killing has resulted in Sikh fundamentalism becoming inextricably involved with terrorism, for the Akali politicians and the temple functionaries have not only not clearly distanced themselves from the terrorists but have generally justified the latter's actions and often collaborated with them. That most terrorists have little interest in religion or piety seems to have dawned on many Sikhs, particularly after the indisputable desecration of the Golden Temple in May 1988, when a group of terrorists occupied it for several days during which they performed ritually polluting bodily functions within it. Details about captured terrorists over the years revealed that many of them were simply criminals or desperate jobless youth, generally of rural origin.

Disillusionment among people in general with regard to the alleged idealism of terrorist fundamentalists, combined with more efficient police operations which are reported to have been often brutal, under the overall direction of a tough chief (who is himself a Sikh), has given rise to the hope that terrorism in Punjab has now been contained. The SGPC also has shown signs of wanting to assert its authority: in October 1988 it announced a ban on the carrying of weapons into the Golden Temple and on residence there. When a demand to this effect was made in May 1988, following Operation Black Thunder, Sikh fundamentalists, including former ministers of the state, had reacted negatively, calling it interference in religious matters and against the basic teachings of Sikhism.

Economic compulsions also reinforce the need for peace and stability. It is noteworthy that despite the unsettled law and order situation, agricultural production in Punjab has continued to soar. Sikh farmers must sell their surplus grain to the government and in the market. Because of the size of the surplus, local consumption is not the answer. While one may be optimistic therefore that the sharp decline in terrorist activities noticed in the last several years will prove lasting, the expectation of a similar downturn in Sikh fundamentalism is perhaps premature. The politicians and the priests keep it alive, although the people show signs of fatigue. The popular image of the Sikh as a hardworking person, who also likes to relax and enjoy life, is reasserting itself. An acute and sober Sikh intellectual, Amrik Singh, observes rather helplessly:

fundamentalism is a fact of life.... The only safe statement that one can therefore make in regard to the next decade or two is that fundamentalism (whatever the term may include or exclude) will continue to be a force and shape the thinking of a substantial number of people, particularly in the younger age group (1988: 440).[16]

Writing over twenty years ago, Khushwant Singh observed pithily, 'there is no such thing as a clean-shaven Sikh' (1966: 303). The

16. The appeal of fundamentalism among the young and the emigré is a subject of much interest. I have talked with several such persons and seen statements by them. An obviously enthusiastic Sikh youth, born and brought up in England, objected to any reference to Guru Nanak's Hindu origin and argued that any Sikh who identifies himself by caste is a hypocrite and anti-Sikh. Such a fundamentalist attitude is of course empirically unsound and sociologically naive. If all Sikhs who acknowledge caste origins were to be excommunicated, there would be hardly any followers of the faith left to live by it.

mid-sixties were marked by the last and successful phase in the agitation for a Punjabi-speaking state. Fundamentalism was present then too, but it was not the kind of overwhelming socio-political phenomenon it has become since then. It follows that the above observation by Khushwant Singh, which many Sikhs themselves would have then characterized as a specimen of the author's engaging style, would today find almost universal support among Sikhs. In the same author's words, 'the sense of belonging to the Sikh community requires both the belief in the teachings of the Adi Granth and the observance of the Khalsa tradition initiated by Guru Gobind Singh' (ibid.).

Sikh fundamentalism today, as in the late nineteenth century, feeds on and is fed by Hindu communalism. While in the earlier period Hindu fundamentalism was linked to the religious revivalism advocated by the Arya Samaj (see Chapter Seven), today it is associated with the Rashtriya Swayam Sevak Sangh, the Bharatiya Janata Party and some other militant Hindu groups, and is predominantly political. The agitation for a Punjabi-speaking state during the fifties and sixties divided the two communities badly. While the Hindus complained that language was being used as a cover for religion, the Sikhs complained that the Hindus had become so hostile that they did not hesitate even to disown their mother tongue, Punjabi (see Kapur 1986: 211–19). There is considerable truth in both charges. The continued killing of Hindus and moderate Sikhs, including widely respected *granthis*, by terrorists occasionally generates incidents outside Punjab (as in the far-off town of Bidar in the state of Karnataka, a thousand or more miles away, where half a dozen Sikh students were killed by Hindu militants in September 1989) and keeps communal tension alive. The ability of Muslim fundamentalists to impose their will on the government (there are six Muslims to every Sikh in India, and they have many areas of population concentration as opposed to one in the case of Sikhs) is an additional factor in the present uneasy political situation in India.[17]

17. Before any Islamic country had done so, the government of India banned on 5 October 1988 Salman Rushdie's novel *The Satanic Verses* at the request of some Muslim politicians who, though they had not themselves seen the book, but had read reviews of it, warned that disturbances would break out if it was made freely available. The government's unwillingness to proceed in the direction of evolving a common civil code in view of the opposition of Muslim fundamentalists is well-known (see Chapter Eight).

Sikh fundamentalism draws sustenance from the deep sense of injury which almost every Sikh feels on account of Operation Blue Star and the massacre of about 3,000 Sikhs in Delhi and elsewhere in the wake of Indira Gandhi's assassination. The government's failure to punish any of the killers does not exactly soothe the wounded Sikh psyche. And as long as the relationship between religion and the state is defined in diametrically opposite ways in the Indian Constitution and by Sikh (and other) fundamentalists, the scope for reconciliation is limited. The government's efforts to neutralize the appeal of militant fundamentalism will obviously be based on removing real as well as perceived economic grievances and on dividing Sikh political opinion. The phenomenon of fundamentalism will not be contained, however, by economic measures and political strategies alone. The appeal of the modern ideology of secularism is limited among the Sikhs. While the processes of secularization affect Sikh society, like they affect other societies, and change individual behaviour in diverse ways, an open affirmation of secularism as a worldview is highly problematic. Some Sikh intellectuals have claimed that their religion is secular, but, as I tried to show in the preceding chapter, this is at best ambiguous. Secularism, if claimed as a value-orientation within the Sikh religious tradition, is amenable to several meanings, some of which, unfortunately, have been claimed as a justification for militancy. The path into a desired, modern, secular, future is not straight either for the Sikhs or for the Republic of India. The latter has to reckon with other fundamentalisms and other secularisms too.

Islam in South Asia
From Orthodoxy to Fundamentalism

This day, O true believers, I have perfected your religion for you, and brought my mercy upon you to its completion. I have chosen for you Islam to be your religion.

THE QURAN (5.3)

Islam desires, above all, that people should commit themselves entirely to God's Truth and that they should serve and worship only God. Similarly, it desires that the law of God should become the law by which people lead their lives.... Only when power in society is in the hands of the Believers and the righteous, can the objectives of Islam be realized.

SAYYID ABUL ALA MAUDUDI, *The Islamic Movement*

Santayana's famous dictum that one compares only when one is unable to get to the heart of the matter seems to me... the precise reverse of the truth. It is through comparison, and of comparables, that whatever heart we can actually get to is to be reached.

CLIFFORD GEERTZ, *Local Knowledge*

Introduction

In Chapter One, I questioned one of the major assumptions underlying the study of contemporary fundamentalist movements, namely that they are essentially antimodern, that their roots lie not so much in their respective pasts as in a worldwide Western cultural hegemony and political dominance.

There are two problems with this way of looking at fundamentalist movements. First, models of modernity other than the Western are excluded. Second, the perspective has a shallow depth in time. When confronted with individual preachings or collective movements from earlier times, which are concerned with *culture*, *scripture*, and *power*, one excludes them by definition from the rubric of fundamentalism because it is said to have 'no ideological precursors' (Lawrence 1989: 100).

If one were to bracket away the criterion of antimodernism, but retain that of a concern with cultural critique and recovery, with scriptural inerrancy and authority, and with power, one could, then, compare, not only synchronically across religious traditions, but also diachronically across different periods of a particular religious tradition over a fairly long period of time. Such an exercise would liberate us from the stranglehold of the peculiar concerns of the present, such as '*gharbzadegi*', that is being smitten or plagued by the West.[1] This malady afflicts not only non-Western societies, spawning fundamentalist movements in reaction, but also to some extent our studies of the latter. It is well to remember the sane advice of Karl Marx that an age is not judged best by relying upon its self-consciousness alone. The introduction of the historical perspective, going beyond the present century, not only would be welcome, but also seems imperative to me in certain cases (see Chapter Three). And this is what I will briefly attempt to do in this chapter with reference to Islam in South Asia.

Islam in South Asia has had an eventful and richly documented history of about 1300 years, and is therefore well suited to the kind of longitudinal inquiry I have suggested. A focus on Islam in South Asia is important also for the comparative study of fundamentalisms. There are more Muslims in South Asia today, numbering well over 300 million, than in any other region of the world; and, although divided into a number of sects (Ahmadiyyas, Bohras, Shias, Sunnis, etc.) and regional communities (such as the Malabari, Bengali, or Kashmiri Muslims), Islam and the 'Indian environment' have played critical roles in the making of their diverse histories. Maulana Muhammad Ali, the Indian political leader, who was one of the key figures in the Khilafat movement (for the restoration of the spiritual and temporal authority of the Ottoman sultan as the caliph of Islam) in the early 1920s (see Minault 1982), thought of India and the

---

1. As described in Chapter One, the theme of *gharbzadegi* was elaborated by certain Iranian scholars. Fazlur Rahman has noted that several Indian writers, notably Abul Kalam Azad, Zafar Ali Khan, and Abul ala Maududi, had used the term *maghrib zadah*, 'West-stricken', in their work to describe 'modern-educated and westernized classes' (1982: 72).

Muslim World as two 'circles of equal size but which are not concentric'. While the historian B.R. Nanda considers the apprehension of irreconcilability, hinted at in this statement, as 'the tragedy of Muhammad Ali's life' (see Nanda 1989: 390), another distinguished Muslim Indian, Maulana Abul Kalam Azad, who served twice as the President of the Indian National Congress, regarded this dual membership as his treasure. He declared in 1940:

> I am a Muslim and profoundly conscious of the fact that I have inherited Islam's glorious traditions of the last thirteen hundred years. I am not prepared to lose even a small part of that legacy.... I am equally proud of the fact that I am an Indian, an essential part of the indivisible unity of Indian nationhood, a vital factor in its total make-up without which this noble edifice will remain incomplete. I can never give up this sincere claim (see Hameed 1990: 161).

What appears as irreconcilability in one statement becomes complementarity in the other.

Both statements—by Muhammad Ali and by Abul Kalam Azad—highlight what many intellectuals, scholars and politicians see as the crucial element of ambiguity or tension in the relation of the Muslims of South Asia to their cultural and political environments. It is a relationship that has, right from the very beginning, carried within itself the potential for the emergence of fundamentalism. As Yohanan Friedman puts it:

> There was, on the one hand, the feeling that the Indian Muslims were constantly in danger of being overwhelmed by an environment which could only be described as an anathema to their ideal of monotheism. The apprehension created an intense desire to preserve Islam in its pristine purity and to protect it assiduously from any encroachment of Indian customs and beliefs.... Diametrically opposed to it was the attempt to find a common denominator for the two civilizations.... This conciliatory trend was always weaker than the orthodox one (1986: 79).

I should like to clarify that I am not here concerned with 'communalism' (more precisely, Hindu-Muslim conflict) in modern India, nor is this discussion a contribution to the history of Islam in India. It is rather an attempt to construct an argument, on the basis of selected materials, about the character of Muslim fundamentalism in South Asia. Briefly, the argument runs as follows: While a concern with *orthodoxy* and *orthopraxis* is only to be expected among the carriers of a religious tradition when they enter an alien socio-cultural environment and make converts, their anxiety about the loss of the pristine purity of belief and practice at a later stage of consolidation expresses itself in the form of efforts at *reform* and *revival*. If and when the reformist-revivalist stage develops into a situation of crisis, so perceived, because of the loss of political power (or, may be, its acquisition)—bringing together the elements of scriptural dogmatism, cultural critique, and the quest for power—one is faced with, I suggest, the phenomenon of *fundamentalism*. The encounter with colonialism and the resultant cultural impact of the West is a particular expression of this crisis and need not be seen as its only true form. To repeat, then, the definition of fundamentalism as the reaction of the bearers of a religious tradition to post-Enlightenment modernity is too restrictive to allow a fuller understanding of even that encounter. We need to look deeper in time and adopt the *longue durée* perspective.

Arrival of Islam in India: Opportunities and Dilemmas

The Western seaboard of India was known to sea-faring Arab traders long before the advent of Islam. The impact of Islam as religion and, presumably, a way of life may have been felt by the Indo-Arab communities within the living memory of the Prophet himself. Islam cast its missionary-cum-military eyes on India during the caliphate of Umar bin al-Khattab, and finally arrived here in AD 712, when Sind was conquered by Muhammad bin Qasim on behalf of Hajjaj bin Yusuf, governor of the eastern provinces of the Umayyad caliphate. Muhammad conquered the kingdom of Dahir, a Hindu raja, and stayed to establish Islam as a political force in Sind. Although the general view is that Hajjaj sent the military expedition because Dahir refused to provide protection to Arab trading vessels against pirates in the Arabian Sea (see Qureshi 1962: 35), it is more likely that the eastward push was also part of a larger plan of a political nature (see Rizvi 1987: 9).

It was one thing to conquer an alien land but quite another, and a difficult one, to establish a stable Muslim state among a people whom Muhammad bin Qasim was obliged by his faith to judge as benighted infidels. These infidels were, however, objectively judged, legatees of Brahmanical and Buddhist cultures with varied achievements to their credit. As Peter Hardy puts it, 'The century following the Arab conquest of Sind was therefore one in which Hindu culture could encounter the Arabs in the hope of giving more than it was forced to receive' (1970: 371).

Immediately, Muhammad's task was to set up an administrative structure and to receive the obedience of the people whose ruler had been defeated. It was obvious that these objectives would be impossible to achieve without the support of the existing administrative functionaries, who happened to be high caste Hindus. While some conversions to Islam were effected, the conqueror had to call upon non-Muslims to continue to hold office under him, and this posed a dilemma. Muhammad would have either to abandon his political mandate and refrain from seeking the co-operation of infidels, or to abandon orthodoxy and seize the opportunity of consolidating the extended dominion of *dar ul-Islam*. As it turned out, political expediency won over orthodoxy.

Muhammad bin Qasim persuaded his religious advisers to allow him to extend the status and rights of 'the protected class' (*zimmi*) to the Hindus of Sind, although they were not, strictly speaking, 'people of the Book' (*ahl-i-kitab*), that is, followers of God-given but superseded religions. This concession was made by him on the basis of the precedent of the 'fire-worshippers' of Iraq and Syria, who already had been accommodated among such 'peoples', although originally only Jews and Christians comprised this special category (see Friedman 1972: 180–2). The Umayyad state adapted the doctrine regarding non-Muslims to purely secular purposes, and the Hanafi school of law, which became preponderant in India, endorsed the view. 'This conciliatory policy was not only desirable but necessary. The Hindus accepted [Muslim] rule on the guarantee that the state would not interfere with the practice of their religion' (Malik 1963: 5).

The Hindus who did not embrace Islam were treated as non-citizens of the caliphate, in it but not of it. They were required under Islamic law (*sharia*), to pay poll tax (*jizya*) on a graduated basis, the propertied classes paying four times as much as the poor. In return, their lives were spared and their properties were exempted from confiscation. They were excused from rendering military service and paying surplus property tax (*zakat*), both essential obligations for Muslims. What is more, Muhammad felt obliged to confirm the privileges of upper caste Hindus, particularly the Brahmans, who traditionally received tribute from lower castes. In conformity with the practice of the Umayyad caliphate, he did not discard the existing administrative structure (see Ahmad 1964: 101), and ruled through

Hindu village headmen (*rais*), chieftains (*dihqans*) and prefects whose work was overseen by Muslim governors. This gave rise, in due course, to the administrative category of Amils in Sind who looked after revenue administration. 'The management of all the affairs of the state, and its administration, I leave in your able hands', Muhammad proclaimed, on a hereditary basis (see Nizami 1989: 96).

Simultaneously, the high ecclesiastical office of *Sadr-ul- Islam al Affal* was created and the secular governors subordinated to it. This gave the arrangement that Muhammad quickly worked out the appearance of an Islamic state. The opportunity for making converts to the new faith was also seized, apparently without great success. Although some chieftains and common people embraced Islam at the invitation of Muhammad, they were, most of them, Buddhists, or Buddhists recently reabsorbed into the Hindu fold. Sind actually became a Muslim majority province only very gradually (see Qureshi 1962: 42, 53–4). In this respect the social dynamics in Sind were no different than in any other area newly conquered on behalf of Islam. It took centuries for even a country like Egypt to have a Muslim majority among its people.

What lay at the core of the new set-up was *compromise* on the part of both antagonistic communities; it was a compromise between religious orthodoxy and political expediency. The Hindus saved their religious faith by submitting to Muslim political power, without acknowledging its legitimacy or authority (see Hardy 1981 on this theme, though for a later period), and consequently agreeing to work for the alien rulers. The nature and extent of the Muslim compromise is indicated by the decree of Hajjaj bin Yusuf, issued on receipt of a petition from the Brahmans to be allowed idol worship, nothing less:

[T]he chief inhabitants of Brahmanabad had petitioned to be allowed to repair the temple of *budh* [the Buddha or *but*, idol] and pursue their own religion. As they have made submission, and have agreed to pay taxes to the *Khalifa*, nothing more can be properly required from them. They have been taken under our protection, and we must not in any way stretch out our hands upon their lives or property. Permission is given to them to worship their gods. Nobody must be forbidden or prevented from following his own religion. They must live in their houses in whatever manner they like (see Malik 1963: 4).

Since the Buddhists and Hindus were grouped together as *zimmis*, their legal status presumably provided them some protection against conversion. In any case, the early Arabs were not enthusiastic proselytisers.

Whatever the *Sadr-ul-Islam* thought of this, the subordination of religious authority to the power of the state at the highest level had been asserted. The compact (if it may be so called) was between two groups of elites—the native and the alien—and the guardians of religious orthodoxy on either side, namely the Brahmans and the *ulama*[2] (the latter were not yet quite a well-defined category or as influential as they became later), apparently kept aloof (see Thapar 1966: 302). Muslim religious authority in India was to be alternately asserted and challenged by Muslim royal power, during the next one thousand years. The tension was internal to the Indian Muslim communities, but the Hindu environment was not an insignificant factor in its ebb and flow.

Simultaneously, the relations between Muslim rulers and the non-Muslim ruled also were to see many ups and downs. In Marshall Hodgson's succinct words, the relations of the Indo-Muslim rulers 'to the indigenous heritage were always a live issue' (1974: 59). On the cultural front, Aziz Ahmad writes in a fairly balanced assessment: 'The history of medieval and modern India is to a very considerable extent a history of Hindu-Muslim religio-cultural tensions, interspersed with movements or individual efforts at understanding, harmony and even composite development. The divisive forces have proved much more dynamic than the cohesive ones' (1964: 73). The foregoing observation, made within a dozen years or so of the partition is, perhaps, insufficiently appreciative of the smooth working arrangements that were worked out at the local level (see, e.g. Bayly 1989; Madan 1972). The prevalence of tensions at the macro-level may not be denied, however, nor indeed the ideological divide.

It would be apposite to point out here that the assimilative character of the Hindu cultural environment was, in the eyes of the Muslim elites (most of them of foreign origin—Arabs, Turks, Iranians, Afghans, etc.), a serious threat to the Muslim way of life as well as to Muslim secular power, and called for 'constant vigilance and effort' (Qureshi 1962: 103). Indian Muslims 'were a people living, as it were, in two worlds; one of their immediate surroundings

---

2. *ᶜUlamā* is the plural of the Arabic noun *ᶜālim*, which literally means 'one who knows', 'a learned person'. It is specifically used to refer to a person who is a formally educated authority on religious and legal matters. The *ᶜulamā* as a body are an essential element of Islamic governance. Their judicial opinions (*fatāwa*) help in the regulation of the domestic and public affairs of a Muslim community.

and the other was the world of the sources of inspiration which sustained their spiritual experience' (ibid.; see also Ahmad 1964: 77 et passim), and there was discord between them. Muslim fundamentalism in India has its roots deep in the twin predicaments of the Indo-Muslim community, namely the perceived threat of the Hindu cultural environment and of Muslim secular power, or, in modern times, of political expediency. But let me not anticipate the modern times. The medieval period claims our attention first.

Religious Authority *versus* Secular Power in Medieval India

When Muhammad bin Qasim was recalled by the new caliph, three years after he had annexed Sind, he had already designed the basic structure of administration in the province, and pushed north-east to conquer Multan, bringing half of what is Pakistan today under Muslim rule. Above all, he had worked out a *modus vivendi* with the Hindu elites. Actually his experiments in administrative and social engineering became the basis for more elaborate and refined arrangements in the following millennium.

The next happening of equal significance from the point of view of Islam in India, in its threefold aspects of religion, culture, and power, was the appearance of Mahmud, king of Ghazni, in 1000 at Lamghan in the north-west (not far from present-day Peshawar). During the next quarter of a century he invaded India seventeen times. He overran the Muslim settlement in Multan, which had been taken over by the Ismaili sect, slaughtered many Ismailis and destroyed their mosques. He pushed eastward towards the Gangetic plain and southward to Gujarat, and ruthlessly pillaged Hindu temples and killed a large numbers of Hindus.

In an astute move, Mahmud submitted himself to the authority of the Abbasid caliphate. 'In his mind the two processes, submission to a "universal" *khilafat* and the invasion and occupation of "infidel" Indian territory were clearly inter-connected' (Ahmad 1964: 5). His vow to cleanse 'pagan' India of its 'ignorance' and false religions had been the occasion for his first investiture at the hands of the caliph al-Qadir; his sack of the rich Hindu temple of Somnath resulted in the honour of a second. Mahmud thus appeared in India as the champion of Sunni orthodoxy, defending it against both the apostate and the infidel. In his concern for orthodoxy he may have appeared to be on the side of the *ulama* rather than secular power, but he did not let down the state: he had Hindus in his multiracial army (see Rizvi 1987: 12–18). Mahmud's successors ruled over north-west India for well over a century and a half making Lahore a kingly city.

The signal for heightened tension between the spokesmen for orthodoxy and the authority of the *ulama*, on the one hand, and the power of the king, on the other, came later during the period known as the Delhi Sultanate (the thirteenth to the early sixteenth centuries). Formally, the Sultanate was a part of the eastern caliphate and the fiction of caliphal source of authority was kept alive beyond the sack of Baghdad in 1258 by the Mongols. Gradually the Delhi Sultans began to call themselves by a title formerly reserved for the caliph, namely *Zillillah* ('the shadow of God'). It was, however, Sultan Ghiyas-ud-din Balban (ruled 1265–87) who apparently realized the potential utility of this concept in the furtherance of the scope and legitimacy of royal power (see Malik 1963: 18).

It has been assumed by many historians that *sharia* was the basis of the medieval Indian states (of the north, the east, and the south), but this was not, in fact, unreservedly so. The Turkish-Afghan connection, which began with the invasions of Mahmud Ghazni, and was extended and consolidated by the Ghurids, ended with the death of Muhammad Ghuri in 1206, when his general, Qutb ud-din Aibak, took over the Indian possessions of the sultan and declared himself the new king. 'The significance of this was that the Sultanate came to be regarded as an Indian state and not as an extension of an Afghan kingdom' (Thapar 1966: 268). The Indo-Muslim kings, however, continued to acknowledge the suzerainty of the caliph and their territories were part of *dar ul-Islam*. However—and this is the point I want to stress—these sultans, with the sole exception of Firuz Tughluq (ruled 1351–88), did not insist on the promulgation of the *sharia*, though they could not have disregarded the consensus (*ijma*) of the *ulama* on doctrinal issues. The distinction between spiritual authority and temporal power is of crucial importance; which has the upper hand in a particular situation depends upon the prevailing circumstances.

Actually, the great empire builder Ala ud-din Khalji (ruled 1296–1316) is reputed to have challenged the authority of the *ulama* who had come into prominence all over the Muslim world after the decline of the Abbasid caliphate in the tenth century. He asserted that he decreed whatever seemed to him to be for 'the good of the state' and 'the benefit of the country', and also 'opportune under the circumstances', without worrying whether it was in conformity with the *sharia*, which he did not claim to know well (see Mujeeb 1967: 73–4). Naturally, the *ulama* did not approve. He was roundly condemned for his disregard of *sharia* by the supporters of clericalism, most notably Zia ud-din Barani (*ca.* 1280–1360), an outstanding historian of medieval India; but the approvers were not absent, and the very distinguished scholar-historian-Sufi, Amir Khusrau addressed the king as *khalifa*.

Referring to the evidence of Barani's classic work *Fatawa-i Jahandari* (religious commandments on rulership) (*ca.* 1358–9), Muhammad Habib writes that the empire of Delhi during the fourteenth century

was not a theocratic state in any sense of the word. Its basis was not *shariat* of Islam but the *zawabit* or the state laws made by the king.... [Their] foundation was ... non-religious and secular.... Barani leaves us in no doubt that in cases of conflict the state-laws overrode the *shariat* (Habib and Khan n.d.: vi).

Habib's own authoritative judgement on the issue of religious orthodoxy *versus* political expediency is noteworthy: 'It is true that Muslim kings, mostly of foreign extraction, sat on Indian thrones for some six or seven centuries [he is obviously counting from the post-Ghaznavid period]. But they could only do so because their enthronement was not the enthronement of "Muslim rule"; had it been otherwise, they could not have lasted for a single generation' (ibid.: v), for 'India could not have been properly governed without help from the sons of the soil' (Habib 1981: 356).

It is obvious from the above that the two tensions—between Islam and its Hindu environment, and between religious authority and secular power—which emerged when Muhammad bin Qasim established a Muslim (but not Islamic) state in Sind early in the eighth century, still persisted in full force in the medieval period. Actually, the tensions came to acquire a sharper edge because of several reasons, of which two are significant for the present discussion. These are: first, the expanding demands of administration; and second, divisions among the ranks of the *ulama*. As for the former, Hindu administrative skills and business acumen, and even military prowess, had become a very strong pillar of the Muslim kingdoms, necessitating adjustments to the Indian environment that have usual-

ly been regarded by modern historians as 'concessions to necessity'.
'Only, it has been suggested, the relatively small numbers of Muslim
invaders and the vastness of the areas to be controlled, inhibited the
Muslim conquerors from seeking to fulfil their true intentions which
were to Islamize the whole country, if necessary by force' (Hardy
1981: 192). Otherwise, the attitude towards Hindus was 'wholly
offensive' and 'virulently hostile' (ibid.: 192, 204). The bending was,
nevertheless, mutual, but that was no consolation to the upholders of
orthodoxy.

The guardians of correct belief and action were themselves
becoming corrupted by proximity to power. A class of *ulama*—
ulama-i su—emerged; they specialized in jurisprudence (*fiqh*), and
became functionaries of the Muslim state. They were not above
time-serving interpretations of the tradition, and even of the Quran,
so long as they were co-sharers of power (see Thapar 1966: 290).
The *ulama* who devoted themselves to religious pursuits (*ulama-i
akhirat*), however, upheld the supremacy of the *sharia*, and kept
aloof from the corridors of power. 'Conscientious theologians were
obliged to condemn the whole system of sultan and qadi and legalis-
tic interpretations' (Mujeeb 1967: 60). The Sufi too were similarly
divided between those who were close to the masses and abhorred
both kings and the *ulama*, and those others (like the early-comer
Suhrawardis) who hobnobbed enthusiastically with kings and courtiers and assumed a variety of roles far removed from those of the
saint and the ascetic (see, e.g., Eaton 1978). The *alim*-Sufi distinction
was not meaningless, however, particularly before the seventeenth
century when significant convergences began to take shape, though
never as deep and clear-cut as the Sunni-Shia divide.

In the midst of these differences, a courtier of aristocratic birth,
whose intellectual passion was historiography, raised his own voice
in defence of religious orthodoxy as he perceived it, and his perspective was not always traditional though it certainly was doctrinaire.
Zia ud-din Barani, a Sunni, puts one in mind of Abu Hamid al-
Ghazali (see Hardy 1978), but unlike the latter he lived and wrote in
the overwhelming presence of Hindus. His attitude towards them was
one of absolute rejection; he even hated Hindus who had embraced
Islam, for religion was for him a matter of birth though this was
contrary to the fundamental teachings of Islam. Some present-day
historians attribute this hostility to the fear that the privileges of the
Muslim nobility (Barani's class) were threatened by the Hindu rural

aristocracy, 'with whom the Sultans had been inevitably led to strike a compromise' (Mukhia 1976: 39).

Emphasizing the class character of Barani's historiography, Habib notes that his attitude towards Hindus has been 'correctly' described as irrational and 'mentally unsound', but queries its sources:

what drove him to madness was the fact that in the empire of Delhi no privileges whatsoever were given to a Musalman as such. He had to find his livelihood in an economic system dominated by the Hindu groups. And the Muslim kings, as Barani laments, were in no mood to challenge a system without which their governments could not have functioned (1981: 424).

In the circumstances, Barani's advice to the Muslim kings on how to deal with Hindus was to offer them the choice between Islam and death and, in the meanwhile, subject them to humiliation. Since he did not believe that conversion could redeem any non-Muslim, or improve the character of the low-born (it was lower caste Hindus rather than their superiors who embraced Islam), there was not a real choice to be offered. Barani wrote that the Muslim king would not be able to establish the supremacy of Islam unless he strove with all his courage to overthrow infidelity and to eliminate its leaders (*imams*), who in India were the Brahmans. Further, if the kings, despite their royal power and prestige, were content to preserve infidelity in return for the tribute and the poll tax, how could they give effect to the tradition of the Prophet, which says: 'I have been ordered to fight all people until they affirm "There is no God but Allah" '? Barani emphasized: 'The religious perfection of the Muslim kings lies in this—they should risk themselves as well as their power and authority and strive day and night to establish truth at the centre' (see Habib and Khan n.d.: 46–7).

Barani's concern was to confront both the threats to religious orthodoxy, from the Hindu environment and from runaway royal (secular) power. Although he was not a theologian himself, his attempt was to bring the royal function and power under the hierarchical control of religious authority. The two functions (or domains) were autonomous but needed to be made complementary. His argument was that, while 'prophethood is the perfection of religion', 'kingship is the perfection of worldly good fortune'. Further, 'these two perfections are opposed and contradictory to each other, and their combination is not within the bounds of possibility' (see Habib and Khan n.d.: 39). Muslim kings, Barani believed, had to follow the policy of pre-Islamic Iranian emperors, 'which breaks the headstrong' and 'subdues the rebels' in order to establish the supremacy of the state. The rulers of Islam, too,

have adopted the policy of unbelievers in God (the Iranian emperors) for establishing their own power so that they may utilise their authority and strength for the protection and promotion of the Faith, for ensuring the greatness of the True Word by constant holy wars (*jihad*) intended to overthrow idolatory and polytheism [both deemed as typical Hindu sins] and for raising the prestige of Islam by killing and slaughtering the enemies of the Faith (ibid.: 39–40).

The kingly function was not self-legitimizing: its legitimacy was derived from the religious function. The exemplary king that Barani presents is, then, a properly instructed, pious sultan, who is 'twin brother' of the 'prophet' (see Hardy 1970: 459–60), and who has virtuous *ulama* for his advisers (see Hardy 1966, 1978). He uses his secular power to eradicate false beliefs (*kufr*) and enforce *sharia*. Barani's grievance was that real-life Muslim kings of India, from Sultan Balban to Ghiyas ud-din Tughluq (1266–1325), had fallen far short of this ideal and therefore orthodoxy was in peril. Royal power had not yet reached the heights it was to attain in the Mughal empire, and departures from orthodoxy, too, had not yet become so alarming as to make the *ulama* give the call for a *return* to the fundamentals of the faith. For this to happen, India had to witness Jalal-ud-din Akbar as the emperor.

Religious Syncretism and Revivalism

The five centuries between the last of Mahmud Ghazni's invasions (1026) and Babur's conquest (1525) saw the spread of Islam far and wide in India and rise and fall of Muslim kingdoms and dynasties. But—and presumably much to the chagrin of the propagators of the faith—it did not see India, though nominally *dar ul-Islam*, become so *de facto*. Those who professed Islam as their religion (*din*), whether immigrants or converts, remained a minority. Those others who, through their association with Muslim aristocracy and administration, came to imbibe Muslim high culture (*adab*) (such as the Amils of Sind, the Pandits of Kashmir, and the Kayasths of the Gangetic plain), though many more, also remained a minority. In the heartland of north India—the Indo-Gangetic plains—where many battles for orthodoxy, and not only for political supremacy, were waged, and from where the twentieth century demand for a separate

Muslim homeland derived its strongest support, Muslims constituted only 14 per cent of the total population at the time of partition. (The figure for India as a whole was about 25 per cent.)

Not that efforts to convert non-Muslims were not made—both persuasion and force were employed—but success was limited. Muhammad Habib concedes that by the medieval times, 'the Muslim faith had made no progress in the rural areas of the provinces that now constitute the Indian Union', but he refers to 'a landslide in favour of the new faith in urban areas' (see Rizvi 1977: 21). Sayid Athar Abbas Rizvi, however, questions this: 'the Hindu architects and masons, who constructed the mosques and minarets of the thirteenth century were not necessarily willing workers. Many worked under duress, although subsequently some of them embraced Islam. The same was the case with the Hindu artisans...' (ibid.: 22). All rulers, beginning with Muhammad bin Qasim himself, forcibly secured converts, some like Firuz Tughluq (Barani's ideal king) more than others, until Akbar forbade the practice: 'Formerly I persecuted men into conformity with my faith and deemed it Islam. As I grew in knowledge, I was overwhelmed with shame. Not being a Muslim myself, it was unmeet to force others to become such. What constancy is to be expected from proselytes on compulsion?' (see Rizvi 1977: 31). Needless to add, this was orthodoxy of the highest order for it was in conformity with the Quranic injunction (10.99) that there should be no compulsion in the matter of faith. For Akbar, 'true Islam meant tolerance and understanding and an extension of the human rights and privileges reserved in earlier Indo-Muslim political philosophy for Muslims alone, to non-Muslims, including the rights of conversion and reconversion, ... freedom of worship and construction of the houses of worship' (Ahmad 1964: 175).

Akbar's catholicity of mind came to flower in a setting which was the handiwork of earlier generations. The upholders of orthodoxy, namely the *ulama* and the Sufi, were divided among themselves. The former included the puritans, who stayed away from the kings and disowned political concerns, as well as the courtiers. Aziz Ahmad has pointed out that the *ulama* tended towards 'fanaticism' and lacked 'character' and 'spiritual sensitivity' (1964: 83). The Sufis, generally of ascetic disposition and closer to the populace, were also divided between a strict adherence to a disciplined way of life and a tendency to pantheistic drift. Not surprisingly, heresies came to be associated with the Sufi more than with the *ulama*. It has been suggested that 'the popularity and success of the Chishti saints in India was due to their understanding of the Indian conditions and the religious attitudes and aspirations of the Indian people' (Nizami 1961: 178), which often meant a willingness to adopt Hindu customs and ceremonies.

The nature and extent of Indian contributions to Sufism are a matter for debate: Did Abu Yazid Tayfur of Iran (d. 874) learn from Abu Ali Sindhi of India the principles of Hindu and Buddhist mysticism? Was Sindhi himself a convert? Was he an Indian at all? Was Abu Raihan al-Biruni right in discerning similarities between Sufi theories of the soul and Patanjali's *Yoga Sutra*? What is not disputed is the fact that the Sufis, who derived their immanentist ideas primarily from Ibin al-Arabi, generally found the Indian cultural environment congenial, and their attraction to certain aspects of Hinduism (notably 'devotionalism' or *bhakti*) resulted in deviations from Islamic orthodoxy which emphasizes the 'otherness' and the 'awesome majesty' (*jalal*) of God. This provoked negative reactions from stricter Sufis and the *ulama*.

The edge to these struggles between Sunni orthodoxy and different kinds of heterodoxy (Shiism, 'erroneous' sufism, 'statism', etc.) was provided by, first, the tendency of Muslim kings to give first preference to their personal or dynastic interests and the interests of the state (usually the former) and to disregard the claims of orthodoxy. Secondly, it was provided by the character of the Muslim masses, who were mostly converts and who never completely forsook their original faiths and ways of life. This is quite understandable because conversions had a multiplicity of causes and were not generally the result of strong religious conviction alone. Coercion, opportunism, economic and ecological pressures, and so forth, were also influential in different degrees in various places and times.

The converted, particularly those in rural areas, did not cut off all social and economic relations with their former co-religionists. Hindu values and practices survived conversion and resulted in a poverty of Muslim mass culture—in terms of a paucity of Islamic belief and practice—that was the source of much dismay to both the *ulama* and the bearers of elite culture (*adab*). Akbar's personal religious beliefs and his respect for religious faiths other than his own 'would have been historically unimportant if they had concerned simply the idiosyncrasies of an imperial mind; they are, however, important because they represent the culmination of trends which had been active in the life of the community for some time' (Qureshi 1962: 137).

Jalal ud-din Akbar (born 1542, ruled 1556–1605) had royal responsibility placed on his shoulders when he was only fourteen years old. He may well have had a precocious teenager's dislike of guardians and tutors and a strong desire to be on his own. The court was certainly not lacking in opinionated advisers including the *ulama*, who happened 'to be represented at this time by corrupt and degenerate men' (Ahmad 1964: 168). Nevertheless, Akbar was in his early years deferential toward these purveyors of traditional orthodoxy (see Hodgson 1974: 66; Nizami 1989: 100– 63). He did not, however, exactly please them by taking an interest, even at that young age, in the teachings and practices of Sufis, Hindu yogis and renunciants. He was particularly close to the Chishti order of Sufis and went on annual pilgrimage to the shrine of Muin ud-din at Ajmer. Akbar encouraged religious controversy at the court and wanted even the Quran discussed and interpreted. For this purpose he actually established the House of Worship (*ibadat khana*) in 1575, which was a debating hall where rationalist inquiry received the emperor's approval. The discussions were at first confined to Sunni Islam, but later other Muslim and non-Muslim religious leaders also were invited to participate (see Ahmad 1964: 168). Akbar gradually came to acknowledge what he considered the revealed and valuable truths of faiths other than his own, and adopted a syncretistic position on religious matters.

Akbar was obviously interested in more than exposing arrogance and charlatanry among the *ulama*; he was also concerned about the legitimation of the imperial state, the majority of the subjects of which were non-Muslim. This is the problem, it may be recalled, that Muhammad bin Qasim had faced in Sind eight hundred years earlier, but it had become much more complex since then. Not only had Islam come of age in India and developed its own internal complexity, complete with divines and mystics and their theological disputations, the caliphate's foothold on the subcontinent, overseen by a governor, had also grown into an empire. While the expanding central authority, was, of course, grounded in 'explicitly Islamic principles', a pluralist legitimation must have seemed appropriate to Akbar (see Hodgson 1974: 66). This would not have been readily possible without the tension between the emperor and his aides and supporters in the court, notably Abul Fazl, and the *ulama* being resolved in his favour. He had to be the principal *alim* ('knower') himself.

Such a resolution was achieved through a declaration, drawn up by Shaikh Mubarak, a maverick of considerable learning who had already earned the wrath of the *ulama* for his unconventional experimental attitude towards religious beliefs (see Rizvi 1987: 107; Mukhia 1976: 48), and signed by a number of high-ranking *ulama*, including the chief *qazi*. Issued in 1579, it held the 'just ruler' (*sultan-i-adil*) to be superior in the eyes of God to any eminent authoritative divine (*mujtahid*), and asserted the emperor's right to settle in favour of a particular interpretation, or opinion, when there was conflict among the appointed divines (*mujtahidun*) on a particular issue (see Qureshi 1962: 140–1; Nizami 1989: 127–31).

It is noteworthy that, while this decree did not deprive the divines of their normal function, nor invest the emperor with arbitrary powers in religious matters,[3] it did combine the two functions that Barani had argued were irreconcilable contraries: the king would no longer be merely a 'twin brother' of the religious scholar but more than his equal; the kingly function thus became pre-eminent. Moreover, the 1579 manifesto defined the principles that would guide the king, and these were secular principles, namely the 'benefit of the people' and 'the betterment of the administration of the country' (see Sharma 1962: 31–2), subject, of course, to conformity with Quranic injunctions as interpreted by Akbar. Incidentally, it may be recalled that these principles had been cited by Ala ud-din Khalji as the guiding principles of his policy.

Two years after the declaration, Akbar went one step further and announced 'divine unity' (*tauhid-i ilahi*), as the basis for the oneness of humankind. He sought to make reason the basis of the approach to religion. Not only were all Muslims to be united—his mosque at Fatehpur Sikri is home to a Chishti shrine—he also affirmed moral principles derived from other religious traditions, 'including the Jain dislike of killing that which possesses life and the Catholic virtue of celibacy' (Ahmad 1964: 171). But he showed, 'surprising indif-

---

3. This is a controversial issue. I.H. Qureshi, who can hardly be called an apologist on behalf of Akbar, writes: 'The decree ... has been wrongly termed a decree of infallibility, which it certainly was not' (1962: 141).

ference to Hinduism' (ibid.: 179).[4] The underlying motive, according to Marshall Hodgson, was 'to create a high inter-confessional moral and even religious level through the example of the court itself and even in some measure through legislation' decreed by the emperor (1974: 67). Muhammad Mujeeb highlights another objective, namely the 'emotional integration of the Indian people' (1967: 258). In this regard the Sufi ideal of universal or total peace (*sulh-i kul*), advocated with great passion by Abul Fazl, Akbar's spiritual counsellor and admiring chronicler, appealed enormously to the emperor (see Mukhia 1976: 77; Alavi 1983: 49). Abul Fazl's strong influence over the emperor can hardly be overstressed, nor indeed his own strongheaded rationalism, which led him along many forbidden paths. To recall but one of the sharpest of his sceptical pronouncements on a mechanical rather than reasoned practice of religion, he warned that, of the five pillars of Islam, prayer and fasting may be but the exertions of the body, charity and pilgrimage to Mecca, the power of the purse, and the affirmation of the creed, mere verbal repetition (see Abul Fazl 1977: III, 364–73).

The importance of the experiment in religious syncretism must not be exaggerated: the new faith was not intended to displace Islam (see Qureshi 1962: 145–7; Ahmad 1964: 171–3; Mujeeb 1967: 263–4; Hodgson 1974: 84). Akbar obviously did not attach too much importance to it, and its tenets were not stated in any detail. Abul Fazl, who became 'the interpreter and expositer of the new faith' (Alavi 1983: 52), does not refer to it by the name of *din-i ilahi* (Divine Faith) even once; Abdul Qadir Badauni, an unsparing and often unjust critic of Akbar, uses the term only once (Mujeeb 1967: 263). Among modern historians, while Aziz Ahmad calls it 'the emperor's spiritual sport' (1964: 172), Sayid Athar Rizvi regards it as a call to spiritual discipline rather than to a new religion (1987: 110). More recently, Irfan Habib has argued that Akbar's goal was more serious: he was against formal religion and wanted to rid true spirituality of religious trappings (1992: 68–72).

Akbar's critics were, however, alarmed by the promulgation of what appeared to be a new faith. They particularly denounced the

---

4. It may be noted here that the fundamentalist Abul ala Maududi asserted the contrary view: 'The new religion... in reality, was intended to favour all religions to the complete exclusion of Islam.... The most favoured creed, however, was Hinduism' (1981: 65).

efforts of enthusiasts like Abul Fazl to bestow on the emperor the mantle of prophethood (he uses for the latter the honorific of 'the Perfect Man', *insan-i kamil*, a term normally reserved for the Prophet among the Sunnis but also used for Sufi masters), and even to suggest a quasi-divine status for him (see Mukhia 1976: 80). According to them, Akbar had already given evidence of wayward tendencies and been guilty of un-Islamic actions. These included abolition of the poll tax (*jizya*) on Hindus, appearing in the manner of Hindu kings before his subjects to be seen by them (*jarokha darshan*), recognition of 'prostration' (*sijda*) as a form of showing reverence for the emperor, wearing of Hindu dress, a visit to the third Sikh guru, Amar Das, and observance of non-Muslim festivals. In the critics' eyes Akbar had ceased to be a Muslim—a judgement rejected by all serious historians except a few obviously prejudiced ones (see, e.g., Malik 1963: 39). In any case, *din-i ilahi* had in Akbar a reluctant proselytizer and it never acquired more than a very limited following. It died with the emperor, but not before it had aroused hostility among the *ulama* who considered Islam to be in danger. The time had come to call a halt to dangerous innovations (*bida*) and reassert the purity of the faith. The concern was not merely with *orthodoxy* but with the imperative of *reviving* the faith and *restoring its purity*.

Akbar's innovations are framed, as it were, by the earlier messianism of Sayyid Muhammad of Jaunpur, and the later revivalism of Shaikh Ahmad of Sirhind.

In the early years of Akbar's efforts to contain the influence of the *ulama*, he had found excellent interlocutors on his behalf in Abul Fazl and Abdul Qadir Badauni, two very able pupils of Shaikh Mubarak. The Shaikh himself had been deeply influenced by the Mahdawi movement of the first half of the sixteenth century, particularly by the role played in its development by Sayyid Muhammad, who introduced messianism in Indian Islam—a radical innovation—and claimed that he was the messiah (*mahdi*) promised to Muslims for the rejuvenation of the faith and the redemption of the faithful. Claiming the authority of Quranic revelation, he called for, among other things, a reassertion of the supremacy of *sharia*, elimination of the *ulama* and the aristocracy, and the reordering of Muslim society in India on a moral basis (see Hodgson 1974: 70; Rizvi 1987: 258–61). Inevitably he came into conflict with the *ulama*. More importantly, he—and perhaps even more the idea of a 'saviour'—had a profound impact on Akbar, and inspired some of his actions in the cause of religious reform mentioned above (see Ahmad 1964: 168).

Akbar's religious reforms did not, however, find favour with the *ulama* and many other self-appointed guardians of orthodoxy. The most notable among these critics was Shaikh Ahmad of Sirhind (1564–1624). He was a brilliant Sufi thinker of the Naqshbandi order and claimed descent from Umar, the second caliph of Islam. He affirmed having mystical experiences suggestive of prophethood and inevitably earned the hostility of the *ulama*. He also claimed divine inspiration for his self-proclaimed mission of restoring Sunni orthodoxy to its pristine glory. His followers bestowed upon him the title of 'the renovator of the second (Muslim) thousand years' (*mujaddid-i alfe-e sani*) (see Hodgson 1974: 84–5).

The Shaikh had acquired a reputation for scholarship early in life, during the last years of Akbar's rule, but resisted efforts to be drawn into the emperor's circle. On the latter's death, he denounced the compromises with Hinduism that, he thought, Akbar had made to the detriment of Islam (see Qureshi 1962: 149–58; Mujeeb 1967: 244–7; Nizami 1989: 261–8). Characterizing the news of the death of Akbar as 'good tidings', he called upon all God-fearing people to put pressure on 'the king of Islam', namely Jahangir (Akbar's successor), to mend the harm done by his father, enforce the Holy Law (*sharia*), and strengthen the community of true believers. He invoked the traditional authority of 'the consensus of the community' (*ijma*) for pronouncing judgement on all 'innovations', as had indeed been the practice 'in the very early days of Islam' (see de Bary 1970: 447), thereby repudiating the authority that Akbar had claimed for himself in his capacity as the just king. Shaikh Ahmad emphasized that the 'example of the Prophet' (*ittiba-i sunna*) alone could be the ultimate guide to righteous behaviour. In relation to non-Muslims, he called for, among other things, the reimposition of the poll tax on infidels, the resumption of cow slaughter (a practice deeply repugnant to Hindus), and the denial of high secular office to Shias as well as to Hindus (see Rizvi 1987: 162, 269–70). He maintained that the power of the state was essential for the maintenance of the holy ways of Islam (see Mujeeb 1967: 247).

The significance of Shaikh Ahmad's call for the restoration of orthodoxy for the argument being developed here is threefold. First, it represented not merely a deep concern with *orthodoxy* (in the manner of, say, Zia-ud din Barani) but also the contention that remedial action in the form of *revival* was called for. A retreat from orthodoxy had occured, in the Shaikh's judgment, owing to the baneful influence of the worldly *ulama*, ignorant Sufis, and heterodox Shias, and the un-Islamic actions of kings, particularly their tolerance of infidels. The enemies of Islam were not only outsiders but also, and more injuriously, insiders. The situation could only be remedied by reviving the original purity and missionary spirit of Islam. Secondly, Shaikh Ahmad stressed the imperative of strengthening the Muslim community by sharply defining its boundaries with reference to infidels (Shias as well as Hindus) and reviving the principle of consensus (*ijma*). Lastly, he underscored the importance of the state as a necessary instrument of renewal. This co-ordinated programme involving the faith, the community, and the state was not merely a restatement of the holistic conception of Islam—as revelation (*din*), as a way of life (*sharia*), and as worldly power (*dawla*)—but also an anticipation of the fundamentalist turn that was to be witnessed from around the middle of the eighteenth century onward.[5]

While Akbar's immediate successors, Jahangir and his son Shahjahan, backed away from the radical religious syncretism that he had set in motion, they did not entirely abandon his attitude of tolerance. It has been said that what Akbar shaped as his 'policy' survived only as 'impulse' in Jahangir's time, and a more deliberate tightening of the Islamic reins occured in Shahjehan's hands. If the latter's eldest son Dara Shikoh had succeeded him as the emperor, the experiment initiated by Akbar would surely have been furthered enormously. More than any other religious thinker in the history of Islam in India, Dara Shikoh produced an original argument for rapproachment between the two religious traditions, arguing that Hindu upanishadic thought held the key to a full understanding of the Quran. As it turned out, he was executed, after he lost the battle of succession to his puritanical brother, Aurangzeb, for his views on the status of Hinduism as a 'twin brother of Islam', which the *ulama* pronounced heretical (see Rizvi 1987: 131). As Qureshi puts it,

The orthodox group had everything to fear if Dara Shikuh came to the throne, because all they had achieved since the last days of Akbar would be undone. Dara Shikuh was

---

5. Irfan Habib (1961) has argued that the influence of Shaikh Ahmad (and later Shah Waliullah, see below) has been exaggerated. This may well be so; but they were not insignificant figures, even if they were not 'giants', and their ideas are important.

a firm believer in the identity of Hinduism and Islam .... The main difference between Akbar and him would have been that whereas Akbar's mind was not disciplined through formal education, Dara Shikuh was a competent scholar. Thus he could injure the interests of orthodoxy more seriously (1962: 160).[6]

Aurangzeb (ruled 1658–1707) was a learned and devout Sunni Muslim. His goal was to govern 'by the precepts of the Sharia for the benefit of the Indian Muslim community'. Conversion of the 'infidel' population was to be encouraged, and, 'failing that, [he] would rule fairly but sternly over the majority population. Increasingly, the political culture of the empire would be defined in exclusive Muslim terms' (Richards 1993: 172). Gradually, he abolished laws and conventions, or prohibited practices, that offended against orthodoxy as defined by the *ulama*. A major landmark was the reimposition of poll tax in 1679, with a view to 'curb the infidels and distinguish the land of the faithful from the infidels' (see Malik 1963: 67). This is an over-simplification, and there were other, if not more important (economic, political) reasons too (see Chandra 1993: 171, 181). Be that as it may, *jizya* 'was often a heavy tax, and was exacted in a humiliating manner' (Hodgson 1974: 95). 'One of the most spectacular expressions of [Aurangzeb's] policy was the widespread destruction of Hindu temples on various pretexts' (ibid.).[7] Many historians believe that the most significant development that influenced the emperor's religious policy was the emergence, in western India, of the Maratha challenge to Muslim hegemony. This of course does not mean that the Marathas were concerned exclusively about religion any more than the Mughals were. Power was the

6. Akbar Ahmed, an anthropologist, observes perceptively: 'From the late seventeenth century onwards Muslims faced two choices: they could either firmly re-draw the boundaries of Islam around themselves, shutting out the emerging realities, or allow the boundaries to become elastic and porous thereby effecting synthesis with non-Muslim groups. The two alternatives ... emerged in the person and character of Aurangzeb and Dara Shikoh' (1988: 79).

7. Two contributors to 'The New Cambridge History of India' take somewhat different positions on this thorny subject. While John Richards (1993) endorses the view adopted here, Catherine Asher suggests that 'when Aurangzeb did distroy temples, he did so not out of bigotry but as a political response when his authority was challenged' (1992: 254).

Romila Thapar writes: 'To the Muslims the Hindu temple was not only a symbol of a pagan religion and its false gods, but [also] a constant reminder that despite their political power there were spheres of life in the country over which they ruled to which they were strictly denied access' (1966: 279).

key element of this historic confrontation. Eventually it became 'a vicious circle' (Ahmad 1964: 198–9) with discriminatory measures against non-Muslims acting as both cause and effect of Maratha, Jat and Sikh rebellions. Aurangzeb 'may have felt that the answer to such threats was greater discipline within the Muslim camp, which for him would include tighter religious discipline' (Hodgson 1974: 93). The foregoing observation is most noteworthy for drawing attention to the role of external *and* internal threats to the religious life of a community in the emergence of alarmist responses including an insistence on orthodoxy.

Although Aurangzeb was still the emperor of Hindustan, and the country was very much a part of *dar ul-Islam*, apprehensions that all was not well were widespread, and not only confined to his close circle. His responses were based on the recognition of the plural character of Indian society. 'Aurangzeb's pluralism had a positive and negative side. Its positivism was directed towards a reformulation of the Muslim society in India. Its negative aspect was the denial to his non-Muslim subjects of the social and spiritual rights conceded earlier by Akbar' (Ahmad 1964: 197). In the event, pluralism degenerated into communalism. To quote Marshall Hodgson again, Aurangzeb not only failed to prevent the disintegration of the empire, but also 'failed' in what he had perceived as his 'first task', viz. 'the preservation or establishment of Shari'ah-minded Sunni rule' (1974: 98).

Loss of Power: *Dar Ul-Islam* to *Dar Ul-Harb*

Aurangzeb died in 1707. His heirs were small men, and within a dozen years the empire was beginning to break up into regional kingdoms. The mantle of the moral leadership of the Muslim community of the subcontinent was now donned by a far-seeing intellectual of high calibre, Shah Wali-Ullah (1703–1762). Muhammad Mujeeb calls him a 'religious leader of real significance' (1967: 277). At the young age of sixteen this precocious scholar assumed the headship of the Delhi branch of the Naqshbandi order of Sufis, and applied himself single-mindedly to the task of saving Indian Muslims. The foundations of his scheme were, first, 'purification' of the prevailing Muslim way of life, corrupted by survivals from pre-Islamic Arab religions, borrowings from Hinduism, and general laxity and, second, the revival of Muslim political power (see Rizvi 1980). In his judgement, the fundamental cause of both the moral and the political decline of Indian Muslims was their ignorance of the Quran and the Prophetic tradition. He was not, however, intolerant towards other religions as such (see Ahmad 1964: 209).

Wali-Ullah considered Sunni-Shia differences and the scholasticism and mutual exclusiveness of the four schools of Islamic law, or *mazhab* (Hanafi, Hanbali, Shafii, and Maliki), largely injurious. His advice to his co-religionists was to overcome dissensions of all kinds, including the theological differences among the three Sufi orders (Qadiri, Chishti and Naqshbandi). He exhorted them to put their trust in a rational and broad-minded interpretation of the fundamentals of Islamic belief, thought and practice, and in their light, to try to evolve a new legal system. To promote such an endeavour, he broke with tradition and translated the Quran into Persian (in 1737–8), and followed this up with a formulation of the elements of Quranic hermeneutics, emphasizing the exercise of independent judgement on an individual basis (*ijtihad*). As for the larger Indian society, he adhered to the pluralist model, classifying the citizenry into three mutually exclusive classes, namely unquestioning acceptors of Islam, followers of Islamic laws with mental reservations, and infidels/*zimmis*, and advocated the realization of *jizya* from the third category. In other words, while divisions within Muslim society were to be cemented, the boundaries separating Muslims from non-Muslims were to be given sharper definition.

To overcome both kinds of foes of the faith, internal as well as external, possession of political power was, in his judgement, essential. But Wali-Ullah looked in vain toward Delhi, Hyderabad, and elsewhere for the revival of the Islamic state. Ultimately he invited Ahmad Shah Abdali (of Afghanistan) to invade north India, which had by then come under the control of non-Muslims, notably the Marathas.[8] The Marathas were defeated at Panipat in 1761 by the combined forces of Abdali and two Indian Muslim chieftans, and the Mughal emperor Shah Alam was reinstated in Delhi. The political fortunes of Islam in north India, however, continued to decline. Abdali, whose sole interest was to consolidate his position in his homeland, failed to fill the political vacuum in north India (see Rizvi

8. Irfan Habib (1961) writes that there is no definitive evidence of Wali-Ullah having invited Abdali to invade India.

1982: 15), although he tried to bring together different Muslim chieftains of the area. As Wilfred Cantwell Smith has written, Abdali's invasions 'proved hardly a contribution to the glory of Islam' (1963: 46). A year after the battle at Panipat, Wali-Ullah died in 1762.

The significance of Wali-Ullah's contributions to Islamic renewal for the present discussion does not lie so much in their success or failure as in their form—combination of several strategies. Unlike Barani and Sirhindi, who believed that the true Islamic way of life had not been supported adequately by the sultan or the padishah—indeed Akbar had promoted what Sirhindi considered reprehensible innovations—the Shah was faced with the collapse of the state. This was an unprecedented crisis and called for a many-sided response. His concern was not only with the revival of the faith in its pristine purity, but also with the re-establishment of the state. The new situation included all three elements—namely, reassertion of scriptural authority, revival of the true way of life, and re-establishment of the religious state—that were employed earlier in this chapter to distinguish fundamentalism from revivalism and orthodoxy. The key variable here is the quest for power.

Wali-Ullah's eldest son, Shah Abdul Aziz (1746–1823), carried forward his father's attempted work of Islamic revival with the help of his brothers, one of whom, Abdul Qadir, went a step further than their father, and translated the Quran into Urdu in the hope of reaching out to the Muslim masses. The most important decision that Abdul Aziz had to take was to pronounce on the character of non-Muslim rule, which primarily meant British and incidentally Sikh rule. Unlike the Marathas, the British followed an interventionist policy, replacing *sharia* by new laws, particularly in the area of crimes. The very year in which the British established their control over Delhi, without doing away with the powerless Mughal 'emperor', that is in 1803, Abdul Aziz declared that the areas under non- Muslim rule had become *dar ul-harb*, 'the house or land of war'.

It may be recalled here that Sind had been included in *dar ul-Islam* early in the eighth century, and Muhammad bin Tughluq had six hundred years later regarded his empire as part of it. It was indeed more than a thousand years of *dar ul-Islam* in India that were being said to have ended. As Aziz put it in his *fatwa* (judicial opinion), 'Islamic law did not prevail any more in Delhi and the law of the Christian overlords was current without any hinderance' (see Mujeeb

1967: 390–1). He did not, however, call for migration (*hijrat*) or holy war (*jihad*), which were, according to his father's teaching, the only legitimate options available in such an imperfect state (*madinat al-naqisa*). Actually, Abdul Aziz softened his attitude towards the British, and English education in particular, after the initial denunciation (see Rizvi 1982: 236).

These options were, however, availed by Abdul Aziz's disciple, Sayyid Ahmad Barelwi (1786–1831), known by the honorifics of *mujaddid* (renewer) and *shahid* (martyr) among his followers. As a pupil he proved himself more strictly orthodox and less gradualist than his mentor. Continuing the earlier efforts to unify the Muslims and to purify their way of life of its Hindu elements and superstitions, he gave a call to follow the example of the Prophet of Islam (*tariqa-i-Muhammadiya*) (see Ahmad 1964: 210–12). Not content with his religious studies, he obtained military training by joining the army of a Muslim chieftain of Rajasthan. Deeply concerned about the moral and political decline of the Muslims, he set two goals for himself, namely the purification of the lifestyles of all strata of Indian Muslims and the realization of the ideal state (*madinat al-tamma*).

While he and his followers tried to reach out to the masses, through the written and the spoken word, 'the establishment of an important Muslim state had by far the highest priority, [for it] was only in such a state that true Islam, freed from semi-pagan practices, could be practised. This necessitated the supreme act of sacrifice, *jihad*, or a religious war' (Ahmad 1964: 214). In preparation for it, he went on pilgrimage to Mecca and Medina in 1822, where he stayed for a year and a half, and even dared challenge the orthodoxy of the Wahhabis, provoking their hostility. Sayyid Ahmad and his companions returned home in 1824.

Two years later, he set out on *jihad*. Travelling westward through Gwalior and Rajasthan, then heading north-west through Sind and Baluchistan, the 'warriors', or *mujahidin* (as they were called), reached Kabul in Afghanistan at the end of the year. Having gained a foothold on Muslim soil, from where alone *jihad* could be launched, and having enlarged the size of his army threefold (from 500 to 1500), Sayyid Ahmad sent an ultimatum to Ranjit Singh, ruler of the Sikh kingdom of Punjab, and almost immediately thereafter attacked a Sikh camp. An early victory here enabled him to establish a theocratic dispensation among the Pathan tribesmen whom, too, he set out to make better Muslims. This was not easily done for the

Pathans were unwilling to give up such elements of their traditional culture as were considered violative of the fundamentals of Islam by Indian judges (see Rizvi 1982: 484–93). Beset with many problems of reform and reorganization, Sayyid Ahmad tried to expand his territorial base, and expand the social space available for his experiments, by wresting Kashmir from the Sikhs. An attack was launched from the west in 1831, but it failed and he was killed in the hostilities. The *mujahidin* movement, although much weakened, lingered for many decades but it changed the focus of its interest and became increasingly involved in the situation in Afghanistan. It was finally crushed by the British in 1858 when the 'warriors' allied themselves with the Indian 'mutineers'. They had failed to establish the ideal Muslim society and state in India.

Contemporary with the north Indian developments, but independent of them, militant reformist movements, with similar political agendas, arose among the Muslims of Bengal also. The most prominent of these was initiated by Shariat-Ullah (1781–1838) after his return to East Bengal in 1820 from Hijaz, where he had spent twenty years, during which he had been exposed to the fundamentalist scripturalist movement of Abd-ul Wahhab. Shariat-Ullah's movement was called Faraizi because of the insistence upon *farz*, the fundamental obligations of a Muslim derived from the Quran and the *sunna* (orthodox tradition). Its leaders rejected Shiism, were more wary about Sufism than the north Indian reformists, and prohibited customary practices suspected to be of Hindu derivation. Their attitude to Hindus was deeply coloured by the economic situation resulting from the land settlement policies of the British, which had led to the expropriation of Muslim landlords and the impoverishment of Muslim peasantry. In view of the resentment against both the Hindus and the British, Shariat-Ullah unhesitatingly declared Bengal to be *dar ul-harb*, and even prohibited the Friday community prayers and the celebration of the Id festivals. But he did not advocate migration or *jihad* (see Ahmed 1981: 39–71; Khan 1965). The anti-British attitude was softened later on, during the leadership of the movement by Shariat-Ullah's son. West Bengal too witnessed a reformist movement during 1827–1831. More militant and more openly anti-Hindu, its leaders were the disciples of Sayyid Ahmad Barelwi (see Ahmad 1964: 216–7).

These nineteenth-century Bengali movements did not achieve their objective of cultural renewal (Islamization) in the desired measure, partly because of the composite character of Bengali society. The great majority of the Muslims of Bengal were descendants of Hindus converted to Islam. It has been argued that Islam flourished in Bengal only when certain Muslim cultural mediators of the medieval period interpreted it to the masses in a locally familiar and originally Hindu idiom (see Roy 1983). The nineteenth century reformers' concept of Islam was West Asian. They did not succeed in their political objective of recapturing power either. They did, however, generate a social and political awakening among the masses, which bore rich fruit a hundred years later when Bengali Muslims chose to cast their lot with the Pakistan movement. Rafiuddin Ahmed has stressed the narrowness of the objectives of the nineteenth century movements, saying that they were 'essentially the response of the *ulema* to the loss of their world [of privilege] which they sought to regain by a return to the primitive society of Islam' (1981: 41). In the event both the prizes—the religious-cultural and the political—eluded the grasp of those who led or participated in these movements. A new India was taking shape in which power equations were to be renegotiated and new strategies for cultural survival formulated.

The Revivalist Hope: Redemption by Education: Tradition *Versus* Modernity

With the collapse of the so-called Mutiny of 1857, and the banishment of the nominal Mughal 'emperor', who had served as its figurehead, Muslim rule in India on a subcontinental scale finally ended. It was replaced by British supremacy—direct rule in the conquered territories and 'paramountcy' in the surviving 'native' states, which included some Muslim principalities, notably the dominions of the Nizam of Hyderabad. The new ground realities also highlighted in Indian Muslim consciousness the overwhelming numerical preponderance of Hindus. A question that had first been posed in 712, namely how the Muslim state in India was to deal with Hindus—and which had not received many answers beyond a pluralist non-equalitarian or a pluralist equalitarian one (Barani *versus* Abul Fazl)—had now lost significance. The new question was, how the Muslims were to hold their own alongside or against the Hindus *under* British rule. In other words, how the Islamic way of life could be safeguarded in a non-Muslim environment and in the absence of political power.

Sayyid Ahmad Khan (1817–98) of Delhi shaped and spear-headed the modernist response. He attached greater importance to Western rationalism, science, education, and pedagogy (use of English as the medium of instruction was a basic tenet of his faith in modern education) than to traditional Islamic knowledge. He did not, however, reject the latter altogether. Moreover, Sayyid Ahmad was second to none in demanding a return to Islam in its pristine purity. He also attached greater importance to co-operation with the British than confrontation with them over who should rule and how, that is the issues of legitimacy and character of the state. He was anxious that Muslims should not lag behind Hindus in seizing the new opportunities that were opening in public life for educated Indians. He saw the future of the Muslim community in India to lie in the pursuit of these religious and secular goals. The alternatives of unquestioning retreat into tradition in fundamentalist style and opposition to the British *imperium*, would, he argued, mean spiritual and material ruin.

Actually Sayyid Ahmad Khan initially sought to further the reformist ('purificationist') programme of Shah Wali-Ullah in the direction of 'limitless rationalist speculation' (Ahmad 1967: 41) in order to build a bridge between Islam and post-Enlightenment Western thought. In a bold move, he called for the rejection of all the 'sayings' attributed to the Prophet, that is the classical *hadis*, that were repugnant to human reason. He even introduced a distinction between Muhammad's personal opinions, which he did not consider binding, and the revelations made by God to him. He went on to trace the roots of modern thought in the revelation itself. A key idea on which he built his thought was 'that the Work of God and the Word of God can never be antagonistic to each other' (see de Bary 1969: 192). Therefore, the 'word' could be interpreted by the 'work'. This made the study of nature by the methods of inductive and experimental sciences imperative and earned for Khan the sobriquet of *nechari* (the 'naturist') from the shocked *ulama* and other critics. Moreover, adaptation to the modern world demanded, according to him, the liberalization of Islamic law.

Sayyid Ahmad Khan operated on several fronts, social as well as political, but attached the greatest importance to modern education, alongside which traditional studies could be pursued critically. He declared: 'The Muslims have nothing to fear from the adoption of the new education if they simultaneously hold steadfast to their faith, because Islam is not irrational superstition; it is a rational religion which can march hand in hand with the growth of human knowledge' (see de Bary 1969: 193–4). Ideas such as these became the basis for the establishment of a Scientific Society and a modern school for Muslims in 1864 and the Anglo-Muhammadan Oriental College at Aligarh in 1874. The College was modelled on Cambridge, and grew in due course to become the celebrated Aligarh Muslim University (see Lelyveld 1978). It should be noted that the teaching of theology was, in the hope of not alienating the *ulama* altogether, left in their hands. Sayyid Ahmad Khan's radical ideas were not fully thought out, and the results that could be reasonably expected from his educational experiments were not clearly spelled out. It would seem that towards the end of his life Sayyid Ahmad was himself disappointed with the first generation of Aligarh graduates, who 'prided themselves on a smattering of modern ideas but were either a-religious or anti-religious' (Rahman 1958: 84). A synthesis of tradition and modernity was more problematic than Khan had anticipated.

Meanwhile, the revivalist hope continued to generate scripturalist responses in north India along sectarian lines, well into the late nineteenth century. They all attributed the decline of political and social fortunes of the Muslims to the failure of the community to live within the bounds of *sharia*. Mention may here be made of the *Ahl-i Hadis* and *Ahl-i Sunnat wa Jammat* movements, the former emphasizing adherence to the Prophet's sayings, and the latter to his example, as the basis of correct belief and practice (see Metcalf 1982: 264–314). They mainly depended upon interpretations of Islamic law in their efforts for renewal (*tajdid*) and reform (*islah*), and vacillated between contextualized traditionalism and scripturalist universalism, producing different varieties of fundamentalist doctrine. This vacillation also marked various educational experiments that preceded and followed Sayyid Ahmad Khan's efforts, but remained opposed to them.

The most distinguished of the traditionalist educational programmes of this kind, though not the oldest, was a seminary, Dar ul-Ulum, founded by a group of *ulama*, led by Muhammad Qasim Nanotawi, in 1867 at Deoband, not far from Delhi. The institutions at Aligarh and Deoband both derived inspiration from the theological teachings of Wali-Ullah. While the college at Aligarh developed the element of religious speculation, the Dar ul-Ulum stressed orthodoxy (see Ahmad 1967: 104). The latter was to attain 'great distinction, unrivalled, except for al-Azhar' (ibid.: 105). Its goal was to return to the tradition of 'the two main streams of Islamic tradition, that of intellectual learning and that of spiritual experience' (Metcalf 1982: 139)—that is, the traditions of the *ulama* and the Sufis. The strategy adopted was to 'return to the tradition of "the tongue and the pen"' and train *ulama* 'dedicated to reformed Islam' (ibid.: 87, 100). They were expected to preach in mosques, issue *fatwas* (judicial opinions) on specific theological and social questions, and provide spiritual guidance to those fit to receive it. In a radical departure from past practice, they were to serve the community rather than the state.

Accordingly, a fairly wide-ranging but fixed curriculum stressed the study of jurisprudence (*fiqh*) and the Prophetic tradition (*hadis*), but also asserted that the *sharia* could not be subjected to rational inquiry. The Deobandi *ulama* were actually against the teaching of the rational sciences of logic, philosophy, and jurisprudence. 'No single concern was more central to them than the quest for correct belief and practice in the light of the classical texts' (ibid.: 140). They adhered to the Hanafi school of law, disapproved of interscholastic eclecticism of the kind advocated by Wali-Ullah, and prescribed strict conformity. They also limited severely the scope of individual interpretation (*ijtihad*) to such injunctions as were characterized by a revealed inner meaning but a flexible outer form.

In short, the Deoband ulama were intellectual isolationists and 'denied the need and value of further knowledge' (Mujeeb 1967: 522–3). New ideas were suspect and innovation was considered a bad thing. The *fatwas* they issued expressed their puritanical zeal.[9] Thus, they were critical of the Ahl-i Hadis for not being orthodox enough, disapproved of Sufi excesses, discouraged social relations and religious disputations with Hindus, and denounced the Ahmadiyya notion of secondary prophets after Muhammad. Some of them went to the extent of opposing the celebration of the Prophet's

9. In the first hundred years of its existence the Dar ul-Ulum claimed to have issued 269, 215 *fatwas*, many of which went into the minutest details of everyday life (see Metcalf 1982: 146). They were too many, and all too often banal as well, to be described as the enunciation of the fundamentals of Islam.

birthday on the gound that it reflected Hindu influence and encouraged false beliefs (see Metcalf 1982: 150).

On the whole, the Deobandi *ulama* steered clear of controversies: thus, they did not attack the Aligarh experiment although they did not approve of it. They kept a low political profile, which does not mean that they did not appreciate the uses of political power. Actually they were deeply concerned with the shaping of ways of being Muslim under colonial rule. This amounted to pulling away from the state until such time as the *ulama* may rule again. The retreat from an active programme of re-establishing the Muslim state was more a tactic than the enunciation of a new principle. The Deobandis' conception of the Dar al-Ulum was of an institution 'from where *jihad* for observance of the *shari'ah* could be carried on' (Mujeeb 1967: 522). This expectation referred to not only the 'greater *jihad*' of self-purification but also to the 'lesser' one against non-believers. The seminary discretely maintained contact with the Caliph-Sultan of Turkey and entertained a pan-Islamist view of the future. They even visualized the possibility of active collaboration in the event of hostilities breaking out between Britain and Turkey (see Malik 1963: 192). At home, they were suspected to have supported the largely Sikh *ghadr* rebellion of 1915 (see Smith 1946: 295), and, ultimately, they 'formed the spearhead of the nationalists among the Muslims' (Mujeeb 1967: 558).

In 1919, after the end of the First World War, the *ulama* of Deoband joined hands with those of Farangi Mahal and Nadwat ul-Ulama, both of Lucknow, to establish a political organization that they called the Jamiyyat-ul-Ulama-i-Hind, the party of the *ulama* of India. It aligned itself with the Indian National Congress and supported the Khilafat movement which protested the imposition of the treaty of Sevres on Turkey (see Minault 1982). Ironically, it was the modernist Aligarh Muslim University which turned out to be the cradle in which the leaders of the Muslim separatist movement were nourished. In fact, one of the reasons the Jamiyyat was founded was that the leadership of the All-India Muslim League (founded in 1906) was too modernist for the liking of the *ulama*. While the League leadership was expected to strive for a modern, presumably secular, state, the Congress was known for its pluralist orientation, in terms of which one could hope to make room for Muslims to live according to their own lights. In short, the Deobandis' twin quest for a scriptural religion, combined with eventually the rule of the *ulama* marks them as moderate fundamentalists.

In the event, it was the Muslim League which worked for the founding of Pakistan and restored political power into the hands of Muslims, though not on an all-India basis (see Shaikh 1989). Moreover, a homeland for Muslims did not automatically resuscitate *dar al-Islam*. In fact, some concerned Muslims looked upon the demand for Pakistan as un-Islamic because of its emphasis upon the Western notions of 'nation' and 'nationalism'. Such critics emerged as the Muslim fundamentalists of twentieth-century South Asia, widely influential but until now (the 1990s) not wholly successful.[10]

Islamic Fundamentalism
in South Asia in the Twentieth Century

The tallest of the Indian Muslim intellectuals of the early twentieth century, Muhammad Iqbal (1876–1938) and Abul Kalam Azad (1888–1958), shared the Deobandis' distrust of the modernists. The youthful Azad, educated at home on traditional lines, sought answers to all significant questions about the universe and the place of humanity in it in the Quran, and called for a return to it in the pages of his widely circulated magazine *Al-Hilal* (see Chapter Five). The older Iqbal, who studied philosophy in Cambridge and Munich, called for 'the reconstruction of religious thought in Islam' (in his poetical works generally and specifically in a set of lectures published in 1934). He cautioned his listeners and readers that such reconstruction was a more 'serious' enterprise than 'mere adjustment to the modern conditions of life' (1980: 178). The task of interpreting the Islamic tradition involved, according to Iqbal, the full realization of the Prophetic message and example. The ultimate principles were unchanging, but their significance in a changing world was open to exploration through reasoned judgements (*ijtihad*). He regarded

10. For the purposes of the present discussion, it is not necessary to also discuss other reformist-revivalist movements that took shape among the Muslims of north India during the second half of the nineteenth century. Barbara Metcalf (1982) has provided an excellent account of the same. They shared with the Deoband *ulama* the political environment of the times, the most significant characteristic of which for the Muslims was the loss of political power. They were concerned with matters of orthodoxy, reform and revival.

Islam as a 'cultural movement' and not at all static, and considered *ijtihad* 'the principle of movement' (ibid.: 148).

Both Azad and Iqbal were revivalists and advocates of pan-Islamism, but otherwise intellectually quite unlike each other. Azad modified his pan-Islamism by adopting a pluralist view of nationalism (see Azad 1959; Hameed 1990) and a comparativist position in the field of religion (see Azad 1962). Iqbal overcame an early romantic view of the love of the land of one's birth to proclaim Islamic universalism and argue for a cultural space for Indian Muslims, which in other hands became the demand for Pakistan (see Malik 1971).

While agreeing with the Deobandis' anti-modernist stance, Azad and Iqbal disapproved of the tendency of the *ulama*, from the earliest times, to place their own opinions and interpretations above the original text. As Azad put it, 'when the commentators found that they could not rise to the heights of the Quranic thought, they strove to bring it down to the level of their own mind' (see Ahmad 1967: 176). A third critic who joined in the criticism of the *ulama* was the gifted editor of the official organ of the Jamiyyat-ul-Ulama-i-Hind, Abul ala Maududi (1903–1979).

Maududi's principal grievance against the Deobandi *ulama*, and the others who together with them comprised the Jamiyyat, was their support of the movement for independence under the auspices of the Indian National Congress. In his judgement, no well-educated and honest Muslim could subscribe to the Western ideology of nationalism, for his worldview would be religious. The very notion of the nation was, according to him, a Western and a false concept. While the political attitudes of the so-called nationalist Muslims were bad enough, the situation became quite alarming in his eyes when the All-India Muslim League, building upon the ideas of Iqbal and others, adopted a separate Muslim homeland in the subcontinent as its political goal. Such a state, Maududi declared, would 'safeguard merely the material interests of Indian Muslims' and neglect their spiritual life as none of the leaders, including Mohammad Ali Jinnah, had 'an Islamic mentality or Islamic habits of thought' (see Ahmad 1967: 214).

From 1933 onward, Maududi's journal *Tarjuman-ul-Quran* was the principal vehicle of his ideas. In 1941, he founded an organization, socio-cultural and religious rather than directly political in character, and called it Jamaat-i-Islami, (literally, the Islamic Association). Arguing that there could be no Islamic state without an Islamic revolution, he concentrated on expounding the fundamentals of Islam and announced that he was opposed to the demand for Pakistan. When Pakistan was established in 1947, Maududi migrated there, and started a campaign for the establishment of an Islamic state. 'Indeed', he wrote, 'if a secular and Godless, instead of Islamic, constitution was to be introduced and if the Criminal Procedure Code had to be enforced instead of the Islamic Shari'a what was the sense in all this struggle for a separate Muslim homeland?' (see de Bary 1969: 303). He pronounced, Western secular democracy to be the very antithesis of Islam (see Maududi 1989).

Expectedly, Maududi was in and out of prison in Pakistan from 1948 onwards. In 1953, when he assumed the leadership of the anti-Ahmadiyya movement, and counted Pakistani *ulama* among his followers, the government held him responsible for street violence in Lahore, and a military court sentenced him to death. The sentence, which had been imposed on flimsy grounds, was commuted soon afterwards (see Adams 1966: 377–8; Binder 1961: 302 et passim). In India, his followers were denounced by the *ulama* of Deoband, who issued a *fatwa* in 1951 asking Indian Muslims to 'shun the Jama'at-i-Islami and treat it as deadly poison'; supporters of the organization were pronounced sinners (see Agwani 1986: 86–7).

Maududi's importance as a twentieth century exegete of the fundamentals of Islam, who has been influential not only among the Muslims of South Asia, but also in the heartland of Islam in West Asia, lies not so much in any profundity of thought as in the compelling sincerity and simplicity of his message and its apparent clarity of argument. He wrote in Urdu and his writings were translated into Arabic and English, contributing to his wide-ranging influence. Among the creative scholars influenced by him the most notable, perhaps, was Sayyid Qutb of the Muslim Brotherhood (al-Ikhwan al-Muslimun) of Egypt (see Binder 1988: 170–205; Sivan 1990: 22–3 et passim). The core of Maududi's message is a call 'for a return to the real and original fountains of the Islamic ideal', dispensing with 'all the excess intellectual and religious baggage accumulated by the community in its journey through the centuries' (Adams 1966: 385). He writes: 'The objective of the Islamic movement, in this world, is... [that] a leadership that has rebelled against God and His guidance [and] is responsible for the suffering of mankind has to be replaced by a leadership that is

God-conscious, righteous and committed to following Divine guidance' (1984: 71). His teaching represented 'a triumph of scriptualist doctrine' (Binder 1988: 171). To elaborate, the Quran and the exemplary life of the Prophet are, according to Maududi, the foundation of the Islamic way of life. The law that God gave is comprehensive and perfect. In Maududi's own words, 'The *shari'ah* is a complete scheme of life and an all-embracing social order—nothing superfluous and nothing lacking' (see Adams 1966: 388). Whatever seems not to be clearly given may be derived from the original sources through personal legal deduction (*taffaquh*). The exercise of personal reason is legitimate for true reason is Islamic. This is a point of fundamental importance: it went beyond the rationalist formulation that Islam conforms to reason.

No individual is, however, an island unto himself: the existence of the social group, of society, is imperative for the Islamic way of life to be pursued. No Muslim society would survive as such if power were not in the hands of reasonable Muslims. Maududi observes:

[I]n human affairs the most important thing is, "who holds the bridle reins?" If these are in the hands of righteous people, worshippers of God, then it is inevitable that the whole of social life be God-worshipping .... None of the purposes of religion can be accomplished so long as control of affairs is in the hands of *kafirs* (see Adams 1966: 389).

This being so, the Islamic state has got to be 'totalitarian', resembling formally even the fascist and communist states, but unlike such ungodly regimes, it is, of course, based upon submission to divine law: that is what Islam means, total submission (see Maududi 1989: 27–34).

Power lies at the very centre of Maududi's concept of true Islamic society, and all varieties of legitimate power are for him only expressions of God's sovereignty (*hakimiyya*). He writes: 'the everlasting truth which the Quran expresses…is that kingship in the heavens and the earth [alike] is kingship of a single essence only' (see Binder 1988: 176). Human beings, like all that God has created, whether animate or inanimate, obey his law by their very nature. Choice is granted to them alone in the sphere peculiar to their state, namely the moral domain. Those who would be saved must submit to God's command here also; only then would they be true 'submitters', that is, Muslims. Maududi interprets the first part of the Muslim confession of faith, 'There is no god other than the God' (*la ilaha illa Allah*), to mean that 'There is none other to be obeyed but God' (see Adams 1966: 381). Those who argue for traditional personal monarchy as an idea *sui generis*, or those who advocate modern secular democracy investing sovereignty in the people, defy God's law, give evidence of their ignorance, and produce total chaos. Ignorance (*jahiliyya*) was the state of society in Arabia prior to the bestowal of the mantle of prophecy on Muhammad. Islam in modern times had, according to Maududi, reverted to the pre-Islamic state of ignorance. Hence the central importance of 'holy war for the spread of Islam' (*jihad*) in his writings.

It was in fact in his 1929 essay on *jihad* that he first stated his fundamentalist position and attracted widespread attention (see Maududi 1980). *Jihad* in his view was total struggle, offensive or defensive as the need may be, against the usurpation of God's sovereignty, whether by pseudo-religious monarchists or Western-ized secular democrats. What is more, its aim was to embrace all of humankind. Just before leaving India for Pakistan in 1947, Maududi appealed to Hindus to resist modernization and search for 'detailed guidance' in their own religious tradition: 'if you do not find [it] it does not mean that God has never given it to you. It means you have lost all or part of it....We are presenting to you the same guidance sent by the same God. Don't hesitate to accept it' (see Cragg 1985: 10).

The significance of the rhetoric of Abul ala Maududi above all was that the fundamentalist concerns of Indian Islam were expressed in general terms, and simultaneously the specificity of the predica-ment of South Asian Muslims was sought to be overcome. I have tried to show here that the major preoccupation of the traditional guardians of Muslim orthodoxy in India, mainly the *ulama*, has been the threat posed by the internal divisions (of sects, schools of law, and Sufi orders) and the external Hindu religio-cultural tradition and social organization. Its enormity was accentuated by large numbers of imperfectly Islamized converts who swelled the ranks of the faithful in India during the heyday of Muslim political power. As long as they enjoyed such power, the guardians were concerned to see that the values of religion would not be sacrificed for the sake of the interests of the state, that kings and emperors did not accommo-date heretics and their Hindu subjects in a compromising manner. Such compromises did occur, however, throughout the thousand years of Muslim suzerainty in India.

The Muslim state had long been defunct when Maududi began his career as reformer in the 1930s. The not-so-new imperial power in the sub-continent was Great Britain, and a national liberation movement, dominated by Hindus, had taken shape over the previous half century. The Muslim response to this development had been, as stated earlier, a divided one. The *ulama* sided with the nationalists against the British, and the modernists, with the British against the nationalists. The radicals among the modernists later spawned the separatists who asked for and won a separate Muslim homeland. Maududi redefined the terms of the choice in religio-cultural rather than political terms, more sharply than Iqbal had done, and rejected all three options. He envisaged a future for Indian, and later Pakistani, Muslims in which they would be co-sharers of Islamic destiny on a global scale: in his own words, 'a rational nationality of believers' constituting 'a world community of Islam' (see Malik 1963: 278). As soon as power appeared to be not only within reach, but also definable in non-secular Islamic terms, he lost no time in stressing its importance. He emerged as a fundamentalist *par excellence*.

Not all of Maududi's South Asian contemporaries thought highly of his incessant efforts for the promotion of Islamic society and government. The extreme hostility of the Deobandi *ulama* and of successive governments in Pakistan (upto the time of President Zia ul-Haq, who was an admirer of Maududi's fundamentalist ideas, notably the notion that sovereignty 'belongs' exclusively to Allah) has been noted above. Among modern scholars esteemed for their deep knowledge of Muslim history and theology, Muhammad Mujeeb accuses him of equating 'assertion' with 'proof' and of the 'disregard of thirteen hundred years of Muslim history' (1967: 402). More forcefully, Fazlur Rahman, who regarded Maududi as 'a journalist rather than a serious scholar', and as a superficial writer, observes: 'Maududi displays nowhere the larger and more profound vision of Islam's role in the world' (1982: 116–17).

Such criticism notwithstanding, Maududi's influence has survived his own life-work, and the Jamaat-i-Islami is an active organization in Pakistan, Bangladesh, and (to a lesser extent) India (see Ahmad 1991: 457–530; Ahmed 1994). Within India, there is a separate Jamaat-i-Islamia in the state of Jammu and Kashmir, which is a major force behind the armed secessionist movement there. It has given the call for Islamic society and government: 'As Kashmiris it is our duty to struggle for…independence…and to establish that social order in the state which we would like to see triumphant in the whole world' (see Agwani 1986: 76).

Concluding Remarks: Lessons of Comparison

This chapter had a limited objective, namely, to review the concern with Islamic orthodoxy in north and north-west India, over the long duration and at the macro-level, with a view to looking for the lessons that such an exercise must have for understanding the contemporary worldwide phenomenon called 'fundamentalism'. Regrettably, this approach has resulted in the neglect, first, of significant regional variations (such as are, for instance, insightfully discussed in Ahmed 1981, Roy 1983, Eaton 1978, and Bayly 1992), and second, of the sociologically interesting accommodations at the microlevel that have been gradually worked out by the people in the course of their everyday life in both the intra-religious (within Islam) and inter-religious (between Muslims and Hindus) contexts. The assumption with which I began the exercise was that all religious traditions are concerned—more in some situations than in others—with safeguarding 'correct beliefs' and 'correct practices'. It was further assumed that, while the guardians of tradition are an identifiable category, attempts to arrogate this role may be made by others, individuals or groups, particularly in times of crisis. The Iranian Revolution of 1979 reaffirmed the role of the Islamic jurist as the guardian of the state and the society (*vilayat-ul faqih*) in the Shia tradition, although this was a minor strand in Shia political thought: constitutionalism was the dominant one (see Chapter One). Similarly, the emergence of militant fundamentalism within the Sikh religious tradition during the 1980s has seen new categories of functionaries don the mantle of the guardians of orthodoxy (see Chapter Three).

Islam, it is often asserted, has been particularly prone to giving rise to fundamentalist movements concerned with restoring the pristine purity of belief and practice. The reasons for this tendency are said to be manifold. Thus, as a way of life ordained by God, revealed in the pages of a single book, reinforced and extended by the exemplary traditions associated with Muhammad (regarded as the last true prophet) and the first four 'rightly guided' *khalifas*, Islam has certain well-defined fundamentals. Belief in the unity of God, in his angels and prophets, and in the revealed book, and submission to his final judgement form the core of orthodoxy. These are supplemented by daily prayers, the month of fasting, charity, and if possible the pilgrimage to Mecca. The clarity of the basic tenets is, however, offset by sectarian divisions, such as the one between Sunnis and Shias which are as old as Islam, by the almost equally ancient conflicts between the *ulama* and the Sufis, by the mutual exclusiveness of the schools of Islamic law, and by the rather ambiguous status of the king, or a substitute secular authority, and of the laws that he makes. The dangers of heterodoxy are further heightened by the absence of a church.

The above characteristics are true of Muslim communities everywhere. Further, the very fact that Islam is a world religion means that it is subject to the pressures of diverse environments. I have tried to show here that, when Islam travelled eastward to India from its *locus classicus* in West Asia, it confronted a highly developed civilization, the religious traditions of which were radically different. The immigrants—whether Arabs, Turks, Mughals, or Pathans—were everywhere in the subcontinent a privileged and self-conscious minority, and depended heavily on proselytization to constitute local Muslim communities. Islam in India, therefore, often generated anxieties and movements for the protection of the purity of the faith.

The tensions that thus simmered at the very core of Muslim society in India never settled down to a stable equilibrium of co-existence. As Francis Robinson puts it, 'there [has been] continual, if sometimes slow and barely perceptible, movement between visions of perfect Muslim life and those which ordinary Muslims lead' (1983: 201). The last two, or two and a half, centuries in particular have been, Robinson says, 'a period of considerable vitality in which versions of high Islamic tradition have come to make noticeable inroads into the custom-centred tradition' (1986: 97–8). Employing the terminology used here, one may say that the eighteenth century witnessed the replacement of an abiding concern with orthodoxy by deeper and more organized fundamentalist movements. How, then, may the difference between orthodoxy and fundamentalism be characterized?

From the evidence presented here, it seems that, despite the differences in the perceptions of the Muslim kings and the guardians of Islam in the medieval period, the state was seen by all concerned ideally as the protector of the true Islamic way of life (*sharia*), even though it did not always discharge its protective role well. The principle of the legitimacy of kingship was given precedence over its actual practice. In Akbar's time, however, it would have appeared to the guardians of orthodoxy that the principle itself was being redefined. When the deviation from orthodoxy involves either large numbers of a community, or its most significant individuals, for example the king, the situation calls for a sterner response than the routine expression of concern about orthodoxy. Such a response came from Shaikh Ahmad Sirhindi, who gave the call for the renewal of the original impulses of Islam.

While Sirhindi's concern at the beginning of the seventeenth century arose from the alleged misuse of royal power, Shah Wali-Ullah's *angst* in the middle of the eighteenth was owing to the loss of political power alongside of the general decline of the moral character of the community. The protective shield of the Islamic way of life had fallen and without it the community was adrift. Political power, then, emerges as the key variable in the transition from orthodoxy to fundamentalism. Fundamentalist movements are Janus-faced: they are as much concerned with gaining (or regaining) power as they are with recovering the purity of the way of life and renewing its impulses. One endeavour is seen as inseparable from the other. In other words, cultural sociology and secular history must be reintegrated. As Wilfred Cantwell Smith puts it, 'The fundamental *malaise* of modern Islam is a sense that something has gone wrong with Islamic history. The fundamental problem of modern Muslims is how to rehabilitate that history ... so that Islamic society may once again flourish as a divinely guided society should and must' (1977: 41).

If power is of critical importance, how do we evaluate Maududi's lack of interest in the political independence of India in the pre-1947 days? It is not at all obscure that for him power, or the quest for it, was not unimportant but had to be subordinated to the right purpose. Since neither the independence of India, nor the demand for Pakistan was intended as the means for the establishment of a true Islamic society, he concentrated on religio-cultural reform. As soon as the establishment of Pakistan opened the way for the establishment of an Islamic state, Maududi lost no time in entering the political arena.

The linkage of culture and power inevitably results in the totalitarian ambition of world domination. Fundamentalist movements lay claim to exclusive possession of 'the truth', brook no dissent, and proceed to show 'the right path' to everybody who is not an 'insider'. Such an attitude comes naturally to Muslim fundamentalists, because Islam does not in principle attach any importance to race, language or nationality. In practice all primordial bonds that separate one Muslim from another are sought to be submerged in the universal brotherhood of Muslims (*umma*). This, at any rate, is the ideal goal.

To carry home the message of *umma* to various peoples, in different places, and at different times, calls for adjustment and innovation. Without these nothing can be done. Paradoxical though it may seem, fundamentalists, who are self-proclaimed renewers, must necessarily be innovators. From Shah Wali-Ullah to Abul ala Maududi, all South Asian Muslim fundamentalists have been innovators. The former's translation of the Quran into Persian, or his plea for eclecticism in the field of Islamic law, and many other exhortations were innovations. Maududi, it has been pointed out, has more in common with the modernist Sayyid Ahmad Khan than with the *ulama*, though he disagreed with them all.

Maududi has been considered the arch conservationist, a scripturalist, claiming *sharia* as an unchangeable, complete and valid way of life for our times, but it would be an error to consider his polemics timeless. He is as much situated in the twentieth century as the modernists he criticizes, and like them he reformulates Islam in the process of protecting it against the spirit of the modern age, which in his opinion is summed up in the notion of rationality. It is this conviction that led Maududi to one of his startling and innovative formulations—one which attracted much attention in West Asian intellectual circles—namely that it will not do to say that Islam accords with reason; one must assert that true reason accords well with Islam.[11]

This formulation is obviously a response to the challenge of the West, for had not the Muslim intellectual luminary al-Ghazali inveighed against reason? Similarly, Maududi's concern with Islamic

11. The credit for this formulation could well be claimed on behalf of Sayyid Ahmad Khan who, in his zeal for the promotion of modern sciences, claimed the Quran as the original source for the inductive method.

governance reflects not an original emphasis in the *sharia*, which is mainly concerned with the regulation of personal matters rather than affairs of the state, but a modern pre-occupation. As Charles Adams puts it, 'it is difficult to avoid the conclusion that Mawdudi ... [was] profoundly determined by historical circumstances' (1966: 395), as indeed was Ayatollah Khomeini.[12] It follows, then, that the confrontation with post-Enlightenment modernity, which I bracketed away at the beginning of this chapter, to enable me to look back a thousand years for the roots of Islamic fundamentalism in South Asia, can now be reintroduced as a characteristic feature of *twentieth-century* fundamentalist movements.

The rearrangement of emphases in the received tradition, in the manner indicated above, is tantamount to a selective retrieval of tradition. Fundamentalist movements appear to be characterized by a tendency first to redefine tradition in the light of perceived contemporary challenges and only then to give the call for a return to the fundamentals of the faith. This is as true of the Sikh and Hindu fundamentalist movements (see Chapters Three and Seven) as of the Muslim.

An attempt to understand developments in the history of Islam in South Asia in the narrative mode yields certain insights into the making of fundamentalism, which is by no means all that there is to this history, but which is the subject of this discussion. These insights include an appreciation of the critical role of, notably, cultural critique, political power, exclusive claims to the possession of the truth, ambitions of domination, and the willingness to innovate and redefine the received tradition. All these, however, will remain inchoate elements in the absence of determined if not charismatic leadership and a formally organized movement. The foregoing commonalities notwithstanding, there will always be critical differences too, and there will be diverse fundamentalisms, even diverse Islamic fundamentalisms. Their 'family resemblance', implied in their being called so, points to 'a oneness residing not in any supposed essential

12. One of Ayatollah Khomeini's closest and learned colleges, Ayatollah Mutahhari in his critique of secularism from the vantage point of Shia Islam, shows a remarkable awareness of the implications of Western science for Islamic thought, and his exposition of the fundamentals of Islam is deeply influenced by this awareness (see Mutahhari 1985, particularly his discussion of evolution, which he accepts and also rejects, ibid.: 205–16).

features of "Islam" ... but in the logic of relations between the meanings given to prescription and those given to circumstance' (Roff 1987: 47).[13]

13. In the context of Islamic fundamentalism, one of the important international movements originating in India is that of purification (*tabligh*) propagated by the Tablighi Jamaat, founded by Muhammad Ilyas (1885–1949) in the 1920s, at a time when some Hindus too had turned their attention to the same goal of purification (*shuddhi*) (see Chapter Seven). The Tabligh is regarded as a political but non-confrontationist, spiritually active, egalitarian movement of moral uplift. Its focus is on religious belief and practice rather than on mundane concerns. It does maintain, however, that parliamentary democracy and the secular state are imperfect institutions (see Metcalf 1994). As of now, I would place it nearer the 'orthodoxy' end of the orthodoxy-fundamentalism continuum, but this is likely to change.

Five

Islam in South Asia
Quest for Pluralism

To you your religion, and to me mine.
THE QURAN (109.3)

But even as your way is excellent in your own eye, so in other people's eyes
their way is excellent. Tolerance is therefore the only way.
ABUL KALAM AZAD, *The Tarjuman al-Quran*

[T]he differences between the root concepts and experiences of the different
religions, their different and often conflicting historical and trans-historical
beliefs, their incommensurable mythologies, and the diverse and ramifying
belief-systems into which all these are built, are compatible with the pluralistic
hypothesis that the great world traditions constitute different conceptions and
perceptions of, and responses to, the [Transcendent] from within the different
cultural ways of being human.
JOHN HICK, *An Interpretation of Religion*

Introduction

In the previous chapter, I discussed the historical roots of Islamic
fundamentalism in South Asia and its flowering in the mid-twentieth
century in the teachings of Sayyid Abul ala Maududi. The core of
the argument was that a dialectic of tensions internal to the Muslim
community, and certain external pressures, gradually led many
ulama and their followers from an early concern with orthodoxy and
orthopraxis to a revivalist *angst* and, finally, to fundamentalism. The
internal tensions that were particularly highlighted by me existed
between the *ulama* as the upholders of orthodoxy and Muslim kings
as the protagonists of dynastic rule. In course of time the worldly-
wise among the *ulama* thought it best to support royal power. The
external pressures were represented above all by the assimilationist

Hindu socio-cultural environment. As subjects of Muslims kings, the Hindus too had to make many compromises in self-interest.

Needless to emphasize, not all *ulama* walked the road to fundamentalism, but since my interest was to examine the emergence of this phenomenon, I focused on those who did so. Ironically, the discussion finally led to a journalist, namely Maududi, rather than to an *alim*. The question that I would like to ask is, whether secularism was ever considered an acceptable alternative? If not, what other courses did the *ulama* or other Muslim ideologues follow? Possible answers to these two questions will occupy us in this chapter. More specifically, we will be concerned with an examination of the evolving position of Maulana Abul Kalam Azad over a period of about thirty years.

As already pointed out in the previous chapter, the person who did most to build bridges between Islam and the Enlightenment in India was Sayyid Ahmad Khan, but he was not a secularist. He attempted to overcome the hiatus between faith and reason without abandoning the fundamentals of Islam (see Malik 1981). In fact no orthodox Muslim thinker has ever treated secularism as anything but an error. As the Pakistani scholar of Islam Fazlur Rahman puts it, 'Secularism is necessarily atheistic' and 'destroys the sanctity and universality (transcendence) of all moral values' (1982: 15).

If Sayyid Ahmad was greatly impressed by the rational experimental sciences of the West, Shaikh Muhammad Iqbal, the poet-philosopher, was deeply influenced by the idealist philosophies. His personal contacts with philosophers in England and Germany, from where he obtained university degrees, exposed him to Western thought much more than Khan ever was, and Iqbal considered the challenge of this thought one of the valid grounds for the reconstruction of religious thought in Islam. He too, however, never considered secularism an option.

The occasion to examine this option arose when Kemalist Turkey gave itself a secular state in place of the caliphate itself. Iqbal wrote (1980: 153–4):

With these [Turkish nationalist] thinkers religion as such has no independent function. The state is the essential factor in national life which determines the character and function of all other factors. They, therefore, reject old ideas about the function of State and Religion, and accentuate the separation of Church and State. Now the structure of Islam as a religio-political system, no doubt, does permit such a view, though personally I think it is a mistake to suppose that the idea of state is more dominant and rules all other ideas embodied in the system of Islam. In Islam the spiritual and the temporal are not two distinct domains, and the nature of an act, however secular in its import, is determined by the attitude of mind with which the agent does it.

He proceeds to argue that the genuinely Islamic attitude of mind is utterly non-dualistic.

The ultimate Reality, according to the Qur'an is spiritual and its life consists in its temporal activity. The spirit finds its opportunities in the natural, the material, the secular. *All that is secular is therefore sacred in the roots of its being....There is no such thing as a profane world....All is holy ground* (ibid.: 155, emphasis added).

A secularist ideology that denies any place to the sacred, or at best privatizes it, is therefore anathema. This is what Iqbal explicitly affirms, and it should suffice for my present limited purpose (see Malik 1971).

One could, of course, show that Iqbal's reconstruction of Islamic thought is self-contradictory in several aspects. Thus, the view of human destiny that he puts forward, in his philosophical as well as poetical works, as humanly realizable possibilities, rather than unrelenting fate, owes more to the influence of Western secular-humanist thought (notwithstanding his stern rejection of the materialism of the West) than Islamic orthodoxy. His assertion that God took a great risk and allowed man the freedom of choice between alternative courses of action dares man to act on his own behalf though in God's name. Iqbal's notion of the relationship of God and the human being as 'co-workers' moves dangerously in the direction of secularism and borders on heresy (see Raschid 1981). But, to repeat what I have said above, at the level of explicit affirmation, Iqbal rejects secularism as a worldview available to the Muslim.

What Iqbal said has since been reiterated by many other modern Muslim thinkers. I will cite only two more authorities, and that too briefly, to emphasize the unanimity of viewpoint that seems to prevail on this crucial issue among Muslims everywhere.

Seyyed Hossein Nasr of Iran maintains that Islam denies history (secular time) though it is itself 'a historical reality of dazzling dimensions' (1981: 1). A secularist perspective on human affairs is illegitimate because, being historicist, it denies the possibility of transcendence. It divides what is whole, denies God, and derives ideas and institutions from a purely human (uninspired) source. Nasr adds (ibid.: 7):

In the unitary perspective of Islam, all aspects of life, as well as all degrees of cosmic manifestation, are governed by a single principle and are unified by a common centre. There is nothing outside the power of God and in a more esoteric sense nothing "outside" his being, for there cannot be two orders of reality…. In essence, therefore, everything is sacred and nothing profane because everything bears within itself the fragrance of the Divine.

It is because modern man thinks that he has succeeded in detaching himself from the Divine that he imagines that secularism will take the place of religion and become 'a competing principle'. Such a position, which in a sense equates man with God, can never be acceptable to a true Muslim. Nasr calls it a 'fantasy', a 'dream of negligence and forgetfulness' (ibid.: 14).

Nasr does, however, acknowledge that in the nineteenth and twentieth centuries intrusions of secularism into the domains particularly of education and law, and even in religious thought itself (interestingly he cites the case of Sayyid Ahmad Khan among others) have occured. It is obvious that in Nasr's view, the limits that may not be crossed by a true Muslim are well-known and defined in terms of a unified view of reality. When this view is abandoned, 'Islam is faced with the mortal danger of "polytheism" or *shirk*, that is the setting up of various modern European ideas as gods alongside Allah' (ibid.: 14). The ideas Nasr has in mind are secular ideas such as nation, state and progress.

A similar but more rigid stand is taken by Syed Muhammad Naquib al-Attas of Malaysia, who rules out any concessions or compromises. He writes: 'Islam totally rejects any application to itself of the concepts of secular, or secularization, or secularism as they do not belong and are alien to it in every respect' (1985: 23). Al-Attas maintains that Islam as the complete and perfect religion (so described in the Quran itself) has already deconsecrated all false (un-Islamic) values, and has itself transcended secular time (historical development). This does not, however, mean that the world is devalued. The Quranic concept of 'the life in the world' (*al-hayat al-dunya*) derives its significance, al-Attas clarifies, from the way it abolishes a supposed distinction between the sacred and the mundane. *Dunya*, the word for 'the world', conveys the meaning of 'bringing near'. Keeping in mind the fact that in Islamic gnosis the world, in fact all of nature, is a Sign of God, it follows that it is the Signs of God that are brought near to us in our worldly lives. 'There can be no excuse, therefore, for those who, struck by the awe of the

Signs, worship them instead of God to whom they point; or those who, seeking God, yet reject the Signs because they see nothing in them but distraction; or again those who, denying God, appropriate the Signs for their own ends and change them in pursuit of illusory "development"' (ibid.: 39). The true Muslim, al-Attas concludes, is one who has found liberation from magical, mythological, national-cultural and universal-secular worldviews.

The views of Islamic scholars may be supplemented by those of distinguished Islamicists from outside the Muslim world. Bernard Lewis (1988: 2–3) writes:

> The distinction between church and state, so deeply rooted in Christendom, did not exist in Islam, and in classical Arabic... there were no pairs of words corresponding to spiritual and temporal, lay and ecclesiastical, religious and secular. It was not until the nineteenth and twentieth centuries, and then under the influence of Western ideas and institutions, that new words were found, first in Turkish and then in Arabic, to express the idea of secular.

More recently, Ernest Gellner, addressing the theme of contemporary change, has characterized Islam as 'markedly secularization resistant' (1992: 6).

An objection may be raised to the above attempt to present the 'Islamic' position by citing authors from different national or intellectual settings. The importance of the historical context should be obvious, particularly to a sociologist. But the point I want to stress is that of the denial of the legitimacy of an autonomous secular domain in Islamic orthodoxy, independent of different time-space frames. According to it—to repeat—the political domain may exist outside the law only surreptitiously. The Quran (4.59) decrees that God, the Prophet, and those in authority over the believers must be obeyed. The authority of the ruler is not absolute, however, for he too is subject to the holy law. Evil rulers that transgress the law are not to be obeyed (ibid.: 26.150–2), as indeed Muhammad himself showed by his own conduct. In short, the Muslim king is not comparable to the Biblical Caesar.

Moreover, the historical evidence is hardly unambiguous. At the formal level, the traditional ideology has been affirmed by all Muslim states except the few that have embraced secularism in the twentieth century. The secular state of Turkey, founded by Kemal Ataturk in the 1920s, has shown unique resilience, unmatched even in the same country at the societal level. Some of the Arab countries that witnessed the rise of socialist movements have also established secular or quasi-secular states, but these are highly vulnerable. They are sustained by a variety of coercive strategies, such as the outlawing of the fundamentalist Islamic Brotherhood in Egypt, the forcible capture of the state by the secularist armed forces in Algeria, and the subjection of Iraq to a harsh dictatorship. In the Islamic Republic of Pakistan, whenever political parties have been allowed by the military to rule, the electorate has kept the fundamentalists out of power, but the two political parties that have held office during the last decade have never acknowledged secularism as their creed. In Bangladesh, the first constitution (1972) explicitly envisaged a secular state, but, five years later, secularism as a principle of state policy was replaced by 'Absolute Trust and Faith in the Almighty Allah as the basis of all actions'. Fundamentalist forces represented by the Jamaat-i Islami have since then gained considerable strength. The point need not be laboured further.

It is obvious from the foregoing necessarily brief discussion that, in the classical Islamic perspective, the key notion of cosmic unity (*tauhid*) does not permit a dualistic sacred *versus* secular dichotomy on the ideological plane. Intrusions of secularism have, however, occured, as Nasr and others have pointed out. Fazlur Rahman, attributes them in large measure to 'the failure of Shari'a law and institutions to develop themselves to meet the changing needs of society' (1982: 43). This failure affected not only law but also, and more particularly, education. In an overall assessment of the latter field, Rahman observes that the emergence of 'a general emphasis on reason' in Shia Islam from the eleventh century onward, building upon earlier Mutazilite foundations, did not become generalized. Moreover, a 'most fateful distinction' came to be made between the religious or traditional sciences, on the one hand, and the secular or rational sciences, on the other, to the detriment of the latter. Sufism too was inimical to the rational sciences and intellectualism generally. Besides, the outcome of certain philosphical debates resulted in important religious personalities, such as al-Ghazali, denouncing objectively valid scientific propositions as heretical (ibid.: 31–9). In short, the secular strand in education emerged but failed to flourish. In India, Sayyid Ahmad Khan attempted in the late nineteenth century to demolish the distinction between Islam and the sciences, but his views were too radical to be implemented even in his own college at Aligarh (see ibid.: 51–2).

Another major source of secularization, as pointed out in the previous chapter, was the tension between the *ulama* and Muslim kings (*salatin*). Although the word 'state' does not occur even once in the Quran, the history of Muslim kingdoms and empires bears ample witness to its importance. Secular authorities did in course of time win recognition for their legislative power, and *urf* and *qanun* came to share space with *sharia*, but they could never pretend to be its equal or replacement. Occasionally, however, the rules that were made might have offended the holy law. From the tenth century onward, it has been noted, temporal rulers in the Muslim world became increasingly independent of the caliphs (see Keddie 1995: 175, 230–1). As noted earlier (see page 115), the first Indian Muslim emperor, Ala-ud-din Khalji, asserted that he did not know the *sharia* well and employed secular criteria, such as public weal and good judgement, to make decisions.

Later, in the nineteenth century, the new political reality that emerged with the consolidation of British rule, after widespread disturbances in 1857 (called the Mutiny by some historians), evoked responses that may be regarded as quasi-secular. As we have seen in the previous chapter, the first such responses were in the field of education, Aligarh and Deoband being the two models. A development that had already taken place was the emergence of Anglo-Muhammadan law: it represented a state-sponsored intrusion of secularization and took the form of fragmentation, protecting personal laws but promoting common criminal and civil laws. The Muslims were divided between those who supported the British (such as Sayyid Ahmad Khan) and those who stood aloof if not in active opposition (notably the Deobandis).

By the early twentieth century Muslim political and economic (that is secular) rights became a salient public concern in India. The Muslim League was founded in 1906 to protect and promote these rights. The Aligarh stance of loyalty was beginning to lose its appeal. Jamal al-din al-Afghani (of Iran), an internationally influential modernist, who was however critical of the Western worldview and particularly imperialism, had visited India several times from about 1858 onwards. In 1859 he began his criticism of Sayyid Ahmad Khan's religious thought, and also attacked his political views, for the fortunes of Muslims all over the world were, in al-Afghani's opinion, inseparable. Sayyid Ahmad's support of British colonial rule in India was, therefore, treachery to the Muslim cause everywhere (see Ahmad 1967: 126–30). Notable among those of the next generation in India whom he influenced were Muhammad Iqbal (1876–1938) and Abul Kalam Azad (1888–1958).

I will not be concerned with Iqbal here beyond what I have said above. This in no way implies a denial of the importance of his unique contributions as poet, philosopher and political thinker (see Malik 1971). I will concentrate, however, on one particular aspect of Azad's many-sided thought. I will discuss the arguments put forward by him, from time to time and from different vantage points, in support of the socio-political co-existence of, and indeed co-operation between, Muslims and non-Muslims (notably Hindus), first in the pursuit of national independence and then under the canopy of a democratic secular (that is non-discriminatory) state. Like any Muslim anywhere, genuinely devoted to the pursuit of his religion, Azad could not have been a secularist except in the limited sense that secularism has come to acquire in post-independence Indian political discourse. Indian secularism, it may be added, stands for religious pluralism in society characterized by mutual goodwill(*sarva dharma samabhava*) under the aegis of a non-discriminatory (*pantha nirpeksha*) state (See Chapter 7).

Before I proceed, I should like to emphasize that what follows is not a biographical essay nor a comprehensive introduction to Azad's religious thought. It focuses on his argument in support of co-operation and goodwill between the different religious communities of India.

Azad: Pluralism as the Politics of National Liberation

Born in Mecca, educated at home in Mecca and Calcutta through a traditional curriculum, Abul Kalam Mohiuddin Ahmed (his given names) began writing poetry as he entered his teens. He discovered Sayyid Ahmad Khan's rationalist discourse when he was about fifteen and was overwhelmed by it. This challenge and a medium for voicing his response, namely journalism, were found around the same time (1905). He learnt to read English and familiarized himself with modern science. He allowed rationalist speculation to lead him into a state of atheism, a kind of logical conclusion, although it had not been thus for Sir Sayyid himself. He thought that he had become free ('*azad*') of that traditional learning and religious worldview of which his father was the most authoritative representative known to him (Azad 1959: 4). He gave himself up to purely secular pursuits and mundane pleasures.

As quickly as he had stepped into the world of disbelief, he retraced his steps back into tradition and recovery of faith in 1910, when he was twenty-two years old. The recovery of faith did not, however, mean that he also abandoned rationalism. It had, in fact, been a part of his traditional scholastic training even before he encountered its modern application in Sayyid Ahmad Khan's works. Nor was Khan's influence completely jettisoned. Even a decade or more later he sometimes wrote what read like footnotes to Sir Sayyid's work: e.g., 'God is one and all His works are integrated', in his *Zikra* of 1925, recalls the latter's assertion that the word and works of God are bound to be in consonance with one another.

During the critical years of loss and recovery of faith, Azad self-confessedly grappled with that most characteristic feature of the Indian cultural landscape, namely pluralism. At first he thought: 'Religion itself, instead of creating harmony, was the greatest cause of dispute in the social history of man. There cannot be either multiplicity or contradiction in the truth. Where there is opposition and dispute, there is no truth' (see Douglas 1988: 66). But then a solution to this problem emerged with the recovery of faith. Azad wrote (see ibid.: 94):

I realized that the religion which the world recognizes by the name of Islam was indeed the solution to the problem of the differences in religion. Islam does not want to establish any new religion, but its mission according to its own testimony, is simply that the followers of all religions in the world be established in their original and unadulterated truth ..... [When this is done, religious conflict will disappear for] the fundamental principle is one and found in all. It is the adulteration which is wrong. It is the cause of difference, and all are involved in it.

This is a clear statement though not without serious problems, most notably the obligation imposed upon the believer to discover the original form of his or her religious faith. Another problem, relevant in the context of the present discussion, is that the passage belongs to the early 1920s but seeks to present Azad's convictions of more than a decade earlier. From his other writings of the earlier period, one gets the impression of an intense preoccupation with Islam and the social concerns of the Muslim community (social reform, promotion of Urdu, etc.) rather than with evolving a philosophy of religious pluralism. At this time when he spoke of the 'nation', he meant the Muslims. Even a sympathetic commentator like Ian Douglas detected a 'communal emphasis' in these early journalistic writings of around 1903 (see ibid.: 73).[1]

Soon after the recovery of faith, it is interesting to observe, Azad evinced interest in political issues, more precisely in the problem of self-determination and opposition to colonialism. In this quest it was the writings of Jamal al-din al-Afghani, with their emphasis on anti-colonialism and pan-Islamism, and the personal influence of Shibli Numani that he found most inspiring. He was also apparently influenced by the religious discussions of the Egyptian scholars Shaikh Muhamad Abduh and Rashid Rida (on such issues as the relevance of Quranic teachings and the caliphate) in the latter's periodical *Al-Manar*. The vehicles of his thought were, first, *Al-Hilal* and then *Al-Balagh*, Urdu magazines that he founded and edited from Calcutta.

Al-Hilal appeared for the first time on 13 July 1912. Two months later, Azad wrote in it that the 'real purpose' of the newspaper was 'no more than to invite Muslims to follow the Quran in their belief and actions, and act according to the precedent set by the Prophet..... It is my belief that any Muslim who seeks guidance in matters of faith and action from any group or ideology other than the Quran is not a Muslim' (see Hameed 1990: 33). Azad went further and said that what applied to the religious life was equally true of secular concerns. 'Nothing can be more demeaning for the Muslims', he wrote in the same editorial article, 'than having to determine their course by submitting to the political precepts of others.' He concluded: 'It must be understood that Islam has taught us two lessons, that of giving freedom, as well as of seeking it. When we were the rulers we bestowed liberty and now that we are the ruled, we demand the same. We believe that it is the Will of God that nations and countries should be given the freedom for self-rule' (ibid.: 33, 35).

---

1. V.N. Datta, historian and biographer of Azad, disagrees with Douglas's judgement and insists that Azad's thought was rooted in civilizational rather than communal considerations. The single most significant influence on Azad's thought, according to Datta, was Sarmad, the Sufi, who was sent to his martyr's death by Aurangzeb (personal communication). It may be added here that Datta has expressed serious reservations about *India Wins Freedom* being a true statement of Azad's views; he is inclined to consider it as Humayun Kabir's work (see Datta 1990). Although I have consulted and quoted from the book in the writing of this chapter, my argument does not depend upon its contents.

Pointing out to his followers that they had nothing to learn from the Hindus in the field of politics—indeed they had something to reject, namely terrorism—he stressed the inseparability of religion and politics: 'For the Hindus patriotism might be a secular obligation, but for the Muslim it was a religious duty' (quoted in Gandhi 1987: 222). He maintained that, in the eyes of God, only that government is 'legitimate which is not individualistic [despotic], but in the hands of a community or nation.' Therefore, 'It should be the duty of the Muslims to make every effort to achieve independence [lawful freedom] and, according to their religious precepts, they should not rest until they have established a parliamentary form of government' (see Hameed 1990: 35).

It is clear that during the *Al-Hilal* days, Azad was a pan-Islamist for whom the political struggle for freedom was a Muslim's religious obligation. He wrote: 'no one can be a Muslim and a believer in the one God unless he undertakes *jihad*'. Moreover, he emphasized, 'Muslims... have only to revive and reaffirm what has been commanded' (see Mujeeb 1967: 458). It was not a secular or multi-religious enterprise, but deference to certain historical and geographical constraints which made Muslims and Hindus partners in the political struggle. It was therefore an external or contingent relationship and not at all an essential or entailed one.

For Azad, there could be no denying the fact that the Quran considered Muslims the chosen people, the 'friends of God', opposed to the non-believers who could only be the 'friends of devil'. Azad thought of organizing a 'party of God' (*Hizbullah*) for the establishment of the perfect society and affirmation of God's sovereignty, and hoped that he might even be the Imam of India (*Imamul-Hind*), or the supreme leader who would guide the faithful (see Shakir 1970: 143). As Peter Hardy explains, the plan was for the creation of a Muslim '*imperium in imperio*', or 'jurisdictional apartheid', in India under the control of the *ulama*, for 'only thus could the ideal of the true Islamic life in accordance with the *sharia* be pursued' (1971: 34).

Exhorting Indian Muslims to stand on their own feet as 'the army of God', Azad reminded them that they were not a minority—that 400 million believers in the unity of God (the reference being to the world population of Muslims) had little to fear from 220 million 'idol worshippers' of India. 'You must realize your position among the peoples of the world. Like God Himself, look at every one from a lofty position'. The reality of life, however, was that they had to live in India: '*so embrace your neighbours*' (*Al-Hilal*, 1,8, 1912: 2–3, quoted in Douglas 1988: 144, emphasis added). As late as 1920, Azad had issued a *fatwa* ('considered opinion') that Indian Muslims could exercise the option of *hijrat*, or migration to a free land, as India under the British, who had emerged as foes of the Khilafat, was not a place where they could live with honour (see Gandhi 1987: 227). What seemed to bother him then was more the condition of his own community than of his country.

Although he was not concerned with non-Muslims with any sense of positive involvement beyond the sharing of a common homeland and a common political goal, he was no bigot. He wrote in *Al-Hilal* in 1913: 'Islam does not commend narrow mindedness and racial and religious prejudice. It does not make the recognition of merit and virtue, of human benevolence, mercy and love dependent upon and subject to distinctions of religion and race' (see Mujeeb 1967: 458).

Azad's political views got him into trouble with the British. He had graduated from being a newspaper publisher-editor to being a politician. *Al-Hilal* was banned in 1916. He started *Al-Balagh*. He was interned for four years. Released in 1920, he plunged into political activity, involving himself with the concerns of the Jamiat-ul-Ulamai-Hind, the All-India Khilafat Committee, and the Indian National Congress. He also met Mahatma Gandhi. By now he had begun to move beyond the view that co-operation between Muslims and Hindus was merely a political necessity, a means for achieving a political end, viz., freedom from foreign rule, which he believed to be a religious obligation. In his address to the Khilafat conference in Calcutta he observed: 'the tragedy is the world worships words instead of meanings, and even though all are seeking and worshipping but one truth, they quarrel with one another over differences in mere names' (see Douglas 1988: 289).

This was indeed a new, radically different, leitmotif in Azad's religio-political thought. Islamic fundamentalism was now to make way for religious pluralism. Citing the example of the Prophet Muhammad himself, who had entered into a covenant with the Jews of Medina, Azad envisaged a similar 'single nation' (*ummah al-wahidah*) of Muslims and Hindus in India. He wrote: 'if I say that the Muslims of India cannot perform their duty unless they are united with the Hindus, it is in accordance with the tradition of the Prophet' (ibid.: 226). The conservatives among the *ulama*, of course, rejected Azad's argument by analogy as being contrary to Islamic jurisprudence (*fiqh*). 'It would not be an exaggeration to say', comments Mujeeb (1967: 463), 'that in holding this view Maulana Azad stood absolutely alone'.

It was not long before Azad was arrested again. In an original and impressive written statement, 'The Final Verdict', submitted to the judge (in 1921), he spoke in two voices. He spoke as a Muslim, deriving his inspiration from the Quran: 'Islam does not permit that Muslims should live after having surrendered their freedom. They should either remain free or perish. There is no third path in Islam' (see Hameed 1990: 61). But he also spoke as a nationalist whose inspiration came from the likes of Mazzini and whose companions included Gandhi and C.R. Das (all three are mentioned). He was sentenced to a year's rigorous imprisonment.

Out of the prison, Azad became, at the age of 35, the youngest man invited to preside over the Indian National Congress at its special session in Delhi in 1923. For the man who envisaged a 'party' of God, and expected to be chosen as the Imam of Indian Muslims, this was indeed a most dramatic turn in his political career. In memorable words, he spoke of the imperative of Hindu-Muslim unity, without which he warned there could be no freedom from British rule.

Today, if an angel were to descend from the Qutab Minar, [and say] that India will get Swaraj within twenty-four hours, provided she relinquishes Hindu-Muslim unity, I will relinquish Swaraj rather than give up Hindu-Muslim unity. Delay in the attainment of Swaraj will be a loss to India, but if our unity is lost, it will be a loss for entire mankind.

Bemoaning Hindu-Muslim hostilities, he said in words that read like they have been written in 1993 rather than in 1923: 'When the order of the day is, "Protect Hindus" and "Protect Muslims", who cares about protecting the nation?' (see Hameed 1990: 145).

Although Azad claimed in this address that he had been voicing these views since 1912, one should note the radical departure in his views. The Azad of *Al-Hilal*, 1912–16, was a Muslim concerned about the religious life and the political misfortunes of Indian Muslims, who were the 'nation' that he had in mind. Azad's messages, which were earlier clearly addressed to Muslims as Muslims, and in which he told them that there was something higher than universal goodwill for the true believer, and that was the worship of Allah and the establishment of right mindedness and justice, were now recorded in terms of the primary principles of national liberation and universal goodwill (in his own words, 'of humanity within ourselves') as the guiding principles for political action. Pluralism which had earlier been derived from political necessity was now presented as religious humanism.[2] A Muslim had to be concerned about the freedom and well-being of non-Muslims too. This could not be mere expediency. It would have to be a principled stand. Since Azad derived all his principles ultimately from the Quran, the new political philosophy would have to be provided with a religious, and indeed Quranic, foundation.

Azad: Pluralism as a Religious Philosophy

After the 1923 Congress session, with the Khilafat issue behind him, Azad's political activities lost some of their salience until they were revived again in the late 1930s. In the meanwhile he devoted himself to completing the translation and commentary on the Quran (actually he never completed it) which he had announced in the *Al-Balagh* days. It is a moot question whether the commentary would have been the same as it is, had it been written before 1921–23. Be that as it may, I am here interested in making only two points, and I will do this on the basis of Azad's commentary on the introductory seven verses of Islam's holy book.[3]

Two sections are noteworthy from the perspective of the present discussion : section VI, 'The Concept of God: *Tawhid*', and section VII, 'Divine Guidance: *Hidayat*'. I am interested in the former for Azad's method and in the latter for his substantive conclusions. Both

2. Opinion is divided whether co-operation with Hindus was really a new development in Azad's religio-political thought. I guess the middle position perhaps captures the truth better than unqualified affirmative or negative assessments. Thus Douglas writes: 'Co-operation with Hindus had always been a part of Azad's political thought, but *it only entered the realm of action after 1920s*' (1988: 192, emphasis added).

3. I have consulted the original text in Urdu (see Azad 1964–70), but quote here from Syed Abdul Latif's excellent English translation (see Azad 1962).

point in the direction of religious pluralism or, viewing the same conclusions from another perspective, religious syncretism.

But some preliminary considerations first. Azad opens his commentary with the three principal attributes of God that are enshrined in the opening verses of the Quran. These are *rububiyat*, *rahmat* and *adalat*, i.e. (in Azad's interpretation) divine providence, mercy, and justice. For the limited purposes of the present discussion what is noteworthy is the fact that Azad's manner of interpretation tends to focus the reader's attention on humanity, and indeed the entire creation, rather than on Muslims alone. The perspective offered is unitarian.

Thus, Azad emphasizes throughout section III of the *Tarjuman* (Azad 1962: 17–44), entitled 'Divine Providence', that God provides for, nurtures, and sustains all creation. He writes: 'The strangest thing about this scheme of Providence, though the most patent, is its uniformity and the harmony underlying it. The method and manner of providing means of sustenance for every object of existence are the same everywhere. A single principle is at work in all things' (ibid.: 24). Corresponding to this universalism is the uniform capacity or 'inward talent' of all created beings and things 'to make the right use of the provisions afforded' (ibid.: 27). This would seem to mean that not only is Allah the God of all creation, but also that all creation is one in its uniform capacity for responding to what God has intended for his creatures through the twin processes of assignation (*taqdir*) and guidance (*hidayat*).

It is only within this framework that the differences between Muslims and non-Muslims may be properly assessed. The relevant attribute of God in the context of difference (as against the uniformity discussed above) is mercy (see ibid., section IV, 'Divine Benevolence': 45–85). The central points of this exposition are that not only has God sent prophets and warners to all peoples, and given them the benefit of revelation in one form or another, but also, and perhaps more importantly, that the 'opportunities for improvement' are 'afforded to everyone without distinction' (ibid.: 70). Such indeed is the quality of God's mercy. Non-Muslims may well consider Azad's interpretation presumptuous, but what is significant is that he emphasizes that the Quran teaches the Muslim that the path of righteousness is open to one and all, including those who are currently 'disbelievers', 'transgressors', or even 'wicked'. Nobody will be 'wilfully misled'.

From the manner in which 'divine providence' and 'divine benevolence' are interpreted by Azad, it follows that the third attribute, 'divine justice' (ibid., v: 87–95) too must signify the oneness of humanity, derived from the oneness of God. Azad writes: 'Even as the world of creation owes its existence to the forces of Rububiyat and Rahmat, even so does it need for its maintenance the force of justice' (ibid.: 93).

Section VI of the *Tarjuman* is centrally concerned with the Quranic concept of God, but it is presented in a comparative framework. Azad presents a rapid survey of the emergence of the study of comparative religion in the nineteenth century, briefly mentioning some of the views of sociologists like Herbert Spencer, the cultural anthropologists E.B. Tylor and R.R. Marrett, and the ethnologist W. Schmidt. It is apparent that he did not make a close study of these authors nor was he, perhaps, concerned about their theoretical presuppositions. He then comments on a wide variety of religious traditions including the Chinese, Greek, Judaic, Christian, Buddhist and Hindu. Ian Douglas, a Christian missionary, has contended that Azad's treatment of Judaism and Christianity is not as sympathetic or detailed as that of Hinduism (see Douglas 1988: 207). Personally, I find his exposition of Hindu religious ideas also wanting in several respects.

As an anthropologist, I find his distinction between 'High' and 'Low' or popular Hinduism, and his outright denunciation of the latter, highly unsatisfactory.[4] He was obviously fascinated by the so-called Vedantic monism and for obvious reasons, namely that he found it in consonance with the Islamic concept of '*tawhid*' though not identical with it. The point I wish to make is that Azad's discussion in the *Tarjuman* shows his genuine desire and intellectual effort to familiarize himself with various religious traditions and to use the notion of '*tawhid*' as the organizing principle. How well he

4. The crux of the matter for Azad, as indeed for any orthodox Muslim, is the presence of polytheistic and idolatrous elements in popular Hinduism. Azad would have wanted the Vedantist to reject these elements. He wrote: 'The beauty of the Indian mind and all its great achievements have been clouded by superstition and image worship' (1962: 141). As Mujeeb has noted, this was an aspect of Hindu tolerance which Azad did not consider 'virtuous or even morally justifiable' (1967: 462). In fact, Azad also found the upanishadic procedure of defining the Absolute through negation (*neti, neti*), detrimental to the cultivation of positive religious belief.

succeeds in this is not important for the present discussion. What matters is the effort itself.

In Section VII (pp.145–89) of the book, we have Azad's substantive conclusions on the notion of religious pluralism. His subject is 'divine guidance' or *hidayat*. He writes that what is distinctive about human beings is that they derive guidance not only from 'instincts' and 'the senses', but also from 'reason'. But even reason has its limitations. Perfect guidance ultimately comes from revelation: it is called *'al-huda'*. It comes from God. Azad comments:

> It [the Quran] says that even as instincts, senses and reason are provided to man without distinction of race or colour or circumstances, even so, the directive force of Divine Revelation is meant to afford guidance to everyone without distinction, and has to be distinguished from all other forms of so-called guidance which have become the exclusive preserves of particular communities and have divided mankind into a variety of rival religious groups. It gives to this universal guidance of Revelation the name of *Al-Dīn* or the religion or way of life appropriate to the nature and function of man or *Al-Islām* (1962:152).

Having emphasized in the earlier discussion of the godhead the rectitude of the notion of a single true God of all creation, he now explains:

> The way of God has been one and the same everywhere…. It is the law of "belief and righteous living, of belief in one Supreme Lord of the Universe and of righteous living" in accordance with that belief. Any religion other than this or conflicting with it is not religion in the strict sense of the term (ibid.: 154–5).

He adds: 'So the *Qur'ān* says : The message that all the prophets delivered was that mankind should follow one way, the way of God, *Al-Dīn*, and should not differ from each other in respect of that way' (ibid.:156). Azad called this the doctrine of unity of all religions, *wahdat-e-din*.

Whatever differences exist between different true faiths, he clarified, are differences of 'law' (*sharia*) or the path (*minhaj*), and not of 'faith' (*din*). It is the latter that is of primary importance and constitutes the 'spirit' of religion; the former is only its 'outward manifestation' and therefore 'secondary'. It is not difficult to understand why this should be so. While 'the essential purpose of religion is the progress and well-being of humanity', the social conditions in which human beings find their existence are not 'the same in every clime and at all times'. 'Intellectual and social aptitudes' also differ. Hence the differences of path and practice (see ibid.: 258).

Azad concludes that, according to the Quran, 'Real religion is to offer devotion to God and live a righteous life' (ibid.: 159). The implication of this conclusion is that, since all true religions hold this fundamental belief—in his judgement Upanishadic Hinduism too does so—all of them are equally valid, and there should be no conflict between them : 'the *Qur'ān* asks, "Why should one fight another in the name of God and religion"?' (ibid.:182). All that the followers of each and every true religion have to do is to recover the original purity of their faith, and to realize that the oneness of humankind is rooted in the oneness of God and in the oneness of their original spiritual condition.[5]

Azad's formulation of a religious philosophy of pluralism is beset with several difficulties. On the one hand, the objection may be raised, as Douglas has done, that Azad's 'seeming sympathy towards other religions incorporates an unmistakable opposition to them in their present form' (1988: 210). It should be added, though, that he was also dissatisfied with Islam as generally professed and practised in his own time. On the other hand, the criticisms that were directed by some *ulama* at the *Tarjuman*, soon after the publication of the first volume in 1931, such as the alleged devaluation of some fundamental beliefs (like the Prophet's intermediacy) and essential practices (for example, formal prayer), implied in Azad's emphasis upon personal devotion to God and the pursuit of righteousness, led him to affirm categorically that the Quranic law supersedes those given in other religions. This concession, Douglas asserts, 'undermined his argument... in favour of the accommodation of other living faiths. In spite of this... the *Tarjuman* and Azad's... commentary [on the introductory verses] particularly, show a broadening of this vision' (ibid.: 211).

Once again, I would like to emphasize that what matters is the effort that Azad initiated to build a religious philosophy of pluralism,

---

5. Azad's religious pluralism invites comparison with Gandhi's. This is a large theme, and a brief comment should suffice here. Both believed all religions to be true in their essentials, and stressed the transcendental character of the Divine in which they found the warrant for the unity of religions. The errors of living faiths were, in the judgements of both Azad and Gandhi, the result of the limitations of human reason and the corrosive effects of time. To cite but a single statement by Gandhi which Azad would have readily endorsed: 'All religions are divinely inspired, but they are imperfect because they are products of the human mind and taught by human beings' (see Iyer 1986: 543; see also Chatterji 1983).

grounding it in the unity of all faiths. He was never able to elaborate and refine this exercise, because politics claimed him again in 1937 and remained his sole preoccupation for the next two decades until his death in 1958. During this last period of his life he had to respond to the call of, first, national unity (1937–47) and, then, of contributing to the making of a modern secular state (1947–58).

Azad: Pluralism as Cultural History

In 1940 Azad was called upon a second time in his political career to be the president of the Indian National Congress. Inevitably, at this critical juncture, when the idea of the partition of the country was gaining rapid acceptance among the Muslims, and creating a Hindu backlash, he devoted part of his address to the problem of pluralism and national unity. The English translation from the Urdu was made by Jawaharlal Nehru, and some commentators think it and even the original Urdu text read more like Nehru than Azad's compositions. This must be due to the fact that the argument for national unity that Azad put forward was formulated in terms of the inner dynamics of the cultural history of India. Nehru too had presented a similar analysis two years earlier in an article entitled 'The Unity of India', published in the American journal *Foreign Affairs* (see Nehru 1941). The text of Azad's address is well known and it should suffice for the present purpose to highlight the core of his argument regarding the character of Indian history. He declared:

I am a Muslim and profoundly conscious of the fact that I have inherited Islam's glorious traditions of the last thirteen hundred years. I am not prepared to lose even a small part of that legacy.... I am equally proud of the fact that I am an Indian, an essential part of the indivisible unity of Indian nationhood, a vital factor in its total make-up without which this noble edifice will remain incomplete. I can never give up this claim (see Hameed 1990: 161).

Moving from this personal affirmation, Azad offered a historic statement of India's cultural pluralism.

It was India's historic destiny that its soil should become the destination of many different caravans of races, cultures and religions.... This vast and hospitable land welcomed them all and took them to her bosom.... This fusion was a notable historic event.... These common riches are the heritage of our common nationality and we do not want to leave them and go back to the times when this adventure of a joint life had not begun (ibid.: 162).

The passages quoted above, and certain other speeches and writings of Azad during the 1940s and 1950s, have been cited by some scholars as evidence of a secularist turn in his mode of thinking. I do not agree wholly with this interpretation. In the 1940 speech, as in the 1923 presidential address, Azad's intended audience consisted of both Hindus and Muslims, particularly those among them who conceived of the freedom struggle in national (as opposed to communal) terms. The readers of *Al-Hilal* and *Al-Balagh*, and later of *The Tarjuman al-Quran*, may have included non-Muslims, but the readership Azad had in mind was that of Muslims. His writings in these two journals were manifestly scripturalist and revivalist, and rooted exclusively in his conception of Islam as (in the words of the Quran itself) the religion chosen and perfected by God for those who submit to His will. But, to reiterate what has already been said above, even in this phase of his intellectual and political careers, Azad had never espoused an attitude of hostility towards non-Muslims. Indeed, two years before he launched *al-Hilal* in 1912, he had written in an original essay on the mystic Sarmad that, 'In his search for the goal, he [Sarmad] discarded the distinction between temple and mosque', and asked 'which person of genuine mystical experience would quarrel with this principle?' (see Douglas 1988: 287). Having stated this pluralist credo (at the age of 22), he abided by it until the very end of his life half a century later. The importance of Sarmad's influence on Azad's intellectual and spiritual growth can hardly be exaggerated.

The *Tarjuman* was a fruit of Azad's explicit syncretistic quest and, understandably, he drew upon the tenets and insights of other religions too, notably Vedantic Hinduism, and not Islam alone. It is also obvious that in his speeches and addresses as a leader of the Indian National Congress, from the early 1920s onward, his theses and arguments had to be grounded in a pluralist or, at times, even a seemingly non-religious, secular, idiom.

The assertion that it was in the 1940 address that Azad adopted a 'fully secular basis for Indian nationhood... implicitly repudiating the search for a religious definition' (Ahmad 1992: 165) is, it seems to me, questionable. The 1940 address is undoubtedly a major milestone on the road that Azad took in 1920–21, but it is not a new departure. Moreover, it cannot be construed as a repudiation of his religious worldview, although it could be described as his advocacy of secular (in the sense of religiously pluralist) nationalism. In fact, it is clear from the text that the cultural synthesis that Azad considered the hallmark of the history of India after the arrival of the Muslims in the subcontinent included the dialectic of the religious traditions. Nehru did indeed consider 'culture' as a much broader category than 'religion' in his 1938 article: 'The Indian background and unity were essentially cultural; they were not religious in the narrow sense of the word' (Nehru 1941: 15). He could therefore be said to have repudiated a religious definition of the unity of India. To assert the same in the case of Azad would, however, be at variance with the essential strands of his intellectual biography. He may or may not have, in Muhammad Mujeeb's evocative phrase, always talked the Quran (see Mujeeb 1967: 457), but he never ceased to be, even momentarily, a man gifted with a finely tuned religious sensibility. This does not of course mean that he was a strictly orthodox Muslim.

It may be added here that Mujeeb too detects an overly secularist tone in the posthumously published *India Wins Freedom* (1959), but he clarifies: 'it is indeed undeniable that he could eliminate irrelevant religious considerations when thinking of or discussing purely political issues' (ibid.: 441). In this regard, the crucial passage in Azad's book would seem to be the following, appearing at the very end of his narrative (ibid.: 227):

It is one of the greatest frauds on the people to suggest that religious affinity can unite areas which are geographically, economically, linguistically and culturally different. It is true that Islam sought to establish a society which transcends racial, linguistic, economic and political frontiers. History has however proved that after the first few decades, or at the most after the first century, Islam was not able to unite all the Muslim countries into one State on the basis of Islam alone.

This passage does indeed deny religion a primacy over secular aspects of social life in the making of the histories of Muslim societies, and also plays down the pan-Islamism of the *Al-Hilal* and *Al-Balagh* years, but it can hardly be said to repudiate the crucial importance of religion, which is what a secular approach (in the Enlightenment sense of the word 'secular') would imply. We do not take away anything from Azad's greatness by insisting that he was steadfast throughout his life in his adherence to a religious-pluralist, and in some respects syncretist, outlook. In his own eyes, Azad's endeavour was one of being a true Muslim.

Despite Azad's and Gandhi's opposition, the subcontinent was partitioned in 1947 on the basis of religious difference, the so-called 'two nations theory' of Mohammad Ali Jinnah.[6] Convinced that the partition could and should have been avoided, Azad continued his explorations of India's cultural history which was, in his judgement, characterized by the spirit of pluralism. Addressing the convocation of Patna University a few months after partition (on 21 December 1947), he declared:

[F]rom the dawn of history the Indian mind has been comprehensive and tolerant of every kind of thought... what we actually do not find is the clash of opinions or the breaking of heads merely because of the differences of opinion. This is the one grand feature of ancient Indian culture which has been recognized by a great many thinkers of the modern world (see Nizami 1990: 340).[7]

This image of 'assimilation and synthesis' and of 'unity in diversity' became a refrain, as it were, of his speeches. He also continued to point to similarities and convergences between Islam and Vedantic Hinduism, overplaying his hand on occasion. He claimed (in a 1951 speech) that the Upanishads embodied the earliest exposition of pantheistic thought, and elsewhere maintained that Dara Shukoh (the seventeenth century Mughal prince who translated the Upanishads into Persian in the belief that they were revealed scripture) had been right in pointing out cognitive identities between the Quran and the Upanishads (see ibid.: 39, 45). In an address delievered at Shantiniketan in 1951, he mentioned how attractive he found the Vedantic conception of the One Supreme Being as *Shan-*

6. Delivering his presidential address at the 1940 session of the All-India Muslim League at Lahore, Jinnah observed:
    [Islam and Hinduism] are not religions in the strict sense of the word, but are, in fact, different and distinct social orders. It is a dream that the Hindus and Muslims can ever evolve a common nationality, and this conception of one Indian nation has gone far beyond the limits.... The Hindus and the Muslims belong to two different religious philosophies, social customs, and literatures. They neither intermarry, nor interdine together, and indeed they belong to two different civilizations with are based mainly on conflicting ideas and conceptions.... To yoke together two such nations under a single State... must lead to growing discontent and final destruction of any fabric that may be so built up for the government of such a state (1946: 83).
It may be added that the practice of referring to Hindus and Muslims as 'nations' (*qaum*) goes back to Sayyid Ahmad Khan.
    7. In fact, this characteristic of India's intellectual tradition was noted quite early in the history of the Hindu-Muslim encounter by al-Biruni, who accompanied Mahmud Ghazni to India at the beginning of the eleventh century. In his judgement, unwillingness to die for one's religious beliefs was not exactly a Hindu virtue.

tam (peace), *Shivam* (goodness), and *Advaitam* (ontological one-ness). He even provided an Arabic equivalent for the idea of *advaita*, namely *wahidaha la-shariq*, that is one or that without a second. The sympathetic critic Douglas comments:

If one ignores his unfortunate attempt to identify advaita and tawhid as simply a ceremonial nicety, one can still commend Azad for emphasizing these two tenets of faith, monotheism and the unity of mankind, in another religious tradition. Undoubtedly, these two summarized what Islam meant to him, but they were fundamental in Tagore's faith too (1988: 241–2).

Concluding Remarks

My objective in this chapter has been to argue that, although a secular, anti-theistic worldview is difficult to reconcile with Islam, many South Asian Muslim thinkers and spiritually inclined seekers have, over the centuries looked for what is common between Islam and India's indigenous religions and commended the pluralist attitude. Dara Shukoh may have been the most famous of such seekers, but he certainly was not the only one. In the first half of the twentieth century Abul Kalam Azad was undoubtedly the most distinguished and ardent, though not systematic, exponent of the pluralist position: indeed some of his work is marked by strong syncretistic tendencies.

For Azad the co-existence of religious communities in the Indian subcontinent was a theme of abiding interest all through his adult life. It was first dictated by his politics at a time when he thought of himself as primarily a Muslim who belonged to a worldwide community of believers. Nationalism in the Western sense of the term was of little interest to him. Like his senior contemporary, Muhammad Iqbal, he was a pan-Islamist. It was the political liberation of Muslims in India, conceived of as a religious obligation, rather than that of India, which made co-operation with Hindus (with whom Indian Muslims shared geographical and political space) imperative. From being a political strategy, Hindu-Muslim unity was given a religious foundation in the post-Khilafat days (1923–37). The audience still was Indian Muslims primarily but not exclusively. They were now invited to graduate from a marriage of convenience with Hindus to a harmonious union and to look upon all human beings as the children of one God from who they derived their being and their religions, which are therefore not only all of them true but also actually one.

Finally, came Azad's discovery of India, as it were, as a product of the dialectic of historical forces, containing in its cultural synthesis, or composite culture, diverse cultural, linguistic and religious communities. The distinguished Islamicist, Wilfred Cantwell Smith, has written that the fundamental problem of modern Muslims is how to rehabilitate their Islamic history with which something seems to have gone wrong (1977: 41). Azad, one could say, tried to do this for Indian Muslims by asking them to be part and parcel of the history of India without abandoning their Islamic heritage. 'But', in the words of Aziz Ahmad, 'the *ijma* in the modern sense, of the elite and the masses of the Muslims in the subcontinent, rejected his political views, even though a section of the elite respected his religious thought' (1967: 184). The irony is that Azad derived his political views from religious thought, though in the end he sought justification for them in historical terms too.

Aziz Ahmad's assessment is by no means an isolated instance of its kind. Another noted historian, I.H. Qureshi, regards Azad's pan-Islamist days as 'otherworldly' and 'romantic', and the post-Khilafat nationalist phase of his political activity as of no use in the furtherance of Muslim interests (see Qureshi 1962: 258–60). More recently, Aijaz Ahmad, a sympathetic commentator, has observed: 'Azad remains a strict Islamic theologian—though unsatisfactory to most of the theological elite, whom he primarily addresses [in the *Tarjuman*] precisely because of his ecumenism' (1992: 139). Incidentally, it may be noted here that, Aijaz Ahmad regards Azad's exposition of the 'complementarities' between India's two major religions as involving the selective 'incorporation' of Hinduism within Islam. I would substitute 'hierarchical incorporation' for simple incorporation, in keeping with the emphasis upon relations rather than entities or substances that characterizes the analytical approach of this book.

It may be added here that Azad was painfully aware of his limited and after 1940 (when the demand for partition was formally made) waning following among the Muslims. Mohammad Ali Jinnah publicly denounced him as a 'showboy' of the Congress. The bitterness of Azad's feelings may be guaged by his address to the Muslims of Delhi from the Jama Masjid on 23 October 1947. It is a short address, in Urdu prose of high quality, clear, and directly from the heart (see Azad 1990); the English translation from which I quote is by Hameed (1990: 170–1): 'Do you remember? I hailed you, you cut off my tongue; I picked my pen, you severed my hand; I wanted to move forward, you broke off my legs; I tried to turn over, you injured my back.... The partition of India was a fundamental mistake...'.

After partition and independence, India opted for a secular (in the sense of non-discriminatory) state. All the recognized ideologues in the government—including Sarvepalli Radhakrishnan, Jawaharlal Nehru, and Abul Kalam Azad—clarified that in the Indian conception, the secular state was not against religion (in the sense that, say, the Soviet state was) but only neutral. The Constitution included under Fundamental Rights the right of every citizen to profess, practise, and propagate the religion of his or her cultural heritage or choice (Article 25). Indian Muslims generally welcomed this conception of the secular state. Even the Jamaat-i-Islami (founded by Abul ala Maududi) did so. It declared:

Secularism as a state policy which implies that there should be no discrimination or partiality on the basis of belief can hardly be questioned. The Jamaᶜat has categorically stated that in the present circumstances it wants the secular form of government to continue.... But if beyond this utilitarian expediency some people have the deeper philosophical connotations in mind, we beg to differ. The philosophical connotations are essentially Western in origin, and carry a spirit and a history which are totally foreign to our temper and needs (see Mushir-ul-Haq 1972: 11–12).

The foregoing statement of the fundamentalist position is clear but not unambiguous. It is silent on the pluralist alternative that Azad espoused and implicitly rejects it. Its acceptance of the secular state resulted from its apprehension that the alternative would be a Hindu state. In fact, Maududi himself had advised the Hindus (apparently, he included Buddhists, Jains and Sikhs among Hindus) to shape the Indian polity on the basis of guidance that they may be able to derive from their own scriptures (see ibid.: 9). His followers in India thought otherwise, but not all Indian Muslims were his followers.

Among those who were not, there have been many intellectuals who have made further contributions to the elaboration of a cultural pluralist, or secular nationalist, argument from a Muslim point of view. They are all of them indebted, though in different degrees, to Azad's earlier formulations.[8] Most of them, emphasize secular nationalist politics and do not pay much attention to the construction

---

8. It is rather ironical that Abul ala Maududi too was influenced by Azad's early writings. Their final destinations, however, turned out to be, as we have seen, quite distant one from the other.

of a philosophical argument also (see Miller 1987). Among those who do so, Hasan Askari's is an interesting attempt, arguing that, 'For a religion to remain a religion it should be inter-religious' (1977: 108). But his concrete concern is with the Muslim-Christian dialogue. India presents a far more complex challenge than the encounter of Abrahamic religions, and we have yet to see a more systematic if not a wholly successful effort to meet it than Abul Kalam Azad's.

Chapter
Six

The Hindu Religious Tradition
Secularism as Pluralism

Personally, I think the world as a whole will never have, and need not have,
a single religion.
MAHATMA GANDHI, 30 May 1913

The worshippers of the Absolute [among Hindus] are the highest in rank;
second to them are the worshippers of the personal God; then come the
worshippers of the incarnations like Rama, Krishna, Buddha; below them are
those who worship ancestors, deities and sages; and lowest of all are the
worshippers of the petty forces and spirits.
S. RADHAKRISHNAN, *The Hindu View of Life*

On the level of pure religious thought, the Hindus are the group who have
gone furthest in interpreting religious diversity, in making room in their
religious philosophy for the fact that other people have their faiths.... But the
Hindus with their caste system, negate their intellectual breadth by a social intolerance that is the most rigid in the world.
WILFRED CANTWELL SMITH, *Islam in Modern History*

Introduction

An exploration of the ideologies of secularism and fundamentalism
as defined in this book in the context of the Hindu religious tradition,
immediately runs into two problems. First, it has been asserted by
historians that Hinduism is a 'deceptive term', 'difficult to define',
and special care has to be exercised in its 'proper use' (von
Stietencron 1991). Thus, if it has no identifiable founder, no single
canonical text so acknowledged by one and all, no church-like
organization, and no fundamentals of belief and practice, how valid
is it to speak of Hindu fundamentalism? Second and, I think, more
importantly, many scholars have questioned whether the sacred-

secular dichotomy of domains is at all present in the Hindu religious tradition, or present only in a sense which is different from that of the Christian perspective on the subject, so that secularism in the sense in which it is generally understood in the West, and in social science literature, may not be a relevant category of description here. Although I do not want to get enmeshed in these definitional controversies, some elaboration of the two problems, and a brief response to the sceptical attitude that underlies them, would be in order.

Historians generally seem to agree that the English term 'Hinduism' (and its equivalents in other European languages, notably French and German) came to be used only around 1830 A.D. It was in all probability coined, or at least given currency, by Christian missionaries, who emphasized the dark side of the religion of the Hindus, with its 'superstitious beliefs' and 'sordid practices'. Indologists, who acclaimed the Hindus' intellectual and literary achievements, were quick to pick up and popularize the word 'Hinduism'. Functionaries of the East India Company, and later of the British Government of India, imbued with the utilitarian ideas of the times, also found it convenient for administrative purposes. Ethnographic notes on Hindu castes and 'animist' tribes began to be compiled in Bengal early in the nineteenth century. When the first large-scale census operations got under way in 1881, religion was considered an obvious basis for social classification. Hinduism and Islam, and other faiths too, were thus accorded official recognition, the former two as the major religions of the provinces comprising British India, and indeed of the entire subcontinent. Hindus were thus found to constitute almost four-fifths of the total population, and the notions of Hindu *majority* and Muslim *minority* were born.

Those who were counted as Hindus included many religious communities and sects, often highly localized, such as the Jains and the Sikhs. Some of these groups did not call themselves Hindus and were not given access to high-caste temples because they were considered ritually impure. They were not, however, drastically different from their Hindu neighbours in terms of religious belief and practice. The census enumerators and other lower-level employees of the government were mostly Brahmans, or drawn from the upper castes and Brahmanized to different degrees, and they were instrumental in establishing a new Brahmanical hegemony and the notion of Hinduism as an 'all-India' religion (see Thapar 1989; Inden

1990; Oberoi 1994). Some historians find the idea of a well-defined and monolithic Hindu community infuriatingly 'erroneous' and even 'dangerous' (Frykenberg 1991), but it has taken root.

Actually, many Brahmans themselves were frankly puzzled by the notion of Hinduism as a religion in the same sense as Christianity or Islam. One of the tallest Indian intellectuals of the second half of the nineteenth century, Bankimchandra Chatterji, wrote: 'There is no Hindu conception answering to the term "Hinduism", and the question..."What is Hinduism?" can only be answered by defining what it is that the foreigners who use the word mean by the term' (see Bagal 1969: 231). Such early reservations notwithstanding, Hinduism gained rapid currency. As Romila Thapar has observed, 'The need for postulating a Hindu community became a requirement for political mobilization in the 19th century when representation by religious community became a key to power and where such representation gave access to economic resources' (1989: 210).

By the early twentieth century, Hinduism was well established in both political and scholarly discourses. Max Weber commented upon its recency, but freely used 'Hinduismus' (in German) in his studies of world religions in the second decade of the century. The word occurs in the English translation of M.K. Gandhi's autobiography (*My Experiments with Truth*) and in S. Radhakrishnan's Hibbert Lectures at Oxford (*The Hindu View of Life*), both published in 1927. The number of scholars—Indologists, historians, social anthropologists, and others—who have since used the term is literally legion, and includes such distinguished names as Ananda Coomaraswamy, R.C. Zaehner, Louis Dumont, and M.N. Srinivas. They all recognize the internally heterogenous character of modern Hinduism, with its 'all-India', regional, and local versions—a classification first used by Srinivas in his classic work on the Coorgs (1952)—and with its elements derived from the classical textual tradition, going back to the Vedic period of three thousand or more years ago, and from oral folk cults or 'popular Hinduism', so-called. These traditions have been dynamically interrelated over the millennia, through such processes as 'parochialization' (or percolation) of elements derived from the Great Tradition, and 'universalization' of those derived from the Little Traditions (see Marriott 1955). Depending upon what the purpose of a particular inquiry is, one may focus on the congeries that is Hinduism, or on its constituent religions, individually or collectively, which share a 'family resemblance' (having some but not necessarily the same features, or a key feature, in common).

The terminological issue apart, the idea of a religion of the Hindus generally is historically well established. Al-Biruni characterized it by, among other features, belief in the divinity, soul, *samsara* or metempsychosis, and *moksha* or liberation; the existence of sacred books and divinely instituted *varnas* or social classes; and the practice of idol worship, pilgrimages, etc., in his celebrated *Tarikhul Hind* early in the eleventh century (see Al-Biruni 1983). As a term of self-ascription, the word 'Hindu' has been traced to the fifteenth century (Thapar 1989: 224).

Whether Hinduism as the religion of the Hindus generally is a nineteenth century invention, or has deeper roots in time, does not seem to be a very significant question for the purposes of the present work. As the distinguished French Indologist, Louis Renou, insightfully puts it, 'In India everything is in one sense older, and in another sense of more recent origin than is generally supposed' (1953: 46). Moreover, it should be obvious that those scholars, Indian or Western, who describe Hinduism as a figment of the Orientalist imagination, are closed-minded in their denial of the validity of developments within the religious traditions of the Hindus that have actually occured during the last one hundred and fifty years and to which the Hindus themselves have contributed actively. To conclude, then, it is futile and rather pedantic to insist on the artificial character of modern Hinduism,[1] as if all reality were not socially constructed. I have no doubt that it makes good sense to pose questions about the ideologies of secularism and fundamentalism in the context of the Hindu religious tradition in its textual if not oral versions.

---

1. Some authors go further and question whether 'dharma', used as a synonym for 'religion', is religion at all in the sense in which Judaism, Christianity and Islam, and even Sikhism, are so. This is an important and interesting query and was raised by, for example, Wilfred Cantwell Smith (1978: 51–118), who argued that calling Hinduism a religion amounts to reifying an abstraction. S. Radhakrishnan (1927) avoided the word religion and instead spoke of 'the Hindu way of life'. I am not interested in pursuing this question here, but recognize the need for caution against uncritical comparison and hasty generalization. Those who have specialized in Indian cultural studies speak and write of Hinduism as a religion, and I follow this practice. I do not think there is much scope for misunderstanding unless, of course, one is interested in creating it.

The Unity of the Sacred and the Secular

The more significant of the two problems mentioned at the beginning of this chapter is, I think, that of the sacred-secular dichotomy. This is an ideological question, and an answer to it must be sought in the first place in the work of those persons who formally engage in such discussions. In other words, what light does the textual tradition throw on this issue?

Basing his discussion mainly on the texts called the Brahmanas, but also on the *Rig Veda*, Ananda Coomarswamy (1942) developed a crucial distinction between 'spiritual authority', or Sacerdotium (*brahma*), and 'temporal power', or Regnum (*kshatra*). According to the texts (see especially *Shatapatha Brahmana* 4.1.4.2–6), originally the two functions were distinct, but later a union was effected at the initiative of Varuna the Regnum, for Varuna 'could not subsist apart from Mitra the Sacerdotium'. It was thus that the Sacerdotium came to have precedence assigned to it: 'I assign to you the precedence; quickened by thee I shall do deeds'. The point to stress is that the so-called Oriental despot is not an absolute or arbitrary ruler, but 'subject of another King ... the Law (*dharma*), than which there is nothing higher'. In other words, 'The Regnum is not its own principle, but is controlled by another, the Eternal Law, the Truth (*dharma, Satyam*)'. This *'Reductio regni ad sacerdotium'* is, Coomaraswamy points out, effected through the rituals of kingship (see Coomaraswamy 1978: 8, 16, 46, 50, et passim).[2]

2. The *Rig Veda* (IV.50.8) says: 'He lives prosperous in his abode, to him the earth is prodigal of all its gifts, to him the people are obedient of their own accord, that *rājan* [king] in whose house the Brahman walks in the first place'. Describing this as an instance of a 'bipartite conception of sovereignty' found among Indo-Europeans, Georges Dumezil observed more than half a century ago: 'In India, in the very earliest times, *rāj* (or *rājan*) and *brahman* existed in a true symbiosis in which the latter protected the former against the magico-religious risks inherent in the exercise of the royal function, while the former maintained the latter in a place equal to or above his own' (1988: 22).

Jan Gonda also draws repeated attention to 'the unmistakable existence of a belief [in Vedic texts] in a complementary relation between both components of this divine duality [Mitra-and-Varuna].... I would even say that this is a very early and clear instance of a curious trend in the history of Indian religions, viz. the tendency to view and represent ideas, figures, or divine powers as complementary and co-operative' (1974: 155–6).

This central Brahmanical theme of the union of the sacred and the secular (see *Aitareya Brahmana* 3.11, *Jaiminiya Upanishad Brahmana* 2.2.8; *Shatapatha Brahmana* 2.5.4.8) has been discussed by some modern scholars, who implicitly reject the notion of a dichotomy of domains, though they qualify the rejection in various respects. Thus Louis Dumont gives an interesting interpretation. Drawing upon the same textual sources as Coomaraswamy, namely the *Rig Veda* and the *Brahmanas*, he points out that the king depends on the Brahman priest (*purohita*, he who is placed in the front) for the success of all that he does as king. 'Temporal authority is guaranteed through the personal relationship in which it gives preeminence over itself to spiritual authority incarnated in the *purohita*' (Dumont 1962: 51). By this act, the king loses his 'hierarchical preeminence in favour of the priests, retaining for himself power only.' Now comes the crucial element of the argument:

Through this dissociation, the function of the king in India has been *secularized*. It is from this point that a differentiation has occured, the separation within the religious universe of a sphere or realm which is opposed to the religious, and roughly corresponds to what we call political. As opposed to the realm of values and norms it is the realm of force. As opposed to the *dharma* or universal order of the Brahman, it is the realm of interest or advantage, *artha* (ibid.: 55).

Having introduced the dichotomy of domains, Dumont feels the need to enter a caveat. First, he maintains that, the very core of the notion of kingship is everywhere, including India, permeated with magico-religious ideas. Secondly, and more importantly, in the absence of the emergence of the ideologies of individualism and nationalism, 'in India the autonomy of the [secular] domain remains relative, and within it economics and politics remain undifferentiated'. In contrast to what happened in the West, the emergence of an autonomous political domain in India 'took place *within* the given framework without altering it or emancipating itself from it' (ibid.: 76). It did not become 'absolutely autonomous in relation to religion', and failed to ascend to the level of 'universal value'.

Using the idiom which Dumont developed fully after his essay on kingship in ancient India was written, we may say that the relationship between the domains or principles of *dharma* and *artha* is hierarchical: although *artha* is opposed to *dharma*, it is not completely separated from the latter, like Weber (1958) mistakenly believed it was, but is encompassed by it. It may be noted here parenthetically that Dumont does not refer to Weber's contrast of China and India in terms of, respectively, an alleged complete fusion or total separation of political authority and priestly power. In an earlier statement on the traditional (Hindu) theory of goal-oriented action, Dumont had written:

> To say that *artha* [which he translated as 'calculating egotism' or 'instrumental action' and categorized as an 'inferior ideal'] corresponds to the royal function should not be taken to mean that the king is not subject to *dharma* ['moral universalism' or 'moral action', the 'superior ideal']: the hierarchy of ends governs all, but *artha* defines the particular sphere of royal activity (1960: 41–2, fn. 14).

Two points in Dumont's formulation call for discussion. First, how autonomous is 'relatively autonomous'? Second, is the language of 'superior and inferior' appropriate? Apparently, Dumont considers relative autonomy to be significant enough to write of the secularization of kingship. Indeed, in the general context of the caste system as a whole, he writes of an absolute dysjunction of 'status and power, and consequently spiritual authority and temporal authority' (1980: 71–2). This dysjunction does not, however, by itself amount to the secularization of power. Such a conception has been questioned by Indologists who write with authority on the subject.

Dumont's French colleague, Madeleine Biardeau, for instance, echoes his basic formulation when she writes: 'the svadharma of the king and that of the Brahman are more than ever complementary and opposed'. She acknowledges that the domain of *artha* has its own 'techniques' and 'norms', but clarifies: 'It would be unacceptable for the royal function, so central to the maintenance of the social order, not to be fully integrated into the socio-economic order, dharma, which unites heaven and earth, the gods and men' (1989: 54). Elsewhere, writing about the concept of king's *svadharma* (that is, dharma appropriate to one's inborn nature and station in life) in the *Mahabharata*, Biardeau points out that, 'the Kshatriya gained access to salvation through his specific and impure [secular] activities', and thus his traditional roles, including that of the warrior, were included in 'the realm of ultimate values' (1982: 97). In short, Biardeau recognizes the secular content of kingship, but hardly allows it any autonomy.

Jan Gonda and Jan Heesterman, two distinguished Dutch Indologists, present a more complex picture of the nature of kingship.

Gonda writes (as indeed do all authorities on the subject) that the key to the king's manifold functions is that he, far from being arbitrary, is the upholder of dharma and thus maintains social order. I would like to point out that it is in this sense that the well-known proclamation in the Shantiparva of the *Mahabharata* (63, 25ff.) that *rajadharma* is the premier dharma is to be understood. Indeed, the epic itself says so quite early (3, 207, 26). Citing the *Brihadarnyaka Upanishad* (I, 4, 11ff.), Gonda writes (1969: 20):

In the beginning this world was brahman. As it did not flourish because it was alone, it created ksatra power, or rather *that emanated from it*, and afterwards the third and fourth classes. Yet "he" (i.e. brahman viewed as a creator and as the universe) did not yet flourish. He therefore created dharma, that is to say: *this too emanated from brahma*. That dharma is the ruling power of the ksatriya class (*kṣtrasya kṣtram*).

What is being stressed here is the presence of a single principle of social integration; there is no separate principle governing the political realm. 'It is therefore from the Indian point of view quite reasonable', Gonda adds, 'that the king's power is checked by the brahmans who are brahman incarnate' (ibid.: 67). Emphasizing the traditional point of view as elaborated in such key texts as the *Mahabharata* (1, 3), Gonda further observes that 'king and purohita are, for the sake of the well-being of the kingdom, an inseparable pair; they are each other's complement' (ibid.: 66; see also Gonda 1974: 156).

Heesterman is of the opinion that, originally, the roles of the Brahman priest and the king appear to have been interchangeable, and the warrior-Brahman is a respected figure in the *Atharva Veda*. A subsequent split brought about by Brahman ritual-reformers created an ambiguity, if not an asymmetrical dependence, which was never overcome in the literature on the subject. Although 'the religious aspect of kingship' was recognized as 'primary', yet 'a consolidated theory of sacral kingship' was not developed. Kingship remained, Heesterman writes, 'suspended between sacrality and secularity, divinity and mortal humanity, legitimate authority and arbitrary power, dharma and adharma' (1985: 111). It was denied 'authority and legitimacy of its own' by the texts. Thus, according to the *Shatapatha Brahmana*, our author notes, 'the *brahman* can stand on its own, the *kṣatra*, however cannot and depends on the *brahman*' (ibid: 112). Pointing out that traditional theory does not permit the king to derive his authority from the community—it has to be derived from a transcendent source—Heesterman concludes: 'The king, therefore, desperately needs the brahmin to sanction his power by linking it to the brahmin's authority' (ibid: 27).

Read together, the views of Coomaraswamy, Dumont, Biardeau, Gonda, and Heesterman point to the conclusion that the autonomy of the king as the supreme symbol of secular power, although present, is, in fact, so bounded in the Vedic corpus as to provide no obvious grounds for constructing a theory of the secular state for our times that might legitimize the autonomy of secular power by invoking traditional non-religious values.[3]

The post-Vedic *Smriti* or *Shastra* texts introduce important variations on the theme of the *brahma-kshatra* relationship, with *brahma* as the encompassing principle, but basically confirm the earlier position outlined above. The most crucial development, which seemingly proposed the concept of pure power (power for the sake of power, self-legitimized), is a formulation in the very first book of Kautilya's *Arthashastra* (AS, *ca.* 300 BC). It reads as follows: *Artha eva pradhāna iti Kauṭilyaḥ, arthamulau hi dharmakāmav iti* (AS I. vii. 6,7): '"Material well-being alone is supreme", says Kautilya. For, spiritual good and sensual pleasures depend upon material well-being' (Kangle 1972:14). The categories in terms of which the argument is constructed are not *brahma* and *kshatra*, but *dharma* (spiritual good), *artha* (material well-being), and *kama* (sensual pleasures). That Kautilya wanted this statement about the primacy of *artha*, which denotes both economic and political power, to be

---

3. Cf. Smith 1994: 27: 'In the Veda, at least, such dichotomies are probably misapplied—the Kshatriya's royal and military power are infused with "spirituality", and the Brahman's "spirituality" is represented as one kind, indeed the best kind, of coercive power'.

It may be pointed out here that classical formulations find echoes in contemporary beliefs and practices. Writing about the notion of kingship on the basis of intensive observation of temple rituals in Puri (Orissa), in which the king takes active part even now (after the integration of princely states in the Indian Union), Frédérique Marglin questions Dumont's thesis of the secularization of kingship, although she acknowledges that 'kingship is subordinated to as well as outside of the principle of pure and impure' (1982: 156). In other words, Marglin finds the relationship of religious status and royal power more complex than Dumont recognizes it to be. Further, it may be noted that, many of the symbols and functions of traditional Hindu (and Muslim) kingship have been taken over by the modern state (see Appadurai 1981 and Mayer 1982), which is not therefore wholly an innovation.

regarded as crucially significant is obvious from the literary device of self-quotation.

The text presents us with a problem, however, in the form of the immediately preceding formulation (AS I. vii. 4,5). Writing of the king, Kautilya prescribes that, '(he should devote himself) equally to the three goals of life which are bound up with one another. For, any one of (the three, viz.,) spiritual good, material well-being and sensual pleasures, (if) excessively indulged in, does harm to itself as well as the other two' (Kangle 1972:14). There is an obvious contradiction between the two formulations (in verses 4–5 and 6–7). The translator I have quoted comments tersely but correctly: 'It appears that Kautilya was the first to assign a high place to *artha* as against *dharma* and *kāma*' (ibid.). Many a commentator has tried to overlook the contradiction, and surreptitiously ignores the formulation that does not find favour with him. R. Shamasastry, who discovered the text and published it in 1909, observes more helpfully than Kangle that, 'one or two passages embodying the opinions of others seem to have been omitted' (1967: 12,n.1), but he does not say by whom. The conclusion that emerges is that Kautilya first states the traditional position on the important subject of the mutual relationship of the three goals or orientations of human endeavour, and then proclaims his own radically different opinion, elevating *artha* above *dharma*.

A contemporary philosopher, K. J. Shah, insists, however, that the second formulation (AS, verses 6–7) must be read in the light of the first (AS, verses 4–5), that is we must read backwards to reach the conclusion that, 'artha will not be artha if it is not in accordance with dharma' (Shah 1982: 60). He argues that 'The four goals [he includes moksha or liberation as the fourth goal] constitute one single goal, though in the lives of individuals the elements may get varying emphasis for various reasons'. Summing up, Shah observes: 'artha alone as a goal is greed, kama alone is lust, dharma alone is mechanical ritual, and moksa alone is escapism' (ibid.: 59). He concludes that a reading of the *Arthashastra* such as he suggests is in consonance with the temper of the text as a whole, which was underlined by Kautilya himself at the end (before he signed off): 'This science brings into being and preserves spiritual good, material well-being and pleasures, and destroys spiritual evil, material loss and hatred' (AS XV.i.72; Kangle 1972: 516).

Shah's insistence that Kautilya's *Arthashastra* should not be read as proposing a thesis about the autonomy or priority of secular power, totally at variance with the tradition, is justified by the fact that Kautilya himself conforms to the Vedic tradition in many formulations such as the ones defining caste duties and the relationship between the king and his domestic chaplain (*purohita*). It may be noted here that, at the very outset, the *Arthashastra* includes the Vedas in the list of the sciences, alongside of economics and politics (AS I. 2.1). As for the chaplain, Kautilya writes (AS. I. 9.9) that, after appointing a person of noble family and character, well-trained in the Vedas, as his domestic priest, the king should 'follow him as a pupil (does) his teacher, a son his father, (or) a servant his master' (Kangle 1972: 18). This is explicit enough. In any case, scholarship on the subject is agreed that 'among the *artha* treatises only the Kautilya *Arthashastra* ... emphasizes the general priority of *artha*', and that in the post-Kautilya literature, 'there is a tendency to reinstate the priority of *dharma*' (Wilhelm 1978: 70,69).[4]

The *Manusmriti* (MS, 100 BC?–AD 100?) does not alter the above position, but only confirms it. Thus, having placed *danda* (coercive force, punishment) at the very centre of socio-political order—'The whole world is kept in order by punishment' (MS VII.22; Buhler 1886: 219)—the treatise draws attention of the king to his twin roles

---

4. Kautilya is often compared with Machiavelli. U.N. Ghosal finds many parallels between the contents of the works of the two authors (if one may write of the *Arthashastra* as having a single author), but concludes that, while Kautilya's 'statecraft' was 'limited and selfish, for it consisted in ensuring the security and stability of the king's rule inside the kingdom and its progressive advance towards the goal of universal dominion outside the same', the impulse that animated Machiavelli's work was 'a burning patriotism which sought passionately for the deliverance of his unhappy motherland' (1966: 154).

J.C. Heesterman points to another contrast, however, rejecting the generally held view that the 'notorious *Arthashastra*' formulates an amoral science of politics: 'Herein, it would seem, lies the essential difference with Machiavelli, who decisively breaks away from the concept of politics as part and parcel of the scholastic *philosophia ethica* (or *moralis*). Kautilya's sobriquet "Indian Machiavelli" is all too glib' (1985: 111, 231 n.30).

The issue is indeed contentions. Pitrim Sorokin, a Harvard sociologist, wrote that he did not find in the *Arthashastra* 'a purely secular, empirical and morally cynical standpoint so pronounced as in many Western works beginning with Machiavelli's *Prince*' (quoted in Sarkar 1985: 639). Benoy Sarkar, his Calcutta contemporary, called it 'a secular work with vengeance' (ibid.). Sarkar asserted that 'materialism' was 'the foundation' of 'Hindu civilization' (ibid.: 635), but this is hardly proven. Even the old Charvaka school of philosophy never became ascendant.

as protector and dispenser of punishment (that is justice), and advises him to worship Brahmans first thing in the morning, learn the Vedas and other sciences from them, and take counsel with the most distinguished of all learned Brahmans on matters of royal policy. He is further asked to appoint a domestic chaplain (*purohita*) and officiating priests (*ritvig*) so that all the appropriate domestic rituals are performed. Finally, he is told that his happiness lies in vanquishing his enemies, protecting his subjects, and honouring the Brahmans (MS VII. 28, 37, 43, 58, 78, 88). All these directions point to the dependence of the king on the Brahman, or, in other words, the primacy of *dharma* over *artha*.

Robert Lingat (1973: 217) has summed up the position of the *smriti* texts on this issue quite succinctly: 'The role of the *purohita* is multiple.... He is far from being simply a priest with the duty to see that the king fulfils his religious obligations.... In reality the *purohita* is the brain of the king. As servant of *dharma* he is a servant of the state' (1973: 217; see also Kane 1973: 117–9). It may be clarified here that the Brahman serves the state because the ordering principle of the polity is dharma rather than force which is its instrument. Lingat (ibid.: 217–18) rightly concludes:

It would be vain to look in Indian tradition on the relations between the two powers for an analogy with the Christian theory of the Two Swords. True, the Brahman is master when the question is one of ritual and... of penance. But his scope extends in reality over all the field of royal activity, as much on its political side as on its religious. There are no two powers here each functioning in its proper sphere, the sacred to one side, and the profane [secular] to the other. Secular power alone has the capacity to act, but it is a blind force which needs to be directed before its application can be effectual.

It is not necessary to continue this exposition of what the classical texts say on the interdependence of *dharma* and *artha* (and *kama* too), with *dharma* ordering or encompassing the other two orientations. One may well conclude by recalling what the *Mahabharata* (*ca.* BC 400–400 AD), the great epic about kingship, has to say on the subject: 'He who wishes to achieve *kama* and *artha* must first concentrate on *dharma*, for *kama* and *artha* are never separate from *dharma*' (V.124. 37). More to the point, (and as already noted earlier) the *Mahabharata* (12.63. 25–9) acclaims the king's dharma as the premier dharma, but this only underscores his duty to uphold all dharmas, those that are context-sensitive (such as *jati dharma*) and those that are general (*sadharna*).[5]

To conclude, the relative autonomy that Dumont grants to the political function seems to be severely circumscribed, more than might at first seem manifest. He is quite right, therefore, to express the relationship of spiritual authority and temporal power in terms of superiority and inferiority, or encompassing and encompassed, and not complete separation *à la* Weber who presented Hindu kingship as self-sufficient and fully secular.

Religious Pluralism

In view of the above, one would only expect that the scholars who want to present the traditional Hindu point of view on today's problems, notably a widely acknowledged crisis of secularism in India, will have difficulties finding a time-honoured basis for even the secular state, completely detached from religious values and the authority of the Brahman-priest, not to speak of ideological support for a fully-fledged secularist worldview. Mahatma Gandhi, arguing from an avowedly traditional point of view, rejected secularism as a

5. It would be appropriate to cite the opinion of Pandurang Vaman Kane, the most distinguished contemporary authority on *dharmashastra* literature, on this subject, but he does not formulate his commentary in terms of a separation or union of functions or powers. This is of course in itself instructive. The following observations sum up Kane's point of view. 'Arthaśastra ... is properly speaking a part of the dharmaśastra... [and] is supposed to have like dharmaśastrā a divine source' (1973: 8–9). As for the dictates of dharma, the king was obliged to consult his chaplain (*purohita*) and other learned Brahmans (ibid.: 96–7). Kane acknowledges, however, that the formal position notwithstanding, both the *Mahabharata* and the *Arthashastra* 'support in several places the adoption of means entirely divorced from all rules of fair dealing and morality' (ibid.: 10).

I will not discuss A.M. Hocart's idiosyncratic view that the 'kings' are the 'first caste', for not only does he too acknowledge that 'royalty and priesthood form a pair' (1950:38), but also acknowledges the superiority of the sacred when he proclaims that 'every occupation is a priesthood' (ibid.:16).

A final comment. The conceptualization of the relationship of spiritual or priestly authority and temporal power in the Hindu tradition is essentially the same as in the early Christian formulation of Pope Gelasius, noted earlier (see page 8). It is comparable to the medieval Muslim theologian Zia-ud-Din Barani's notion of prophets and kings as 'twin brothers' (see page 118).

preferred way of life if it stood for the divorce of politics from religion; but he endorsed the idea of a secular state which did not interfere in the religious lives of the people and was in that manner impartial (see Chapters Seven and Eight).

It has been asserted by many modern Hindu intellectuals, however, that the Hindus do not need to take lessons from other cultural traditions, for their own tradition is in fact secular. Nirad Chaudhuri, an acute commentator on the course and significance of contemporary events in India, writes: 'In India secularism of even the highest European type is not needed, for Hinduism as a religion is itself secular and it has sanctified worldliness by infusing it with moral and spiritual qualities. To take away that secularism from the Hindus is to make them immoral, and culturally debased' (1987: 881).

This may seem to be basically a restatement of the kind of holism which Gandhi espoused, although with a characteristic verbal twist that can only be confusing. But Chaudhuri does not mean to say that, contrary to what is often alleged, Hinduism is this-worldly but its worldliness is religious. He rather argues that the religious life of the Hindus is worldly in orientation, and that the world of gods reflects the world of men, a position vaguely reminiscent of the classical Durkheimean (sociologistic) position on the subject (see Durkheim 1965; see also Dumont 1970b). In the event, 'Hinduism is a social contract between two acquisitive communities' (1979: 14), and *artha* rules everywhere; but *artha* has its rules, its specific morality, and Hinduism is not wholly 'sordid'. Chaudhuri acknowledges the supremacy of dharma, in all domains including the material, but calls it a moral rather than a religious 'entity' (ibid.: 17). The distinction between morality and religion is of only limited interest in the present context, and I will not further examine it.

A more familiar line of argument discards the notion of secularism as a rationalist worldview, according to which religion is excluded from societal space or, at best, granted legitimacy only in the privacy of individual lives. This argument adopts the idea of secularism as *religious pluralism*, which stands for non-preferentialism as state policy and of inter-religious tolerance as social philosophy. Moreover, religious pluralism is said to be a traditional Brahmanical idea that was revived and restated by Hindu social reformers of the late nineteenth and twentieth centuries. Swami Vivekananda (1863–1902) was perhaps the first modern intellectual to vigorously present tolerance, and indeed acceptance, as the correct Hindu position on the phenomenon of religious difference. Addressing the Parliament of Religions at Chicago in 1893, he declared (Vivekananda 1972: 3):

I am proud to belong to a religion which has taught the world both tolerance and universal acceptance. We believe not only in universal toleration, but we [also] accept all religions as true. I am proud to belong to a nation which has sheltered the persecuted and the refugees of all religions and all nations of the earth.

Vivekananda's spiritual mentor, Sri Ramakrishna (1836–86), had in his own life and teachings tried to realize the oneness of the religious quest, not only by affirming the truth of all available paths of spiritual realization within the Hindu world, but also by temporarily suspending his Hindu identity and living the life of a practising Muslim (see Isherwood 1965: 124–5). Needless to stress, there is a continuity from Rammohun Roy's consensual theology (see Chapter Seven) to Vivekananda's universalist praxis via Ramakrishna's pluralist personal experience (*siddhi*). In fact, Roy's early endeavour appears modest in retrospect compared to the immensity of Ramakrishna's spiritual quest and the vast scope of Vivekananda's 'mission', which was to establish the supremacy of Vedantic Hinduism on a worldwide basis.

In his younger years as a temple priest and religious devotee, Ramakrishna had shown an amazing openness of mind in respect of religious beliefs and practices, embracing Vedic-Puranic texts and rituals, Vaishnava-Shakta concepts and worship, *Tantra*, and even obscure rustic cults (see Sarkar 1993: 47). But, as he grew older, and emerged as a revered guru among the gentry of Calcutta, he tended to be more selective, and favoured the higher tradition of Brahmanism and *bhakti* (theistic devotionalism). Further, he stressed that once a path had been chosen, one should stick to it and not risk failure in the spiritual quest. Sumit Sarkar observes that Ramakrishna's teaching reflected the medieval, pluralist, Brahmanical doctrine of difference (*adhikara bheda*) and, indeed, had deeper roots in the classical notion of *svadharma*, that is the spiritual path appropriate to one's social status (caste) (ibid.: 48) and, I may add, personal nature (*svabhava*). The seer's familiarity with other religious traditions, his 'foray' into Islam notwithstanding, was 'fairly minimal' (ibid.: 46). In other words, inter-religious pluralism was not a dominant theme of Ramakrishna's religious quest: he was indeed eclectical in his approach but primarily within the Hindu fold.

Vivekananda's message of tolerance and indeed acceptance was formally addressed to the followers of all religious faiths, but it was given from a Hindu platform, as it were:

[W]e not only tolerate, but we Hindus accept every religion, praying in the mosque of the Mohammedans, worshipping the fire of the Zoroastrians, and kneeling before the cross of Christians, knowing that all the religions, from the lowest fetishism to the highest absolutism, mean so many attempts of the human soul to grasp and realise the infinite, each determined by the conditions of its birth and association, and each of them marking a stage of progress (Vivekananda 1972: 331–2).

As a statement of ideals which Vivekananda may have truly held dear, the foregoing declaration (contained in a lecture delivered in America in 1894) is indeed laudable; but as a statement of prevailing Hindu practice of the time, it was inaccurate and misleading. Even as a statement of personal ideals, it concealed more than it revealed, for Vivekananda's specific references to religions other than his own were not always flattering.

Take, for example, the case of Buddhism. In his paper on Hinduism presented to the Parliament of Religions, he proclaimed that there was a place for 'the agnosticism of the Buddhists and the atheism of the Jains... in the Hindu's religion' (ibid.: 6). Exactly a week later, he clarified at the same forum that the Buddha had taught 'nothing new', that 'he was the fulfilment, the logical conclusion, the logical development of the religion of the Hindus'. He complained that the Buddha 'was not understood properly by his disciples', and called for a rapproachment: 'Hinduism cannot live without Buddhism, nor Buddhism without Hinduism' (ibid.: 21, 23). Elsewhere he clarified that, like 'everything else in India', Buddhism was based on Vedanta and had, in turn, influenced developments in the latter (see Vivekananda 1973b: 279).

Needless to emphasize, the foregoing views are not of tolerance or acceptance but of absorption or inclusion. It may be added that Vivekananda held similar views about Jainism and Sikhism (see, e.g., Vivekananda 1973a: 379–80). Actually he was kinder to the Sikhs than to the Buddhists and Jains, obviously because he considered them a Hindu sect, an attitude common to most Hindus of the time. Vivekananda deplored the influence of the Buddhists and Jains as conducive to passivity, inaction and, worse, ignorance (*tamas*, darkness). Some of his most negative remarks were reserved for the Buddha (he 'ruined us' by his stress on nirvana) and the Buddhists (they 'for want of right means have degraded India') (see Vivekananda 1963: 13–15).

It is remarkable that Vivekananda once spoke on the Prophet Muhammad in the course of his travels in America, but the remarks he made, while respectful, do not reveal a close familiarity with the basic teachings of Islam. What is more, the idea of Hindus learning from Islam is politely brushed aside: 'the great messengers of light… are our great teachers, our elder brothers. But we must go our own way!' (1972: 484). Elsewhere he paid rich tribute to Islam, for 'the peculiar excellence of Mohammedanism', namely its message of equality among the believers (1976: 371), and for its patronage of learning (1963: 91–2). The attitude is patronising, however, and sometimes even critical and paradoxical as, for instance, when he disapproves of the Islamic doctrine of 'the same law and the same rule for all' (1963: 7). He obviously preferred the context-sensitivity characteristic of Hindu society. He is said to have prayed that India may have 'an Islamic body and a Vedantic heart' (see Raychaudhuri 1988: 244). The reference presumably is to the egalitarian Muslim social organization, but as just indicated, he was rather ambivalent about the Islamic ideal of all being made equal by the confession of faith.

Vivekananda's attitude to Christianity was more complex, being influenced by his keen awareness of the threat of Christian evangelicalism and Western cultural domination. How deep Christian influence could penetrate, even without the efforts of the missionaries, was known to him from his personal contacts with Brahmos such as Keshub Sen (see Chapter Seven). The attitude he adopted could be simply but not inaccurately described as aggressive. At the broadest level, he considered the East and the West irreconcilably different in their core values (see Vivekananda 1973a: 375). The West, he said, was unable to rise above the notion of the 'mind' (*manas*), while the Hindus knew the higher reality of 'the inner self' (*atman*) (ibid.: 459). While Indians should 'learn', he advised, 'from the West her arts and sciences', in the domain of religion, 'Hindus must believe that we are the teachers of the world' (ibid.: 443). His assessment of Christianity was that it was an inferior religion: 'with all its boasted civilization [it] is but a collection of little bits of Indian thought', 'a very patchy imitation' of 'our religion' (ibid.: 275). He even believed that the veneration of Virgin Mary had been borrowed from Hinduism's Kali worship (1963: 5).

Vivekananda considered the Bible a text suitable for 'ordinary devotees', preferring Vedanta for 'the spiritually advanced' (see Raychaudhuri 1988: 247).

Vedanta was indeed in Vivekananda's judgement India's gift to the world. He called it 'truer than any other religion, because it never conquered, because it never shed blood, because its mouth shed on all words of blessing, of peace, words of love and sympathy' (1973a: 274). He exhorted his Indian followers to 'go out' and 'conquer the world through our spirituality and philosophy. There is no other alternative, we must do it or die' (ibid.: 277). It is unnecessary to elaborate Vivekananda's negative views about religions other than Vedanta—he considered many contemporary forms of Hinduism including the Puranic and Tantric, which Ramakrishna had embraced, degenerate and strongly condemned caste taboos and prejudices—to raise serious doubts about his claims about tolerance and acceptance.

In view of the above, how may we interpret Vivekananda's very frequent quotation in his speeches and writings of the Rigvedic aphorism about the Absolute being one despite it being described variously? To cite but one example (ibid.: 112–13):

In India the same competing gods had been struggling with each other for supremacy, but the great good fortune of this country and of the world was that there came out in the midst of the din and confusion a voice which declared [*ekam sad vipra bahuda vadanti*] "That which exists is One; sages call it by various names". It is not that Shiva is superior to Vishnu, not that Vishnu is everything and Shiva is nothing, but it is the same one whom you call either Shiva, or Vishnu, or by a hundred other names.

Vivekananda's highest concern was to purify Hinduism and to unite Hindus. He found the emergence of 'sects' understandable ('The almost infinite mass of energy in the world cannot be managed by a small number of people', ibid.: 372), but disapproved of contentions and divisive sectarianism. Besides, he envisaged an 'eternal' and 'infinite' religion, based on 'the wonderful truth' that he said he had learnt from his 'master' (Sri Ramakrishna), namely 'that the religions of the world are not contradictory or antagonistic' (1977: 180). Although the text from which I have quoted (constructed from lectures delivered abroad in 1896) does not give a name to this religion, judging by the spirit of his overall position, one may safely conclude that Vedanta was this 'eternal religion' or, at least, the basis for it. And the moral of the discourse was: 'we must respect all religions and we must try to accept them all *as far as we can*' (ibid., emphasis added). The qualification with which this sentence concludes is noteworthy. The doubt in his mind arose, I think, from a solid residue of resistence to the idea of the equality of all religions.

Vivekananda's notion of tolerance, it is reasonable to conclude, was hierarchical in as much as Vedantic Hinduism was regarded as the foundation of all religious ideals of all times. He declared in a speech delivered in India:

Ours ... is the universal religion. It is inclusive enough, it is broad enough to include all the ideals. All the ideals of religion that already exist in the world can be immediately included, and we can patiently wait for all the ideals that are to come in the future to be taken in the same fashion, embraced in the infinite arms of the religion of Vedanta (1973a: 251–2).

It is obvious that Vivekananda's ideas of tolerance, acceptance and harmony, and of the conquest of the world by Hindu spirituality, are more inclusive or synthetic than pluralist. Pluralism requires a transcendental referent in the absence of which either rank relativism will prevail or hierarchy will rule. Vivekananda clearly believed Vedanta to be the transcendental religion; but surely one of the existing religions cannot be so regarded. Gandhi knew this and maintained that the religion which he considered the source of value was not Hinduism or any other known religion, but one that transcended them all.

Apart from the issues of tolerance and pluralism, it may well be argued that, largely in response to the challenge of the West and the nobler aspects of Christianity, Vivekananda gave a secularist orientation to Hinduism through his notion of 'practical', or socially concerned, Vedanta. This stood for applying the truths learnt from the Vedic tradition to an active engagement in social ameliorative activities. He called for a marriage of renunciation (*vairagya*) and service of humanity (*jivanseva*). His concept of service was constituted of several, hierarchically-arranged, strands, beginning with material needs ('It is an insult to a starving people to offer them religion': Vivekananda 1972: 20), but eventually rising above them to the spiritual level. Going beyond orthodox Vedanta and the immediate teachings of Ramakrishna, which focused on the illusory character of the world (*maya*) and self-directed salvation (*mukti*) respectively, Vivekananda was responsible for introducing the ethic of other-directed altruism into modern Hinduism (see Gupta 1974:

25–50). He wrote:'The universal aspect of God means this world, and worshipping it means serving it this indeed is work, not indulging in ceremonial' (see Williams 1995: 389). The Ramakrishna Mission, founded in 1897, became the organizational means through which Vivekananda sought to achieve his objectives. All this is important: in the context of the present discussion it only highlights the fact that the Swami was an innovator and not an agent of tradition.

To return to the distinction between a hierarchical concept of tolerance and equalitarian pluralism, its blurring creates confusion and should be avoided. Thus, when M.N. Srinivas, the distinguished sociologist, writes that 'Hinduism is regarded as a tolerant religion both by its votaries and others' (1992: 122), and proceeds to trace the attitude to the Vedic aphorism 'Truth is one, the sages call it by many names' (the very same that Vivekananda invoked), one is not sure that the conceptual distinction between symmetric mutual tolerance legitimized by a higher ideal and hierarchical pluralism has been observed.[6] Similarly, when S.C. Dube, another leading sociologist, writes that Hinduism 'is a loosely structured federation of faiths' and maintains that 'Hindu civilization represents a pattern of stabilized pluralism' (1983: 1), his formulation raises the same question as Srinivas's.

Other scholars holding similar views cite the authority of classical texts, such as the *Manusmriti*. According to the latter, when two *shruti* (sacred, revealed) texts are in conflict, both are considered valid and lawful (MS II.14). Writing of the *Dharmashastras* (the normative texts of Brahmanism) generally, Romila Thapar notes that, what later came to be seen as a single Hindu society, was earlier 'a variety of communities, determined by location, occupation and caste' (1992: 75). Since these communities lived in a state of close though highly structured interaction, pluralism would have been an obvious basis for developing a general view of everyday life or, if one may so put it, the theory of practice. From neither of these examples is it clear as to how conflicts may have been resolved in real life. Was an arbiter, such as the king, envisaged?

---

6. Srinivas does here what many other authors including myself (see Madan 1989: 115), have done, namely, present a free translation of the aphorism *ekam sad viprah bahudā vadanti*. In the original text (*Rig Veda* I.164.46), the '*ekam*' refers to the Absolute Being known by the names of such divinities as Agni and Yama, rather than Truth.

The royal task indeed was to afford protection to all the ways of life prevalent in the realm. Only in very exceptional circumstances, apprehending disorder, might the king have used his authority to abrogate certain customs and usages (see Lingat 1973: 226). The idea of a state religion was wholly alien to this way of thinking. The *Mahabharata* supports a general pluralist position, as was noted earlier, saying that the king's duty (*rajadharma*) includes in itself all the ways of life (*dharmas*), each of which has the king's way of life as its umbrella (Shantiparva 63.25). One of the criticisms made of Hinduism from the perspective of an absolutist theory of ethical judgement is that it lacks a general notion of morality of virtue and vice, and of reward and punishment. In other words, it is relativist in orientation[7]. While Hindu pluralism produces flexibility and makes private worlds of creed and custom viable, it does not really guarantee that they will be equal.

Writing of contemporary times, Srinivas stresses the institutional framework of religious tolerance in Hindu society, besides scriptural authority (mentioned above) and pantheism, the latter having generated tolerance towards not only 'the great world religions but [also] towards tribal and peasant religions' (1992: 123). He observes: 'it [tolerance] is provided by, strangely enough, caste. It is true that at the level of individual castes, exclusivism is the rule, but if one looks at the system as a whole, an acceptance of [different] life-styles lies at its heart. However, the practice of the latter is the acceptance of hierarchy' (ibid).[8]

---

7. Relativism as the defining characteristic of the Hindu way of thinking, insightfully described by A.K. Ramanujan (1989) as 'context-sensitivity', should not be overstressed, however, as if there were no commonalities and no holistic vision. Thus, Beni Prasad, one of the pioneers of political studies in India, wrote nearly seventy years ago: 'As in medieval Europe, so in ancient India, theory saw the universe as one articulated whole.... In short, there were principles applicable to all, principles which were of a universal nature' (1968: 347).

Lest this formulation be looked upon with suspicion because it is based on texts, let me quote from an ethnographic monograph based on fieldwork in central India in the mid-1950s. The author gives a list of 'the principles of dharma' as described to him by the villagers. The first of these is '*sarva sadharan dharma*, or general rules of *dharma* meant to be observed by all Hindus in the community'. Only then are caste and family *dharmas* and 'special rules' mentioned (see Mathur 1964: 88–95).

8. The way Srinivas refers to hierarchy, rather fleetingly, tends to play down its implications for those castes, constituting in most places the majority of the population, who are at the bottom, often grievously deprived materially and untouchables to boot.

Elsewhere, Srinivas writes: 'The secularism of the Indian republic is an expression of such tolerance' (ibid.: 56), that is tolerance flowing from hierarchical pluralism. He clarifies that not only are the members of each religious community allowed to profess, practice, and propagate their faith, they are also guaranteed protection against discrimination at the hands of the state on the ground of religious identity. The reference is to Articles 25 to 28 of the Constitution of India (see Chapter Eight). In popular debates and discussions also, the protagonists of the liberal Hindu point of view maintain that 'Hinduism is tolerant and, therefore, secular', and further clarify that 'Hinduism ... revels in plurality' (Jain 1994: 105, 106). The questionable equivalence of tolerance and pluralism persists. The caveat that the pluralism of India is the pluralism of the caste system, inegalitarian and exploitative at its very core, mentioned by Srinivas himself, is absolutely crucial. What is more, it has disturbing implications. As the caste order dissolves, Hinduism's structural formula for pluralism also collapses, for it does not have an alternative formula with which to ensure orderly social existence while accommodating diversity. A modernized Hinduism that denounces caste may well end up being fundamentalist and intolerant.

From the foregoing it should be clear that, the specific meaning that has come to be bestowed on secularism in India, and not by Hindu intellectuals and politicians alone (see Chapters Two and Five), is a rather imprecise notion of religious tolerance in society and a similarly unclear idea of non-preferentialism or equal respect for all religions (*dharma nirpekshta* or *sarva dharma samabhava*) as state policy. Whether the state stands apart from the religious concerns of the peoples of India, or involves itself in these is left deliberately vague, I suppose in the interests of political expediency. Religion is thus neither abolished from human life, as it were, nor driven indoors from the public arenas into the privacy of individual lives. Paradoxical though it may sound, Indian secularism is indeed religious.

To conclude. In exploring the possibility of secularism as an ideology, distinct from the on-going processes of secularization, in the setting of an evolving Hindu religious tradition, we find that, definitional controversies apart (Is Hinduism an Orientalist fiction? Is it a religion at all? Etc.), two main conclusions emerge.

First, the classical Hindu religious tradition, enshrined in the ancient texts from the Vedas through the Smritis to the Epics, does not recognize a mutually exclusive dichotomy of the religious *versus* the secular, nor the idea of religion as a private activity. In this respect the Hindu tradition is the very opposite of the Christian tradition before and after the Reformation. The Western ideology of secularism, which was a product of the dialectic of Protestantism and the Enlightenment (see Chapter One), is not, therefore, readily communicable to the Hindus *qua* Hindus. A transfer can surely be effected, but a meaningful translation is difficult to achieve. As Bankimchandra Chatterji put it,'You can translate a word by a word, but behind the word is an idea, the thing which the word denotes, and this idea you cannot translate, if it does not exist among the people in whose language you are translating' (see Chatterjee 1986: 61).

It follows that if we seek to build an ideology of secularism that valorizes human reason and agency, and rejects religion as a 'fake', or at best 'the opium of the masses', that is best privatized, we shall have to look elsewhere than the mainstreams of the Hindu religious tradition for support.[9] The unrelenting processes of secularization in the domains of productive activities, organization of work, provision of health care, dissemination of knowledge and new values, etc. have undoubtedly narrowed the scope of religious faith in Hindu society, but it is still an overwhelming social force. As of now, the resources of the Hindu religious tradition are not available to promote an ideology of secularism that is seen as an antidote to religion.

Second, an alternative ideology of secularism, which stands for a pluralist society and a non-discriminatory state, should be acceptable to the Hindus *qua* Hindus, unless overriding negative circumstances, unforeseen at present, come into play. The Hindu religious tradition has been pluralist in character by reasons of both internal dynamics and external challenges, but in its own hierarchical fashion. Even today, in the closing years of the twentieth century, when the notion of a unified Hinduism has been abroad for well over a century, and is acknowledged widely in principle, it is equally widely denied in practice. The last one hundred years or so have witnessed the birth of new goddess (e.g., Santoshi Ma) or godman (e.g., Satya Sai Baba) cults, and more significantly new religous communities such as the Radhasaomi Satsang (see Juergensmeyer 1991). The continual rise

---

9. The example of the materialistic Charvaka school comes to one's mind, but as stated earlier, it has generally been treated as minor if not aberrant. Buddhism and Jainism, although traditionally designated as atheistic (*nastika*), are not materialistic religious philosophies, however.

of new religions within the country, most notably Buddhism, Jainism and Sikhism, all of which emerged as critiques of Brahmanical orthodoxy and ritualism, and the arrival of Christianity and Islam from abroad, have contributed to a spirit of 'religious liberality' (see von Stietencron 1991: 22).[10] But this liberality too operates within a hierarchical framework. In other words, difference is hierarchised: it is neither abolished nor translated into an ideology of equality. Moreover, a hardening of once- permeable boundaries has occured in modern times. Thoughtful analysts have written about the 'objectification' of communal identities through census enumeration (see Kaviraj 1995) and of the 'substantialization' or 'ethnicization' of castes through politicization (see Dumont 1970b and Gould 1990). It is unwarranted to believe that religious tolerance that once may have been characteristic of the Hindu religious tradition (or the 'harmonious regime' that apparently typified caste-based society) is readily recoverable today. Gandhi's assassination was a result of more than a conspiracy among a dozen men; it represented a contemporary Hindu attitude that is widespread.

While the pluralist orientation of Hinduism at the ideological level has been widely acclaimed, although religious intolerance has not been entirely absent,[11] the inequities of the social order associated with it also have attracted social criticism and even moral condemnation (see Smith 1977: 81, n.68). Nevertheless, sociologists such as Srinivas have made a valid distinction of levels, and argued that at the global level caste itself generates a pluralist, though undoubtedly inegalitarian, orientation. The attitudes that are generated by the caste

10. The followers of Zoroastrianism, the Parsis, are too microscopic a minority to be significant nationally, but at the regional level in Gujarat and Maharashtra, they have been a noteworthy witness to the spirit of religious tolerance in India.

11. Romila Thapar presents a brief rebuttal of 'a persistent, popular belief that the "Hindus" never indulged in religious persecution', drawing attention to the persecution of Buddhists and Jains by various Hindu groups, intersectarian conflicts between Vaishnavas and Shaivas, and the persecution of the lower castes by the upper (1992: 73–5). Curiously, she concludes: 'If acts of intolerance and violence against other religious sects reflecting the consciousness of belonging to a religious community did not form part of a Hindu stand against such sects, then it also raises the question of how viable is the notion of a Hindu community for this early period' (ibid.: 74–5). M.N. Srinivas, after drawing attention to the pluralist implications of Hindu pantheism, observes: 'However, monotheism occurs in Hinduism at the sectarian level, and it is usually accompanied by "intolerance" towards other sects. Mention may be made here of Sri Vaishnavism and Virashaivism, both popular sects in South India' (1992: 123).

system, and in turn sustain it, are extended to cover inter-religious relations also. Indeed, in many a village, Muslims are ranked higher than certain untouchable, nominally Hindu, castes.

In short, the Hindu religious tradition is different from Christianity, and similar to Islam and Sikhism, in denying the religious-secular dichotomy. It is also different from Islam and Christianity in its pluralist though hierarchical orientation, which is reflected in, or may be seen as a reflection of, the caste system. The refusal to grant legitimacy to the change of religious faith, particularly in the form of institutionalized conversion, has been claimed to be a proof of the positive attitude of Hinduism toward religious diversity. On its basis, the followers of Islam, Christianity, Sikhism, Zoroastrianism and numerous other faiths could be accommodated as castes or caste-like groups. Secularization has been called a gift of Christianity to humankind (a Christian but rationalist alternative to Christianity, as it were) (see Chapter One). Religious pluralism may be similarly considered a gift of the Hindu cultural tradition from Vedism onward, through the millennia, including some expressions of neo-Hinduism, most notably the Gandhian (which I discuss in Chapters Seven and Eight), but not others, such as currently Hindutva (see Chapter Seven).[12] As already stated, however, this pluralism is both realized through and maimed by the all-pervasive reign of hierarchy in social thought and social practice and by the spirit of inclusivism/exclusivism. Genuine pluralism requires an appropriate ontology and, besides, the phenomenological and social experience of mutual interdependence expressed institutionally. It is a game that all religious communities must play. The 'imputation or presumption of tolerance' among others may well define 'one's own tolerance in the Gandhian world-view and praxis' (Nandy 1988: 193), it is, I think, insufficient in realpolitik. Presently, the hierarchical pluralism of the Hindu religious tradition combines with the exclusiveness of Islam and Sikhism to produce an impasse because of which, among other reasons, secularism in India is said to be in a crisis. I will examine this phenomenon in Chapter Eight, but want first to take up (in Chapter Seven) the problem of accounting for the emergence of

12. I have avoided any reference to pluralism as a Hindu (Brahmanical) metaphysical doctrine, because of a lack of good understanding of the issues involved. John Arapura (1987) has presented a brief discussion of the response of two modern Indian philosophers, namely K.C. Bhattacharya and S. Radhakrishnan, to the phenomenon of religious pluralism.

fundamentalist movements, so-called, in the setting of the avowedly pluralist Hindu religious tradition.

APPENDIX
The Ashokan State. The Weberian Thesis

Readers will have perhaps missed in this chapter any discussion of the character of the Ashokan state and its ideological foundations. This is a complex issue, and also very interesting, but it tells us more about Ashoka than about any particular religious tradition. As Radhakumud Mookerji observes, the public morality that the king presented to his people could not be 'identified with any of the then prevailing faiths of the country. It certainly was not Buddhism, his own religion' (1989: 68), although influenced by the latter (see Gombrich 1988: 129). Mookerji clarifies: 'the *dharma* of the Edicts is not any particular *dharma* or religious system, but the Moral Law independent of any caste or creed, the *sara* or essence of all religions' (ibid: 69).

Further, as Romila Thapar notes, Ashoka did not want to make Buddhism the state religion. His active promotion of *Dhamma* was on behalf of the moral ethic of social responsibility and respect for human dignity. Toleration, or respect for all religions, and non-violence in the face of intersectarian differences were fundamental to Ashoka's conception. He declared (Rock Edict XII): 'On each occasion one should honour another man's sect, for by doing so one increases the influence of one's own sect and benefits that of the other man...therefore concord is to be commended so that men may hear one another's principles' (see Thapar 1961: 255). Pillar Edict VII, which carries the last and longest of the Ashokan inscriptions, notes that, 'People's progress in *dhamma* is achieved in two ways, by *dhamma* rules and by conviction. Rules count for little; most is by conviction' (see Gombrich 1988: 131). The ideology was humanist and pluralist, but it would be misleading to call it secularist or statist.

The association of the modern Indian state with the Ashokan state, through the highly visible symbols of the wheel of righteousness on the national flag and the lions on the state seal, both taken from the Sarnath Pillar, is somewhat confusing. Ashoka's religious pluralism was, as noted above, born of a deeply religious attitude; the policy of respect for all religions that is intended to guide the state today is based on pragmatism, the rational calculation of neutrality as an instrument of stability or, in other words, secular considerations.

As for the Buddhist religious tradition and its significance for the secular domain (particularly the polity), viewed in comparative perspective, Stanley Tambiah's monumental *World Conqueror and World Renouncer* (1976) is most valuable for both information and analytical insights.

*   *   *

Another deliberate omission is a discussion of the Weberian thesis about Hindu other-worldliness. This is an important and much debated subject. Max Weber's misunderstandings of Brahmanical thought are more than matched by his critics' misunderstandings of the thesis (see Kantowsky 1986). I will restrict myself to a brief comment.

Weber argued that, unlike the Puritans' this-worldly asceticism, derived from the doctrine of predestination, which goaded the actor to strive for worldly success, eschewing immediate gratification, the Brahmans came to place the highest value on other-worldly asceticism, or renunciation. 'Indian religiosity', he wrote, 'is the cradle of those religious ethics which have abnegated the world, theoretically, practically, to the greatest extent' (1948: 323). This was a misleading oversimplification. The doctrinal core of Brahmanical thought, according to Weber, is *karma*, elaborated through the notions of *samsara* (transmigration of souls or rebirth) and *dharma* (in the sense of a morally organized structure of social action or, simply, caste duties). Believers in karma may not strive to change the world, much less master it in the Christian fashion. The ontological reality of the world of human experience is not denied, it is simply relativized. Since the secular domain bears the divine signature just as the sacred does, it is as rational for the clean castes to leave it as it is for the low castes to put up with it, rather than seek to change it; indeed doing so would be, in Weber's phrase, 'senseless' (1958: 122).

The conclusion at which Weber arrived was not that Brahmanical thought is irrational, in fact he greatly admired its intellectual quality, but that its rationality is contemplative rather than practical. It cannot be transformed into scientific rationalism, or lead to the 'disenchantment' of the world, which was a unique expression of rationalization in the West, but has come to be regarded as a crucial element of the ideology of secularism. The passage from worldly endeavour 'in the name of God' to the same striving but 'in the name of man', that is from theodicy to anthropodicy (see Schluchter 1984: 50) was straight in the West. It constituted the self-emancipation of man (see Chapter One). The path was not available in the Brahmanical world because of its qualified ontological dualism or, to repeat what I have written earlier, its practice of hierarchizing difference.

Weber wrote in the absence of ethnographic and sociological studies of the Hindu involvement with the secular world, but he was aware of the gap between ideology and practice: this is obvious from his characterization of Hindus living in conformity with the ideology as 'pious' (see, e.g. Weber 1958: 120–1). His critics wrongly accuse him of maintaining that Brahmanical thought denies the reality of the empirical world and is irrational. Weber's early work on the Protestant ethic and the spirit of capitalism (see Weber 1930) did imply a universal notion of rationalization, but by the time he completed his studies of other world religions, he had come to recognize the importance of 'the vantage point' to the character of rationalization possible in a particular setting: the theoretical model of rationalization developed earlier was relativized (see Mommsen 1989: 162–4). What is more, he recognized that in the disenchanted or secularized world, a pluralism of values also would prevail. This does not mean, however, that a society so pluralized necessarily will become secularized. The contemporary Indian tendency of equating pluralism with secularism amounts to stopping short of the goal, and would seem to be an expression of fatigue if not despair.

Seven

The Hindu Religious Tradition
Revivalism and Fundamentalism

A 'Hindu' means a person who regards the land of Bharatvarsha, from the
Indus to the Seas as his Fatherland as well as his Holyland, that is the cradle
of his religion.

VINAYAK DAMODAR SAVARKAR, *Hindutva*

My own understanding of Hindu civilization is that it is neither absorbtive nor
eclectic, for the truly astonishing factor in Indian civilization is the endurance
and persistence of its stylè and patterns.

AINSLIE T. EMBREE *Utopias in Conflict*

Reform and Revivalism in the Nineteenth Century

Contemporary accounts of Hindu fundamentalism—so-called—
detect its roots in certain developments in Bengal, Maharashtra,
Punjab, and elsewhere in the last quarter of the nineteenth century,
when Hindu movements of reform and revival made their appearance
(see Jones 1989). Particular attention is devoted in these accounts to
the Arya Samaj movement in Punjab (see Jones 1976 and Gold
1991). What happened in the late nineteenth century had its roots in
earlier events, and these may be recapitulated here very briefly.

Historians have recorded the emergence, early in the nineteenth
century, of an awareness of the cultural and religious heritage of the
West among Indian intellectuals of Bengal and Western India. Ironically, a crucial event in the initiation of this process of expanding
consciousness was the lifting of the ban by the British government,
in 1813, on proselytization by Christian missionaries. William Wil-
berforce, a prominent Anglican well-known for his efforts to abolish
slave trade, observed in the course of a debate in the House of
Commons that the conversion of the peoples of India was 'the

greatest of all causes, for I place it before Abolition'. He called the gods of the Hindus 'absolute monsters of lust, injustice, wickedness and cruelty', and their religion, 'one grand abomination' (see Moorhouse 1984: 68). Thereafter, criticism of Hinduism and Hindu culture generally by missionaries, 'often crude and ill-informed' (Raychaudhuri 1988: 2), became the order of the day. Needless to add, the missionaries operated under the supportive aegis of British rule (see Inden 1990).

In the circumstances, it is not surprising that many early Victorian writers considered India to be at the threshold of a new way of life under the combined impact of the new administrative and mercantile dispensations and evangelical Christianity. In their enthusiasm the critics overlooked the vitality of the inner dynamism of Hinduism (see Bayly 1990: 159). The emergence of movements of religious reform and revival in different parts of India during the nineteenth century (from the 1820s onward) was more in the nature of a creative response to a challenge than an unconsidered rejection of, or unqualified surrender to, external influences. The sense of continuity was so strong that some historians have questioned the applicability of the notion of 'revivalism' to late nineteenth century developments in Bengal (see Raychaudhuri 1988: 8–9).[1]

Ironically, again, the links with the past were rendered highly valuable by the positing of a Golden Age of Indian Culture by the Orientalists, beginning in the late eighteenth century with the translations of Sanskrit classics into English by William Jones, H.H. Wilson, H.T. Colebrooke, and others (see Kopf 1969). While a newly aroused cultural pride helped the concerned intellectuals to retain enough self-esteem to embark upon programmes of religious and social reconstruction, they did not allow their anti-missionary senti-

---

1. Amiya Sen has argued against Raychaudhuri's stand that it is inappropriate to refer to certain developments within ways of life 'that were far from dead' (Raychaudhuri 1988: 9) as revivalism. Sen stresses that 'the literature of this period itself is replete with reference to the term "revival" even though there remained inner differences of meaning' (Sen 1993: 10). Further, he points out that 'it is not always easy to ascertain what is "living" and what is "dead" within any given tradition' (ibid.). He concludes:

In the context of late nineteenth century Bengal, the use of the term "revivalism" does not necessarily imply the restoration of ideas that were practically dead and gone or a thoughtless emulation of bygone life-styles but a conscious attempt to use chosen elements of the past for functions that were by and large secular and certainly futuristic (ibid.: 12).

ments, or their repugnance for the Western lifestyle, to develop into a total rejection of Christianity itself, or of British rule, which was generally judged to have been a providential blessing in place of the earlier Muslim rule in its years of decay.

The character of the mixed response of Bengali intellectuals to the cultural impact of the West is best illustrated by the creed and social concerns of the Brahmo Sabha (1828) and its successor, the Brahmo Samaj (1843). The former was intended by its founder, Rammohun Roy (1772–1833), to be the means of eradicating erroneous religious beliefs and degenerate social practices among the Hindus, and of promoting the idea of a universal religion comprising a theological consensus among the followers of major world religions. The outstanding role of Roy and of the Brahmo Samaj in the shaping of the modern Indian mind is well known (see Joshi 1975 and Kopf 1979)— it has even been exaggerated—and I will not go into the details here. My limited purpose is to apply some of the insights derived from the earlier analysis of the Sikh and Muslim religious traditions to the materials at hand in order to examine whether Roy and his major successors in the Brahmo Samaj could be called precursors of the Hindu fundamentalists of today, presuming at this point of the discussion that there is such a phenomenon as Hindu fundamentalism.

From the very beginning of his career as an author (at the age of eighteen), Roy engaged in a critique of Hindu polytheism and ritualism (particularly idolatry). He also gradually developed a critique of what he regarded as repugnant social practices, most notably *suttee*, that is the immolation of a widow at the funeral pyre of her husband. This practice was outlawed in 1829 in large measure due to his efforts, provoking a conservative reaction. Roy's reasonable familiarity with the basic teachings of Islam, and his much closer study of the Christian Gospels, provided him with many key ideas for the reform of Hinduism and Hindu society, including an uncompromising emphasis on monotheism and on the uplift of women.

As for religious reform, he wanted reconstructed Hindus to recover the original purity of their religious thought and knowledge by subjecting it to a rational critique and by returning to its sources for inspiration. It is obvious that he had the example of the European Renaissance in mind. Roy identified the Vedas and the Upanishads as the true source of Hinduism, following a well-established, one thousand year old canonical tradition in this regard. He bewailed that 'the ancient religion' of the Hindus 'had been disregarded by the generality of moderns' (see Kopf 1979: 13). It is important to note, however, that Roy did not consider these scriptures essential to the attainment of true religious belief, or valuable in their entirety (he chose only four Upanishads for translation into Bengali and English). He also did not consider the chosen Brahmanical texts as the sole repository of valid knowledge. In fact, he was deeply impressed by the ethical content of the New Testament—he compiled a book on the subject—which he missed in his own religious tradition.

Moreover, Roy also rejected the notion of the entitlement, or traditional authority (*adhikara*), of the Brahmans to expound religious beliefs and interpret the scriptures. They had in fact concealed the sacred tradition, he complained, behind the 'dark curtain' of Sanskrit (see Halbfass 1988: 205). He subscribed to the Enlightenment idea that every human being has the 'innate faculty' of reason, or rational thought, to be able to 'distinguish the truth from untruth' and 'discern good from bad', 'without the instrumentality of prophets, religious authority, and traditional revelation' (see Pantham 1986: 37). Since he did not consider the true meaning of the chosen texts to be at variance with reason, he could be said to have entertained the idea of not only the primacy but also the infallibility of scripture.[2]

After Roy's death in 1833, the agenda of his successors underwent some significant changes (see Kopf 1979), some of them apparently mutually contradictory. Thus, while Debendranath Tagore (1817–1905) was more self-consciously a Hindu, it was he who declared in 1850 that the idea of the infallibility of Vedanta as the source of true religious belief would have to be discarded, because, contrary to the Upanishadic teaching of monism, he himself was a dualist (denying the unity of *brahman* and *atman*, or, more simply, of the godhead and the human seeker). A notable feature of Tagore's intellectual effort from the perspective of the present discussion was his at-

---

2. Anantanand Rambachan writes:

It is clear...that although Rammohun Roy did not unambiguously reject Vedic authority and infallibility, he had a considerably modified attitude to it.... His view of nature as revelation, his extrascriptural concept of a type of minimal theology, his idea that religious truth is not confined to the text of the Vedas, and his argument that knowledge of the latter is not necessary for a knowledge of God, all mollify the traditional attitude towards the Vedas (1994: 259).

tempt—the first of its kind within the Brahmo movement—to lay down the fundamentals of the Brahmo ethic. This was done in 1850 at the time of the repudiation of Vedanta—which amounted to knocking the bottom out of the Brahmo faith—and again in 1857 when a 'confession of faith' was published in *Tattvabodhini Patrika* (a magazine founded and edited by Tagore). Later, however, he made significant concessions to the prevailing Hindu orthodoxy, advising his followers not to completely cut themselves off from 'the great Hindu community' and the 'highest truths of Hindu Shastras [canonical texts]' (see de Bary 1969: 88; see also Kopf 1979: 105–6, 133–4 et passim).

Tagore's successor, Keshub Chandra Sen (1838–84), completely rejected the Vedas and the Upanishads as infallible scripture. He treated such rejection as the critical line of demarcation between Brahmos and Hindus. He wanted to take Brahmoism closer to Christianity, which he called the 'religion of Humanity', and even strove for an Indian version of it. Intuition replaced Roy's reason and inference from nature's revelations as the source of theistic belief and spiritual knowledge generally. But Sen too underwent a major change in his religious beliefs later in his life when he was drawn into Bengali Vaishnavism and the *bhakti* tradition made its way into Brahmoism. He came under the personal influence of the Hindu mystic-devotee, Sri Ramakrishna, whose spiritual practice (*sadhana*) reinforced and validated his own notion of the 'motherhood of God' and his quest for a 'religion of Harmony' (see Halbfass 1988: 255–6 and Kopf 1979: 264–5).

The foregoing, deliberately brief, presentation of some aspects of the views of Rammohun Roy and the two principal leaders of the Brahmo Samaj before it was overtaken by a Hindu resurgence from the 1870s onwards, provides us a reasonably clear answer to the question whether Brahmo Samaj could be considered a precursor of today's Hindu fundamentalism. The answer has to be in the negative, but the phenomenon is interesting because some of the elements of fundamentalism were present in it. Thus, the efforts of Roy and his successors are inconceivable without the challenge of Christianity and the Western lifestyle, which were seen as positive influences in some respects but primarily as threatening. It should be noted that British rule was considered a benign cultural force rather than a usurpation of political power.

The key element in the Indian reaction under discussion was a deep sense of frustration with the contemporary state of culture, religion and society and a compensatory adoration of the past. Brahman priests were seen as representatives of degeneration and Brahmanical scriptures stood for ancient greatness. A concern with scripture—its character and authority—would have made one suspect a fundamentalist streak in the movement initiated by Rammohun Roy. But the idea of infallibility of scripture, although acknowledged by him, was already weaker in his exposition of it than in Brahmanical orthodoxy. As noted above, it was finally repudiated by Keshub Sen. Moreover, religious syncretism was an ideal to which the Samaj was dedicated in one form or another. The exclusivism characteristic of religious fundamentalism was definitely absent.

Finally, the concern with social reform best exemplified by Roy's efforts on behalf of the oppressed Hindu women was inspired by the contact with the West rather than developed as an element of the ideological opposition to it. In any case, the reformist programme failed to develop into a comprehensive critique of the traditional lifestyle: in fact it weakened with the passage of time. In short, although some of the critical elements that might have given Brahmo Samaj a fundamentalist appearance were present in it in nascent form, they never coalesced into a fully articulated pattern.

What about Hindu revivalism—so-called—of the last quarter of the nineteenth century in Bengal and elsewhere in the country? In Bengal the emergence of a new consciousness among Hindus followed several paths. Thus there was a religious-devotional (Vaishnavite) revival which obviously had individual ecstatic experience as its main focus. In contrast, there was the radical departure in the direction of social service and restructured monasticism that Vivekananda initiated: it was revivalist only in the sense that its third crucial element was a vision of Hinduism as an activist, this-worldly, universal religion. Finally, there was the shaping of a new political consciousness among the Hindu intelligentsia, not only in Bengal but also in western India, which combined the stirrings of nationalist thought with religious sentiments and symbolism, as for instance, and notably, in the work of Bankimchandra Chattopadhyay (1839–94).

For Chattopadhyay political regeneration and cultural and religious reconstruction were two sides of the same coin. He even wrote of a 'national religion', the roots of which lay in the Vedas: 'the Vedas are nothing less than *the basis of our entire religious and social organization*' (see Chatterjee 1986: 61). Added to this emphasis on roots, and on a holist conception of life in which the religious and the social are one and the same reality,[3] is a historical judgement regarding the Hindu indifference to power. He wrote:

Europeans are devotees of power. That is the key to their advancement. We are negligent towards power: that is the key to our downfall. Europeans pursue a goal which they must reach in this world: they are victorious on earth. We pursue a goal which lies in the world beyond [namely salvation through knowledge], which is why we have failed to win on earth. Whether we will win in the life beyond is a question on which there are differences of opinion (see Chatterjee 1986: 57).

The subjection of Hindus to the British and before that to Muslims, for all of eight hundred years, was a consequence of this negligence and of apathy to history. It followed that the way to national freedom and honour lay through a positive attitude to power defined not merely in material but also in cultural terms. The first task then was Hindu cultural regeneration.

Bankimchandra was an erudite intellectual, familiar with Western political philosophy and sociology. His concept of religion as dharma, that is a comprehensive design for living, was borrowed from Auguste Comte. 'I have said', he wrote, 'that religion in its broadest and most legitimate sense is culture. If this be true, the most perfect religion is that which supplies a basis for the most comprehensive development of culture' (see Das 1984: 162). Bankimchandra believed that a 'reformed, regenerated and purified' Hinduism would qualify better for being 'the most perfect religion' than any other world religion, not to speak of European materialist philosophies of life. Purification and regeneration had become essential because of the accumulation of 'the rubbish of the ages': 'The great principles of Hinduism are good for all ages and all mankind... but its non-essential adjuncts have become effete and even pernicious in an altered state of society' (see Chatterjee 1986: 77).

In developing the notion of corruption by passage of time, Bankimchandra was willing to jettison even the Vedas as 'dead': 'they do not represent the living religion of India' (see Das 1984: 160). In his religio-philosophical work, *Dharmatattva*, he gave preference to the Puranas over the Upanishads because of the other-

3. Bankimchandra wrote: 'With other peoples, religion is only a part of life; there are things religious, and there are things lay and secular. To the Hindu, his whole life was religion' (Halbfass 1988: 339).

worldly orientation of the latter. Continuing with his selective retrieval of the past, Bankimchandra drew from the *Mahabharata*—particularly the *Bhagavad Gita*—and the *Bhagavat Purana* to present 'a complete human ideal' for 'all kinds of people' in the person of Krishna whom he regarded as a historical figure—a 'householder, diplomat, warrior, law-giver, saint and preacher' (see Chatterjee 1986: 70). It may be noted that Krishna as the supreme lover is absent in this broad characterization. An idealized 'Krishnaism' (Halbfass 1988: 339) was thus presented as 'purified' Hinduism, shorn of the dross of 'superstitions' and the mindlessness of rituals. It was because of these acquired flaws, Bankimchandra believed, that the Hindu religious tradition had become the target of attacks by Christian missionaries and, earlier, misrepresentation by Muslim theologians.

Bankimchandra's project of national-cultural regeneration, in which patriotism (*svadeshapriti*) and humanism (*manushyatva*) were considered the highest values, incorporated some of the key elements of a fundamentalist ideology—notably, recognition of a crisis (emanating from the challenges of Islam, Christianity, and Western secularism), the idea of cultural regeneration (but not an uncritical return to the tradition), and an emphasis on power as an instrument of a world-affirmative *weltanshauung*. It remained an elitist vision of the future, however, shared by other intellectuals but not transformed into an organized cultural or political movement. As Partha Chatterjee points out, 'Bankim's time' was 'the heyday of colonial rule', and his 'direct disciples were the "revolutionary terrorists"'(1986: 79).

Bankimchandra Chattopadhyay died in 1894: by then the scene of religious activism had shifted out of Bengal into western and northern India.[4] The socio-religious movement that was the most prominent in the 1890s was that spearheaded by the Arya Samaj in Punjab. While some scholars have seen in it the first successful

---

4. The influence of the Brahmo Samaj on Dayanand Sarasvati, the founder of Arya Samaj, will be mentioned below. Here it may be noted that the Prarthana Samaj of Bombay was founded in 1867 mainly under the influence of the Brahmo leader Keshub Chandra Sen who visited Bombay in 1864 and again in 1867 (see Jones 1989: 141–4). The goals of the Prarthana Samaj were rather modest. Its leaders, who included M.G. Ranade and R.G. Bhandarkar, hoped to promote the spiritual and rational elements (as against the 'superstitious') within the Hindu religious tradition.

example of 'organized Hinduism' (see Gold 1991), others simply refer to it as 'a fundamentalist movement' (see Llewellyn 1993).

The Arya Samaj

The Arya Samaj was founded by Dayananda Sarasvati (1824–83) in 1875 at Bombay.[5] He was by that time a well-known *sannyasi* who had in recent years added social reform to his primary concern of religious purism. Besides preaching against 'blind beliefs', idolatry, ritualism and the stranglehold of those Brahmans whose sole claim to perform the priestly role was their caste status, he was now criticizing social evils, such as discrimination against women and the lower castes, that prevailed in Hindu society. A crucial experience had been Dayananda's visit to Calcutta in 1872, and his meeting there with the leaders of the Brahmo Samaj including Debendranath Tagore. The extent to which the teachings of the Brahmo Samaj influenced him is a matter of debate—he must have found the on-going debate about scriptural authority interesting—but there is no doubt about the influence of their methods. After leaving Calcutta Dayananda made a couple of attempts at founding a socio-religious organization, but nothing seems to have come of them. When he arrived in Bombay in 1874, he encountered much interest in some circles in the issue of 'what constituted authentic, traditional Hindu doctrine as against the later innovations and perversions brought about by the sects' (Jordens 1978: 129). This interest had been generated by certain developments within the Vallabhacharya sect since the mid-1850s, and had moved in the direction of a 'Vedic religion'.

The Bombay Arya Samaj was founded by Dayananda with the support mainly of members of trading castes but of Brahmans also. Various rules of membership and conduct were adopted: these included two fundamentals, namely belief in God and in the Vedas as the true source of knowledge. A most significant element was the rejection of the notions of bodily characteristics of God and reincarnation (*avatar*). Dayananda obviously 'wanted to bring together all Hindus who agreed on a couple of very broad issues: a dedication to

5. The main sources for the following discussion are Kenneth Jones's authoritative work *Arya Dharm* (1976) and an excellent biography of Dayananda by J.T.F. Jordens (1978).

religious and social reform, and a conviction that this reformation had to come through a revival of Vedic religion' (Jordens 1978: 144). He denied being a *guru* whose word had to be final and stressed the role of 'rational examination'. The Bombay initiative did not, however, grow into a movement involving large numbers of people: it remained confined largely to the city. A movement emerged in Punjab, however, soon afterwards.

Dayananda arrived in Punjab in 1877. His stay of sixteen months in areas of the province that were under British administration was two months shorter than in Bombay, but the impact he made was truly enormous. It took just two months (compared to six in Bombay) to establish Arya Samaj here, and the organization as well as the movement sponsored by it flourished rapidly. The reasons for this remarkable success are of significance to the present discussion. The most crucial of these reasons obviously was the apprehension of an external threat by upper caste Hindus rather than disquiet arising from internal tensions of various kinds—as was the case in Bombay—which were of course present.

Although Hindus in the southwestern parts of the province had been exposed to Islam as early as the eighth century, one may speak of their being under Muslim political pressure in all but the eastern parts from the eleventh century onwards (see Chapter Four). Later, when Sikhism emerged in Punjab in the medieval period, first as a reformist, pacifist religion and then as a political force (see Chapters Two and Three), Hindus found themselves confronted by two powerful, professedly egalitarian, and proselytizing religions. The situation was aggravated by the arrival of the British in the mid-nineteenth century after the collapse of Maharaja Ranjit Singh's kingdom. The association between British soldiers and administrators, on the one hand, and Christian missionaries, on the other, was closer in Punjab than it had been anywhere else in India. Kenneth Jones observes: 'the Punjab administrator—soldier or civilian-bred—was also religious. An atheist "sahib" was as unthinkable as he would have been intolerable' (1976: 7). In the event, 'Christian missionaries occupied the land in the wake of British conquest' (ibid.: 7–8).

Faced with the Muslims and the Sikhs, and then the British, Punjabi Hindus realized their powerlessness. They did not have the living memory of a political heritage of their own—having lived under non-Hindu rulers since the thirteenth century—with which they could identify in the period of deprivation and fear. The recent arrival of Bengalis—Brahmos and Christians—under the sponsorship of the administration, followed by the founding of the Brahmo Samaj in Punjab in 1863, further complicated matters. The tolerant attitude of the Brahmos towards other religions, particularly Christianity, was not welcome to Punjabi Hindus. The latter, feeling threatened from all sides, were waiting for a saviour, and Dayananda turned out to be the one. Judging by what Jones (1976) and Jordens (1978) write, the missionaries went about their work of saving souls in a loud and self-congratulatory manner that bordered on the aggressive, particularly in the event of conversions from upper castes. Desparate situations call for bold remedies, and these were what Dayananda provided. No sooner had he arrived in Punjab than he mooted the possibility of purification (*shuddhi*), that is reconversion, of Hindus who had been seduced by the missionaries, but were willing to return to their own religion. Within six months this became a key element in the programme of the newly formed Arya Samaj in Lahore. Dayananda provided the ideological justification for this radical innovation through his lectures.

The Lahore Arya Samaj produced a revised and tightly written statement of ten basic principles (*niyam*), on the basis of those adopted at Bombay two years earlier.[6] In the words of Kenneth Jones: 'Stressing the ultimate authority of one formless, omniscient God, the source of all knowledge, and the authority of the Vedas, Arya principles called specifically for social action' (1976: 37). Besides, certain by-laws (*upaniyam*) were drawn up in respect of organizational matters. The second of these stipulates that a member of the Samaj must believe in 'the fundamental principles'. It is important to note that these ten principles have never been altered and have acquired the character of 'fundamentals' comparable to the fundamentals of any other socio-religious movement. The by-laws, however, have not had the same unchanging character.

The significance of the Vedas to the making of the Arya Samaj as a religious and social movement is crucial. The idea of an original

6. Of the ten principles of the Arya Samaj (see Jones 1976: 321), the first two are about God as 'the primary source of all true knowledge', and about his attributes and his relation to the Universe, which is said to be that of the creator to creation. The third identifies the Vedas as 'the books of all true knowledge', which the Aryas are duty-bound to 'read', 'hear them read', and 'recite them to others'. The remaining seven principles have more to do with praxis than pure dogma, and stress the values of truthfulness, virtue, altruism, love, justice, and knowledge in action.

textual source of true knowledge is said to have been received by Dayananda from his guru, but the identification of the four Vedas (*Rig, Yajur, Sama, Atharva*) as that source was the result of his own extensive study of sacred literature and his reflection.[7] He concluded that only the Vedas were self-evidently true (*svatah pramana*), or independently authoritative, and excluded the Upanishads, Puranas, Smritis and the *Mahabharata* from the category of divinely revealed knowledge. What is more, Dayananda regarded Vedic knowledge as both comprehensive and eternal: 'God being eternal, His knowledge and attributes must be eternal' (Sarasvati 1994: 241). In short, God had revealed through the Veda everything once for all.

Claims to revealed knowledge by Christianity and Islam were rudely rejected by Dayananda (in Chapters 13 and 14 of his major work, *Satyarth Prakash*).[8] Having declared the notion of divine intervention in cosmic affairs through the agency of divine incarnation (*avatara*) as contrary to the nature of godhead—'Krishna could never be God' (Sarasvati 1994: 219)—Dayananda opted for the idea of revelation such as found in Abrahamic religions.[9] He declared: 'God instructed human souls by virtue of his Omniscience and Omnipresence without the use of organs of speech...by virtue of his

7. Dayananda authored three major works, an introduction to Vedic commentary (*Rigvedadibhashya Bhumika*), a manual of lifecycle rituals (*Samskara Vidhi*), and a general work (*Satyarth Prakash*) on varied themes, such as the stages of life, education, government, godhead, knowledge, and true and false religions. The first two books are in Sanskrit and the third is in Hindi. The last named (it came out in two editions in 1875 and 1883) is best known, obviously because it is written in Hindi with the general reader in mind and deals with general issues. For Dayananda's views on Hindu scriptures, expressed in his writings, see Llewellyn 1993: 157–263.

8. Gandhi's opinion of *Satyarth Prakash* is worth quoting:

I have profound respect for Dayananda Saraswati. I think that he has rendered great service to Hinduism.... But he has made his Hinduism narrow. I have read *Satyarth Prakash*, the Arya Samaj Bible.... I have not read a more disappointing book from a reformer so great. He has claimed to stand for truth and nothing else. But he has unconsciously misrepresented Jainism, Islam, Christianity, and Hinduism itself (1967: 145).

9. Jordens (1978: 279–80) comments:

Dayananda's restrictive concept of true religion as the religion of one book was no doubt inspired by the concept prevalent among Protestant missionaries. He accepted their premise of a divine revelation given once and for all time, and applied to the four *Vedas*. But he went even further than any Christian fundamentalist would have dared to go by claiming that the *Vedas* contained the totality of all knowledge, spiritual, moral, social, political, and even scientific.

presence in [the human heart]' (ibid.: 236). Needless to emphasize, this was, like his notion of reconversion of lapsed Hindus through purification, a radical departure from the Hindu religious tradition. Having redefined the character of the Vedas, Dayananda called upon all true, 'noble' Hindus (the Aryas) to order their religious and social lives in accordance with the perfect knowledge enshrined in the scripture. Although he wrote an exposition of Vedic knowledge, which clearly amounted to a radical reinterpretation (see Llewellyn 1993), he did not consider his views binding on the Aryas. For their guidance he also prepared a manual on life-cycle rituals which turned out to be a strong binding force among the Arya Samajis.

The seeds of schism were also present in the movement from the very beginning. Not long after Dayananda's passing in 1883, the Aryas divided into moderates and militants. The former were less sectarian and more secular in their orientation, and devoted themselves to the task of social reconstruction through what they called Anglo-Vedic education (see Kumar 1993) and other ameliorative activities. They also became involved in the politics of nationalism. The moderates, Kenneth Jones observes, 'like Jewish intellectuals who founded Zionism, or the anglicized Muslims who dreamed of Pakistan, sought political solutions to the problems that faced the Hindu community. Their Arya Dharm merged with a broader Hindu consciousness' (1976: 315).

The militants—so-called—were more intensely religious in orientation and, therefore, also more exclusive. They believed Dayananda to have been a divinely inspired seer and, therefore, infallible. They 'sought to create a new man, the Arya Hindu, and a new world for him to inhabit' (ibid.: 316). The difference between the two types of Aryas ranged from diet and ritual to education and politics, but should not be exaggerated. It remained confined to Punjab and was more a matter of personal preference than an institutional schism. The really significant division was between the Arya Samajis, on the one hand, and orthodox Hindus (the Sanatanis), on the other. Fundamentalism always is a double-edged sword: while it brings the like-minded closer together (through their precisely defined beliefs and clearly laid-out programmes of action), simultaneously it separates them sharply from those who do not belong with them—in this case the Sanatanis as well as the Sikhs and the Muslims of the province.

Dayananda's explicit concerns had been religious, cultural, and social. His bitterness about the aggressive evangelical activities of the missionaries not only made him very critical of Christianity, but also generated strong nationalistic sentiments in him. The days of nationalist politics were yet to dawn, however; he died in 1883, two years before the founding of the Indian National Congress. It was only with the rise of Mahatma Gandhi as the leader of the Congress, at the end of the first World War, that Arya Samajis were actively drawn into the national movement (see Jones 1976: 40–52). Prominent Arya Samaj leaders such as Svami Shraddhanand and Lala Lajpat Rai, were active in the campaign against the Rowlatt Bills and supported Gandhi's first non-cooperation movement. Simultaneously, the Arya Samaj went ahead with its programme of reconversion: this inevitably intensified communal tensions between the Hindus generally and the Muslims and Sikhs virtually all over north India. The Muslim response to the Aryas' *Shuddhi* (ritual purification) and *Sangathan* (organization) were *tablig* and *tanzim* respectively. The two sets of words, one Sanskrit and the other Arabic, had exactly the same meanings. From that time onward, the Arya Samaj, which spread beyond Punjab, although never in a big way, came to be associated with Hindu rather than nationalist-secular political aspirations.[10]

The above discussion, mainly of the views of Dayananda Sarasvāti, is not by any means an adequate account of his work or of the activities of the various Arya Samajes; it is not intended to be that. My inquiry is focused on exploring the circumstances under which certain fundamentalist ideas, which began to make their appearance in a sporadic manner from the 1820s onwards, first in Bengal and then in western India,[11] matured into a well-articulated ideology and an active organization in Punjab in the last quarter of the century. The free-floating ideas that had been present in earlier movements, or in the writings of particular individuals, and later contributed to the making of this fundamentalist ideology included, notably, the

10. It was in the setting of this communal confrontation that Maulana Abul Kalam Azad made the statement quoted above (p.162) regarding the threat to national interests in his presidential address to the Indian National Congress at Delhi in 1923.

11. I have not gone into the developments in Bombay and Poona—other than the founding of the Arya Samaj—for which see Kumar 1968, Dobbin 1972, and Masselos 1974.

apprehension of corruption of religious belief and practice and of social abuses. This in turn generated efforts aimed at religious reconstruction and social reform. Religious reconstruction emphasized the need to return to a pristine state of purity exemplified by scripture. Dayananda carried these ideas forward to a vedic claim of monopoly over the Truth, since the Veda alone was, according to him, the word of God. He thus denied other religions any legitimacy to exist. Further, he claimed a compatibility between Vedic knowledge and modern science.[12] The transformations of earlier ideas wrought by Dayananda, and the innovations he made, together constitute an ideology which is fundamentalist. It is similar to the views put forward by, for example, Maulana Maududi, which were discussed earlier in this book (see pp. 139ff.).[13]

In conclusion, I would like to point out here that the emergence of fundamentalism in Hindu society is a later development than in Muslim and even Sikh society. Moreover, like Sikh fundamentalism, it took shape in Punjab, and remained a regional phenomenon for several decades. In fact, Hindu and Sikh fundamentalisms fed on each other. The confrontation with evangelical Christianity, increasingly identified in the minds of the people with the British rulers

12. Dayananda's insistence on Vedic knowledge being inclusive of all valid knowledge, including Western science and technology, was based on only a rudimentary acquaintance with the latter. The idea was elaborated by some of his gifted followers. The contributions of Guru Datta appear to have been particularly notable. The holder of a Master's degree in science, he was a member of the faculty at the prestigious Government College in Lahore, and had an influential leadership position in the Samaj. In his writings, 'Vedic knowledge and science complemented each other in a hierarchial arrangement with Vedic truth superior to all other forms of knowledge' (Jones 1976: 162). Jones notes that during these last years of the nineteenth century young educated Punjabis were particularly attracted to science and technology. The presence of intellectuals such as Guru Datta and Ruchi Ram Sahni (of the Punjab Meteorological Service) within the Arya Samaj would have gone a long way in enhancing its appeal among educated people. The similarity of this situation to that in the post-revolution Iran, where Ayotullah Khomeini's inner circle included ayatullahs such as Murtaza Mutahhari who were conversant with developments in modern science, is striking.

13. J.E. Llewylln (1993: 86–153) has presented an extended argument in support of the characterization of the Arya Samaj as a fundamentalist movement. The criteria employed by him are derived directly from a paradigm developed by Martin Mary (1988). There are several similarities between Llewylln's discussion and my own, and I too have found Marty's paradigm instructive. My approach is different, however, in certain crucial respects from both Marty's and Llewylln's. This will be obvious to the attentive reader.

through the nineteenth century, is of key importance in this development. The transformation of a positive attitude towards Christianity
into a negative one occured in the fifty years between the deaths of
Rammohun Roy in 1833 and Dayananda Sarasvati in 1883. Dayananda and Keshub Sen, the third of the great leaders of Brahmo Samaj,
died within a year of each other. While Dayananda left behind him
a vigorous ideology backed by an organization, Keshub bequeathed
no more than a cultural space for Hindu revivalism. In Punjab, the
exclusivist Aryas included the religiously pluralist Brahmos among
the opponents they had to overcome, and this they did quite comfor-
tably.

Hindutva and the RSS

In the development of Hindu fundamentalism, the emergence of the
Arya Samaj in Punjab towards the end of the nineteenth century is a
watershed. From then onward there could be no turning back.
Dayananda Sarasvati had contributed, among others, two key ideas
that I have adopted, as characteristic of religious fundamentalism,
namely a return to scripture or, more precisely, canonical authority,
and reform of an allegedly corrupt way of life. The third key idea,
namely the quest for power, was present only in a subdued or implicit
mode, as a setting for the Arya Samaj movement, rather than as its
announced goal. The emphasis upon the Vedas as books that were in
principle available to one and all, and the rejection of the value of
the ministrations of priests, had of course been a blow to the established pattern of the distribution of power within the caste-stratified
Hindu society. Power as a crucial element in the external order of
Hindu society, that is in the arena of Indian politics, remained outside
the formally adopted programme of the Arya Samaj, although it
absorbed the public life of many of its prominent members.

A Hindu political party, distinct from the Hindu dominated Indian
National Congress, namely the Hindu Mahasabha, was established
in 1915 (see Jones 1995). It began with a modest agenda of the
protection of specifically Hindu interests (most notably, cow-protec-
tion and the promotion of Hindi and the Devanagari script), but failed
to make much of an impact on the politics of the day. Demands for
its activization were made in the early 1920s, following the worsen-
ing of Hindu-Muslim relations and the involvement of the Congress

in the Khilafat movement (1919–20) under Mahatma Gandhi's leadership (see Minault 1982). Not only was the Hindu Mahasabha revived, Hindu *sabhas* cropped up in many parts of the country, including Bengal and Madras. A clear statement about the alleged threat to the Hindu community's interests that militant Muslims posed, and the need for Hindu unity and a show of strength, was made by the prominent Congress leader, Madan Mohan Malaviya (founder of the Banaras Hindu University), who presided over a national meeting of the Mahasabha in August 1923. The prominent Arya Samaj leader, Lajpat Rai of Punjab (he was a Congress leader), too, was involved in the effort to make the Mahasabha a strong political force.

In the context of the present discussion, the most significant development was the publication in the same year (1923) of a book, *Hindutva: Who is a Hindu*? written by a notable Mahasabha leader, Vinayak Damodar Savarkar, while in jail as a political prisoner. Dayananda had presented a restrictive definition of the true followers of the original Vedic religion and named them 'Aryas' ("the noble people"). They were contrasted to the Sanatan Dharmis, that is Hindus who followed religious and social practices which he considered degenerate. As already noted, he also rejected the non-Vedic faiths of Buddhism, Jainism, and Sikhism as false. Savarkar emphatically favoured the term 'Hindu', tracing it back to the geographical designation Sindhu—Hindus being the people who lived in the lands between the river Sindhu (Indus) and the high seas, and whose original scriptures were the Vedas. For them, the country so defined was both their fatherland (*pitribhu*) and their holyland (*punyabhu*), and they constituted one nation, the Hindu nation. The acknowledgement of a common nationality (*rashtra*), a common race (*jati*), and a common culture or civilization (*sanskriti*), constituted, in Savarkar's considered opinion, the ideology of 'Hindutva', that is being a Hindu.[14]

---

14. Savarkar writes (1989: 116):

A Hindu ... is he who looks upon the land that extends from Sindhu to Sindhu—from the Indus to the Seas—as the land of his forefathers—his Fatherland (Pitribhu), who inherits the blood of that race whose first discernible source could be traced to the Vedic Saptasindhus, and which on its onward march, assimilating much that was incorporated and ennobling much that was assimilated, has come to be known as the Hindu people, who has inherited and claims as his own the culture of that race as expressed chiefly in their common classical language Sanskrit, and represented by a common history, a common literature, art and architecture, law and jurisprudence, rites and rituals, ceremonies and sacraments, fairs and festivals; and

Savarkar clarified that Hindutva was a complex whole of which Hinduism (the religion) was only 'a derivative, a fraction, a part' (1989: 3). Further, Savarkar insisted, the term Hinduism 'should be restored to its proper significance to denote the religions of all Hindus', including in this broad category Sanatan Dharmis, Arya Samajis, Buddhists, Jains, and Sikhs (ibid.: 107), and even tribal communities such as the Santals (ibid.: 113). It is not surprising that Savarkar should have concluded that, 'the Bohras and such other Mohammedan or Christian communities [as are descended from converted Hindus] possess all essential qualifications of Hindutva but one, and that is that they do not look upon India as their Holyland' (ibid.: 113). These communities are therefore excluded from the 'nation', although they remain in the 'country'. They can be 'incorporated' into the nation only if they 'look upon our land not only as the land of [their] love but even of [their] worship' (ibid.: 84). The 'choice of love' is open to them, for they are 'our countrymen and our old kith and kin' (ibid.: 115).

Savarkar's momentous declaration—'a coherent and powerful pattern of concepts' (Basu et al. 1993: 6)—has in recent years acquired the undisputed status of the manifesto of Hindu fundamentalism, which is totalitarian in relation to those forcibly grouped together as 'We Hindus', and exclusivist towards those stigmatized as the spiritually alienated 'Others'. Savarkar diluted Dayananda's emphasis upon respect for the scriptures and replaced it by an overwhelming stress upon culture. In the process, the notion of the 'chosen' or 'special' people that is characteristic of fundamentalist movements was broadened as well as sharpened as a political concept. Dayananda's Aryas were called upon to defend the true faith and the true way of life; Savarkar's Hindus were instructed about their pre-eminence as the 'first' citizens of the land by virtue of their

---

who, above all, addresses this land, this Sindhusthan as his Holyland (Punyabhu), as the land of his prophets and seers, of his godmen and gurus, the land of piety and pilgrimage. These are the essentials of Hindutva—a common nation (Rashtra), a common race (Jati), and a common civilization (Sanskriti). All these essentials could best be summed up by stating in brief that he is a Hindu to whom Sindhusthan is not only a Pitribhu but also a Punyabhu. For the first two essentials of Hindutva—nation and Jati—are clearly denoted and connoted by the word Pitribhu, while the third essential of Sanskriti is pre-eminently implied by the word of Punyabhu, as it is precisely Sanskriti including sanskaras, i.e. rites and rituals, ceremonies and sacraments, that makes a land a Holyland.

cultural identity. This shift is not surprising, for the national movement had come a long way since Dayananda's death in 1883, and
Hindu-Muslim political relations had deteriorated considerably.

It is rather paradoxical, therefore, that the public body that apparently was most influenced by Savarkar's ideas about Hindu identity should have disclaimed an interest in politics. Keshav Baliram
Hedgewar, a medical practioner and an active Congressman, and five
collaborators, founded an organization at Nagpur in 1925, two years
after the publication of *Hindutva*, for the protection of Hindu culture.
The name Rashtriya Swayamsevak Sangh (RSS), that is 'the national
organization of volunteers', was given to it two years later. It is
noteworthy that by identifying the organization as 'national'
(*rashtriya*) rather than Hindu, Hedgewar sought to define the nation
in exclusively Hindu terms. He clarified: 'If we use the word "Hindu"
it will only mean that we consider ourselves only as one of the
innumerable communities in this land and that we do not realize our
natural status as the nationals of this country' (see Golwalkar 1980:
177). Further, the justification that Hedgewar provided for the new
organization made it quite clear that Hindutva was being defined
antagonistically as an identity which was under severe pressure from
Muslims, who had been lately politically mobilized during the Khilafat
movement.[15] He also drew attention to the emergent Brahman-non-
Brahman conflict. Expectedly, his first recruits were Brahmans.

Hedgewar's programmatic emphasis was on the character-build-
ing of carefully chosen individuals through physical culture and
ideological instruction.[16] The latter focused on the proclaimed greatness of the Hindu cultural tradition. Although political classes also
were held, organizational objectives were defined non-politically.[17]

15. For a dependable account of the history of the RSS by an insider, see Goyal
(1979a). Also see Andersen and Damle (1987) and Basu et al. (1993).

16. Golwalkar (1980) lists four virtues of the ideal person: invincible physical strength,
character or the commitment to a worthy cause, intellectual acumen, and fortitude.

17. The RSS did not have a written memorandum of association until required by
the Government of India to produce one as a precondition for the removal of the ban
that was imposed upon it following the assassination of Mahatma Gandhi in 1948. In
the written constitution of 1949, the objectives for which the RSS was established are
described as follows: 'To eradicate differences among Hindus; to make them realize the
greatness of their past; to inculcate in them a spirit of self-sacrifice and selfless devotion
to Hindu society as a whole; to build up an organized and well-disciplined corporate life;
and to bring about the regeneration of Hindu society' (Goyal 1979a: 206, translated from
the original text in Hindi, which is more detailed, see Goyal 1979b: 164).

Members were free to participate in politics but not as RSS workers. Hedgewar, who became the 'supreme guide' (*sarsanghchalak*) in 1929, temporarily withdrew from the position in 1931 during his participation in the Civil Disobedience Movement launched by the Congress. By 1934, the RSS had acquired enough visibility, and Hindu-Muslim relations had worsened further, for the Congress to debar its members from formally associating with communal organizations including the Hindu Mahasabha, the RSS, and the Muslim League.

Although bracketed together by others, the Mahasabha and the RSS maintained distinctive identities, the crucial difference being the latter's proclaimed non-participation in political activities. The RSS spread to north India from its Maharashtrian homeground, however, with the help of the established Mahasabha and Arya Samaj organizational networks. Some ideological give-and-take between the three bodies also occured, but they stayed apart. The distance widened further after Hedgewar's death in 1940 when Madhav Sadashiv Golwalkar, designated by Hedgewar as his successor, took over as the 'supreme guide'. In fact, the 1940s saw a clear stiffening of the RSS ideology, marked by, first, an emphatic rejection of political activity; secondly, an enhanced emphasis on the notion of nationality defined in terms of the criteria of 'fatherland' and 'holyland';[18] and thirdly, an implicit exclusion of Christians and Muslims from the 'nation'.

In Golwalkar's definition of it, even more strongly than in Hedgewar's, the RSS was a cultural organization concerned with national rejuvenation. The nation under reference was, in his words, the 'full-fledged ancient nation of the Hindus' (Golwalkar 1980: 182), united by geography, race, religion, culture, and language— 'the famous five unities' (Golwalkar 1938). Earlier, in the Muslim period, this nation had been weakened by internal dissensions and alien influences. In contemporary times, the Congress had denied the reality on the ground, and embraced 'the phantom of unity' between

18. Golwalkar writes (1980: 73–4):

We existed when there was no necessity for any name. We were the good, the enlightened people. We were the people who knew about the laws of nature and the laws of the Spirit. We built a great civilization, a great culture, and a unique social order.... The name "Hindu", derived from the river Sindhu, has been associated with us in our history and tradition for so long that it has now become our universally accepted and adored name.

the sons of the soil and the 'invaders', namely Muslims and Christians. The Jews and the Parsis were 'guests' for they did not entertain political ambitions. Pursuantly, Golwalkar wrote (1938: 52):

[T]he non-Hindu people in Hindustan must either adopt the Hindu culture and language, must learn to respect and revere Hindu religion, must entertain no idea but the glorification of the Hindu nation, i.e. they must not only give up their attitude of intolerance and ingratitude towards this land and its age-long traditions, but must also cultivate the positive attitude of love and devotion instead; in one word they must cease to be foreigners or may stay in the country wholly subordinated to the Hindu nation claiming nothing, deserving no privileges, far less any preferential treatment, not even citizen's rights.

The above is an unambiguous statement about power, couched in cultural and political terms; the relation between culture and politics is obviously regarded as an internal (hierarchical) one. In view of this, the professed non-involvement of the RSS in politics can be seen for what it is, namely a *strategy*. If we recognize the pre-eminence of Hindu culture, Hindu monopoly over power is ensured ideologically. It is, of course, also expressed demographically through the overwhelming Hindu majority in the population and consequently in the electorate. The official census today puts this majority at 83 per cent; if the Scheduled Castes and Tribes are excluded, the proportion is about 20 points lower. In such a situation, politics is the art of the understatement, but when the need arises, words are not minced as the above quotation from Golwalkar shows. And when the time was opportune, the RSS provided all support to Shyama Prasad Mookerjee when he established a new political party, Jana Sangh, in 1951.

It is important to note here that the above statement was made by Golwalkar two years before he became the RSS chief. The assumption of this supreme authority and the responsibility that went with it made him more circumspect in his pronouncements, but the essence of his politico-cultural position remained unchanged. He stressed the limited, instrumental character of politics—he called it 'an external appliance' (1938: 98)—as also its 'lure' and its corrupting influence. He doubted if political power could at all lead to cultural rejuvenation, and even called for 'restraints' on the power of the state (ibid.: 89–100). This call was combined by Golwalkar with an emphasis on the holistic nature of culture, which he defined in psychological ('mental patterns', ibid.: 167) and of course behavioural terms. The quest for 'God realization', the importance of life-cycle rituals (*samskara*) in imprinting true character on the individual, the salience of the traditional goals of human striving (*purushartha*), self-restraint, and altruism are reiterated in his writings and speeches as the key elements of Hindu culture.

The importance of religion in the RSS ideology is unclear. Judging by what the ideologues, notably Golwalkar, have written, or by what the workers do organizationally, rituals and matters of theological import—particularly the latter—do not seem to receive much attention. Scriptural authority was hardly ever employed by Golwalkar to justify any beliefs or actions. The emphasis is consistently on *sanskriti* (culture), which is, however, derived from *dharma* (religion). In the preamble to the constitution of the RSS, it is stated that the rejuvenation of Hindu society should be based on religion and culture, in that order (see Goyal 1979b: 164). From Dayananda to Golwalkar, there is a clear shift from the critical importance of the canon to that of culture or, more precisely 'national' culture.

The issue of 'foreigners', therefore, acquires crucial significance. I have already quoted Golwalkar's 1938 statement. Later pronouncements may be more cautiously worded, but remain essentially unaltered. 'Foreigners' that were 'invaders', but regard themselves as 'victors' and until recently 'rulers and masters', are called 'enemies' and 'traitors' by him, particularly if they are lacking in respect for the 'traditions' and 'historical personages' of the country, and are indifferent to its 'security and integrity' (Golwalkar 1992: 275–6).[19] The identification between Hindus and the country is, however, qualified. After the ban on the RSS imposed following Gandhi's assassination had been lifted in 1949, Golwalkar said that there was no land other than India that the Hindus could call their own, but 'we do not say that Hindusthan is the country of Hindus

---

19. The issue of the attitude of particular communities or organiztions to the history of India is rather complex, and much depends upon what is expected to be the content of this attitude, whether a largely uncritical admiration for the Hindu past, as seems to be the case in the RSS ideology, or a general sense of history as was advocated most notably by Jawaharlal Nehru in *The Discovery of India* (1946) and other writings and speeches. Thus, addressing the convocation of the Aligarh Muslim University in 1948 (a few months after the partition), he asked his largely Muslim audience (Nehru 1987: 25):

I have said that I am pround of our inheritance and our ancestors who gave an intellectual and cultural preeminence to India. How do you feel about this past? Do you feel that you are also sharers in it and inheritors of it and, therefore, proud of something that belongs to you as much as to me?

only' (ibid.: 278). He clarified the RSS position on the issue of religious minorities, for instance in 1969, when he asserted that an invitation to the descendants of converts (Christians and Muslims), to 'rejoin their family' could not be called 'irresponsible'. Making a clear break with Dayananda's religious approach, he played down the importance of 'ritual purification' (*shuddhi*), which he considered only emotionally significant, and spoke in terms of 'return' and 'transformation'. Those returning could, he declared, continue their non-Hindu modes of 'worship' (ibid.: 293–4).

Golwalkar presented four kinds of levels or *dharma*, namely the national (*rashtra*), social (*samaja*), lineage (*kula*), and individual (*vyakti*) (1980: 173). The arrangement is hierarchical, so that the lowest, individual level is subordinated to the others, and *rashtra dharma*, or 'love of the motherland' encompasses the others. *Kula dharma* embodies the value of fraternity and *samaj dharma* that of common culture (heritage, history, ideals, and aspirations). The first three levels, and the values typifying them, constitute the national culture, and are indeed 'the bedrock of national integration' (ibid.: 175). One must conform to them in order to belong to the nation. Freedom of choice is available only at the comprehensively circumscribed individual level. The public arena is homogenized, and pluralism is allowed to operate in the private domain of personal faith and worship. Only in this limited sense are Golwalkar's exhortations that Hindus must be tolerant about religions other than their own to be understood. In 1971, he said: 'The Hindu is born secular. He accepts the truth that there are different paths to God Realization' (1980: 646).

The above discussion of Golwalkar's views should suffice to bring out the fact that, disavowals about politics notwithstanding, the ultimate objective of the RSS is political domination through cultural homogenization. This endeavour inevitably brings the organization into conflict with such Hindus as are the votaries of the political and economic ideologies of liberal democracy, capitalism, and socialism or communism. These ideologies are denounced by RSS ideologues for not only being alien but also materialist. Criticism of Western lifestyles, although somewhat less strident, also is a basic feature of the RSS ideology. The westernized Hindu is deemed to be the internal enemy of the 'national' culture, the 'pure and sublime' character of which is said to have been subject to a 'thousand-year-long corroding influence of foreigners' (Golwalkar 1980: 163). As we have seen earlier (in our discussion of Sikh and Muslim fundamentalisms), the recognition of internal enemies alongside of external foes is a characteristic feature of fundamentalist movements.

In view of the foregoing discussion, what conclusions may be drawn about the RSS ideology in the context of Hindu fundamentalism?[20] To avoid fruitless quibbling, it is best to use the words 'nationalism' and 'fundamentalism' synonymously if the former is used in the manner of the RSS ideologues. In fact, 'nationalism' has the advantage of drawing attention to the concern with power. It is at the same time noteworthy that the emphasis upon culture has resulted in a dilution of interest in religious issues, such as was central to the teachings of Dayananda Sarasvati and to the vision of Arya Samaj.[21] What is more, the critique of lifestyles that are considered alien and corrupt by the RSS, and which therefore have to be purged, does not seem to have the depth of social concern that characterized the Arya Samaj movement. Even the idea of cultural rejuvenation lacks precision: not only is an original source of inspiration like the rigorously defined Vedic corpus in Dayananda's teaching missing, the process of return also is denuded of its ritual character which had bestowed power on it at the turn of the century.

I earlier argued that the Arya Samaj was a fundamentalist movement among the Hindus, which rested upon a radical reinterpretation of the Hindu religious tradition in its cosmological, theological, scriptural, ethical, and socio-cultural aspects. Its organizational pattern also was modern. The RSS ideology is, by comparison, much

20. M.S. Golwalkar was succeeded on his death in 1973 by Madhukar D. Deoras, who in turn handed over the office of 'supreme guide' to Rajendra Singh in 1993 on account of his failing health. I do not consider it necessary to discuss the views of the latter two leaders as they have not made any major additions or alterations to the ideology as formulated by Savarkar, Hedgewar, and Golwalkar. Deoras's only significant contribution has been an explicit interest in politics, and this is expected to be carried forward by Singh. I consider this more a matter of 'form' than of 'substance': the political objectives of the RSS have been present in the ideology right from the very beginning in the early 1920s.

21. Satish Saberwal suggests (in a personal communication) that 'the underplaying of the religious' by RSS perhaps follows from:

recognizing that a rigorous scripturalist stance would be devisive. The Arya Samaj tried, but the Vedas are too remote to strike a wide chord. In Islam, Christianity, and Sikhism, a complex of practices and roles has historically linked scripture with everyday life; in Hinduism there is a great profusion of such complexes and scriptures. The latter day attempt at mobilizing Sadhus for unfamiliar roles is an attempt to overcome that profusion.

narrower, and valorizes what it calls the national culture of India. Its organizational set-up is more regimented than that of the Arya Samaj (see Andersen and Damle 1987: 83–107). Power is exercised within the RSS most systematically employing the instruments of 'discipline', 'training', and 'surveillance'. So perfect is the organization that individual workers do not see themselves as 'the points of application of power' (to continue use of Foucauldian terms) but its 'vehicles' (see Foucault 1980). The RSS shares with the Samaj a formal denial of the importance of the leader—both Hedgewar and Golwalkar wrote and spoke to that effect—but in reality the 'supreme guide' is indeed *supreme* and much more than a guide. In short, the character of the internal organization of the RSS marks it as fundamentalist.

While neither movement formally acknowledges any political goals, the RSS has gradually unravelled its objectives and spawned a family of political organizations that today includes the Bharatiya Janata Party (BJP), which is but the Jana Sangh reborn (see Graham 1990), and the Vishwa Hindu Parishad (VHP) (see van der Veer 1994a and b). The emergence of these bodies has proceeded hand in hand with heightened religiosity among Hindus, particularly the urban middle classes. New deities, new sacred symbols, and new forms of collective religious celebrations, some of which are reminiscent of the elementary forms of the religious life that Emile Durkheim (1965) wrote about, have arisen (see also Babb 1986 and Juergensmeyer 1991). An analysis of the political and electoral dimensions of Hindu nationalism, and an interpretation of such religious movements, however, is beyond the scope of this book.

Gandhi's Hinduism

Continuing my examination of India's religious traditions, I made an attempt in the last chapter to inquire what resources within Hinduism might be identified as supportive of the ideology of secularism that seeks to limit or privatize the role of religion in social life. The discussion focused on the absence of a sacred-secular dichotomy, and led to the Hindu notion of pluralism which is essentially hierarchical and inclusivist. In the present chapter, I have discussed the emergence of religious fundamentalism among the Hindus in some parts of the country in the second half of the nineteenth century, and its transformation into an apparently apolitical but frankly inclusivist/exclusivist cultural nationalism from the 1920s onward, which has been in fact, political from the very beginning, was also noted. In course of time, this nationalism or fundamentalism has generated moderate as well as militant political parties, or other organizations, all over the country.

Now, in the minds of many thoughtful people in India and abroad, the person who best exemplified the modern Hindu sensibility was Mahatma Gandhi. I will conclude this chapter by offering some observations on his thinking on Hinduism, reserving for the next comment on his rejection of a secularist worldview (that denies or severely limits the importance of religion in politics), despite his espousal of the ideal of a secular (non-interventionist) state.[22]

Gandhi was born a Hindu and this fact was for him the very foundation of his life. The family had broad religious sympathies—combining Vaishnava, Jain, and Islamic elements—and imparted to him, during his childhood, a pluralist orientation that was later confirmed by his own mature reflection. This process of maturation led him to gradually abandon dogmatic and ritualistic Hinduism, and to concentrate on deliberately designed practice within a framework defined by morality and reason. Gandhi wrote (in 1927): 'Believing as I do in the influence of heredity, being born in a Hindu family, I have remained a Hindu. I should reject it if I found it inconsistent with my moral sense or my spiritual growth' (see Gandhi 1969: 166). The inner life was not opposed to the outer; the two were rather integrated in a seamless whole.

Time and again, throughout his life, Gandhi emphasized the final authority of moral conscience and rational thought. When a conflict between the two was encountered, the former was treated as superior. He considered the 'inner voice', 'the small voice within', divine guidance. The scriptures, or the remembered tradition, were accorded only conditional authority.[23] Gandhi maintained that the

22. For a handy selection of Gandhi's written or spoken statements on Hinduism, see Iyer 1986. For interpretation of the same, see Chatterji 1983, Iyer 1986, and Parekh 1989a and b. The basic source is, of course, *The Collected Works of Mahatma Gandhi* (vols. 1–100). There is no serious study of Gandhi's life and work that does not discuss his views on Hinduism and on religion generally: see, e.g., Brown 1992. The corpus of shorter works is truly enormous: see, e.g., Nanda 1990.

23. It may be noted here that in the traditional literature, four sources of *dharma* are identified: the Vedas, the conduct of those seers who know the Vedas, the example of righteous men, and 'self-validation' (*atmatushti)* or conscience. See *Manusmriti* II.6 (Buhler 1964: 30).

fundamentals of Hinduism were not to be sought in the 'ample scriptures', which were at no point of time complete or perfect, and much less in a literalist reading of them.[24] He said (in 1924): 'Vedas to be divine must be a living word, ever growing, ever expanding and ever responding to new forces. The priest clung to the letter and missed the spirit' (Gandhi 1967: 85–6). He rejected the notion of a single, once-for-ever, act of divine revelation to a chosen people, whether in the form found in the Abrahamic religious, or in Dayananda's reinterpretation of the Vedic corpus (which I discussed earlier). 'I do not believe in the exclusive divinity of the Vedas,' Gandhi declared (in 1921). 'I decline to be bound by any interpretation, however learned it may be, if it is repugnant to reason or moral sense' (Gandhi 1966: 246). Nothing could be more explicit or emphatic, and I have not found any other, *later*, statement in the *Collected Works* that would indicate a significant change in Gandhi's thinking.

Freedom from dogmas was, in Gandhi's judgement, the best thing about Hinduism. He wrote (in 1927) (Gandhi 1969: 166–7, emphasis added):

I have found [Hinduism] to be the most tolerant of all religions known to me. Its freedom from dogma makes a forcible appeal to me inasmuch as it gives the votary the largest scope for self-expression. Not being an exclusive religion, it enables the followers of [the] faith not merely to respect all the other religions, but *it also enables them to admire and assimilate whatever may be good in the other faiths.*[25]

Gandhi practised what he preached. He acknowledged the enormous influence—joyously received—of the moral content of Christianity on his own thinking summed up best of all in the Sermon on the Mount, in which, Gandhi declared, 'Jesus has given a definition of perfect *dharma*' (see Chatterji 1983: 41–57).[26] Similarly, he

24. Gandhi wrote (1925): 'I am not a literalist. Therefore, I try to understand the *spirit* of the various scriptures of the world. I apply the test of Truth and Ahimsa laid down by these very scriptures for interpretation. I reject what is inconsistent with the test, and I appropriate all that is consistent with it' (Gandhi 1968: 111).

25. It may be noted here that Gandhi consistently maintained that Hinduism includes Buddhism, Jainism, and Sikhism. At the same time he did not deny the followers of these religious traditions the right to consider themselves distinct from Hindus. See, e.g., his views on Sikhism and the Sikh gurus, and on Sikh sensitivities, in Gandhi 1968: 263–4.

26. One of his earliest Christian admirers, the Rev. Joseph Doke of South Africa, who also was his first biographer, wrote (Doke 1967: 106):

praised (in 1929) 'Islam's distinctive contribution to India's national culture [through] its unadulterated belief in the oneness of God and a practical application of the truth of the brotherhood of man for those who are within its fold' (Gandhi 1970: 58).

The core of Gandhi's being, however, was Hindu, as he himself acknowledged throughout his life, and as the most perceptive of his Christian admirers, Charles F. Andrews, also noted. Gandhi's Hinduism was not, however, a stock of fundamentals, but 'a living organism'. A final quotation on this should suffice. It is from an article in *Young India*, 8 April 1926 (see Iyer 1986: 488):

...Hinduism is a living organism liable to growth and decay.... one and indivisible at the root, it has grown into a vast tree with immumerable branches... It is and is not based on scriptures. It does not derive its authority from one book. The *Gita* is universally accepted, but even it only shows the way. It has hardly any effect on custom.... It takes a provincial form in every province, but *the inner substance* is retained everywhere (emphasis added).[27]

In writing of the inner substance within a tradition of dynamism, did Gandhi, after all, think of Hinduism in terms of a set of fundamentals? Yes, he did. Writing in *Young India* (6 October 1921), he presented a definition of *'sanatana* [eternal] Hinduism' in terms of his own belief in: (1) the Hindu scriptures (Vedas, Upanishads, Puranas) and the ideas of reincarnation and rebirth; (2) the *varnashrama* dharma 'but not in its present and crude sense' which included untouchability; and (3) cow protection 'in its much larger sense'; as also (4) his willingness to accommodate idol-worship (see Gandhi 1966: 245–50). Of these he selected the protection of the cow as the

------

I question whether any system of religion can absolutely hold him. His views are too closely allied to Christianity to be entirely Hindu; and too deeply saturated with Hinduism to be called Christian, while his sympathies are so wide and catholic that one would imagine he has reached a point where the formulae of sects are meaningless.

27. Gandhi did not lay down for all Hindus that they should consider any particular text as the holiest and basic scripture comparable to, say, the Bible or the Quran. He observed (in 1927): 'The question, which is the chief religious work, one can only answer for oneself. For me it is the *Gita*' (see Iyer 1986: 85). A decade later, he clarified that his reinterpretation of the *Gita* was 'a new but natural and logical interpretation upon the whole teaching of the *Gita* and the spirit of Hinduism.' He considered this scripture a reinterpretation of the earlier ideas of *karma, sannyasa* and *yajna*. Further, he described the great epics, *Mahabharata* and *Ramayana* as 'undoubtedly allegories' (Gandhi 1976: 339).

'central fact of Hinduism', elaborating it in a manner that elevates it into a master symbol of harmony in the cosmos, plenitude in this world, and compassion in society (ibid.: 248). The spirit underlying this enunciation of fundamentals was, however, explicitly anti-fundamentalist. Gandhi's sights were ultimately set on religious transcendentalism. He wrote in 1920 (see Gandhi 1965: 406):

I have been experimenting with myself and my friends by introducing religion into politics. Let me explain what I mean by religion. It is not the Hindu religion, which I prize above all other religions, but the religion which transcends Hinduism, which changes one's very nature, which binds one indissolubly to the truth and which ever purifies.

In short, Gandhi's emphasis was not on fundamentals of belief and practice mindlessly defined and mechanically enforced, nor indeed was it on reviving tradition *qua* tradition. The stress was rather on the cultivation of an over-arching moral sensibility in which the rational outlook is leavened by recognition of the indispensability of ultimate, moral, values. Gandhi's ideal of 'Ram Raj' did not so much recall a past mythological time as it emphasized the moral foundations of society and derivatively of the state. It recalls Ashoka's doctrine of *Dhamma*.[28] It is obvious that pluralism easily degenerates into cultural, and worse moral, solipsism unless it is redeemed through reference to a higher, transcendental, level, for example in the manner suggested by Gandhi. Secularism as an ideology in which man is the measure of value and instrumental

28. See the earlier discussion of the Ashokan state (p. 201). It may be pointed out here that, while Gandhi's Ram Raj has been suspected to signify Hindu political domination, the symbols of *Dhamma* have been adopted to underwrite the religious neutrality of the Indian state. Gandhi's religious symbolism was contaminated by the poison of communalism that marked his time, although not his own attitude, and suffered from the demographic preponderance of Hindus in the country's population. As even Nehru observed (with obvious anguish), in his autobiography, Gandhi's continual stress on the religious and spiritual side of the national movement, although not dogmatic, did bestow upon it a revivalistic character among the masses. In contrast, the Ashokan state is very remote in time (the middle of the third century BC) and Buddhists have virtually vanished from the country. The glory of Gandhi's life lies in his assassination at the hands of a Hindu extremist with RSS associations, who considered him an enemy of Hindu cultural ideals and political interests (see Nandy 1980: 70–97). In more recent times, the notion of Ram Raj has indeed become a menacing symbol of Hindu intolerance exemplified by the destruction of the so-called Babri mosque in Ayodhya on 6 December 1992 by the followers of the RSS-BJP-VHP combine (see van der Veer 1994b: 2–11, 152–62).

values are deemed to be ultimate values, was, in his opinion, only a form of hedonism. The contemporary worldwide disenchantment with secularism as a worldview would not have come as a surprise to Gandhi.[29]

Anticipating the argument, I will only note here that the pluralist, and indeed syncretist, tradition, emanating within the Hindu religious tradition in modern times from the life and work of Rammohan Roy, and culminating in a radical reinterpretation by Gandhi, seems to have weakened following the emergence of so-called democratic, mass politics, and the rise of new middle classes in both rural and urban areas. For them, the insular religiosity of the RSS-BJP-VHP type is said to hold a strong appeal, although state-assembly elections in 1994–95 have not provided evidence of a massive or widespread electoral swing in its favour. It commands the allegiance of no more than about one-fifth of the electorate and remains a primarily north Indian party that is gaining strength in the west. The threat of Hindutva is real however, like a gathering storm, and Nehruvian secularism, although still a powerful force, is no longer unquestioned: indeed it is in a crisis.

29. The philosopher Mrinal Miri (1995) has convincingly argued that the epistemology characteristic of modern secular humanism 'is unable to provide a basis for belief in the reality of values' and that in Gandhi 'we have an alternative epistemology... that accounts for the possibility of self-knowledge, which is also... knowledge of moral truths'. He concludes that within, 'the Gandian epistemic scheme, the ideal relationship between different religions of the world is one of international [intercommunal/ intercommunity?] fellowship'.

Chapter
Eight

The Crisis of Indian Secularism

India will be a land of many faiths, equally honoured and respected, but of one
national outlook.
JAWAHARLAL NEHRU, 24 January 1948

I am convinced that every nation and every people come to some form of
religious self-understanding whether the critics like it or not.
ROBERT N. BELLAH, *Beyond Belief*

'When I use a word', Humpty Dumpty said, in rather a scornful tone, 'it
means just what I choose it to mean—neither more nor less.'
'The question is', said Alice, 'whether you can make words means so many
different things.'
'The question is', said Humpty Dumpty, 'which is to be master—that's all.'
LEWIS CARROLL, *Through the Looking Glass*

Introduction

In the present Chapter, I will explore the nature of Indian secularism
and discuss the difficulties into which it has run. This is a large
undertaking and could well be the theme of a book rather than of a
chapter in one. The most that I can hope to do here is to pose some
critical questions and make suggestions for rethinking the answers.

Three basic assumptions are implicit in the apprehensions about
Indian secularism having run into difficulties. There is, first, the
assumption that secularism as an anti-religious or, at any rate, non-
religious ideology has universal applicability, but that it has culturally specific expressions. This is how many intellectuals consider it
permissible to speak of *Indian* secularism. In other words, secularism
is not an Indian ideology, but there is an Indian ideology of
secularism. The *general* ideology of secularism, it is asserted, has

been historically validated by the experience and achievements of the so-called modern societies of the West in the last four hundred years, and it should have succeeded in India too. Secondly, it is assumed that secularism will be welcomed by all right-thinking persons, for it shows the way to the making of rational plans for social reconstruction and state action, placing ultimate faith in the adequacy of human agency. Finally, there is the assumption that, with appropriate corrective measures, ideological secularism can still be made to succeed in India, notwithstanding all the faltering of the last five decades.

All three assumptions, I think, should be subjected to critical scrutiny, without conflating on-going processes of secularization with the ideology of secularism. The virtues claimed for ideological secularism are not unquestionable nor does it provide answers to all questions about life and living. It has not been a complete success anywhere, and we do not know of any wholly secularized societies. Our times are witness to both secularization and fundamentalism. There are obvious limits to what the theoretical and experimental sciences can enable human beings to know; and there are even more obvious limits to what technology and the bureaucratic organization of work can enable us to do. These limits are the limits of the historic process of 'rationalization', valorized in the ideology of secularism, even in the West, which is said to bring to the non-Western countries intimations of their future as modernizing societies.

I have already discussed (in the first chapter) the emergence of the ideology of secularism in the West in the seventeenth century. Some later developments, including most significantly the rise of religious fundamentalism, were also noted. I drew pointed attention to the Christian setting and, indeed, described secularism as an outcome of the dialectic of the Enlightenment and Protestantism. Finally, I mentioned the distinctiveness of the religious traditions of India including Islam. Three major traditions—Sikhism, Islam and Hinduism—were discussed at considerable length. I concluded the last chapter, which was devoted to Hindu fundamentalism, with a critical summary of Gandhi's conception of Hinduism and his ideal of inter-religious harmony. I will now take up his views on secularism as a backdrop for a discussion of Jawaharlal Nehru's ideology of secularism, which is the main theme of this chapter.

A Gandhian Perspective

Secularism in India is a multivocal word: what it means depends upon who uses the word and in what context. There is, therefore, no single or straight answer to the question as to why secularism in India has run into difficulties. Let me then attempt to present two possible answers which are based on my understanding of Mahatma Gandhi's and Jawaharlal Nehru's views on the relationship of religion, politics and the state. Needless to emphasize, I do not pretend that my answers are what Gandhi and Nehru themselves would have said had they been alive today.

Obviously, we must begin with Mahatma Gandhi because he is often referred to as the spiritual father of Indian secularism. He has even been inaccurately and unjustly called a secularist. If the essence of all varieties of secularism is the demarcation of boundaries between the sacred and secular domains *per se*, then Gandhi would have had no use for any such ideology. Its success would have been a moral disaster. His vision, as has been noted so often, was holistic, with religion as its constitutive principle—as the source of value for judging the worth of all worldly goals and actions. Religion here means, above all, altruism (*sevadharma*), self-assurance arising from inner conviction (*atmatushti*), and the putting of one's faith in the saving grace of God (*Rama nama*).

'For me', Gandhi observed, 'every, the tiniest, activity is governed by what I consider my religion' (see Iyer 1986: 391). Like religious pietists generally, he believed that God permeates every fibre, nook and corner of human experience. This for him was a timeless principle and yet he was very sensitive to the conditions and demands of particular times and places, in conformity with the *kala-desha* (time-place) sensitivity of Indian classical tradition. 'Every age', Gandhi wrote, 'is known to have its predominant mode of spiritual effort best suited for the attainment of *moksha*. ... In this age, only political *sannyasis* can fulfil and adorn the ideal of *sannyasa*'. Consequently, 'No Indian who aspires to follow the way of true religion can afford to remain aloof from politics' (see Parekh 1989a: 100). Gandhian politics, in short, were inseparable from religion. He wrote in 1940:

I cannot conceive politics as divorced from religion. Indeed religion should pervade every one of our actions. Here, religion does not mean sectarianism. It means a belief in ordered moral government of the universe. It is not less, because it is unseen. This religion transcends Hinduism, Islam, Christianity, etc. It does not supersede them. It harmonises them and gives them reality (see Mohan Rao 1968: 34–5).

Now, Bhikhu Parekh asserts in an insightful and thought-provoking discussion of Gandhi's political philosophy that, 'there was hardly a Hindu religious category and practice to which [Gandhi] did not give a worldly and secular content'. In other words, 'Gandhi secularized Hinduism as much as it was possible to do *within* a spiritual framework' (ibid.: 109). The emphasis upon the word 'within' is Parekh's and it is of crucial importance. It signifies that the relationship of the sacred and the secular—of *dharma* and *artha*, or religion and politics—is 'hierarchical' (in the Dumontian sense): the latter category is opposed to the former but also encompassed by it. Did Gandhi, then, secularize religion or did he sacralize politics? Both positions have strong adherents. I would rather side with Margaret Chatterji's judgement that 'Gandhi seems almost a secularist', but judged by his handling of concrete issues, notably the communal (Hindu-Muslim) problem, he 'was not secularist, if by this we mean an attempt to prune away all religious considerations from political matters' (1983: 85).

Gandhi was very careful with his use of words and so must we be in attempting to construct an answer to our question on the basis of first principles such as the above. Politics were sacralized by Gandhi, they became the dharma of the age (*yugadharma*) and, consequently—*not* contradictorily—the state was devalorized, for its constitutive principle is power or coercion. In his conception of the moral or perfect society, Gandhi emphasized that its enduring basis can only be the moral calibre of the individuals who constitute it. He extended the principle to the relationship of the citizen to the state. As Parekh puts it, 'For Gandhi it was the citizen's sense of moral responsibility for his actions that ultimately determined the character of the state' (1989a: 124). In itself, the state, in Gandhian reckoning, is amoral, impersonal, distant, coercive, and even violent. Although Gandhi's views on the modern state became less negative over time, he never warmed up to this institution. In Parekh's summing up, 'It took him a long time to appreciate its moral, regenerative and redistributive role and even then his acceptance of it remained half-hearted and unintegrated into his general perspective' (ibid.: 204). Gandhi did not set much store by Western liberal democracy either, considering it to be rooted in individual selfishness and a materialist conception of the good life (see Parekh 1989b: 74).

A Gandhian, it seems to me, would have to say that secularism has run into difficulties in India because the modern state is too much with us, and intrudes into areas of life where it has no business even to peep. That state is best which governs the least. The ideal to strive for is that of morally sensitive individuals actively promoting civil society. Talking with a Christian missionary in September 1946, Gandhi said: 'If I were a dictator, religion and state would be separate. I swear by my religion, I will die for it. But it is my personal affair. The state has nothing to do with it. The state would look after your secular welfare, health, communications, foreign relations, currency and so on, but not your or my religion. That is everybody's personal concern!' (see Iyer 1986: 395). A year later, soon after independence and a few months before his death, he said : 'The state should undoubtedly be secular. Everyone in it should be entitled to profess his religion without let or hindrance, so long as the citizen obeys the common law of the land' (see Bose 1948: 256). But he was totally against the idea of a state religion or state support for any religion. 'A society or group', he said, 'which depends partly or wholly on state aid for the existence of its religion, does not deserve or, better still, does not have any religion worth the name' (ibid.: 287).

To the extent to which Indian secularism, even though it stands for equal respect for all religious faiths (*sarva dharma samabhava*), is a state ideology, enshrined in the Constitution in which it is linked to the materialist ideology of socialism, and to the extent to which it has nothing to say about the individual except in terms of his or her rights, it is from the Gandhian perspective a hedonistic ideology, and bound to fail. In Judith Brown's excellent summing up, 'In Gandhi's eyes men and women were human in virtue of their capacity for religious vision. ... [If] this was stifled by the individual or by political and economic structures then people were degraded and dehumanized. This was so strong and striking an attack on secular materialism as could be made' (1992: 392).

A Gandhian critique of secularism in terms of ultimate values and individual responsibility is in some respects similar to Max Weber's concern with the problem of value. What Gandhi and Weber are saying is that a secularized world is inherently unstable because it elevates to the realm of ultimate values the only values it knows and these are instrumental values. 'Natural science', Weber said, 'gives us an answer to the question of what we must do if we wish to master life technically. It leaves quite aside, or assumes for its purposes, whether we should and do wish to master life technically and whether it ultimately makes sense to do so' (1948: 144).

Nehru on Religion, Politics and Secularism

Gandhian remedies are believed by modernist Indians to be far-fetched and impractical, if not obscurantist. The fact that he was not a systematic thinker, attaching greater importance to action (*acara*) and experience (*anubhava*) than to formal thought (*vicara*), does not make the task of examining the contemporary relevance of Gandhi's views any easier.[1] In any case, there was hardly anyone among the leaders of independent India who could be said to want to build on the basis of Gandhi's political and economic philosophy. In relation to the character of the new state, Sardar Patel (the powerful Deputy Prime Minister) and Rajendra Prasad (the first President) were no closer to Gandhi than was Nehru (the first Prime Minister, 1947–64), which does not mean that their notions of a strong state were identical. It is perhaps ironic that Gandhi's public designation of Nehru as his political heir added strength to and bestowed legitimacy on Nehru's own independent position as a national leader. Let us then turn to Jawaharlal Nehru for a diagnosis of the malady that has afflicted Indian secularism. Before we proceed let us look again at the words 'religion' and 'secularism' in the context of Nehru's views, abiding by the good advice that we must pay a word extra when we make it do a lot of work!

By intellectual preference Nehru's concept of secularism was the same that I wrote about earlier in this book in the context of the Enlightenment. He was against institutional religion, ritual, and mysticism and did not consider himself a religious person. He was not, however, uninterested in spiritual matters. Any impressions of his boyhood experiences of Brahmanical belief and ritual were erased by the powerful impact of his father's personality and, later, by his reading of the works of Karl Marx, Bertrand Russell and other

1. I owe this framework for the interpretation of traditional Indian thought to the late Professor K.J. Shah. It is a great pity that Shah died (in 1994) without bringing together his original reflections, some of them unpublished, on Gandhi.

similar thinkers.[2] Nehru's study of world history and his encounters
with the Indian masses in the 1920s and '30s made him feel very
negative about the role of religion in human affairs and he looked
forward to a secularized society. He was an agnostic who subscribed
to a rationalist, and even a historicist, worldview.

Gandhi's religiosity, to put it mildly, puzzled and annoyed Nehru.
It caused him to write (in his autobiography) one of his clearest and
most mature statements on the subject of religion. Referring to the
anguish that the news of Gandhi's fast (in September 1932) on the
subject of separate electorates (in Nehru's judgement 'a side political
issue') had caused him while he was in prison, Nehru wrote: 'I felt
angry with him at his religious and sentimental approach to a political
question, and his frequent references to God in connection with it'.
He further observed (1980: 374):

India is supposed to be a religious country above everything else .... [And yet] I have
frequently condemned [religion] and wished to make a clean sweep of it. Almost
always it seemed to stand for blind belief and reaction, dogma and bigotry, superstition
and exploitation, and the preservation of vested interests. And yet I knew well that
there was something else in it, something which supplied a deeper inner craving of
human beings.

Indian religiosity had been on Nehru's mind for quite some time,
though he refused to be unduly worried about it. It was more a

2. Nehru grew up in a divided home. He recalled in his autobiography that, when
he was a child, religion seemed to be 'a woman's affair' that his father and other men
in the house 'refused to take seriously' (1980: 8). B.R. Nanda has written of
Jawaharlal's mother's 'attachment' to the Hindu scriptures, *pujas*, orthodox rituals
and pilgrimages (1962: 41). As for his father, Nanda describes him as 'a product of
the late Victorian "free thinking" rationalism, which was learning to dispense with
divine explanations of the working of the universe and to pin faith in the human
intellect and on science to lead mankind along vistas of progress' (ibid.: 43).
   Henny Sender (1988) describes the composite culture of the Kashmiri Pandit
community of the United Provinces, of which the Nehrus were distinguished members,
and the personal unorthodoxy of Motilal Nehru. She also quotes from the senior
Nehru's presidential address to the Congress at Calcutta (1928): '[The] association
[of religion] with politics has been to the good of neither. Religion has been degraded
and politics has sunk into the mire. Complete divorce of one from the other is the only
remedy' (see ibid.: 295). Jawaharlal's political world, too, like his home, was a divided
one, with Gandhi taking the place of his mother, as it were, and insisting on the validity
and indispensability of religious values. Gandhi's influence, however, never succeeded in erasing the earlier and deeper influence of Motilal. Incidentally, it has been
recorded that the senior Nehru used to tease both his wife and Gandhi about their
religiosity (see Nanda 1962: 41; Akbar 1988: 229).

nuisance than a real problem. In 1928 he had declared: 'If religion, or rather what is called religion, in India continues to interfere with everything, then it will not be a mere question of divorcing it from politics, but of divorcing it from life itself' (Nehru 1972: 233). The Gandhian imperative of religion as the guide to all, even 'the tiniest', activities was not what Nehru believed in. As for the Gandhian notion of divince grace, Nehru considered the idea of 'a personal god' 'very odd' (1961: 28). Like all modern intellectuals he had implicit confidence in the processes of secularization.

Proclaiming this confidence in his presidential address to the Lahore (1929) session of the Congress, he said:

I have no love for bigotry and dogmatism in religion, and I am glad that they are weakening. Nor do I love communalism in any shape or form. ... I know that the time is coming soon when these labels and appellations will have little meaning and when our struggle will be on the economic basis (1973a: 188).

Two years later—in fact again and again during the next two decades—he reaffirmed the primacy of the economic factor: 'the real thing to my mind is the economic factor. If we lay stress on this and divert public attention to it we shall find automatically that religious differences recede into the background and a common bond unites different groups. *The economic bond is stronger than even the national one*' (1973b: 203, emphasis added). These concluding words underlined Nehru's secular position and his socialist convictions.

Given this position, it is no wonder that Nehru was dismissive about the Hindu-Muslim problem: 'the question does not exist at all for us', he declared (ibid.: 282). When he did acknowledge the seriousness of communalism, he looked upon it as an expression of class interests. In 1928 he said: 'It may be a giant today, but it has feet of clay.... It is really the creation of our educated classes in search of office and employment' (see Akbar 1988: 217). Later, and more thoughtfully, he said in his presidential address at the Lucknow (1936) Congress: 'First of all the Congress always put independence first and other questions, including the communal one, second, and refused to allow any other of those questions to take the pride of place'. He added: 'I am afraid I cannot get excited over the communal issue, important as it is temporarily. It is after all a side issue, and it can have no real importance in the larger scheme of things' (1975: 190).

The same train of thought was given considered expression in *The Discovery of India* (written in prison during 1944). Nehru wrote (1961: 543):

The belief in a super-natural agency which ordains everything has led to a certain irresponsibility on the social plane, and emotion and sentimentality have taken the place of reasoned thought and inquiry. Religion, though it has undoubtedly brought comfort to innumerable human beings and stabilized society by its values, has checked the tendency to change and progress inherent in human society.

He confessed candidly in the same work, that religion did not 'attract' him for 'behind it lay a method of approach to life's problems which was certainly not that of science' (ibid.: 26). Just three years before he became the Prime Minister of India, Nehru looked forward to the future and exhorted Indians that they face life 'with the temper and approach of science allied to philosophy and with reverence for all that lies beyond' (ibid.: 547).

Out of prison in 1945, Nehru faced a rapidly changing political situation and, much to his chagrin, the 'side issue' moved fast to occupy the centre of the stage. He was disbelieving and appalled. 'To think in terms of Pakistan when the modern trend is towards the establishment of a world federation is like thinking in terms of bows and arrows as weapons of war in the age of the atomic bomb' (1981: 187). The viceroy, Lord Wavell, recorded in his journal on 14th July 1945, 'the theme of [Nehru's] discourse was that... [Pakistan was] a narrow medieval conception; and that the eventual cleavage when India's freedom was secured would be between classes rather than communities, between poor and rich, between peasant and landlord, between labourer and employer' (Wavell 1977: 155–6). India's freedom was secured two years later, but the country was partitioned on the basis of religion.

I have quoted fairly extensively from Nehru's writings, statements and speeches to highlight the consistency of his thinking over two decades and more. It is obvious that the decisive element in this thinking was, at the broadest level, an Enlightenment view of religion, which was against revelation and dogmatism rather than religion as such, if it did not offend against reason, and, more specifically, the Marxian position on religion, though considerably diluted. It is thus that we find Nehru attacks the bigotry and dogmatism of religion, but acknowledges that religion stands for higher things of life too. He wrote of the comfort that religion had brought to innumerable people and did not dismiss the phenomenon as 'the opium of the people' as Marx had done.

But the idea of economic issues having precedence over even the question of independence from colonial rule is in accordance with the Marxian position. As is well known, in their discussion of the role of ideologies, Marx and Engels observed in *The German Ideology* that any attempt to understand an epoch of history in terms of political and religious issues is to 'share the illusion of the epoch' (see Marx and Engels 1959: 259). Similarly, Engels in his graveside summary of Marx's thought, had said that Marx had 'discovered the simple fact, hitherto concealed by an overgrowth of ideology, that mankind must first of all eat and drink, have shelter and clothing, before it can pursue politics, science, religion, art, etc.' (see Acton 1955: 143). Actually, Marx believed that religion had already been dissolved by the circumstances prevailing in Europe in his own time (Marx and Engels 1959: 260). And Lenin had affirmed that even while the socialists must fight against religion, doing so did 'not mean that the religious question must be pushed into the foreground where it does not belong' (n.d.: 16). Nehru acknowledged his indebtedness to the teachings of Marx and Lenin in his autobiography, *The Discovery of India* and elsewhere; but he was too much of a liberal to be called a copybook Marxist.

In short, Nehru's position on religion, religious conflict and the significance of the processes of secularization was what would be called rationalist and modern, whether one sees it derived from Marxian or Lockean roots. It was also idealist in the sense that it reflected more the ideals of the European Enlightenment than the hard facts of society, culture and politics in India. The latter generated compulsions at variance with these ideals. It is remarkable that it was Nehru who in the same year, 1931, in which he gave the hopeful message of the recession of religious differences (quoted above) persuaded the All-India Congress Committee (at its Karachi session) to insert in the resolution on fundamental rights 'Freedom of conscience and of the profession and practice of any religion' (see Nehru 1973a: 512). Further, all citizens of free India would be equal before the law, irrespective of religious (and other similar) differences, and the state would observe neutrality with regard to all religions (*dharma nirpekshata*). 'This', Nehru's biographer S. Gopal tells us, 'was the first breakdown, in concrete terms, of the concept of secularism in the Indian context and formed the basis of the [relevant] articles in the constitution many years later' (1987: 12).

The Constitution did not, however, contain the word 'secularism' anywhere, and 'secular' only once, but that too to denote an aspect of religious practice.[3] The addition of the words 'secular' and socialist' to the description of India as a 'sovereign republic' in the Preamble of the Constitution came through the 42nd Amendment in 1976 (during Indira Gandhi's Emergency rule).[4] It is important to note that the Hindi version of the Constitution uses *panth nirpeksha*, 'neutral in relation to religious denominations' (i.e. non-sectarian) as the equivalant for 'secular'. Was specific reference to secularism considered unnecessary earlier, when the Constitution was being framed (1946–49)? Or was it too controversial ? Perhaps both; which exactly would depend upon whose views one has in mind.[5] The transcript of the debate in the Constituent Assembly reveals that there

3. While Article 25 of the Constitution grants 'Freedom of conscience and free profession, practice and propagation of religion' as a fundamental right to the citizens of India, its sub-clause 2(a) makes room for 'regulating or restricting any economic, financial, political or other secular activity which may be associated with religious practice'. The Hindi version of the Constitution uses *laukika*, literally 'worldly', for 'secular'.

4. A further amendment to specify the secular and democratic character of the state, and to define the word 'secular' (in Article 366) was passed in 1978 by the newly elected Lok Sabha but failed to receive the approval of the Rajya Sabha where the Congress Party had a two-thirds majority. It is ironical that the same party proposed in 1993 to amend the Constitution to include in it a definition of secularism as the state policy of equal respect for all religions.

5. A prominent member of the Constituent Assembly, K.T. Shah, tried, through two amendments to the Draft Constitution, to have India declared a secular state, specifying that it would have nothing to do with any religion, creed or faith. According to the first of these amendments India would have been described as a 'Secular Federal Socialist Union of States'. Dr B.R. Ambedkar, who was piloting the draft, rejected both amendments on the ground that it was not advisable to prescribe a particular form of social organization for future generations. On another occasion he denied that the Indian state was secular because he wanted it to have the right of intervention in religious matters in the same manner as in secular affairs.

It may be added here that another vocal member, H.V. Kamath, proposed that the Preamble to the Constitution begin with the words 'In the name of God'; this too was found unacceptable by the majority of the members present, because such an invocation would not be in consonance with the secular spirit of the Constitution. The consensus of opinion among the members was that the reference to 'liberty of thought, expression, belief, faith and worship' in the Preamble was comprehensive enough to cover all reasonable points of view. Subsequently, after the Kesavananda Bharati case of 1973, the Preamble came to be formally recognized as an essential part of the Constitution, proclaiming its philosophy, and secularism as one of its 'basic' (that is unalterable) features.

was considerable difference of opinion on the right of propagation of one's religion, in addition to its profession and practice, but it was ultimately approved. The following statement by the well-known Congressman, H.V. Kamath, perhaps represented the general feeling of the members of the house (Constitutent Assembly of India Debates, 6 December, 1948: 825):

The State represents all the people who live in its territories, and, therefore it cannot afford to identify itself with any particular section of the population. ... We have certainly declared that India should be a secular State. But ... a secular state is neither a Godless State nor an irreligious, nor an anti-religious, state.

Already, one can see, the notion of the secular state, and of secularism, were being enveloped in ambiguity, meaning what one wished the terms to mean.

More about the Constitution below. Let me first recall how Nehru, having seen his confidence in the primacy of the economic over the religious factor proven premature, if not wholly misplaced, looked to the future after partition and independence. A few months after these cataclysmic events he posed the key question (in 1949): 'Do we believe in a national state which includes people of all religions and shades of opinion and is essentially a secular state, or do we believe in the religious, theocratic conception of the state'? His answer was unequivocal: 'we shall proceed on secular and national lines' (Nehru 1987: 26). This then became the guiding principle that animated the Constitution (then on the anvil) and became the basis of state policy in all relevant areas of action. The great Indian experiment of nation building, or national integration, had thus entered its most crucial phase.

It, however, suffered from a critical infirmity. Given Nehru's lifelong aversion to religion as practised by common people—the so-called popular religion—he could not have suddenly begun to see virtues in it. Moreover, within the Western liberal tradition, the modern state had emerged as secular in the specific sense that the maintenance of the 'true faith', or any faith, was none of its concerns (see Skinner 1978: 352). Nehru's definition of the secular state in terms of religious pluralism (quoted above) was, it seems obvious to me, a compromise, a strategy to deal with an awkward problem, namely the all-pervasive influence of religion in society, that would not go away. Nehru had made such compromises more than once in his political career: on one historic occasion (the 1936 presidential address to the Congress) he had called them 'temporary expedients of a transition rather than as solutions of our vital problems' (1975: 182). Like his attitude to *khadi* (hand-spun and hand-woven cloth) defined thus on this occasion, his attitude to religious pluralism was, it seems to me, an arrangement *ad interim*, a strategy rather than a surrender.

It was not an ideological commitment to religion or spirituality comparable to, for instance, Sarvepalli Radhakrishnan's, who thought that it would be 'strange that our government should be a secular one while our culture is rooted in spiritual values'. 'Secularism', Radhakrishnan believed, had to be given a new, *appropriate*, definition 'here' (in India), namely 'stress on the universality of spiritual values which may be attained in a variety of ways' (1956: vii–viii). Constitutionally, this translates as the principle of (to use a term from the legal discourse in the USA) 'non-preferentialism' between different religions rather than 'neutrality' between spirituality and materialism or religion and agnosticism. And Nehru was a self-proclaimed agnostic.

The paradox of Indian secularism lies not only in that religious pluralism is meaningless in the absence of a positive attitude to religion, but equally significantly in that the idiom of its articulation is trapped in a double-bind. Nehru wrote that ideas like 'socialism' and (I should think) 'secularism' must be communicated to the people in 'the language of the mind and the heart... the language which grows from a complex of associations of past history and culture and present environment' (1975: 182). Needless to add, this would not easily have been the language of India's westernized educated elite, whom Gandhi had called 'hard hearted'.

Eleven years after independence, and eight years after the adoption of the Constitution, Nehru was visited by André Malraux in Delhi and asked what his greatest problem had been during his years of power. Nehru replied, 'Creating a just state by just means', and, after a pause, 'Perhaps, too, creating a secular state in a religious society' (see Malraux 1968: 145). I detect a sense of dismay in Nehru's observations on the subject in his later years. Sorrowfully, he wrote in 1961, just three years before his death (see Gopal 1980: 330–1):

We talk about a secular state in India. It is perhaps not very easy even to find a good word in Hindi for "secular". Some people think it means something opposed to

religion. That obviously is not correct .... It is a state which honours all faiths equally
and gives them equal opportunities.

Having written this, he proceeded more in line with his earlier
thinking on the subject:

Our Constitution lays down that we are a secular state, but it must be admitted that
this is not wholly reflected in our mass living and thinking. In a country like England,
the state is ... allied to one particular religion ... Nevertheless, the state and the people
there function in a largely secular way. *Society, therefore, in England is more
advanced in this respect than in India,* even though our constitution may be in this
matter more advanced (ibid., emphasis added).

It is clear from this that Nehru had not given up his trust of the
processes of secularization and of the secularization thesis. The
chasm between him, on the one hand, and Gandhi and Radhakrishnan, on the other, was deep. For Gandhi religious pluralism
entailed inter-religious understanding and mutual respect: it was the
strength of Indian society while communal politics tied to statism
would be its bane. For Nehru, however, religiosity and the attendant
conflicts were the badge of social backwardness. Secularism in the
sense of neutrality as state policy was a strategy to cope with a
difficult situation. And the state was potentially a very important
instrument of public welfare and social advancement, very much on
the lines J.S. Mill and other liberals had advocated.[6] I am puzzled by
those intellectuals who speak of a hyphenated Gandhi-Nehru view
of secularism or, for that matter, of development. It is high time we
accepted the authoritative verdict of B.R. Nanda, biographer of both
Gandhi and Nehru: 'The working partnership of Nehru and Gandhi
lasted till the end, but their philosophies of life never really converged' (1974: 103).

A Nehruvian answer to the question why secularism has run into
difficulties in India would, then, be that the people are not yet ready
for it. It requires a level of general education that is yet beyond them,
and a liberal outlook on life and scientific temper which unfortunately they lack. I will not discuss here the larger and more complex issue
of the lack of a sense of Indian history. Not only did Nehru consider

6. 'In many parts of the world, the people can do nothing for themselves which
requires large means and combined actions; all such things are left undone, unless
done by the state': John Stuart Mill *Principles of Political Economy,* II, pp.602–3,
quoted in de Schweinitz, Jr. 1983: 125.

such a sense vital to the cultivation of the spirit of nationalism, he also stressed the importance of comparison: this is obvious from his historical reflections. His reading of Indian history (see Nehru 1946) has come under attack recently for allegedly being tainted by a soft Hindutva ideology (see, e.g., Abdullah 1993: 74). This is absurd, for Ashoka and Akbar receive the highest honour from him, and neither was a Hindu. Religious intolerance has, meanwhile, intensified in recent years and fundamentalisms of various names and hues stalk the land today. The question that strikes one is that, if Nehru understood what India's problem in this regard was, why did he not strive harder than he did to remove the obstacles that stood in the way of a modern, secular, society? One can never be sure, but I could venture a reasonable guess.

In the early years after independence Nehru remained firmly wedded to the belief that state-sponsored economic growth was the key to social development. Hence, in his eyes, dams and factories were India's new temples.[7] In believing so in the 1950s he was in excellent company. Confessional statements by economists on the 'sins' of a narrow concept of the contents of the growth basket and of the quantitative approach to development were not to come before another decade would pass. By the time this approach to development ran into a crisis Nehru was a sick man and he died soon afterwards in 1964. He had bet on what had then seemed a sure winner, but after a good early run, it turned out to be a lame horse. The most serious failure of the 1950s from the point of view of the present discussion was the shocking neglect of investment in health and of radical educational reform. Gunnar Myrdal (1968) was one of the early critics of the Nehruvian experiment to draw pointed attention to this failure. More broadly, and more fundamentally, there was a dangerous dependence on the state. As Edward Said subtly puts it, 'Nehru's accomplishment was to take the Indian nation as liberated from modernity by Gandhi and deposit it entirely within the concept of the state' (1993: 262).[8]

---

7. Thus, in 1953, Nehru described the laying of the foundation stone of the Nagarjun-Sagar dam by himself as a 'sacred ceremony' and called the dam itself 'a temple dedicated to the humanity of India'.

8. Said's judgement is based on Partha Chatterjee's insightful analysis of what the latter calls 'the moment of arrival' in Indian nationalist thought. According to it: 'Once established, this state will stand above the narrow interests of groups and classes in society, take an overall view of the matter and, in accordance with the best scientific

Secularism and the Constitution

As an aspect of his basic approach, Nehru also put his faith in the Constitution and the legislative process, and this turned out to be a case of excess rather than neglect. I have already referred to some of the features of the Constitution bearing upon the contemporary crisis of secularism. There are other problems too to which I now turn briefly. I am not a jurist any more than I am an economist, but I find certain unresolved tensions in the Constitution. An examination of Articles 13 to 17, 19, 23, 25 to 30 (all from Part III dealing with 'Fundamental Rights'), and of Articles 44, 48 and 51 (from Part IV on 'Directive Principles') brings these out clearly. Thus, Articles 25 to 30, which are the most crucial in this regard, guarantee 'freedom of conscience and free profession, practice and propagation of religion' (25), 'freedom to manage religious affairs' (26), 'freedom as to payment of taxes for promotion of any particular religion' (27), and 'freedom as to attendance at religious instruction or religious worship in certain educational institutions' (28). They protect the 'interests of minorities' (29), including their 'right ... to establish and administer educational institutions' (30). Article 44 directs that 'the State shall endeavour to secure for the citizens a uniform civil code throughout the territory of India'. The way things have proceeded reveals the contradiction between Articles 25 to 30 and Article 44. The jurists may well argue that Directive Principles do not have the same force as Fundamental Rights and, therefore, the question of contradiction does not arise. It would be undeniable, however, that the former have contributed enormously to the strengthening of inward-looking, communal feelings and attitudes, and obstructed the spread of modern, secular education and attitudes among the cultural minorities.

It is not at all surprising that the state has so far failed to implement the constitutional directive of evolving a uniform civil code. The resistance has come principally from Muslims, some of whose

---

procedures, plan and direct the economic processes in order to create enough social wealth to ensure welfare and justice to all' (Chatterjee 1986: 133). Hindsight is a chastening perspective, and we know today the limitations of the socially aware but historically mistaken view of the state that Nehru and others of his generation embraced. To repeat, they expected too much of the state, and not in the economic domain alone.

leaders claim that their social life cannot be governed by any laws other than the *sharia*. It may be recalled that the Constituent Assembly had, by a resolution in 1948, rejected the contention that Muslim personal law was inseparable from Islam and, therefore, protected against legislative interference. The British had greater success in this regard as the Criminal Procedure Code that they enacted—it is still largely in force in India, but has been modified in Pakistan—overrode traditional laws and conventions.

The framers of the Constitution, it seems to me, overlooked the possibility that in a democratic polity the state may reflect the character of the society, and that a communally divided society and a secular state could be mutually contradictory. On the one hand, there is the danger of majoritarianism and, on the other, that of vesting the religious minorities with a kind of veto power. In other words, there is a tension here that must be resolved deliberately; it will not go away by itself. One is reminded of Karl Marx's perceptive observation, in his tract on 'The Jewish Question', that 'the emancipation of the state from religion is not the emancipation of the real man from religion' (1975: 146–74); needless to add, the real man he spoke of is the socially situated person.

There are other contradictions in the Constitution that bear upon the present discussion. I mentioned Articles 17 and 48. The former was a triumph for what Gandhi would have called moral reason: it abolished the practice of untouchability 'in any form'. This was intended to promote the cause of the so-called low caste Hindus, who had been exploited and humiliated by upper caste Hindus for as long as any one could remember, actually for centuries. But Article 48 represented a concession to high caste sentiment, 'prohibiting the slaughter of cows and calves and other milch and draught cattle', though the reason given is a secular one, namely the organization of 'agriculture and animal husbandry on modern scientific lines'. The record of the debate on this issue in the Constituent Assembly reveals that Nehru had to threaten resignation in order to have this ban given a secular character. The Hindu lobby, which had the informal patronage of the President, Dr Rajendra Prasad, had wanted a general ban, and Nehru none of it. As early as 1923, when he was the mayor of Allahabad, he had persuaded the Municipal Board to reject a proposal to prohibit cow slaughter (see Gopal 1987: 24). It may be argued that the ban on cow slaughter is no more Brahmanical than Article 47, which includes a directive about prohibition on the consumption of intoxicants, is Islamic. This would be legal quibbling, for we know the strong sentiment against cow slaughter, generated among Hindus generally during the last one hundred years, to be a politically explosive issue.

It is noteworthy that, in the furtherance of the objectives of a secularized society and the establishment of a secular state, Nehru showed a much greater willingness to oppose what he considered reactionary elements among the Hindus than among the other communities. This was best illustrated by his stand on the Hindu Code Bill. The Hindu Marriage Act, 1955, the Hindu Succession Act, 1956, and the Hindu Adoption and Maintenance Act, 1956, were enacted by the Parliament, despite opposition by conservative Hindu leaders, including President Prasad, mainly because of Nehru's insistence. I agree with Bhikhu Parekh's insightful observation that:

Nehru's state acted as, and claimed all the rights of a *Hindu* state in its relation to the Hindus ... because he and his colleagues were and thought of themselves as Hindus ... they [thus] both dared take liberties with the Hindus and *dared not* take them with respect to the Muslims and even Sikhs (1991: 42).

The Majority-Minority Conundrum

Nehru's firm stand apparently contrasts with the vacillating attitude of the Rajiv Gandhi government, which rushed through Parliament the Muslim Women (Protection of Rights) Act in 1986, to nullify the Supreme Court's verdict in the Shah Bano case upholding the legal liability of a Muslim male to provide maintenance support for the wife he divorces. The new law was a concession to the conservative Muslim lobby according to which Muslim society is subject to *sharia* everywhere and for all time (see Baxi 1992: 95 and Sathe 1991: 39–59). But there is a sense in which Rajiv Gandhi was simply continuing with the Congress legacy of providing special treatment and protection to religious minorities in accordance with their own wishes. This had been endorsed by both Gandhi and Nehru before independence, and represented 'the benign elder brother' attitude. In any case, the 1986 happenings could hardly be cited as the best way of using the legislative process as an instrument of secularization. This is particularly regrettable in view of the directives incorporated in Article 44 ('to secure for citizens a uniform civil code') and in Article 51 (by Amendment in 1976) 'to promote scientific temper'

(51-A[a]) and to 'preserve the rich heritage of our composite culture' (51-A[f]). One could, however, well argue that these additions to Article 51 are so vague and trite that those responsible for their inclusion in the Constitution could hardly have been serious about them.

Why did Nehru treat Hindus and Muslims differently? And why have successive governments at the Centre since Nehru's death in 1964 often done so? Should not non-discrimination between different religious communities be one of the first principles of the policies of a secular state? The answer, it seems to me, lies largely in the fact that, as observed earlier, non-discrimination may not be sufficient to meet the requirements of the situation. The anxieties and sensitivities of the minorities must be recognized. But where does the state draw the line? There is no easy answer to this question. Consequently, the majority-minority conundrum has become an almost insoluble problem. In a democratic polity being in a majority betokens public approval and signifies legitimate electoral success for the group concerned. Such majorities represent interest groups and ideological positions. In Thomas Jefferson's celebrated phrase, 'the will of the majority' is 'the Natural law of every society' and 'the only sure guardian of the rights of man' (see Cunningham Jr. 1991: 133). The legitimacy of majority rule disappears, it must be stressed, if it takes away or abridges the rights of the minorities or, for that matter, of the individual. It becomes tyranny. Nobody should be in a majority or out of it, because of ascribed, or near-ascribed, attributes of race, gender, language or religion. Majorities so defined are rightly judged to be unfair winners in political games.

A questionable assumption, however, underlies the existence of majorities of this kind, namely that they are internally undifferentiated in terms of social customs, economic interests and political loyalties, and are, therefore, able to appear and even act as monoliths, as it were. No religious community of India—the Hindus least of all—is, however, internally undifferentiated. So much so, indeed that, as a sociologist, I find little warrant for using the word 'community' in referring to the Hindus. But politically motivated Hindus have learnt the immense usefulness of the term and non-Hindus never let go of it, whether in reference to themselves or the threatening Hindus. The majority-minority differentiation in religious terms has thus become an integral part of Indian political rhetoric: it is the language of communalism rather than liberalism.

[handwritten margin notes: Majoritarianism (we are all minorities!!)]

We need to go back a little in time to appreciate how things have come to such a pass. It is perhaps ironic that primordially defined majorities and minorities entered the Indian political idiom in the context of granting representation to people in local self-governance. The conceptualization of the people of India as quantitatively defined tribes, castes, and religious communities was made possible by yet another instrument of modern governance, namely the periodic census, begun in 1872 and made into a decennial exercise from 1881 onward. The best known critics of the introduction of Western liberal notions of elective representation in the 1880s, when the viceroy, Lord Ripon, brought forward his Local Self-Government Bill (1883), were Sayyid Ahmad Khan and Amir Ali, who maintained that such a measure would be unsuitable to a heterogenous society such as the Indian, characterized as it was by not only differences of race and religion, caste and creed, but also of numbers. Speaking in Lucknow on 28 December 1887, Sayyid Ahmed presented his thesis of Hindus and Muslims as 'two different nations'. The Muslims, he declared, would come under Hindu domination because of their fewer numbers: 'It would be like a game of dice, in which one man had four dice and the other one' (see Akbar 1988: 46–7). Arguments were backed by action: for instance, the influential *ulama* of the newly founded seminary at Deoband (in north India) issued *fatwas* discouraging social and economic contacts between Muslims and Hindus (see Chapter Four). The notion of a Muslim minority, threatened by a socially mobile and politically assertive Hindu majority was thus born. It accorded well with the official British perception of India as a country of discordant religious communities, castes and tribes.

Moreover, several historians have argued that, at the core of the Muslim opposition to Western style political representation lay several religious and political convictions. Thus, Muslims are said to be ever conscious of belonging to a divinely constituted religious brotherhood, entitled to wield political power over non-Muslims by virtue of their moral superiority. In India, in the late nineteenth century, they also considered themselves—at least the descendents of immigrants and the aristocrats among them did so—the legatees of the Mughal empire. Indeed, M.A. Jinnah himself said in 1942 that if the British hand over power to the Muslims, they will be making full amends to [those] from whom they have taken it' (see Nanda 1974: 177). Finally, the political domain is seen by Muslims as the arena *par excellence* for the expression of religious values, and not a domain apart (see Shaikh 1989).

Unable to stop the idea of representative government, even in its most limited form, in the tracks, Sayyid Ahmad put forward the notion of 'separate electorates', based on religious identity, towards the end of the nineteenth century. The idea of 'weightage' also was mooted in course of time to overcome the disadvantage of numbers. The new principle that came to dominate the thinking of certain sections of Muslim political leadership in the twentieth century was that of 'parity'. This notion was finally embraced by Jinnah in the crucial final years leading to partition and independence in 1947. Had the principle of parity at the federal level been conceded, treating Muslims on par with Hindus, and providing safeguards for the others, some historians believe, partition may have been avoided (see Jalal 1985). In its absence, emphasis upon the character of Muslims as a 'minority', or as a separate 'nation', depending upon the context was Jinnah's trump card.[9]

Addressing the All-India Muslim League in Lahore in 1940 at the Lahore session, which later adopted the separate Muslim states resolution, Jinnah echoing Sayyid Ahmad's 'game of dice' argument, ridiculed Gandhi's protestations of brotherly feelings towards non-Hindus and Jinnah himself: 'The only difference is this, that brother Gandhi has three votes and I have only one vote' (see Wolpert 1988: 181). This was, of course, a reference to the arithmetic of Hindu and Muslim populations in the 1941 census.

A decade later, the Constitution of India acknowledged the concept of minorities, but did not define it precisely, leaving a good deal

---

9. It is noteworthy that, alongside of the characterization of the Muslims as a minority, there have also been repeated denials of its appropriateness. Thus, Abul Kalam Azad wrote in the very first volume of *Al-Hilal* (1912) that the preoccupation with their status as a minority was 'the root' of the Muslims' problem: 'members of a brotherhood of four hundred million believers in the unity of God are afraid of two hundred and twenty million idol worshippers of India'. He exhorted them: 'You must realize your position among the peoples of the world. Like God himself, look at everyone from a lofty position' (quoted in Douglas 1988: 144). Similarly, Rahmat Ali, to whom we owe the word Pakistan, denounced the idea of Muslims being considered a minority, and believed that it had been invented by the Hindus to ensure their domination over the Muslims (see Malik 1963: 245–6). And Jinnah himself denied the relevance of minority status (merely a demographic fact) when he stressed the principle of parity between Hindus and Muslims in the political arena in recognition of what he regarded as the significant facts of history.

to be inferred. Thus, Articles 29 and 30 specifically refer to the rights (in fact, Fundamental Rights) of 'minorities' to conserve their languages, scripts and cultures, have free access to state-aided educational institutions, and to establish and administer their own educational institutions. Although it seems perverse to me to place an interpretation on these constitutional provisions to the effect that *only* the minorities have such rights, mischievous politicians have not been reluctant to cite them as evidence of 'minorityism'. The forthright views of Dr B.R. Ambedkar, hailed as 'the father of the Indian Constitution', do not exactly help in removing such doubts. The minorities, he said in the Constituent Assembly, 'have loyally accepted the rule of the majority which is basically a communal majority and not a political majority. It is for the majority to realize its duty not to discriminate against minorities. Whether the minorities will continue or will vanish must depend upon this habit of the majority. The moment the majority loses the habit of discrimination against the minority, the minorities can have no ground to exist' (CAD, vol.7, I: 39). The majority and the minorities thus stood defined, though in a somewhat Humpty Dumpty fashion.

Without any regard for the social reality of the multiplicity of economic interests and political opinion among Hindus as well as Muslims and Sikhs, *imagined* majorities and minorities were said by these political leaders to be pitted against each other in a life-and-death struggle. For Jinnah, who claimed to be 'the sole spokesman' on behalf of the Muslims, the Congress was a Hindu organization and Maulana Azad its 'show-boy' President; Gandhi was merely the leader of the Hindu 'community', an opinion which he reiterated in his condolence message on Gandhi's death, ignoring the circumstances of the assassination. And for Ambedkar, Gandhi was a usurper who unjustly claimed to speak on behalf of low-caste Hindus.

Not everybody, however, agreed, then or later, with such views of dominant and dominated majorities and minorities. Frank Anthony, at that time the acknowledged leader of the Anglo-Indians, repudiated, on the floor of the Constituent Assembly itself, the allegation that the minorities were being deprived of their rights and otherwise oppressed. On the contrary, he said, the minorities had made demands that were not tenable (see CAD, vol.8: 333–8, 346–9). But he did not abandon the concepts of majority and minority. Professor V.V. John, a distinguished Indian intellectual who happened to be a Christian, and many others like him, have done precisely this, and asked for the protection of *human rights* rather than minority rights. According to him, the leaders of the minority communities practice 'selective secularism' and demand from Hindus what they do not themselves practice.[10] One ingenious argument in this regard is that minority communalism is a half-way house to secularism (see Baig 1967: 164–80).

It will be recalled that, after partition, the Muslim fundamantalist organization, Jamaat-i-Islami (Hind), through a series of pronouncements, accepted 'in the present circumstances', which meant conditionally, 'the secular form of government', but rejected secularism as an ideology. It described its decision quite explicitly as one dictated by 'utilitarian expediency'. Many other Muslim organizations and leaders took up the same position (see Mushir-ul-Haq 1972: 6–21). Similarly, fundamentalist Sikh leadership used to say that the Sikh religious tradition does not permit the separation of religion and politics and that, unless this right is recognized, the state in India is not truly secular but under Hindu domination. Some of them have, of course, since opted for the demand for an autonomous theocratic Sikh state (see Chapter Three).

The notion of minority status as privilege is of course a gross exaggeration, but many governmental actions based on political expediency have given it currency. How far people will go in the abuse of this idea was well illustrated by the successful effort of the Ramakrishna Mission members in Calcutta to get themselves recognized by a court of law as a non-Hindu minority (see Smith 1993). This decision was, however, set aside by the Supreme Court in July 1995. Meanwhile the Hindu-Muslim problem which had eased, more than somewhat, in the years following independence has become salient again. While the aggressive elements among the leaders of the so-called minorities raise cries of alarm that India is fast degenerating into a Hindu country, their counterparts among the Hindus cry foul and accuse the government of 'minorityism'. Addressing the 1923 session of the Congress at Delhi, its President, Maulana Abul Kalam Azad, had observed about the then prevailing political differences and slogans: '"Save the Hindu from Muslims", says one group, "Save Islam from Hinduism", says another. When the order of the day is, "Protect Hindus" and "Protect Muslims", who

10. From notes taken by the author at a lecture given by Professor John in New Delhi on 28 November 1979.

cares about protecting the nation (see above page 162)? That was said seventy-odd years ago, but could have been said today.

Within this overall framework of majority-minority politics, there are variations and ramifications. Thus the violent student agitation of 1990 against reservations (vide Articles 330 and 332 of the Constitution) being sought to be raised to the level of nearly 50 per cent was the protest of a minority—those classified neither as scheduled caste or scheduled tribe nor as 'other backward classes'—against a majority of allegedly uniformly non-privileged people, although many among them were by no means economically deprived. Limitations of space do not allow me to discuss the thorny issue of reservations, which deserves detailed discussion (see Béteille 1992). But I should point out that, although the exploitation of certain castes and communities at the hands of others over the centuries down to this day, cannot be denied, the idea of reservation quotas—notwithstanding the fact that it was intended to be a temporary protective measure for thirty years only (Article 334)—does not fit well with the idea of secularism, understood as non-discriminatory state policy, particularly if it threatens to become a permanent vested interest. The hope that compensatory discrimination will transform communal groups into 'components of a pluralistic society in which invidious hierarchy is discarded while diversity is accommodated' (Galanter 1984: 561) in a kind of 'principled eclecticism' (ibid.: 567) is far from being realized.

Ironically, Nehru anticipated the danger. Speaking on the subject of reservation in the Constituent Assembly, he warned (Nehru 1991: 54):

I would like you to consider this business, whether it is reservation or any other kind of safeguard for the minorities objectively. There is some point in having a safeguard of this type ... when there is autocratic or foreign rule. As soon as you get ... political democracy, then this kind of reservation, instead of helping the party to be safeguarded or aided, is likely to turn against it. ... [In] a democracy ... it is the will of the majority that will prevail. ... Frankly, I would like ... [to] put an end to such reservations as there still remain.

Nehru was obviously thinking of the 'majority' in the Jeffersonian sense, which is of course inseparable from individual rights.

Another critical issue for Indian secularism that I will only mention, but not discuss at any length, is the problem of the Kashmir Valley. Through Article 370, the Constitution gave to Jammu and

Kashmir a special status, making it impossible for the Parliament to make laws for this state without the concurrence of its legislature in respect of subjects other than those mentioned in the Instrument of Accession or corresponding to them. This too was intended as a temporary measure, as the future of the state had become an international dispute by India's appeal for UN intervention to end Pakistani aggression. This specific legal context was soon overgrown by political considerations: the Kashmir Valley with its Muslim majority was vital to secular India's interests as a token of the repudiation of the two-nation theory which was the basis of Pakistan.

Since Sheikh Muhammad Abdullah, the acknowledged leader of the majority of Kashmir Muslims, had explicitly rejected this theory, the position of Indian leadership did not then seem unreasonable (see Abdullah 1993). But with the passage of time, Kashmiri Muslims came to be seen as hostages, and a special status was needed for retaining the state within the union for still newer considerations. Article 370 is now said to protect 'Kashmiriyat' or Kashmiri identity. Why Kashmiri identity needs special protection any more than, say, Bengali or Tamil identity is difficult to understand, unless it is taken to mean Kashmiri *Muslim* identity and brought under the rubric of minority rights and privileges (see Madan 1994c).

Although the state was ruled between 1947 and 1990 by a succession of elected governments, headed by Muslim chief ministers, they have not been of like mind regarding the nature of the state's relation with the Union (see Abdullah 1993; Qasim 1992). Administrative inefficiency and political corruption in the state have been matched by the machinations of the Union government. Although the representation of Muslims in the bureaucracy and the professions and the overall economic situation, had improved considerably, yet a secessionist movement erupted there in the mid-1980s. It turned violent in 1989, and the state has been under the rule of the Union government since early 1990. Well-trained and heavily armed militants, supported by Pakistani authorities, are being fought by the security forces and there is blood-letting on both sides. Innocent people of all communities are caught in the crossfire, literally and figuratively, and suffer. What the turbulent elements are asking for is, in effect, another partition, and this fans the fires of Hindu reaction elsewhere in the country, resulting in such politically bizarre happenings as the 'unity march' (*ekta yatra*) of the Bharatiya Janata Party president, Dr Murli Manohar Joshi, in January 1992.

In the Valley itself, the Hindus were a 3 per cent minority of about 200,000 people, several thousand of whom have been reportedly killed or critically injured, and many of whose homes or properties have been plundered or burnt. Most of them have fled their homes and live in refugee camps in Jammu and Delhi, or with relatives, outside the Valley. They are another example of a non-privileged minority. Not only Hindus, but those Muslims too, who do not seem to be in full agreement, are the targets of fundamentalists and secessionists. In fact, about three times as many Muslims as Hindus are reported to have been killed.[11]

The silence of Muslim political leadership in India about the happenings in Kashmir underscores the tragic fact that all is not well with Indian secularism.[12] For Jawaharlal Nehru, Kashmir had been India's answer to communalism, the shining token of her secularism. He had been encouraged in this belief by the leaders of the Muslim masses of Kashmir, including the tallest of them all, Sheikh Abdullah. Today Abdullah's is not a universally honoured name in the Valley and his grave has to be guarded by police to prevent its desecration by his own people. He had led these people in a liberation struggle that had been conspicuously socialist and secular in its ideological stance and action programmes, and had been actively supported by Nehru (see Abdullah 1993).

The militant secessionism of Kashmiri Muslims is more inspired by religious and ethnic (Mulsim-Kashmiri) considerations than by pure Islamic fundamentalism, but the influence of the latter (particularly after the Iranian Revolution) is not absent. There have been clashes between Islamic fundamentalists and devout Kashmiri Muslims because the former regard the relic and saint worshipping, and *urs* celebrating, Kashmiri Muslims as imperfectly Islamized (see Khan 1994). Whatever is judged to be the character of Kashmiri

11. These estimates are based on newspaper reports which are the only figures available to me.

12. Syed Shahbuddin, a prominent Muslim leader and parliamentarian (formerly a member of the elite Foreign Service), clarified (in a letter to the Editor, *The Times of India*, New Delhi, 30 August, 1994):

On militancy in Kashmir they [Indian Muslims or, as the author prefers, Muslim Indians] have been largely silent primarily because the government of India has treated Kashmir as a law and order problem and there has been massive and indiscriminate use of force against our own citizens in Kashmir. Muslims face a moral dilemma of speaking out on both aspects and being misunderstood.

separatism, it is perfectly clear that it is against pan-Indian secular nationalism (see Varshney 1992). It is not going to be easy, therefore, to accommodate Kashmiri nationalism within the Indian state without imposing a very severe strain upon Indian secularism. A restatement of Kashmiri aspirations in terms of cultural pluralism and administrative decentralization of which a national state would be seen as the guarantor is not yet in sight (at the beginning of 1995).

Kashmir alone is not a cause of the crisis of Indian secularism. The destruction of the Babri mosque in Ayodhya in December 1992 by right-wing Hindu extremists, including prominently the so-called RSS family (*sangh parivar*), was an unprecedented and crippling blow to Indian secularism. The events leading upto the demolition are well-known (see Gopal 1991; Srivastava 1991). There was a widespread sense of foreboding;[13] yet the Indian state, at the state and national levels, became an accomplice, through acts of omission and commission, in this act of betrayal of both traditional cultural pluralism and modern secularism. As Prime Minister P.V. Narasimha Rao put it, the demolition posed a 'grave threat' to 'the institutions, principles and ideals on which the constitutional structure of [the Indian] republic has been built' (quoted in Larson 1995: 273). The communal riots that followed (in January 1993) in different parts of the country, particularly the cities of Bombay and Surat, far away from Ayodhya, were widely described as anti-Muslim pogroms. Subsequently, Bombay had also to witness retaliatory bombings by Muslim gangsters and their accomplices. These events revealed as nothing else until then the fragility of Indian secularism.

In the two years since then (1993–95), a semblance of communal peace has returned to the country, even Punjab seems to be well set on the road to recovery, but Kashmir continues to be in turmoil. State legislative assembly elections, involving more than half of the total

---

13. Anticipating damage to the mosque, I wrote just a week before the demolition (see Madan 1992):

Today's purveyors of *hindutva*, who speak of righting old wrongs, and do not believe that a mosque, which may have been built after demolishing a temple on the site four and a half centuries ago, deserves to exist as a place of Muslim worship, may or may not succeed in bringing it down. They have certainly diminished the very cultural tradition they seek to protect by making it appear intolerant.... It is said that the Babri Masjid is a symbol of oppression and must go. Did the great Hindu temples that were a symbol of the oppression of the so-called low castes have to go? Or, for that matter, the palaces of British Raj?

country-wide electorate, have produced both defeats and victories for the Bharatiya Janata Party, but it is not clear whether its success has been due to its Hindutva appeal. It is noteworthy that in Uttar Pradesh, the home state of the Babri mosque, and in Bihar, caste solidarity rather than religious identity has won at the hustings. It would be very short-sighted to consider casteist politicians as the soldiers of Indian secularism simply because in certain situations they establish alliances with Muslims against upper caste Hindus. The most dangerous portent is the coming to power of the ultra-chau-vinistic Shiva Sena, in coalition with BJP, in Maharashtra. Nothing is more inimical to the spirit of Indian secularism (cultural pluralism in society and a non-discriminatory state) than the vituperations of the Sena chief, Bal Thackeray, against non-Maharashtrians and those Muslims whom he considers anti-national. The end of the crisis of Indian secularism is not yet in sight.

Concluding Remarks

I began this chapter by recalling that secularism as an explicitly formulated ideology was born of the dialectic of religion and science, and was not simply an anti-religious ideology, though many intellec-tuals have desired and even believed it to be so. There is much rethinking these days about the standard accounts of the Enlighten-ment, and the misleading preoccupation with what Stephen Toulmin (1990) calls its 'sunny side', to the neglect of its dogmatism and of the narrowing of rational debate by seventeenth century scientists. Attention has also been drawn to the fact that the notion of the self-emancipation of humankind, which lies at the very core of the secularization thesis also implies the sacralization of the secular. Such reconsiderations are bound to affect our appreciation of secularism also, for it was, as already pointed out, partly an expres-sion of the Enlightenment.

It is important to recognize that one of the major reasons for the rise of religious fundamentalism all over the world today is the excesses of ideological secularism, and its emergence as dogma, or a religion, just as Karl Marx, Max Weber, and some other social theorists had anticipated. By subverting religion as generally under-stood, secularism sets off a reaction in the form of fundamentalism, which usually is a perversion of religion, and has less to do with the purity of faith and more with the acquisition of political power.[14] The temple and the mosque lovers of today's India are, first and foremost, power-hungry politicians. In their hands, religion no longer is concerned with value, but only with instrumentalism; that is, religion is a means among others for the achievement of whatever goals are adopted.

If secularism is not essentially anti-religious, but only against revelation and unreason, Indian secularism with its ideal of respect for all religions would be much less so. Why then did Nehru complain to Malraux that it was difficult to establish a secular state in a religious country such as India? Elsewhere in this book I have attempted an answer to this question, which could hardly have been Nehru's own answer, too, though it does perhaps come within recognizable distance of a Gandhian position. My main argument is that neither India's indigenous religious traditions nor Islam recognize the sacred-secular dichotomy in the manner Christianity does so and, therefore, the modern processes of secularization (in the sense of expanding human control over human lives) proceed in India without the support of an ideology that people in general may warm up to, such as one legitimized by religion. What exists empirically, but not also ideologically, exists but weakly (see Madan 1987 and 1994a). The conclusion is not that the secular state should be jettisoned, or, more absurdly, all Indians should become Christians, but that special efforts are needed to give it clear definition, work out its relation to civil society, and reinforce it ideologically.

More generally, one recognizes that, as Louis Dumont (1994: 6, 14–15) has argued, the alternatives available in situations of civilizational contact are not limited to mutual exclusion or unilateral surrender. Most often a 'synthesis' takes place; of what kind is the key question. Such syntheses have a universalistic potential; they characterize not only particular cultural spaces but many also enter into 'the world culture of the time'. Hence the immense importance of what happens in India.

---

14. While philosophers do not seem to find this distinction difficult to accept, some sociologists reject it as sophistry (see Bailey 1991). I would like to recall here an observation by Wittgenstein that echoes Gandhi's views closely. Gandhi wrote: 'Religion is outraged when an outrage is perpetrated in its name' (1961: 47). And this is what Wittgenstein noted: 'Religion as madness is a madness springing from irreligiousness' (1984: 13e).

India is not entirely lacking in its own resources to cope with the processes of secularization in the midst of much religiosity and to find support for its evolving notion of secularism as inter-religious understanding. What I have in mind is not so much the medieval religious syncretism—there are differences of opinion about both its significance and recoverability[15]—as the fact that none of India's indigenous religions has been considered by its traditional thinkers a revealed religion in the sense in which the Abrahamic religions are so. The call recently given by certain intellectuals to 'Semitize' Hinduism bears witness to the lack of confidence that assails the innermost spirit of Hindutva. The Indic religious traditions are more or less open to questioning from within and reformulation through interpretation. Also, they have been subject to considerable pressure from outside, producing a flexibility of attitudes if not always religious liberality. In the not too distant past, Gandhi showed that reinterpretation through questioning and receptiveness to outside influences was still possible.

For these resources to be turned into strength we have to substitute a clearly defined religious pluralism for a narrow secularism and also to further explore India's cultural traditions for suitable ideas. The Indic religions share crucial metaphysical presuppositions about 'being', 'knowing', and 'value', contribute significantly to the over-all cultural *ambiance* of the country, and provide the foundation for regional composite cultures. Their followers share many attitudes and have many social practices in common. Islam and Christianity are non-indigenous in origin, but can hardly be considered alien today. It may not be denied that there are significant theological, metaphysical, cognitive, and ethical differences between Indic and classical Islamic worldviews. But differences alone do not characterize their relationship. Considerable ethnographic and historical evidence bears witness to cultural exchanges, shared value-orientations, and compatible lifestyles evolved over the centuries (see, e.g., Madan 1989; Bayly 1989).[16] The task of socio-cultural reconciliation is daunting but not beyond reach.

15. For a richly documented account, see Roy 1983. A sceptical assessment will be found in Ahmad 1964.

16. The character of Muslim society in India has been the subject of an important debate in recent years. While some scholars (mainly anthropologists and sociologists) have focused on local level accommodations and adjustments, emphasizing cultural

At the same time, we have to recognize, first, the limitations of an ambiguous concept of pluralism and, then, the real dangers of Hindu communalism and the insensitivity of the Hindus generally to the feelings of those who consider themselves non-Hindus. It has been noted that these non-Hindus are treated as permanent outsiders if they happen to be Christians or Muslims, or are denied a sense of separate identity if they are 'tribals' or Sikhs (see Oommen 1990: 11). Gandhi no less than Nehru was conscious of the greater harm that majority communalism might do in India though neither could be said to have approved of minority communalism. As Ashis Nandy (1980: 70–98) has insightfully argued, Gandhi was the sterner foe of Hindu communalism and paid for it with his life.

If India is to be saved from religious discord reinforced by fundamentalist tendencies present in all three traditions, and the resultant political divisiveness, we need rigorous rethinking and concerted action. What is at stake is the very survival of the Indian state. Social backwardness in the form of a weakly developed sense of civic ties—the bond of responsible citizenship—that would moderate if not replace the divisive primordial loyalties of religion, language and caste, is indeed a very severe handicap. Nehru saw this clearly and articulated it forcefully. What he did not see well was that when the state is made to take on too much out of the ambition and hubris of those who take charge of it, they run the risk of making it totalitarian or seeing it fall flat on its face. The emergency regime of Indira Gandhi (1975–77) revealed the limitations and the heavy costs of the totalitarian option in a large, internally diverse, and politically conscious country, such as India. The events that have unfolded since then have shown that the state in India has become increasingly ineffective in coping with caste and communal violence, just as its achievements in bringing about social and economic development have been meagre and uneven.

---

borrowing between Hindus and Muslims and survivals of pre-Islamic beliefs and customs among the latter, others (mainly historians) have asserted that Muslim communities in South Asia have been subject to the efforts of their religious leaders to attain perfection as practising believers. The relations of these Muslims with their cultural environment have been marked, it is said, more by 'tension' than 'equilibrium' (see, e.g., Ahmad 1964, 1967, Ahmad 1978, Das 1984, Madan 1995, Robinson 1983, and Roy 1983). The current salience of fundamentalism itself bears witness to the accommodations and adjustments mentioned above.

It may be argued that Nehru failed to realise fully the importance of the symbolism of the sacred in a secular society. His reference to the dams and factories of modern India as 'temples' (noted above) showed his awareness of the symbolic value of the sacred, but, perhaps, he remained content with too little. The example of the USA may be cited to underscore the importance of the aura of the sacred. An American President may not be at all personally religious, yet he must publicly acknowledge the religious foundations of American society. It is not any particular religion or church that is valorized, but the embodiment of the historical and spiritual experience of the American people, called 'civil religion' by Robert Bellah (1970) and others. The presence of civil religion, it has been suggested, has made the separation of the Church and the state successful in the USA.

The situation in India is significantly different, however, because of the prevailing religious plurality, which turns into antagonism only too readily. Moreover, the partition of India in the name of religious and cultural differences made the secular nationalists recoil from the idea of associating the state with religion, which in the circumstances could only have meant Hinduism. Contrary to what some scholars have suggested optimistically (see Larson 1995), there are no signs of an Indian civil religion taking shape.[17] The late

17. Larson is of the opinion that the Indian secular state is 'basically Neo-Hindu' in origin, and has generated a 'Gandhian-Nehruvian Indic civil religion', the 'cognitive base or belief system' of which is 'the loose conglomeration of Neo-Hindu notions and liberal-democratic-cum-socialist ideas'. He detects in the contemporary Indian rhetoric of '"secular" traditions of tolerance, non-violence', etc., and in the pride in 'the Indic heritage', echoes of the rhetoric about the 'American way of life', 'the religion of the Republic', and 'the promised land'. He concludes: 'In both instances one is dealing with much more than rhetoric or a political idiom with a religious tint. One is also dealing with the religious idiom of an institutionalized civil religion' (ibid.: 202–3).

I know of no other interpretation of the same kind and am not sure that the comparison is wholly defensible. The Biblical heritage in America is far more internally harmonious than the Indo-Islamic legacy. Moreover, the one-half century after partition, itself a divisive act, that has been witness to many kinds of inter-community conflicts (based on religion, language, caste, etc.), is much too short a period for the shaping of significant common aspirations and expressive national symbols and rituals. Larson reads more into the ceremonies associated with the Independence and Republic Days—particularly those held in Delhi—and in the observance of a multitude of religious holidays. The strength of the state in the USA is matched by the strength of the civil society (Alexis de Tocqueville noticed this more than a century and a half ago); in India we can only speak of a double weakness—of the state and of civil society.

twentieth century is, perhaps, too late in the day for such a development. Nehru proceeded only as far as he did because he was very much a creature of his times. In short, even when we recognize clearly the problems we face, and envisage possible solutions, the passage from thought to action is fraught with serious difficulties. The future of India as a civic society, and the character of its polity in the years to come, are as yet far from settled issues. All those who cherish the values of democracy and cultural pluralism—of human freedom and dignity—can hardly afford to be complacent.

Epilogue

One does not ask plain questions.
There aren't such things.
E.M. FORSTER, *Howards End*

We shall not cease from exploration/And the end of all our exploring/Will be
to arrive at where we started/ And know the place for the first time.
T.S. ELIOT, 'Little Gidding'

Of all the public debates that engage intellectuals in India today, the
most significant, I think, and also the most contentious, is the debate
about secularism. It concerns not only the kind of polity we want to
build but also the character of the society we wish to live in. Needless
to stress, these are not plain questions. The manner in which the
interrelatedness of culture, society and politics has unfolded in India
over the last hundred years or so has made the secularism debate
today also a debate about religious nationalism and fundamentalism.
Its contentiousness comes partly from ideological differences concerning the place of religion in society and partly from conceptual
ambiguities that are common in such situations. Thus, while
everyone agrees that secularism in India is in a state of crisis,
interpretations of the crisis vary according to each exponent's
preferred ideology and favoured vocabulary.

I write of a century of the debate mindful of the fact that use of
the word 'secularism' has gained currency only since independence,
and that the terms 'religious nationalism' and 'fundamentalism' are
even more recent. Concepts have a way of shedding their skins. The
nationalism of the pre-independence days and today's secularism are
essentially the same ideas: while the former seemed appropriate in
the context of the struggle for freedom, secularism points to post-independence visions of society and polity. Communalism repudiated

the secular notion of an *Indian* nation and installed in its place religious communities seeking statehood. The term was a coinage of the secular nationalists and used pejoratively. In their own eyes, the so-called communalists too were nationalists, and not all of them considered themselves religious. Religious fundamentalism is of course a far more complex phenomenon than religious nationalism.

The debate about secularism in India abounds in ironies. If we go back to the 1880s to look at its beginnings, these will be found partly rooted in the self-contradictory character of the social processes generated by colonialism, and partly in the religio-cultural plurality of India. On the one hand, British rule contributed to the making of a national, secular identity on a subcontinental scale through administrative, judicial, economic, educational and other measures. The country saw the emergence of a new middle class, which, notwithstanding critical deficiencies owing to its planted character, represented a secular culture. On the other hand, the colonial rulers not only insisted on describing India as a land of disparate religious communities, castes, sects and tribes, but also contributed to the consolidation of such primordial identities through the codification of Hindu and Muslim family laws, compilation of ethnographic notes, and enumeration of the 'peoples of India' through decennial censuses from 1881 onward. These measures encouraged communalism.

A major development in the administrative organization was the introduction of local self-government in 1883. Its progress was, however, frustrated by a recalcitrant bureaucracy. To remedy this situation, the Indian National Congress was established in 1885 by, among others, a retired English civil servant. A 'fuller development and consolidation' of 'sentiments of national unity' was one of its stated objectives. In today's idiom, the Congress had a secular agenda. Or so its leaders, mostly Hindus, believed.

There were Muslims too in the Congress, but not very many of them, nor from all parts of India. Sayyid Ahmad Khan, one of the most notable public figures of the time in the north, considered the goals of the Congress inimical to the interests of the numerically smaller and educationally backward Muslim community. He refused to join the Congress and advised Muslims generally to do likewise. Sayyid Ahmad's opposition to the Congress was formally proclaimed in 1887, the year in which a Muslim leader from Bombay, Badruddin Tyabji, was its president. Tyabji, in his presidential address, hoped that there was nothing in the mutual relations of the different religious communities that would make anyone of them refrain from joining with the others 'to obtain those great general reforms' and 'rights' that were 'for the common benefit'. Through an exchange of letters in the early months of 1888, these two distinguished Muslims opened the secularism debate of India without coming to any agreement. Tyabji argued that community and national interests were both equally legitimate and non-antagonistic in character; Khan insisted on the priority of the former and questioned the validity of the latter in the Indian setting.

Sayyid Ahmad's argument survived his death in 1898; indeed it gained much strength. The government partitioned the Bengal Presidency in 1905, avowedly for reasons of administrative efficiency. The Congress saw in it the imperial design to divide and rule, but Bengali Muslims generally welcomed the measure as a means of escaping Hindu economic domination. There was a direct connection between the partition of Bengal (later revoked in 1912 under pressure of the 'nationalists') and the founding of the Muslim League in 1906 at Dacca. In the years that followed, the League leadership developed its separatist agenda on the basis of an arguable incompatibility of the Muslim and Hindu interests. It envisaged India as a 'federation of religions' within which each community would 'carve out its own political space'.

There were other Muslim leaders, however, who supported the national, secular platform. One of the most prominent among them, a member of both the Congress and the League, was Mohammad Ali Jinnah. In his address as the president of the League in 1916, he spoke of 'affairs of our common secular existence' and of the 'new appeals of territorial patriotism and nationality'. This must be one of the earliest instances of the use of the term 'secular' in the public discourse of modern India. Jinnah's efforts to build bridges across the lines of religious cleavage had their most notable success in the form of the Lucknow Pact of 1916. According to it, the Congress and the League agreed that, after providing for a sufficiently large quota of elected legislative council seats for the Muslims, the two organizations were to make a united demand for self-governance. The Pact, which has been called 'the highpoint of Indian nationalist unity', was, however, never implemented.

The specifically Indian expression of secularism in politics as Hindu-Muslim unity or, more generally, as inter-communal harmony

Jinnah.
& secularism.

(in contrast to communalism or the notion of community-wise exclusiveness of material interests and cultural concerns), took an unexpected turn in 1920 when Mahatma Gandhi made support for the claim of the Ottoman sultan to the status of the caliph (*khalifa*) an integral part of the non-cooperation movement. He wrote of *khilafat* as a question that concerned nearly 'one-fourth of the nation', that is the Muslims, and therefore 'must concern the whole of India'. Muslim participation in the national movement reached unprecedented heights during the Khilafat agitation, but the abolition of the caliphate in 1924 by the secular nationalists of Turkey knocked the bottom out of Hindu-Muslim co-operation. In fact, inter-community hostility resurfaced with renewed intensity. The ideology of Hindutva was proclaimed and the Rashtriya Swayamsevak Sangh established. In the hope of winning the support of Muslims for the national cause through the acknowledgement of *noblesse oblige*, Gandhi ended up as a loser twice over. As the leader of the Muslim League, Jinnah kept aloof from the Khilafat agitation, although he had not hesitated to raise issues of special concern to Muslims. His antipathy to Gandhi's ideas and political style was complemented by his distrust of Muslim religious leaders. And he warned Gandhi about the risks of bringing religious matters into secular politics.

Jinnah's transfer of loyalty from secular nationalism to Muslim separatism was made in the name of Muslim interests, rather than Islam, but he could not have been unconscious of the irony of the situation. Jawaharlal Nehru was struck by it, and he wrote in his autobiography how 'the old Ambassador of Unity associated himself with the most reactionary elements in Muslim communalism'. The objective achieved, Jinnah called for the burying of the communal 'hatchet' on the eve of the birth of Pakistan, and declared (on 11 August 1947 in his presidential address to the Constituent Assembly in Karachi) that a citizen of Pakistan 'may belong to any religion or caste or creed—that has nothing to do with the business of the State'. Looking ahead, he envisaged a time when 'Hindus would cease to be Hindus and Muslims would cease to be Muslims, not in the religious sense, because that is the personal faith of each individual, but in the political sense as citizens of the State' (see Wolpert 1988: 339–40). It is noteworthy that attempts have been made to suppress this secularist speech from the very day on which it was delivered: such was the gap between the leader and his followers and between his own ideals and actions.

As for Nehru, his relationship with Gandhi has its own elements of irony. While, at the commencement of his political career, he acknowledged Gandhi as a uniquely powerful leader—and Gandhi was a wholly religious person—he also gave anguished expression to the incursion of religion into politics. In his autobiography, Nehru observed that, although Gandhi's stress on the religious and spiritual dimensions of the national movement was not couched in dogmatic terms, 'it did mean a definitely religious outlook on life', as a result of which the national (non-cooperation) movement took on 'a revivalist character so far as the masses were concerned'. He confessed: 'I used to be troubled sometimes at the growth of this religious element in our politics, both on the Hindu and the Muslim sides. I did not like it at all…. Even some of Gandhiji's phrases sometimes jarred upon me—thus his frequent reference to *Rama Raj* as the golden age which was to return' (1980: 72). Nehru never compromised on the issue of the secular state and, by and large, on the ideology of secularism (in the Enlightenment sense of the term), until he too was constrained by the prevailing circumstances in independent India to embrace the notions of religious pluralism in society and a non-discriminatory state as the substance of secularism. The inconclusive Gandhi-Nehru dialogue on the issue of the place of religion in politics is as significant an aspect of the secularism debate in India as the Congress-League differences earlier.

In his celebrated midnight ('Tryst with destiny') speech in the Indian Constituent Assembly on 14–15 August 1947, Nehru lauded the fulfilment of the goals of the struggle for freedom from colonial rule, 'not in full measure' but 'substantially'. Freedom had indeed been achieved, but at what was considered an unbearable price until the very end, namely the partition of the subcontinent on the basis of religious difference. According to Nehru and other Congress leaders, and of course Gandhi, the notion of two nations, that is the irreconcilability of Hindu and Muslim cultures and interests, was grossly exaggerated if not wholly mistaken. While Gandhi did not consider Indian Muslims, the great majority of whom were descended from Hindus converted to Islam, culturally very distinct from the latter, Nehru regarded religion and culture largely as epiphenomena that reflected the underlying economic reality. According to both points of view, the elevation of religious and cultural differences to the level of a first principle in politics violated the very spirit of the national movement. A dozen years later, Nehru acknowledged that the aging and tired leaders of the Congress had agreed to partition as 'a way out' of the political impasse. Moreover, at least some of them, including Nehru himself, believed that it would be temporary.

It was perhaps much too soon in August 1947 for Nehru to make an accurate assessment of any but the short term costs of the critical choice that he and his colleagues had made. Today, half a century later, it is irrefutable that partition was a concession to religious nationalism that was not yet a lifting of the curse of communalism. Perhaps Jinnah realized this, for he spoke of the unavoidability of the creation of religious minorities in each country.

It has been argued that not all Hindus were opposed to partition. The resultant demographic profile of the successor state of India, raising the proportion of Hindus in relation to Muslims from about three-quarters to above four-fifths, gave Hindus a more dominant position than before. This fact was used by Pakistani leadership to brand India as 'Hindustan', a Hindu country.

While the League leadership proceeded to build an Islamic state, India affirmed its commitment to secularism in conformity with the ideology of secular nationalism that the Congress had throughout proclaimed to be the basis of its struggle for freedom. The constitution adopted in 1949 envisaged a secular state. The widespread revulsion generated by the assassination of Gandhi at the hands of a Hindu helped contain Hindu communalism for a while. The realization of the grievous harm that partition had done to their fortunes at the subcontinental level, made the 43 million Muslims, who remained in India by choice or the compulsion of circumstances, opt for a low political profile. The establishment of the Bhartiya Jana Sangh in 1951, and its noteworthy performance in the 1951–52 general elections (it won 12 per cent of the votes cast), signalled the return of Hindu religious nationalism, particularly in north India. Muslim attitudes began to change in tandem, as it were. Before long, communal riots too began to recur. Nehru summed up his anguish when he said in 1958 that his two hardest tasks as Prime Minister had been the building of a just society and of a secular polity (see page 245). By the time he died in 1964, his experiment of planned economic development within a socialist framework also had run into serious difficulties. The vision of a secular, socialist India, so full of promise at the dawn of independence, was now clouded by uncertainty.

While a radical restructuring of the processes of economic development in the recent past (since 1991) in a 'market-friendly' mould seems to have accelerated the processes of diversification and growth—opinions on this are expectedly divided along ideological lines—the crisis of Indian secularism has, it is generally agreed, deepened. The weakness of the secular state to overcome the challenge of communalism is symbolized by the destruction of two places of worship, namely, the Akal Takht in Amritsar in 1984 and the Babri Masjid in Ayodhya in 1992. The former had been converted into a fortress by fundamentalist and militant Sikhs under the nose, as it were, of the Union government, which ultimately had to use too much force because it acted too late. In the event, the shrine was all but completely destroyed. The mosque had been converted into a 'disputed structure' by Hindu communalists, who ultimately demolished it, while the state government looked the other way and even provided covert help. The claim of the Bhartiya Janata Party, which had come to power in Uttar Pradesh in 1991, that it was the upholder of genuine secularism, as against the 'pseudo secularism' of the Congress, was exposed as no more than political chicanery. The Congress could well be accused of appeasing the Muslim 'vote bank', but the BJP had revealed, through its rhetoric and actions, its communal character and earned the dismissal of the state governments it had formed. The electorate too administered a rebuff to it in 1993 by voting non-BJP governments to power in the three of the four states where it had ruled, including Uttar Pradesh. The parties that came to power in the state, namely, Samajwadi and Bahujan Samaj Parties, fumed against BJP's communalism, but were themselves openly casteist and wooed the Muslim voters. Ironically, these caste leaders were hailed as 'the new champions' of secularism by some reputed intellectuals, for they had placed 'material matters above matters of faith'. The public debate about secularism has become curious indeed.

*   *   *

From the days of the Khilafat agitation in the early 1920s and onward a large corpus of scholarly writing on nationalism and communalism has accumulated. It has been contributed mostly by historians and political scientists. The contribution of sociologists is meagre. As

intellectual styles and theoretical paradigms have changed, interpretations of the phenomena also have changed. It is no longer
considered adequate to invoke the 'divide and rule' policies of the
imperial power to explain communal conflict: it is now *de rigueur* to
argue that the very existence of communal identities was an aspect
of the larger hegemonic enterprise of the construction of the 'other'.
Similarly, reductionist explanations in the Marxist mode also are
now considered inadequate, and the call has gone out from the
'subalternist' circles to recognize the importance of religion as a
crucial element in the situation. Since the scholars who produce these
interpretations are themselves secularists, one detects a lack of not
only ethnographic detail but also ease in the writings of some of them.

Be that as it may, one of the most significant insights of the
literature on communalism, I think, is that it reveals how religion
itself is devalued when it becomes a significant means of mobilizing
people for the furtherance of certain secular objectives, most notably
the acquisition of power. The religious element that enters into the
making of communalism has been described as 'but the shadow of
religion, i.e. religion taken not as the essence and guide of life in all
spheres, but only as a sign of the distinction of one human, at least
virtually political, group against others' (Dumont 1970a: 91). The
transformation of ends into means, allegedly in furtherance of the
very same ends, is intensely ironical.

The partition of the subcontinent for the creation of Pakistan, it
was generally hoped, would help the secular-minded in India to put
the distraction of communalism behind them. The great task that lay
ahead was the making of a secular state and the first steps toward
this goal were taken by the Constituent Assembly (1946–49).
Scholarly writing too turned to the exploration of this theme. In an
early and perceptive dissertation, prepared in the late 1950s, Ved
Prakash Luthera argued that, in the prevailing socio-cultural and
political milieus, the only feasible option for India was to have a
'jurisdictionalist' rather than a secular state; and this indeed was what
the constitution-makers had provided. Under jurisdictionalism, he
explained, all religions are treated as equal by the state, which
guarantees freedom of conscience and worship to everybody;
moreover, the state assumes a supervisory and vigilant role toward
religious institutions (see Luthera 1964: 21–3). In short, Luthera did
not consider an orthodox secular state feasible in India. He did not,

however, entertain any doubts about the viability of the kind of state provided for in the constitution.

Whatever its deficiencies, the Luthera thesis highlighted some significantly specific and fairly explicit features of the Indian constitution. Its publication in 1964 was preceded by a year by Donald Eugene Smith's *India as a Secular State,* which instantaneously and deservedly achieved the status of a premier authoritative work on the subject. Smith's answer to the question whether India was a secular state was a qualified 'yes'. He maintained that one could be cautiously optimistic but not absolutely sure about the future of secularism. 'The forces of Hindu communalism' were the potential threat that would have to be watched carefully, for there was 'much that could go wrong' (1963: 493–501).

These early reservations and warnings received less attention, perhaps, than they deserved. The 1950s and early 60s, upto Nehru's passing in 1964, were the years of high hope, and even heady enthusiasm, for the votaries of the ideologies of secularism and socialism. When anxieties began to emerge, and later in the 1970s to thicken, these concerned the slow pace of secularization and the recurrence of communal conflict rather than the suitability or viability of received ideas and institutions. A widely discussed public document, voicing serious concern about 'the accelerating pace of retreat from reason' and 'the decay of rationality' was 'A statement on scientific temper', issued in 1981 by a galaxy of intellectuals (see Bhaduri et al. 1981). It called for the fostering of 'scientific temper' (the phrase was attributed to Jawaharlal Nehru) and the recognition of science and technology as 'viable instruments of social transformation'. It drew a spirited retort from the cultural psychologist Ashis Nandy in the form of a 'Counter-statement on humanistic temper' (1981), in which he focused attention on the role of science in 'the institutionalization of suffering' and promotion of modern 'superstitious' and 'authoritarianism'.

Subsequently, Nandy published a radical critique of ideological secularism, pointing out that the Indian national movement had stressed that religious tolerance may be derived from an attitude of respectfulness toward all religions, and did not have to depend upon the devaluation of religion. If secularism 'is not to become a reformist sect within modernity, [it] must respect and build upon the faiths and visions that have refused to adapt to the modern worldview' (1985: 2). It is not people of faith, Nandy added, but religious zealots and secularists who are respectively against religious tolerance and religion itself. His critique points to the imperative of the recovery of religious tolerance (see Nandy 1988).

I have followed Nandy's writings on the theme of religious tolerance, and am in sympathy with the main thrust of his arguments. I agree that, paradoxical though it may seem, religion itself can be a resource in the fight against religious bigotry. I also agree that modernity (including secularism), being hegemonic in character, narrows rather than enlarges the domain of significant choice-making. I do not, however, agree with all the claims Nandy makes on behalf of abstract religion as against historical religions. He tends to idealize tradition, and does not recognize the enormous philosophical doubts and practical difficulties that will attend any serious attempt at the recovery of religious tolerance.

Let me hasten to add, I am not against the making of such efforts by intellectuals and others, and indeed support them. I only want to stress that doing so is not going to be easy. Considering, for instance, the lack of success of the three-language formula, because most of us are reluctant to seriously learn a second Indian language, what are the chances of religious-minded people in this country taking a genuine interest in faiths other than their own? Is religious tolerance possible unless it is based on engagement and dialogue rather than indifference or avoidance? And what about the secularists? Moreover, historical memories of the pasts of India as shaped by, among other things, the century-old debate about secular and religious nationalisms, have tended to be divisive rather than cohesive. Today, the call has gone forth from some of Europe's leading intellectuals to overcome the bitter legacy of the past through such means as the 'exchange of memories', 'promotion of plural readings of founding events', 'narrative hospitality', and, above all, 'forgiveness' (see Ricoeur 1992). If the West which we like to call materialist can think in such terms (Ricoeur writes of 'spiritual density'), maybe Indian intellectuals can do the same. Whatever is difficult is not impossible, but it is important to recognize the difficulties as far as possible in advance.

Starting off from a different point of departure than Nandy's, I have presented a critique of ideological secularism in several essays. In an address (see Madan 1987), I emphasized, first, the rootedness of secularism in the dialectic of Protestant Christianity and the Enlightenment and, second, its incompatibility with India's major religious traditions. Consequently, I expressed scepticism about an easy passage of unreformed secularism to India. The construction of an Indian ideology of religious pluralism and tolerance, I added, had been rendered problematic by the processes of secularization which tend to, if they do not actively seek to delimit and devalue the role of religion in society.

In two crucial passages I observed:

Secularism is the dream of a minority which wants to shape the majority in its own image, which wants to impose its will upon history but lacks the power to do so under a democratically organized polity. In an open society the state will reflect the character of the society. Secularism therefore is a social myth which draws a cover over the failure of this minority to separate politics from religion in the society in which its members live. From the point of view of the majority, "secularism" is a vacuous word, a phantom concept, for such people do not know whether it is desirable to privatize religion, and if it is, how this may be done, unless they be Protestant Christians but not if they are Buddhists, Hindus, Muslims, or Sikhs. For the secularist minority to stigmatize the majority as primordially oriented and to preach secularism to the latter as the law of human existence is moral arrogance and worse—I say "worse" since in our times politics takes precedence over ethics—political folly. It is both these—moral arrogance and political folly—because it fails to recognize the immense importance of religion in the lives of the peoples of South Asia (Madan 1987: 748–9).

In the prevailing circumstances secularism in South Asia is impossible as a credo of life because the great majority of the people are in their own eyes active adherents of some religious faith. It is impracticable as a basis for state action either because Buddhism and Islam have been declared state or state-protected religions or because the stance of religious neutrality or equidistance is difficult to maintain since religious minorities do not share the majority's view of what this entails for the state. And it is impotent as a blueprint for the future because, by its very nature, it is incapable of countering religious fundamentalism and fanaticism (ibid.: 748).

I concluded:

I have been sceptical about the claims that are made for secularism, scientific temper, etc., and I have suggested a contextualized rethinking of these fuzzy ideas.... I have suggested that the only way secularism in South Asia, understood as interreligious understanding, may succeed would be for us to take both religion and secularism seriously.... Secularism would have to imply that those who profess no religion have a place in society equal to that of others, not higher or lower (ibid.: 758).

I have quoted at length from the address: the readers of the present work will notice that, retrospectively, it reads like a prospectus of the book. But I have also moved beyond it. The printed text attracted widespread reference and comment, some of it positive and fair (see, e.g., van der Veer 1994b and Larson 1995), some of it critical (see, e.g., Bailey 1991, Baxi 1992 and Béteille 1994), and some of it rather amusing (in 1992 a columnist in *The Economic Times* recommended it as essential reading for the Indian Prime Minister!). The criticisms focused on my scepticism about ideological secularism and its easy universalizability, which worried the secularists. I was misunderstood to be against secularization (as if that makes sense), and wrote a short rejoinder to clarify my position (see Madan 1994a; see also 1994b).

It is reassuring that the notions of secularism and fundamentalism are now the subject of a serious debate. Significant questions are being raised. For example, whether secularism is 'an adequate, or even appropriate ground on which to meet the challenge of majoritarianism' (Chatterjee 1994). Does the present Indian situation hold the possibility of interventionist secularization being employed to promote cultural and religious intolerance? Similarly, analytically interesting distinctions have been proposed in the attempt to find out 'how not to defend secularism' (Bhargava 1994). It has been suggested that the immediate objective of 'political secularism' and the higher, more distant goal of 'ethical secularism' both 'insist upon the separation of religion and politics without undermining either', and, therefore, both should be 'invoked to justify a secular state'. What the religious justification of the state might imply could be, I think, a matter of substance (content) or style (form). These are complex questions, not settled issues, that call for a reproblematization of secularism.

The present work is offered as a contribution to these ongoing debates on secularism and fundamentalism. It is a book about India, but cannot be lacking in comparative interest. The Indian social reality is vast and complex, and any study of it, no matter how focused, will reflect a wide range of phenomena and possibilities. The daunting task that I have had to face has been how to pursue the inquiry without being submerged in detail. I have had to resort to selection, abridgement and abstraction. Thus, I have not written about South India, but the north-south contrast in respect of the emergence of Hindu and Muslim fundamentalisms surely demands exploration. I have written about the defining orientations or central tendencies of India's major religious traditions, risking the criticism that I homogenize and essentialize phenomena that are synchronically diverse and diachronically dynamic. The notion of tradition posits continuity as well as change, and I have tried to explore both. Insofar as I have been concerned with the building of 'ideal types' (nearly in the Weberian sense), the discussion focuses more on recognizable profiles than on the flux of events.

In the study of the religious traditions, I have been concerned primarily with ideas (and ideologues) and events, rather than with institutions, in the interests of what seemed feasible within the covers of one book. I am not asserting a methodological position that bestows priority or primacy on ideas over interests—on idealism over materialism—in the study of society. Nevertheless, a theoretical perspective is emphasized, namely that, whatever exists empirically (e.g., the processes of secularization), and not also ideologically, exists but precariously. This does not mean, for instance, that Indians have to become Protestant Christians *en masse* to achieve reasonable and viable secularization of society. The chosen perspective only draws pointed attention to the need for greater effort on the part of Indian intellectuals to clarify the meanings of secularization (as process and as thesis) in a context-sensitive manner. Contrary to what many of us believe, there is considerable historical and ethnographical evidence that the common people of this country, whatever their religious background, are comfortable with religious pluralism in one form or another and practise it. The traditional elite of the nineteenth century, from whom today's intelligentsia have descended, excoriated such pluralism as the superstitious ways of the masses. The intelligentsia would rather opt for an encompassing ideology of modernity, which limits the role of religion to the private domain and therefore admits of plurality. The two pluralisms—the people's and the intellectuals'—are obviously different, even opposed, but the hiatus has not been explored.

Religious pluralism as ideology—as secularism—is more than the recognition of plurality; it is an intellectual and moral commitment, and has emerged as a key issue in contemporary India (and in this book). A causal relationship between pluralism and secularism has been noticed since long. Voltaire welcomed religious pluralism, hoping that, in the end, it would eliminate religion by eroding its credibility. In our own time, the social theorist Peter Berger has persuasively argued that '"pluralism" is a social-structural correlate of secularization of consciousness' (1973: 131). He points to the 'demonopolization' of religious traditions that secularization produces, which then leads to pluralism and ecumenicity. The relationship is symmetrical: secularization produces pluralism;

pluralism produces secularization. This argument bears the imprint of the Western experience; interestingly, it apparently supports the Indian definition of secularism as religious pluralism and also the contention that, given the prevailing plurality of religions, India provides a congenial environment for secularization.

Closer exploration of the thesis raises doubts about both its appropriateness vis-à-vis India and its logical soundness. Plurality in a setting where hierarchy is present is not likely to produce a crisis of credibility, nor egalitarian pluralism, for all religions are deemed to be true, but one is more true than the others and encompasses them. For Vivekananda, Vedanta was the mother of all religions; for Abul Kalam Azad, Islam was the faith perfected by God for humanity to embrace and Vedanta measured up to it. Moreover—and this is sociologically very important—secularization produces uniformity in the areas it liberates from the reign of religion, and the process knows no limits in principle. Modernization homogenizes all that it surveys. A simple-minded equation of secularism with pluralism is therefore problematic.

I find it ironical that, through its definition as equal respect for all religions, secularism in India becomes a religious idea: it underscores the importance of religion, and not in private life alone, but also in the public domain. As a religious idea, pluralism may not evade the question of value. Hierarchy is the notion that some religious liberals find most acceptable as the means to deal with the phenomenon of the plurality of religious and sub-religious traditions. A back-to-back pluralism is the more general choice: it is easy, but it too evades the issue—unless it implies a religious apartheid, usually benign, sometimes malign. One has to be a Mahatma Gandhi to venture coming near to being a radical pluralist (in the sense of considering each religion a complement to the others) and look beyond the abyss of rank relativism. But is *that* what secularism is all about? What about its relation to secularization? Is pluralism too, then, a social myth? These are not plain questions and must be asked, lest it should be said that there are locks on our minds. Meanwhile, in the writing of this book, I have (in Spinoza's words) 'made a sedulous effort not to deride, not to deplore, not to denounce human actions, but to understand them'.

Glossary

Nearly all the key words from India's religious traditions that have been used in this book are glossed in the text itself. The purpose of the glossary is limited to providing standard transliteration of selected terms along with additional explantory notes. Since the transliteration of Arabic, Persian and Urdu words follows different principles from that of words from Sanskrit and other north Indian languages, the glossary is divided into two parts.

I. Arabic, Persian, and Urdu Words

ahl-i kitab, ahl-i kitāb. People who are in possession of a revealed though superseded book of knowledge. They are entitled to protection as the *ẕimmī* (q.v.) under Islamic law.

alim, ᶜālim. Pl. *ᶜulamā.* A learned man; religious and legal scholar.

bida, bidᶜah. Reprehensible innovation in religious belief.

dar-al harb, dār-al ḥarb. The land of war, where Muslim institutions do not prevail.

dar-al Islam, dār-al Islām. The land of Islam where Muslim institutions prevail irrespective of the religion of the ruler(s).

din, dīn. Prophetic religion.

faqih, faqīh. See *fiqh* (q.v.).

fatwa, fatwā. Judicial pronouncement; advisory opinion expressed by a *muftī*, i.e., one qualified to do so.

fiqh. Islamic jurisprudence. Hence *faqīh,* jurist.

hadis, ḥadīs. The sayings of the Prophet Muhammad inspired by divine revelation.

hakimiyya, ḥakimiyya. Sovereignty; the notion that temporal sovereignty ultimately vests in God, who is the most just of rulers, *ahkam'l-ḥ ākimīn* (*Qur'ān* xcv.8).

hijrat. Migration; the departure of Muslims from a country under non-Muslim rule (*dār-al ḥarb*, q.v.) in the manner of the Prophet Muhammad's departure from Mecca (Makkah).

hukam, ḥukam. Divine commandment in the Sikh tradition.

hukam nama, ḥukam nāma. Instructions of the Sikh gurus or of the *jathedār* (head) of the five *takht* (q.v.).

ijma, ijmāᶜ. The unanimous opinion of a council of learned men (*faqih, ᶜulamā,* q.v.)

ijtihad, ijtihād. Exertion; the considered and logically argued opinion of a learned man (*mujtahid*) on an issue relating to the *sharīᶜat* (q.v.).

imam, imām. Leader, exemplar of Muslims; leader of the congregational prayer; among the Shīᶜah, each of the twelve leaders succeeding the Prophet Muhammad.

jahiliyya. State of ignorance (*jahl*). Pre-Islamic state of false knowledge; erosion of true knowledge.

jihad, jihād. Endeavour; the obligation of a Muslim to wage war against unbelievers (*kāfir,* q.v.). Hence *mujāhid,* warrior in the cause of religion. The Sufi tradition refers to the striving to overcome one's vices or lusts as the greater *jihād, al-jihādu'l akbar.*

jizya, jizyah. Poll or capitation tax exacted from non-Muslims in *dār-al Islām* for protection of person and property.

kafir, kāfir. One who hides the truth; one who is not a Muslim and believes (misbelieves) in that which is not true (e.g., the divinity of Jesus or polytheism).

khalifa, khalīfa. Successor (from *khalf,* to leave behind); successor to the Prophet Muhammad. Hence *khilāfat,* caliphate.

khalsa, khālsā. The community of baptized Sikhs.

mahdi, mahdī. The leader who shall appear on earth at the end of time to guide Muslims.

maulana, maulānā. Master. Title of Sunnī religious scholar.

mazhab. Sunnī school of law; more generally religion.

padshah, pādshah. King of kings. Title of each of the ten Sikh Gurus (with the prefix *sachā,* true), stressing the unity of spiritual and temporal lordship.

pir, pīr. Sufi spiritual master. In the Sikh tradition *pīrī-mīrī* conveys the unity symbolized in the notion of *pādshah* (q.v.); *mīr* is temporal lord.

qanun, qānūn. Statute, canon law.

qazi, qāzi. Judge administering *sharīᶜat* (q.v.).

Quran, Qur'ān. The Muslim holy book containing divine revelations, for the believers to read and recite, from the Arabic *qara',* cp. the Hebrew *kīrī.*

sharīa, sharīᶜah, sharī ᶜat. Muslim law comprising the Qur'ān, *hadiṣ* (q.v.), and *ijmāᶜ* (q.v.) (from *sharh,* exposition, to expound).

Shia, Shī͑ah. Followers; partisans of ͑Ali, cousin and son-in-law of the Prophet Muhammad, who was, according to the Shī͑ah tradition the legitimate *imām* (q.v.).

sultan, sultān. Pl. *salatīn*. Power, authority; king.

Sunni, Sunnī. One who follows the path shown by the Prophet Muhammad.

tajdid, tajdīd. Renewal. Hence *mujaddid*, renewer.

takht, takht. Throne. Seat of temporal authority in the Sikh tradition. The Akāl Takht at Amritsar, and certain *gurdwārās* (q.v.) at Damadama Sahib, Keshgarh (both in Punjab), Nanden (Maharashtra), and Patna (Bihar) are designed as *takht*.

tauhid, tauhīd, tawhīd. Unity of godhead, one of the fundamentals of Islam. Polytheism is *bid ͑ah* (q.v.).

ulama, ͑ulamā. See *͑alīm* (q.v.).

umma, ummah. A people. The universal community of Muslims.

urf, ͑urf. Customary law.

vilayet-i-faqih, vilāyet-i-faqīh. The Shī͑ah doctrine of the guardianship of the state held by the most learned jurist.

zimmi, zimmī. Non-Muslim subject protected by the Islamic state on payment of *jizyah* (q.v.).

II. Sanskrit, Hindi, and Punjabi Words

advaita. Non-dual, non-dualism; the doctrine of the unity of the universal and individual souls (*brahman* and *ātman*, q.v.). A metaphysical system taught by Shankarcharya (Śaṅkarācārya) in the eighth century.

ahamkara, ahaṁkāra. Egoism; the claim that human agency is self-sufficient. Considered as one of the five cardinal vices in the Hindu and Sikh religious traditions, the other four being *kāma* (lust), *krodha* (anger), *lobha* (greed), and *moha* (attachment to illusory things). See *haumai*.

artha. Wealth. Hence *arthashastra* (*arthas͑āstra*), the science of material prosperity.

atma, ātmā, ātman. Inner, unconditioned self; spirit; soul.

Bhagavad Gita, Bhagavad Gītā. 'The Song Celestial'. A philosophical dialogue in verse in the sixth book of the great epic *Mahābhārata*, dealing with the paths to self-realization through knowledge (*jñāan*), action (*karma*), and devotion to God (*bhakti*).

brahma. Sacerdotium; *brahman*, the primary principle which is the source of all that exists; infinite spirit; the Absolute.

brahman, brāhmaṇa. Liturgical text; ritual specialist, priest.

dharma. A key word with multiple connotations, ranging from the over-arching notion of cosmo-moral order to duties and laws of various kinds (e.g., *varṇa dharma*, caste duties; *rāja dharma*, king's duties) and, most generally, religion in the narrow Western sense of the term. *Dharam* in

Punjabi. Hence *dharma yuddha*, war in the cause of righteousness, or *dharam yudh* (in Punjabi), employed by the Sikhs to legitimize secular political action. See *purusārtha*.

granth, granth. Book. The Sikhs call their holy book *Ādi Granth*, the original book, or *Granth Sāhib, Guru Granth Sāhib*, i.e., the honoured book that is the *guru*. It mainly comprises hymns by the Sikh Gurus (*gurbānī*) and saints from many parts of India, such as Kabir, Sheikh Farid and Ravidas. Those who learn to read the multilingual holy book in the prescribed manner are called *granthī*.

grihastha, grhastha. Householder, the state of domesticity. *Grhastī, gristhi* in Punjabi.

gurdwara, gurdwārā, gurudvāra. The guru's abode. In the Sikh tradition God is the *guru*. Hence *gurdwārā* is the place of worship and prayer for the Sikhs. The principal object of veneration is the *Granth Sāhib* (q.v.).

gurmat, gurmattā. A community decision arrived at a general gathering of the Sikhs (*sarbat khālsā*), in the presence of the *Granth Sāhib* (q.v.), that is binding on all members of the community.

haumai. The term for egoism in the Sikh tradition. *Haumai* makes one *manmukh* (self-willed); liberation from it makes one *gurmukh* (obedient to the word of the Guru).

hindutva. Being a Hindu. Hindu cultural identity. The key slogan employed by the Hindu right wing for total mobilization of the peoples of India.

Japji, Japjī. The first of Guru Nanak's hymns, found at the very beginning of *Granth Sāhib* (q.v.), it contains the 'foundational formula' (*mūl mantra*) of the Sikh faith, affirming the unity, immanence and nurturing character of the Supreme Being. *Jap* means meditation.

kshatra, ksatra. Regnum; temporal power represented by the king.

nirpeksha, nirpeksa. Neutral. Hence *nirpeksatā*, neutrality, as in *dharma nirpeksatā*, religious neutrality as state policy. See *samabhāva*.

purushartha, purusārtha. Ends of life; goals of purposive action; usually three, namely, *dharma* (moral orientation), *artha* (rational pursuit of economic and political goals), and *kāma* (aesthetic and sensual enjoyment). *Moksha* (*moksa*), liberation from the foregoing, is often listed as the fourth *purusārtha*.

rahitnama. rahitnāma. Rules governing a baptised (*amrtdhārī*) Sikh's life. Several such manuals are extant, all claiming to be based on Guru Gobind Singh's injunctions.

rashtra, rāstra. Nation.

samabhava, samabhāva. Similar attitude or equal respect, as in *sarva dharma samabhāva*, equal respect for all religions. See *nirpeksa*.

sanatan, sanātan. Timeless, eternal, as in *sanātan dharma*, orthodox, un-reformed religion (Hinduism).

shabad, sabad. The 'holy word' or hymn in the Sikh tradition. From the Sanskrit *sabda* for word, sound, verbal testimony.

shastra, śāstra. Science, knowledge; treatise. See *smrti.*

shruti, śruti. That which is heard; revealed knowledge. The Brahmanical notion of revelation is different from that of the Abrahamic religions as it is internal and timeless, for the Truth itself is timeless. See *sanātan, veda* and *smrti.*

smriti, smrti. Memory; remembered tradition; written texts, e.g., *Manu smrti* which is also called *Mānav dharma s'āstra,* the science of (human) righteous conduct.

taksal, taksāl. 'Mint'; Sikh religious school.

upanishad, upanisad. 'Secret knowledge'; Brahmanical metaphysical texts. See *vedānta.*

veda. Knowledge, the highest knowledge received through *śruti* (q.v.); sacred lore; the texts (*Rg, Yajur, Sāma, Atharva*) embodying such knowledge and providing guidance to ritual performances with a view to attaining it. From *vid,* to know; cf. *vidyā,* knowledge in general.

vedanta, vedānta. The culmination (or end) of vedic knowledge; metaphysical texts containing discussions about being, knowing and value. Vivekananda called *vedānta* the mother of all religions.

References

Abdullah, Sheikh M. 1993. *Flames of the chinar: An autobiography.* New Delhi: Viking.

Abul Fazl. 1977. *Akbar Nama.* English trans., H. Beveridge. 3 vols. New Delhi: Munshiram Manoharlal.

Acton, H.B. 1955. *The illusion of the epoch: Marxism-Leninism as a philosophical creed.* London: Cohen and West.

Adams, Charles, J. 1966. The ideology of Mawlana Mawdudi. *In* Donald Eugene Smith, ed., *South Asian politics and religion.* Princeton, N.J.: Princeton University Press.

Agwani, M.S. 1986. *Islamic fundamentalism in India.* Chandigarh: Twenty-first Century India Society.

Ahmad, Aijaz. 1992. Azad's careers: Roads taken and not taken. *In* Mushirul Hasan, ed., *Islam and Indian nationalism: Reflections on Abul Kalam Azad.* New Delhi: Manohar.

Ahmad, Aziz. 1964. *Studies in Islamic culture in the Indian environment.* Oxford: Clarendon Press.

———. 1967. *Islamic modernism in India and Pakistan 1857-1964.* London: Oxford University Press.

Ahmad, Imtiaz, ed. 1976. *Family, kinship and marriage among Muslims in India.* New Delhi: Manohar.

———. 1978. *Caste and social stratification among Muslims in India.* 2nd ed. New Delhi: Manohar.

Ahmad, Mumtaz. 1991. Islamic fundamentalism in South Asia: The Jamaat-i-Islami and the Tabhlighi-Jamaat. *In* Martin E. Marty and R. Scott Appleby, eds., *Fundamentalisms observed.* Chicago: University of Chicago Press.

Ahmed, Akbar S. 1988. *Rediscovering Islam: Making sense of Muslim history and society.* London: Routledge and Kegan Paul.

Ahmed, Rafiuddin. 1981. *The Bengal Muslims 1871-1906: A quest for identity.* Delhi: Oxford University Press.

————. 1994. Redefining Muslim identity in South Asia: The transformation of Jamaat-i-Islami. *In* Martin E. Marty and R. Scott Appleby, eds., *Accounting for fundamentalisms.* Chicago: The University of Chicago Press.

Akbar, M.J. 1988. *Nehru: The making of India.* London: Viking.

al-Attas, Syed Muhammad Naquib. 1985. *Islam, secularism and the philosophy of the future.* London: Mansell.

al-Biruni, Abu Raihan. 1983. *India.* Abridged ed. of Edward C. Sachau's English trans., ed., Qeyamuddin Ahmad. New Delhi: National Book Trust.

Alavi, Azra. 1983. *Socio-religious outlook of Abul Fazl.* Delhi: Idarah-i Adabiyat-i Delhi.

Amrik Singh. 1988. Sikhs at the turn of the new century. *In* Joseph T. O'Connell, et al., eds., *Sikh history and religion in the twentieth century.* Toronto: University of Toronto.

Amuzegar, Jehangir. 1991. *The dynamics of the Iranian Revolution.* Albany: State University of New York Press.

Anderson, Walter K. and Shridhar D. Damle. 1987. *The brotherhood in saffron: The Rashtriya Swayam Sevak Sangh and Hindu revivalism.* New Delhi: Vistar.

Appadurai, Arjun. 1981. *Worship and conflict under colonial rule: A south Indian case.* Cambridge: Cambridge University Press.

Arapura, J.G. 1987. India's philosophical response to religious pluralism. *In* Howard G. Coward, ed., *Modern Indian responses to religious pluralism.* Albany: State University of New York Press.

Archer, John Clark. 1946. *The Sikhs in relation to Hindus, Muslims, Christians and Ahmadiyas.* Princeton, N.J.: Princeton University Press.

Arjomand, Said Amir. 1988. *The turban for the crown: The Islamic revolution in Iran.* New York: Oxford University Press.

Arkoun, Mohamed. 1987. *Rethinking Islam today.* Centre for Contemporary Arab Studies, Occasional Papers. Washington D.C.: Georgetown University.

Arthas'āstra. See Sastry, R. Shama 1967.

Asad, Talal. 1993. *Genealogies of religion: Discipline and reasons of power in Christianity and Islam.* Baltimore: Johns Hopkins University Press.

Asher, Catherine B. 1992. *The new Cambridge history of India. I: 4. Architecture of Mughal India.* Cambridge: Cambridge University Press.

Askari, Hasan. 1977. *Inter-religion.* Aligarh: Printwell.

Attar Singh. 1973. *Secularism and the Sikh faith.* Amritsar: Guru Nanak Dev University.

Augustine, St. 1948. *The city of God,* 2 vols. New York: Hafner.

Ayer, A.J. 1986. *Voltaire.* New York: Random House.

Azad, Abul Kalam. 1951. Speech on 22 September 1951, inaugurating the Vishva Bharati as a central university.

———. 1959. *India wins freedom*. Bombay: Orient Longman..

———. 1962. *The Tarjuman al-Quran*. Vol. 1. Ed. and trans., Syed Abdul Latif. Bombay: Asia Publishing House.

———. 1964, 1966, 1968, 1970. *Tarjumān al-Qur'ān* (in Urdu). Vols.1, 2, 3, & 4. New Delhi: Sahitya Academy.

———. 1990. *Intikhābāt Mazāmīn* (in Urdu). Ed., Syeda S. Hameed. New Delhi: Indian Council of Cultural Relations.

Babb, Lawrence A. 1986. *Redemptive encounters: Three modern styles in the Hindu tradition*. Berkeley: University of California Press.

Bagal, J.C. ed. 1969. *Bankim-rachanāvalī*. Calcutta: Sahitya Samsad.

Baig, M.R.A. 1967. *In different saddles*. New Delhi: Vikas.

Bailey, F.G. 1991. Religion and religiosity: Ideas and their use. *Contributions to Indian sociology* (n.s.) 25, 2: 211-32.

Barr, James. 1978. *Fundamentalism*. Philadelphia: Westminster Press.

Barrier, Gerald N. 1970. *The Sikhs and their literature*. Delhi: Manohar.

———. 1988a. The Sikhs and Punjab politics 1882-1922. *In* Paul Wallace and Surendra Chopra, eds., *Political dynamics and crisis in Punjab*. Amritsar: Guru Nanak Dev University.

———. 1988b. Sikh politics in British Punjab prior to the Gurdwara Reform Movement. *In* Joseph T. O'Connell, et al., eds., *Sikh history and religion in the twentiety century*. Toronto: University of Toronto.

———. 1995. The Singh Sabhas and the evolution of modern Sikhism, 1875-1925. *In* Robert Baird, ed., *Religion in modern India*. New Delhi: Manohar.

Basu, Tapan, P. Datta, S. Sarkar, T. Sarkar, and S. Sen. 1993. *Khaki shorts and saffron flags*. Hyderabad: Orient Longman.

Bauberot, Jean. Forthcoming. *France as a secular state: Past and present*.

Bayly, C.A. 1990. *Indian society and the making of the British empire*. Hyderabad: Orient Longman.

Bayly, Susan. 1989. *Saints, goddesses and kings: Muslims and Christians in South Indian society, 1700-1900*. Cambridge: Cambridge University Press.

Baxi, Upendra. 1992. Secularism: real or pseudo. *In* M.M. Sankhder, ed., *Secularism in India*. New Delhi: Deep and Deep.

Becker, Carl. 1932. *The heavenly city of the eighteenth century philosophers*. New Haven: Yale University Press.

Bellah, Robert N. 1964. Religious evolution. *American sociological review* 29: 358-94.

———. 1967. Civil religion in America. *Daedalus* 96. Reproduced with a prefatory footnote in Bellah 1970.

———. 1970. *Beyond belief: Essays on religion in a post-traditional world*. New York: Harper & Row.

Berger, Peter L. 1973. *The social reality of religion*. Harmondsworth: Penguin Books.

Béteille, André. 1992. *The backward classes in contemporary India*. Delhi: Oxford University Press.

————. 1994. Secularism and the intellectuals. *Economic and political weekly* 29, 10: 559-66.

Bhaduri, Amit et al. 1981. A statement on scientific temper. *Mainstream* July 25.

Bhargava, Rajeev. 1994. How not to defend secularism. *South Asia bulletin* 14,1: 33-41.

————. 1995. Religious and secular identities. *In* Upendra Baxi and Bhikhu Parekh, eds., *Crisis and change in contemporary India*. New Delhi: Sage.

Biardeau, Madeleine. 1982. The salvation of the king in the Mahabharata. *In* T.N. Madan, ed., *Way of life: King, householder, renouncer. Essays in Honour of Louis Dumont*. New Delhi: Vikas.

————. 1989. *Hinduism: The anthropology of a civilization*. Trans., Richard Nice. Delhi: Oxford University Press.

Binder, Leonard. 1961. *Religion and politics in Pakistan*. Berkeley: University of California Press.

————. 1988. *Islamic liberalism. A critique of development ideologies*. Chicago: The University of Chicago Press.

Bipan Chandra. 1984. *Communalism in modern India*. New Delhi: Vikas.

Bose, N.K., ed. 1948. *Selections from Gandhi*. Ahmedabad: Navjivan.

Brown, Judith M. 1992. *Gandhi: Prisoner of hope*. Delhi: Oxford University Press.

Buhler, G. 1964 [1886]. *The laws of Manu*. Delhi: Motilal Banarsidass.

CAD. 1948-49. *Constituent Assembly of India Debates*, Vol.7 and Vol.8, India Official Reports. New Delhi: Lok Sabha Secretariat.

Campbell, Colin. 1971. *Towards a sociology of irreligion*. London: Macmillan.

Cassirer, Ernest. 1968. *The philosophy of the Enlightenment*. Princeton, N.J.: Princeton University Press.

Census of India. 1991. Series - 1 India. Religion (*Paper 1 of 1995*). New Delhi: Office of the Registrar General, Government of India.

Chadwick, Owen. 1975. *The secularization of the European mind in the nineteenth century*. Cambridge: Cambridge University Press.

Chandra, Satish. 1993. Jizyah and the state in India during the 17th century. *In* Satish Chandra, *Mughal religious policies, the Rajputs and the Deccan*. New Delhi: Vikas.

Chatterjee, Partha. 1986. *Nationalist thought and the colonial world: A derivative discourse?* Delhi: Oxford University Press.

————. 1994. Secularism and toleration. *Economic and political weekly* 29, 28: 1768-77.

Chatterji, Margaret. 1983. *Gandhi's religious thought*. London: Macmillan.

Chaudhuri, Nirad C. 1979. *Hinduism: A religion to live by*. New Delhi: B.I. Publications.

———. 1987. *Thy hand, great anarch! India 1921-1952*. London: Chatto & Windus.

Chopra, Surendra. 1988. Ethnicity, revivalism and politics in Punjab. *In* Paul Wallace and Surendra Chopra, eds., *Political dynamics and crisis in Punjab*. Amritsar: Guru Nanak Dev University.

Coomarswamy, Ananda. 1978 [1942]. *Spiritual authority and temporal power in the Indian theory of government*. New Delhi: Munshiram Manoharlal.

Cox, Harvey. 1965. *The secular city: Secularization and urbanization in theological perspective*. New York: Macmillan.

Cragg, Kenneth. 1985. *The pen and the faith. Eight modern Muslim writers and the Quran*. London: George Allen & Unwin.

Cunningham, J.D. 1955 [1916]. *A history of the Sikhs*. Delhi: S. Chand & Co.

Cunningham Jr., Noble E. 1991. *In pursuit of reason: The life of Thomas Jefferson*. New Delhi: Affiliated East-West Press.

Das, Sisirkumar. 1984. *The artist in chains: The life of Bankimchandra Chatterji*, New Delhi: New Statesman.

Das, Veena. 1984. For a folk theology and theological anthropology of Islam. *Contributions to Indian sociology* (n.s.) 18, 2: 292-305.

Datta, V.N. 1990. *Maulana Azad*. New Delhi: Manohar.

de Bary, Wm Theodore, gen. ed. 1969. *Sources of Indian tradition*. Vol. II. Compiled by Stephen Hay and I.H. Qureshi. New York: Columbia University Press.

———. 1970. *Sources of Indian tradition*. Vol. I. Compiled by A.L. Basham et al. New York: Columbia University Press.

Demerath, N.J. and W.H. Rhys. 1992. *A bridging of faiths. Religion and politics in a New England city*. Princeton, N.J.; Princeton University Press.

Dobbin, Christine. 1972. *Urban leadership in western India*. Oxford: Clarendon Press.

Doke, Joseph J. 1967. *An Indian patriot in South Africa*. New Delhi: Publications Division, Government of India.

Douglas, Ian Henderson. 1988. *Abul Kalam Azad: An intellectual and religious biography*. eds., Gail Minault and Christian Troll. Delhi: Oxford University Press.

Dube, S.C. 1983. Harmonizing dimension in Hindu civilizational processes. *In* S.C. Dube and V.N. Basilov, eds., *Secularization in multi-religious societies*. New Delhi: Concept.

Dumezil, Georges. 1988. *Mitra-Varuna: An essay on two Indo-European representations of sovereignty*. New York: Zone Books.

Dumont, Louis. 1960. World renunciation in Indian religions. *Contributions to Indian sociology* IV: 33-62.

———. 1962. The conception of kingship in ancient India. *Contributions to Indian sociology* VI: 48-77.

———. 1970a. *Religion, politics and history in India*. Paris and Leiden: Mouton.

———. 1970b. *Homo hierarchicus: The caste system and its implications*. London: Weidenfeld and Nicholson.

———. 1980. *Homo hierarchicus: The caste system and its implications*. Rev. ed. Chicago: University of Chicago Press.

———. 1983. A modified view of our origins: The Christian beginnings of modern individualism. *Contributions to Indian sociology* (n.s.) 17: 1-26.

———.1986. *Essays on individualism: Modern ideology in anthropological perspective*. Chicago: University of Chicago Press.

———. 1994. *German Ideology: From France to Germany and back*. Chicago: University of Chicago Press.

Durkheim, Emile. 1965 [1915]. *The elementary forms of the religious life*. Trans., J.W. Swain. New York: The Free Press.

Eaton, Richard. 1978. *The sufis of Bijapur 1300-1700: Social roles of sufism in medieval India*. Princeton, N.J.: Princeton University Press,

Eliot, Charles. 1954. *Hinduism and Buddhism*. Vol.II. London: Routledge and Kegan Paul.

Elster, Jon, ed. 1986. *Karl Marx: A reader*. Cambridge: Cambridge University Press.

Embree, Ainslie T. 1990. *Utopias in conflict: Religion and nationalism in modern India*. Berkeley: University of California Press.

Engels, Friedrich. 1959. *Anti-Duhring*. Moscow: Foreign Languages Publishing House.

Evans-Pritchard, E.E. 1965. *Theories of primitive religion*. Oxford: Clarendon Press.

Fauja Singh. 1969. Development of Sikhism under the Gurus. *In* Fauja Singh et al., *Sikhism*. Patiala: Punjabi University Press.

Field, Dorothy. 1914. *The religion of the Sikhs*. London: John Murray.

Foucault, M. 1980. *Power/knowleage: Selected interviews and other writings, 1972–77*. Ed., Colin Gordon. Brighton: Harvester.

Fox, Richard G. 1985. *Lions of the Punjab: Culture in the making*. Berkeley: University of California Press.

Friedman, Yohanan. 1972. The temple of Multan. A note on early Muslim attitudes to idolatory. *Israel Oriental studies* 2: 176-82.

———. 1986. Islamic thought in relation to the Indian context. *In* Marc Gaborieau, ed., *Islam and society in South Asia (Puruṣārtha* 9). Paris: Editions de l'Ecole des Hautes Etudes en Sciences Sociales.

Frykenberg, Robert E. 1991. The emergence of modern 'Hinduism' as a concept and as an institution. *In* Gunther D. Sontheimer and Hermann Kulke, eds., *Hinduism reconsidered*. New Delhi: Manohar.

Gadamar, Hans-Georg. 1975. *Truth and method*. New York: Continuum, The Seabury Press.

Galanter, Marc. 1984. *Competing equalities*. Berkeley: University of California Press.

Gandhi, Mohandas Karamchand. 1927. *An autobiography or the story of my experiments with truth*. Ahmedabad: Navjivan.

———. 1961, *The way to communal harmony*. Ahmedabad: Navjivan.

———. 1965. *The collected works of Mahatma Gandhi* [CWMG], Vol.17. New Delhi: Publications Divisions, Government of India [PD, GOI].

———. 1966. *CWMG*, Vol.21, New Delhi: PD, GOI.

———. 1967. *CWMG*, Vol.24, New Delhi: PD, GOI.

———. 1968. *CWMG*, Vol.25, New Delhi: PD, GOI.

———. 1969. *CWMG*, Vol.35, New Delhi: PD, GOI.

———. 1970. *CWMG*, Vol.58, New Delhi: PD, GOI.

———. 1976. *CWMG*, Vol.63, New Delhi: PD, GOI.

Gandhi, Rajmohan. 1987. *Understanding the Muslim mind*. New Delhi: Penguin Books.

Gay, Peter. 1966. *The Enlightenment: An interpretation. The rise of modern paganism*. New York: Vintage Books.

Gellner, Ernest. 1992. *Postmodernism, reason and religion*. London: Routledge.

Ghoshal, U.N. 1966. *A history of Indian political ideas*. Madras: Oxford University Press.

Gill, Sucha Singh. 1988. Contradictions in the Punjab model of growth and search for an alternative. *Economic and political weekly* 23: 436-37.

Glasner, Peter. 1977. *The sociology of secularization*. London: Routledge and Kegan Paul.

Gold, Daniel. 1991. Organised Hinduisms: From Vedic truth to Hindu nation. *In* Martin E. Marty and R. Scott Appleby, eds., *Fundamentalisms observed*. Chicago: University of Chicago Press.

Golwalkar, M.S. 1938. *We or our nationhood defined*. Nagpur: Bharat Prakashan.

———. 1980 [1966]. *Bunch of thoughts*. Bangalore: Jagarna Prakashana.

———. 1992. *Rāshtra* (in Hindi). Compiled by Gaurinath Rastogi, ed., Bhanu Pratap Shukla. New Delhi: Janaki Prakashan.

Gombrich, Richard. 1988. *Theravada Buddhism: A social history from ancient Benaras to modern Colombo*. London: Routledge and Kegan Paul.

Gonda, J. 1969 (1966). *Ancient Indian kingship from the religious point of view*. Leiden: E.J. Brill.

————. 1974. *The dual deities in the religion of the veda*. Amsterdam: North Holland.

Gopal, Sarvepalli, ed. 1980. *Jawaharlal Nehru: An anthology*. Delhi: Oxford University Press.

————. 1987. *Nehru and secularism*. Occasional Papers, No.42 (mimeo). New Delhi: Nehru Memorial Museum and Library.

————, ed. 1991. *Anatomy of a confrontation: The Babri Masjid–Ram Janmabhumi issue*. New Delhi: Viking.

Gopal Singh. Tr. and annotator. 1978. *Sri Guru Granth Sahab*. 4 vols. Chandigarh: World Sikh University Press.

————. 1987. *The religion of the Sikhs*. New Delhi: Allied.

————. 1988. *A history of the Sikh people*. New Delhi: World Book Centre.

Gould, Harold A. 1990. *Politics and caste*. Delhi: Chanakya.

Goyal, D.R. 1979a. *Rashtriya Swayamsevak Sangh*. New Delhi: Radhakrishna Prakashan.

————. 1979b. *Rāshtriya Swayamsevak Sangh* (in Hindi). New Delhi: Radhakrishna Prakashan.

Graham, B.D. 1993. *Hindu nationalism and Indian policies. The origins and development of the Bharatiya Jana Sangh*. Cambridge: Cambridge University Press.

Greene, Everts B. 1941. *Religion and the state: The making and testing of an American tradition*. New York: New York University Press.

Grewal, J.S. 1979 [1969]. *Guru Nanak in history*. Chandigarh: Punjab University.

Grewal, J.S. and S.S. Bal. 1987 [1967]. *Guru Gobind Singh: A biographical study*. Chandigarh: Punjab University.

———— and P.S. Rangi. 1983. Imbalance in growth in Punjab agriculture. *In* R.S. Johar and J.S. Khanna, eds., *Studies in Punjab economy*. Amritsar: GND University.

Gupta, K.P. 1974. Religious evolution and social change in India: A study of the Ramakrishna Mission Movement. *Contributions to Indian sociology* (n.s.) 8: 25-50.

Habib, Irfan. 1961. The political role of Shaikh Ahmad Sirhindi and Shah Walliullah. *Enquiry* 5: 35-55.

————. 1992. Observations on Akbar and his age: A symposium. *Social scientist* 20, 9-10: 68-72.

Habib, Muhammad. 1981. *Politics and society during the early medieval period*. Collected works of Professor Muhammad Habib. Ed., K.A. Nizami. New Delhi: People's Publishing House.

———— and Afsar Umar Salim Khan. n.d. [1961?] *The political theory of the Delhi sultanate. (Including a translation of Ziauddin Barani's Fatwa-i Jahandari, circa 1358-9 A.D.)*. Allahabad: Kitab Mahal.

Halbfass, Wilhelm. 1988. *India and Europe: An essay in understanding*. Albany: State University of New York Press.

Hameed, Syeda Saiyidain., ed. 1990. *India's Maulana Abul Kalam Azad. Centenary volume II. Selected speeches and writings.* New Delhi: Vikas & Indian Council for Cultural Relations.

Hans, Surjit. 1985. Historically changing modes of thought in Sikhism in the over-all social context. *New Quest* 52: 211-21.

Harbans Singh. 1964. *The Heritage of the Sikhs.* Bombay: Asia.

———. 1966. *Guru Gobind Singh.* Chandigarh: The Guru Gobind Singh Foundation.

———. 1983. *The Heritage of the Sikhs.* Rev. ed. New Delhi: Manohar.

Hardy, Peter. 1966. *Historians of modern India. Studies in Indo-Muslim historical writing.* London: Luzac & Co. Ltd.

———. 1970. The foundations of medieval Islam. *In* Wm. Theodore de Bary, gen. ed., *Sources of Indian tradition.* Vol. I. Compiled by A.L. Basham et al. New York: Columbia University Press.

———. 1971. *Partners in freedom and true Muslims.* Lund: Studentlitteratur.

———. *The Muslims of British India.* Cambridge: Cambridge University Press.

———. 1978. Unity and variety in Indo-Islamic and Perso-Islamic civilization: Some ethical and political ideas of Diya al-Din Barani of Delhi, of al-Ghazali and of Nasir al-Din Tusi compared. *Iran* 16: 127-35.

———. 1981. The growth of authority over a conquered political elite: The early Delhi sultanate as a possible case study. *In* J.F. Richards, ed., *Kingship and authority in South Asia.* (South Asia Studies, no.3, second ed.) Madison: University of Wisconsin.

Heesterman, J.C. 1985. *The inner conflict of tradition.* Chicago: University of Chicago Press.

Herrin, Judith. 1987. *The formation of Christendom.* Oxford: Basil Blackwell.

Hick, John. 1989. *An interpretation of religion.* New Haven: Yale University Press.

Hobbes, Thomas. 1991. *Leviathan.* Ed., Richard Tuck. Cambridge: Cambridge University Press.

Hocart, A.M. 1950 [1938]. *Caste.* London: Methuen.

Hodgson, Marshall G.S. 1974. *The venture of Islam. Conscience and history in a world civilization. Vol. three: The gunpowder empires and modern times.* Chicago: University of Chicago Press.

Hopfl, Harro, ed. and trans. 1991. *Luther and Calvin on secular authority.* Cambridge: Cambridge University Press.

Inden, Ronald. 1990. *Imagining India.* Oxford: Basil Blackwell.

Iqbal, Muhammad. 1980 (1944). *The reconstruction of religious thought in Islam.* Delhi: New Taj Office.

Isherwood, Christopher. 1965. *Ramakrishna and his disciples.* Calcutta: Advaita Ashrama.

Iyer, Raghavan. 1986. *The moral and political writings of Mahatma Gandhi. Vol.I: Civilization, politics, and religion.* Oxford: Clarendon Press.

Jain, Girilal. 1994. *The Hindu phenomenon.* New Delhi: UBS Publishers and Distributors.

Jalal, Ayesha. 1985. *The sole spokesman: Jinnah, the Muslim League, and the demand for Pakistan.* Cambridge: Cambridge University Press.

Jinnah, M.A. 1946. *Presidential addresses of Quaid-e-Azam M.A. Jinnah.* Delhi: All India Muslim League.

Jodh Singh, Bhai. 1967. Structure and character of the Sikh Society. *In Sikhism and Indian society.* Simla: Indian Institute of Advanced Study.

Jones, Kenneth W. 1968. Communalism in the Punjab. *The journal of Asian studies* 28, 1:50

———. 1976. *Arya dharm: Hindu consciousness in 19th-century Punjab.* New Delhi: Manohar.

———. 1989. *Socio-religious reform movements in British India.* Cambridge: Cambridge University Press.

———. 1995. Politicized Hinduism: The ideology and program of the Hindu Mahasabha. *In* Robert D. Baird, ed., *Religion in modern India.* New Delhi: Manohar.

Jordens, J.T.F. 1978. *Dayananda Sarasvati: His life and ideas.* Delhi: Oxford University Press.

Joshi, V.C., ed. 1975. *Rammohun Roy and the process of modernization of India.* New Delhi: Vikas.

Juergensmeyer, Mark. 1988. The logic of religious violence: The case of the Punjab. *Contributions to Indian sociology* (n.s.) 22, 65-88.

———. 1991. *Radhasaomi reality: The logic of a modern faith.* Princeton, N.J.: Princeton University Press.

———. 1995. Antifundamentalism. *In* Martin E. Marty and R. Scott Appleby, eds., *Fundamentalisms comprehended.* Chicago: University of Chicago Press.

Kane, Pandurang Vaman. 1973. *History of dharmas'āstra (ancient and medieval religious and civil law).* Vol.III, 2nd ed. Poona: Bhandarkar Oriental Research Institute.

Kangle, R.P. 1972. *The Kauṭilya arthas'āstra.* Part II. An English translation with critical and explanatory notes. Delhi: Motilal Banarsidass.

Kant, Immanuel. 1991. *Political writings,* 2nd ed., ed., Hans Reiss, trans., H.B. Nisbet. Cambridge: Cambridge University Press.

Kantorowicz, Ernst. 1981 [1957]. *The king's two bodies: A study in medieval political theology.* Princeton, N.J.: Princeton University Press.

Kantowsky, Detlef, ed. 1986. *Recent research on Max Weber's studies of Hinduism.* Köln: Weltforum Verlag.

Kapur, Rajiv. 1986. *Sikh separatism: The politics of faith.* London: Allen and Unwin.

Kapur Singh. 1959. *Parasharprasna or the baisakhi of Guru Gobind Singh.* Jullundur: Hind Publishers.

Kaviraj, Sudipta. 1995. Religion, politics and modernity. *In* Upendra Baxi and Bhikhu Parekh, eds., *Crisis and change in contemporary India.* New Delhi: Sage.

Keddie, Nikki R. 1995. *Iran and the Muslim world: Resistance and revolution.* London: Macmillan.

Khan, Abdul Majid. 1967. The impact of Islam on Sikhism. *In: Sikhism and Indian society.* Simla: Indian Institute of Advanced Study.

Khan, M. Ishaq. 1994. *Kashmir's transition to Islam: The role of Muslim rishis.* New Delhi: Manohar.

Khan, Muin-ud-Din Ahmad. 1965. *History of the Faraidi movement in Bengal (1818-1906).* Karachi: Pakistan Historical Society.

Kher, V.B. comp. & ed. 1962. *In search of the supreme.* Vol. II. Ahmedanagar: Navjivan.

Khomeini, Ayotollah Ruhollah. 1979. *Islamic government.* New York: Manor Books.

Khushwant Singh. 1953. *The Sikhs.* London: Allen and Unwin.

———. 1963 and 1966. *A history of the Sikhs.* Vol. I and Vol. II. Princeton, N.J.: Princeton University Press.

Kolakowski, Leszek. 1990. *Modernity on endless trial.* Chicago: University of Chicago Press.

Kopf, David. 1969. *British Orientalism and the Bengal renaissance.* Berkeley: University of California Press.

———. 1979. *The Brahmo Samaj and the shaping of the modern Indian mind.* Princeton, N.J.: Princeton University Press.

Kumar, Krishna. 1993. Hindu revivalism and education in North-central India. *In* Martin E. Marty and R. Scott Appleby, eds., *Fundamentalisms and society.* Chicago:University of Chicago Press.

Kumar, Ravinder. 1968. *Western India in the nineteenth century: A study in the social history of Maharashtra.* London: Routledge & Kegan Paul.

Larson, Gerald James. 1995. *India's agony over religion.* Albany: State University of New York Press.

Lawrence, Bruce. 1989. *Defenders of God: The fundamentalist revolt against the modern age.* San Francisco: Harper & Row.

Laycock, Douglas. 1994. Free Exercise and the Religious Freedom Restoration Act. *Fordham law review.* 62: 883-903.

Leaf, Murray, J. 1985. The Punjab crisis. *Asian survey* 25, 5: 494.

Lelyveld, David. 1978. *Aligarh's first generation: Muslim solidarity in British India.* Princeton, N.J.: Princeton University Press.

Lenin, Vladimir Ivanovich. 1962. *Collected works.* 5th ed., Vol.4. Moscow: Foreign Language Publishing House.

———. n.d., *Religion.* Calcutta: Burmon Publishing House.

Lerner, Daniel. 1958. *The passing of traditional society.* Glencoe, Ill.: The Free Press.

Lewis, Bernard. 1988. *The political language of Islam.* Chicago: University of Chicago Press.

Lingat, Robert. 1973. *The classical law of India.* Berkeley: University of California Press.

Llewellyn, J.E. 1993. *The Arya Samaj as a fundamentalist movement.* New Delhi: Manohar.

Locke, John. 1967. *Two tracts on government.* Ed., Philip Abrams. Cambridge: Cambridge University Press.

———. 1991. *A letter concerning toleration.* Eds., John Horton and Susan Mends. London: Routledge.

Lowith, Karl. 1949. *Meaning in history.* Chicago: University of Chicago Press.

———. 1982. *Max Weber and Karl Marx.* Trans., H. Fantel. London: Allen and Unwin.

Luthera, V.P. 1964. *The concept of the secular state and India.* Calcutta: Oxford University Press.

Mabbott, J.D. 1973. *John Locke.* London: Macmillan.

Macauliffe, M.A. 1909. *The Sikh religion: Its gurus, sacred writings and authors.* 6 vols. Oxford: Clarendon Press.

Madan, T.N. 1972. Religious Ideology in a plural society: The Muslims and Hindus of Kashmir. *Contributions to Indian sociology* (n.s.) 6: 106-41.

———. 1987. Secularism in its place. *The journal of Asian studies,* 46, 4: 747-59.

———. 1989. Religion in India. *Daedalus* 118: 115-46.

———. 1991. The double-edged sword: Fundamentalism and the Sikh religious tradition. *In* Martin E. Marty and R. Scott Appleby, eds., *Fundamentalisms observed.* Chicago: University of Chicago Press.

———. 1992. Menace of intolerance: National interests get short shift. *The Times of India* (New Delhi), 30 November.

———. 1993. Whither secularism in India? *Modern Asian studies,* 27, 3: 667–97.

———. 1994a. Secularism and the intellectuals. *Economic and political weekly* 19: 1095-6.

———. 1994b. Secularism and pluralism: Towards a clearer perspective. *The Times of India* (New Delhi), 8 January.

———. 1994c. Meaning of Kashmiriyat. *The Times of India* (New Delhi), 4 June.

———. 1995. From orthodoxy to fundemantalism: A thousand years of Islam in South Asia. *In* Martin E. Marty and R. Scott Appleby, eds., *Fundamentalisms comprehended.* Chicago: University of Chicago Press.

———, ed. 1995. Muslim communities of South Asia: Culture, society, and power. New Delhi: Manohar.

Malik, Hafeez. 1963. *Moslem nationalism in India and Pakistan.* Washington, D.C.: Public Affairs Press.

———, ed. 1971. *Iqbal: Poet-philosopher of Pakistan.* New York: Columbia University Press.

———. 1981. *Sir Sayyid Ahmad Khan and Muslim modernization in India and Pakistan.* New York: Columbia University Press.

Malraux, André. 1968. *Antimemoirs.* London: Hamish Hamilton.

Manusmriti. See Buhler, G., 1964.

Marglin, Frédérique A. 1982. Kings and wives: The separation of status and royal power. *In* T.N. Madan, ed., *Way of life: King, householder, renouncer.* New Delhi: Vikas.

Marriott, McKim, ed. 1955. *Village India: Studies in the little communities.* Chicago: University of Chicago Press.

Martin, David. 1965. Towards eliminating the concept of secularization. *In* Julius Gould, ed., *Penguin survey of the social sciences.* Harmondsworth: Penguin Books.

———. 1978. *A general theory of secularization.* Oxford: Basil Blackwell.

Martinich, A.P. 1992. *The two gods of Leviathan: Thomas Hobbes on religion and politics.* Cambridge: Cambridge University Press.

Marty, Martin E. 1986. *Modern American religion,*Vol.1. *The irony of it all. 1893-1919.* Chicago: University of Chicago Press.

———. 1988. Fundamentalism as a social phenomenon. *Bulletin of the American Academy of Arts and Sciences* 42: 15-29.

Marty Martin E. and R. Scott Appleby, eds. 1991, 1992, 1993, 1994, 1995. *I. Fundamentalisms observed. II. Fundamentalisms and society. III. Fundamentalisms and the state. IV. Accounting for fundamentalisms. V. Fundamentalisms comprehended.* Chicago: University of Chicago Press.

Marx, Karl. 1975. On the Jewish question. *In* Karl Marx and Friedrich Engels, *Collected Works.* Vol.3. Moscow: Progress Publishers.

Marx, Karl and Friedrich Engels. 1959. *Basic writings on politics and philosophy.* Ed., Lewis S. Feuer. New York: Doubleday, Anchor.

Masselos, J. 1974. *Towards nationalism.* Bombay: Popular.

Mathur, K.S. 1964. *Caste and ritual in Malwa.* Bombay: Asia Publishing House.

Maududi, Abul ala. 1980. *Four basic Quranic terms.* Delhi: Markazi Mak taba Islami.

———. 1981 [1973]. *A short history of revivalist movement in Islam.* Delhi: Markazi Maktaba Islami.

———. 1984. *The Islamic movement: Dynamics of values, power and change,* Ed., Khurram Murad. London: The Islamic Foundation.

———. 1989 [1965]. *The political theory of Islam.* Delhi: Markazi Maktaba Islami.

Mayer, A.C. 1982. Perceptions of princely rule: Perspectives from a biography. *In* T.N. Madan, ed., *Way of life: King, householder, renouncer.* New Delhi: Vikas.

McLeod, W.H. 1968. *Guru Nanak and the Sikh religion.* Delhi: Oxford University Press.

———. 1976. *The evolution of the Sikh community.* Oxford: Clarendon Press.

———. 1987. The meaning of sant in Sikh usage. *In* Karine Schomer and W.H. McLeod, eds., *The Sants: Studies in a devotional tradition of India.* Delhi: Motilal Banarsidass.

Metcalf, Barbara Daly. 1982. *Islamic revival in British India: Deoband, 1860-1900.* Princeton, N.J.: Princeton University Press.

———. 1994. "Remaking ourselves": Islamic self-fashioning in a global movement of spiritual renewal. *In* Martin E. Marty and R. Scott Appleby, eds., *Accounting for fundamentalisms.* Chicago: University of Chicago Press.

Miller, R.E. 1987. Modern Indian Muslim responses. *In* Harold G. Coward, ed., *Modern Indian responses to religious pluralism.* Albany: State University of New York Press.

Minault, Gail. 1982. *The Khilafat movement: Religious symbolism and political mobilization in India.* Delhi: Oxford University Press.

Miri, Mrinal. 1995. *Gandhi on the moral life and plurality of religions.* Paris: UNESCO.

Mohan Rao, U.S. 1968. *The message of Mahatma Gandhi.* New Delhi: Goverment of India Press.

Mohinder Singh. 1978. *The Akali movement.* Delhi: Macmillan.

———. 1988. Akali struggle: Past and present. *In* Joseph T. O'Connell, et al., eds., *Sikh history and religion in the twentieth century.* Toronto: University of Toronto.

Mommsen, Wolfgang J. 1989. Rationalization and myth in Weber's thought. *In* W.J. Mommsen, *The political and social theory of Max Weber: Collected essays.* Cambridge: Polity Press.

Mookerji, Radhakumud. 1989 [1928]. *As'oka.* Delhi: Motilal Banarsidass.

Moorhouse, Geoffrey. 1984. *India Britannica.* London: Paladin.

Mujeeb, Muhammad. 1967. *The Indian Muslims.* London: George Allen & Unwin.

Mukherji, Partha N. 1984. Gandhi, Akalis and non-violence. *Man and devleopment* 6,3:58-77.

Mukhia, Harbans. 1976. *Historians and historiography during the reign of Akbar.* New Delhi: Vikas.

Mushir-ul-Haq. 1972. *Islam in secular India.* Simla: Indian Institute of Advanced Study.

Mutahhari, Murtaza. 1985. *Fundamentals of Islamic thought: God, man and the universe.* Trans., R. Campbell. Berkeley: Mizan Press.

Myrdal, Gunnar. 1968. *Asian drama.* 3 vols. New York: Pantheon.

Nanda, B.R. 1962. *The Nehrus—Motilal and Jawaharlal.* London: Allen & Unwin.

———. 1974. *Gokhale, Gandhi and the Nehrus: Studies in Indian nationalism.* London: Allen & Unwin.

———. 1989. *Gandhi: Pan-Islamism, imperialism and nationalism.* Delhi: Oxford University Press.

———. 1990. Gandhi and religion. *Gandhi Marg* 12, 1: 5-23.

Nandy, Ashis. 1980. *At the edge of psychology: Essays in politics and culture.* Delhi: Oxford University Press.

———. 1981. Counter-statement on humanistic temper. *Mainstream*, October 10: 16-18.

———. 1983. *The intimate enemy. Loss and recovery of self under colonial rule.* Delhi: Oxford University Press.

———. 1985. An anti-secularist manifesto. *Seminar* 314 (October): 1-12.

———. 1988. The politics of secularism and the recovery of religious tolerance. *Alternatives* 13, 2: 177-94.

Narang, G.C. 1960. *Transformation of Sikhism*, 5th ed. New Delhi: New Book Society of India.

Nasr, Seyyed Hossein. 1981. *Islamic life and thought.* Albany: State University of New York Press.

Nayar, Baldev Raj. 1966. *Minority politics in the Punjab.* Princeton, N.J.: Princeton University Press.

Nehru, Jawaharlal. 1941. *The unity of India.* London: Lindsay Drummond.

———. 1946. *The discovery of India.* Calcutta: The Signet Press.

———. 1961 [1946]. *The discovery of India.* Bombay: Asia Publishing House.

———. 1972. *Selected works of Jawaharlal Nehru* [SWJN], vol.3. New Delhi: Orient Longman.

———. 1973a. *SWJN*, Vol.4. New Delhi: Orient Longman.

———. 1973b. *SWJN*, Vol.5. New Delhi: Orient Longman.

———. 1975. *SWJN*, Vol.7. New Delhi: Orient Longman.

———. 1980 [1936]. *An autobiography.* Delhi: Oxford University Press.

———. 1981. *SWJN*, Vol.14. New Delhi: Orient Longman.

———. 1987. *SWJN*, Second series, Vol.5. New Delhi: Jawaharlal Nehru Memorial Fund.

———. 1991. *SWJN*, Second series, Vol.11. New Delhi: Jawaharlal Nehru Memorial Fund.

Nizami, Khaliq Ahmad. 1961. *Some aspects of religion and politics in India during the thirteenth century.* Aligarh: The Muslim University.

———. 1989. *Akbar and religion.* Delhi: Idarah-i-Adabiyat-i Delli.

———. 1990. *Maulana Azad: A Commemoration Volume.* Delhi: Idarah-i-Adabiyat-i Delhi.

Oberoi, Harjot S. 1987. From Punjab to Khalistan: Territoriality and metacommentary. *Pacific affairs* 60,1: 27-28.

———. 1988. From ritual to counter-ritual: Rethinking the Hindu Sikh question, 1884-1915. *In* Joseph T. O'Connell, et al., eds., *Sikh history and religion in the twentieth century*. Toronto: University of Toronto.

———. 1993. Sikh fundamentalism: Translating history into theory. *In* Martin E. Marty and R. Scott Appleby, eds., *Fundamentalisms and the state: Remaking politics, economics and militance*. Chicago: University of Chicago Press.

———. 1994. *The construction of religious boundaries: Culture, identity and diversity in the Sikh tradition*. Delhi: Oxford University Press.

O'Connell, Joseph T., et al., eds., 1988. *Sikhs history and religion in the twentieth century*. Toronto: University of Toronto.

Oommen, T.K. 1990. *State and society in India: Studies in nation-building*. New Delhi: Sage.

Pandey, Gyanendra. 1990. *The construction of communalism in colonial north India*. Delhi: Oxford University Press.

Pantham, Thomas. 1986. The socio-religious and political thought of Rammohun Roy. *In* Thomas Pantham and K.L. Deutsch, eds., *Political thought in modern India*. New Delhi: Sage.

Parekh, Bhikhu. 1986. Some reflections on the Hindu tradition of political thought. *In* T. Pantham and K.L. Deutsch, eds., *Political thought in modern India*. New Delhi: Sage.

———. 1989a. *Gandhi's political philosophy*. London: Macmillan.

———. 1989b. *Colonialism, tradition and reform: An analysis of Gandhi's political disocurse*. New Delhi: Sage.

———. 1991. Nehru and the national philosophy of India. *Economic and political weekly* 5-12 Jan. 26, 1:35-48.

Passmore, John. 1970. *The perfectibility of man*. London. Duckworth.

Patwant Singh. 1988. The Sikhs and the challenge of the eighties. *In* Joseph T. O'Connell, et al., eds., *Sikh history and religion in the twentieth century*. Toronto: University of Toronto.

Pelikan, Jaroslav. 1987. *Jesus through the centuries: His place in the history of culture*. New York: Harper and Row.

Pettigrew, Joyce. 1975. *Robber noblemen: A study of the political system of the Sikh Jats*. London: Routledge and Kegan Paul.

———. 1984. Take not arms against the sovereign. *South Asia research* 4,2:113.

———. 1987. In search of a new kingdom of Lahore. *Pacific affairs* 60, 1:25.

Pickering, W.S.F., ed. 1975. *Durkheim on religion*. London: Routledge and Kegan Paul.

Prasad, Beni. 1968. *Theory of government in ancient India*. 2nd rev. ed. by A.D. Pant. Allahabad: Central Book Depot.

Preus, J. Samuel. 1987. *Explaining religion. Criticism and theory. From Bodin to Freud.* New Haven: Yale University Press.

Puri, B.N. 1988. *The Khatris: A socio-historical study.* New Delhi: M.N. Publishers and Distributors.

Qasim, Syed Mir. 1992. *My life and times.* New Delhi: Allied.

Qureshi, Ishtiaq Husain. 1962. *The Muslim community of the Indo-Pakistan subcontinent (610-1947).* 'S-Gravenhage: Mouton & Co.

Radhakrishnan, S. 1927. *The Hindu view of life.* London: Allen & Unwin.

———. 1956. Foreword in S. Abid Hossain, *The national culture of India.* Bombay: Jaico.

Rahman, Fazlur. 1958. Muslim modernism in the Indo-Pakistan subcontinent. *Bulletin of the School of Oriental and African Studies* (London) 21: 82-99.

———. 1982. *Islam and modernity: Transformation of an intellectual tradition.* Chicago: University of Chicago Press.

Ramanujan, A.K. 1989. Is there an Indian way of thinking? An informal essay. *Contributions to Indian sociology* (n.s.) 23, 1: 41-58.

Rambachan, A. 1994. Redefining the authority of scripture: The rejection of Vedic authority by the Brahmo Samaj. *In* Laurie L. Patton, ed., *Authority, anxiety, and canon.* Albany: State University of New York Press.

Raschid, M.S. 1981. *Iqbal's concept of god.* London: Kegan Paul.Intl.

Ray, Niharranjan. 1970. *The Sikh gurus and the Sikh society.* Patiala: Punjabi University.

Raychaudhuri, Tapan. 1988. *Europe reconsidered: Perceptions of the West in nineteenth century Bengal.* Delhi: Oxford University Press.

Reardon, Bernard M.G. 1985. *Religion in the age of romanticism.* Cambridge: Cambridge University Press.

Renou, Louis. 1953. *Religions of ancient India.* London: The Athlone Press.

Richards, John F. 1993. *The new Cambridge history of India: I:5. The Mughal empire.* Cambridge: Cambridge University Press.

Ricoeur, Paul. 1992. Quel éthos nouveau pour l'Europe. *In* Peter Koslowski, *Imaginer l'Europe.* Paris: Editions du Cerf.

Rizvi, Sayid Athar Abbas. 1977. Islamic proselytisation (seventh to sixteenth centuries). *In* G.A. Oddie, ed., *Religion in South Asia.* New Delhi: Manohar.

———. 1980. *Shah Wali-Allah and his times.* Canberra: Marifat Publishing House.

———. 1982. *Shah Abdal-Aziz. Puritanism, sectarian polemics and jihad.* Canberra: Marifat Publishing House.

———. 1987. *The wonder that was India. Vol.II. A survey of the history and culture of the subcontinent from the coming of the Muslims to the British conquest 1200-1700.* London: Sidgwick & Jackson.

Robinson, Francis. 1983. Islam and Muslim society in South Asia. *Contributions to Indian sociology* (n.s.) 17: 185-203.

————. 1986 Islam and Muslim society in South Asia: A reply. *Contributions to Indian sociology* (n.s.) 20: 97-104.

Roff, William R. 1987. Islamic movements: One or many. *In* William R. Roff, ed., *Islam and the political economy of meaning*. Berkeley: University of California Press.

Roy, Ashim. 1983. *The Islamic syncretistic tradition in Bengal*. Princeton, N.J.: Princeton University Press.

Royle, Edward. 1974. *Victorian infidels: The origins of the British secularist movement, 1791-1866*. Manchester: Manchester University Press.

————. 1980. *Radicals, secularists, and republicans: Popular free thought in Britain, 1866-1915*. Manchester: Manchester University Press.

Russell, Bertrand. 1946. *A history of western philosophy*. London: Allen & Unwin.

Rustamji, K.F. 1988. Why terrorism has seized Punjab. *The Telegraph* Calcutta, 5 June, p.8.

Saberwal, Satish. 1995. *Wages of segmentation: Comparative historical studies on Europe and India*. Hyderabad: Orient Longman.

Said, Edward W. 1993. *Culture and imperialism*. London: Chatto and Windus.

Samundari, Bishan Singh. 1973. Foreword. *In* Attar Singh, *Secularism and the Sikh faith*. Amritsar: Guru Nanak Dev University.

Saran, A.K. 1982. The meaning and forms of secularism. *The journal of social studies* (Jodhpur) 1, 1: 1-30.

Saraswati, Swami Dayanand. 1994. *The light of truth*. An English translation of the Satyarth Prakash. Trans. C. Bharadwaja. New Delhi: Sarvadeshik Arya Pritinidhi Sabha.

Sarkar, Benoy Kumar. 1985. *The positive background of Hindu sociology*. Delhi: Motilal Banarsidass.

Sarkar, Sumit. 1993. *An exploration of the Ramakrishna Vivekananda tradition*. Shimla: Indian Institute of Advanced Study.

Sathe, S.P. 1991. *Secularism, law and the constitution of India. In* M.S. Gore, ed., *Secularism in India*. Allahabad: Vidya Prakashan.

Savarkar, V.D. 1989 [1923]. *Hindutva: Who is a Hindu?* New Delhi: Bharatiya Sahitya Sadan.

Schluchter, Wolfgang. 1984. The paradox of rationalization: On the relation of ethics and world. *In* Guenther Roth and Wolfgang Schuluchter, *Max Weber's vision of history*. Berkeley: University of California Press.

Schomer, Karine and W.H. McLeod, eds.. 1987. *The sants: Studies in a devotional tradition of India*. Delhi: Motilal Banarasidass.

Schweinitz Jr., Karl de. 1983. *The rise and fall of British India: Imperialism as inequality*. London: Methuen.

Sen, Amiya, P. 1993. *Hindu revivalism in Bengal, 1872-1905*. Delhi: Oxford University Press.

Sender, Henny. 1988. *The Kashmiri Pandits: A study of cultural choice in north India.* Delhi: Oxford University Press.

Shah, K.J. 1982. Of artha and arthaśāstra. *In* T.N. Madan, ed., *Way of life: King, householder, renouncer.* New Delhi: Vikas.

Shahabuddin, Syed. 1994. Muslim task. Letters to the editor. *The Times of India* (New Delhi), 30 August.

Shaikh, Farzana, 1989, *Community and consensus in Islam: Muslim representation in colonial India, 1860-1947.* Cambridge: Cambridge University Press.

Shakir, Moin. 1970. *Khilafat to partition.* New Delhi: Kalamkar Prakashan.

Shamasastry, R. 1967. *Kauṭilya's arthas'āstra.* Mysore: Mysore Publishing House.

Shariati, Ali. 1979. *On the sociology of Islam.* Berkeley: Mizan Press.

Sharma, S.L. 1981. Student politics in Punjab. *In* Paul Wallace and Surendra Chopra, eds., *Political dynamics of Punjab.* Amritsar: Guru Nanak Dev University.

Sharma, Sri Ram. 1962. *The religious policy of the Mughal emperors.* Bombay: Asia Publishing House.

Shiner, Larry. 1964. *The secularization of history: An introduction to the theology of Friedrich Gogarten.* Nashville: Abingdon Press.

———. 1965. Towards a theology of secularization. *Journal of religion* 45: 279-95.

———. 1967. The concept of secularization in empirical research. *Journal for the scientific study of religion* 6, 2: 207-20.

Sivan, Emmanuel. 1990. *Radical Islam, medieval theology and modern politics.* New Haven: Yale University Press.

Skinner, Quentin. 1978. *The foundations of modern political thought: The age of reformation.* Cambridge: Cambridge University Press.

Smith, Brian. 1993. How not to be a Hindu: The case of the Ramakrishna Mission. *In* Robert D. Baird, ed., *Religion and law in independent India.* New Delhi: Manohar.

———. 1994. *Classifying the universe: The ancient Indian varna-system and the origins of caste.* New York: Oxford University Press.

Smith, Donand Engene. 1963. *India as a secular state.* Bombay: Oxford University Press.

Smith, Harry. 1968. *Secularization and the university.* Richmond, VA: John Knox Press.

Smith, Wilfred Cantwell. 1946. *Modern Islam in India. A social analysis.* London: Victor Gollancz Ltd.

———. 1963. The *ulama* in Indian Politics. *In* C.H. Philips, ed., *Politics and society in India.* London: George Allen & Unwin.

———. 1977 [1957]. *Islam in modern history.* Princeton, N.J.: Princeton University Press.

———. 1978 [1962]. *The meaning and end of religion.* New York: Harper and Row.

Somerville, C. John. 1992. *The secularization of early modern England: From religious culture to religious faith.* New York: Oxford University Press.

Southern, R.W. 1970. *Western society and the Church in the middle ages.* Harmondsworth: Penguin.

Srinivas, M.N. 1952. *Religion and society among the Coorgs of south India.* Oxford: Clarendon Press.

———. 1992. *On living in a revolution and other essays.* Delhi: Oxford University Press.

Srivastava, Sushil. 1991. *The disputed mosque: A historical inquiry.* New Delhi: Vistaar.

Swomley, John M. 1987. *Religious liberty and the secular state.* New York: Prometheus Books.

Talib, Gurbachan Singh. 1969. The basis and development of ethical thought. *In* Fauja Singh et al., eds., *Sikhism.* Patiala: Punjabi University.

Tambiah, S.J. 1976. *World conqueror and world renouncer: A study of Buddhism and polity in Thailand against a historical background.* Cambridge: Cambridge University Press.

Thapar, Romila. 1961. *Aśoka and the decline of the Mauryas.* London: Oxford University Press.

———. 1966. *A history of India.* Vol. One. Harmondsworth: Penguin Books.

———. 1989. Imagined religious communities? Ancient history and the modern search for a Hindu identity. *Modern Asian studies* 23, 2: 209-31.

———. 1992. *Interpreting early India.* Delhi: Oxford University Press.

Thompson, John B. 1990. *Ideology and modern culture.* Stanford: Stanford University Press.

Tierney, Brian. 1980. *The crisis of Church and state, 1050-1300.* Englewood Cliffs, N.J.: Prentice-Hall.

Tillich, Paul. 1957. *The Protestant era.* Chicago: Phoenix Books.

———. 1968. *A history of Christian thought. From its Judaic and Hellenistic origins to existentialism.* Ed. Carl Braaten. New York: Touchstone.

Toulmin, Stephen. 1990. *Cosmopolis: The hidden agenda of modernity.* New York: The Free Press.

Toynbee, A.J. 1954. *A study of history,* vol. VII. London: Oxford University Press.

———. 1960. Foreword. *In* Trilochan Singh et al., trans. *The sacred writings of the Sikhs.* London: Allen and Unwin.

———. 1979. *An historian's approach to religion,* 2nd ed. London: Oxford University Press.

Trilochan Singh et al., trans. 1960. *The sacred writings of the Sikhs.* London: Allen and Unwin.

———. 1969. Theological concepts of Sikhism. *In* Fauja Singh, et al., eds., *Sikhism.* Patiala: Punjabi University.

Tully, Mark and Satish Jacob. 1985. *Amritsar: Mrs. Gandhi's last battle*. New Delhi: Rupa.

Uberoi, J.P. Singh. 1991. The five symbols of Sikhism. *In* T.N. Madan, ed., *Religion in India*. Delhi: Oxford University Press.

van der Veer, Peter, 1994a. Hindu nationalism and the discourse of modernity: The Vishva Hindu Parishad. *In* Martin E. Marty and R. Scott Appleby, eds., *Accounting for fundamentalisms: The dynamic character of movements*. Chicago: University of Chicago Press.

————. 1994b. *Religious nationalism: Hindus and Muslims in India*. Berkeley: University of California Press.

Varshney, Ashutosh. 1992. Three compromised nationalisms: Why Kashmir has been a problem. *In* Raju G.C. Thomas, ed., *Perspectives on Kashmir: The roots of conflict in south Asia*. Boulder: Westview Press.

Vivekananda, Swami. 1963. *The East and the West*. Calcutta: Advaita Ashrama.

————. 1972. *The complete works of Swami Vivekananda*. [CWSV], Mayawati Memorial Edition, Vol.I, 14th ed. Calcutta: Advaita Ashrama [AA].

————. 1976. *CWSV*, Vol.II, 13th ed. Calcutta: AA.

————. 1973a *CWSV*, Vol.III, 11th ed. Calcutta: AA.

————. 1973b. *CWSV*, Vol.V, 10th ed. Calcutta: AA.

————. 1977. *CWSV*, Vol.IV, 11th ed. Calcutta: AA.

von Stietencron, Heinrich. 1991. Hinduism: On the proper use of a deceptive term. *In* G.D. Sontheimer and H. Kulke, eds., *Hinduism reconsidered*. New Delhi: Manohar.

Wallace, Paul and Surendra Chopra, eds., 1988. *Political dynamics and crisis in Punjab*. Amritsar: Guru Nanak Dev University.

Ware, Timothy. 1973. *The Orthodox Church*. Harmondsworth: Penguin Books.

Waterhouse, Eric S. 1921. Secularism. *Encyclopedia of religion and ethics*, XI. New York: Charles Scribner's Sons.

Wavell, A.P. 1977. *The viceroy's journal*. Ed., Penderel Moon. Delhi: Oxford University Press.

Weber, Max. 1916. The social psychology of world religions. Included in Weber 1948.

————. 1930. *The Protestant ethic and the sprit of capitalism*. London: Allen Allen and Unwin.

————. 1948. *From Max Weber: Essays in sociology*. Trans. and eds., H.H. Gerth and C.W. Mills. London: Routledge and Kegal Paul.

————. 1958. *The religion of India: The sociology of Hinduism and Buddhisim*. Trans. and eds., Hans H. Gerth and Don Martindale. Glencoe Ill: Free Press.

————. 1978. *Economy and society*, 2 vols. Eds., G. Roth and C. Wittich; trans., E. Fischoff et al. Berkeley: University of California Press.

Wilhelm, Freidrich. 1978. The concept of dharma in artha and kama litera-
    ture. *In* Wendy D. O'Flaherty and J.D.M. Derrett, eds., *The concept of
    duty in South Asia*. New Delhi: Vikas.
Williams, G.M. 1995. Svami Vivekananda. *In* Robert D. Baird, ed., *Religion
    in modern India*. Third ed. New Delhi: Manohar.
Williams, Raymond. 1977. *Marxism and literature*. New York: Oxford
    University Press.
Wittgenstein, Ludwig. 1984. *Culture and value*. Chicago: University of
    Chicago Press.
Wolpert, Stanley. 1988. *Jinnah of Pakistan*. Delhi: Oxford University Press.
Wright, T.R. 1986. *The religion of humanity: The impact of Comtean
    positivism on Victorian Britain*. Cambridge: Cambridge University Press.
Wuthnow, Robert. 1989. *The restructuring of American religion*. Princeton,
    N.J.: Princeton University Press.

INDEX